D0793514

Simulating Minds

PHILOSOPHY OF MIND

Series Editor
David J. Chalmers, Australian National University

Self Expressions
Minds, Morals, and the Meaning of Life
Owen Flanagan

The Conscious Mind
In Search of a Fundamental Theory
David J. Chalmers

Deconstructing the Mind
Stephen P. Stich

The Human Animal
Personal Identity without Psychology
Eric Olson

Minds and Bodies
Philosophers and Their Ideas
Colin McGinn

What's Within?
Nativism Reconsidered
Fiona Cowie

Purple Haze
The Puzzle of Consciousness
Joseph Levine

Consciousness and Cognition
A Unified Account
Michael Thau

Thinking without Words
José Luis Bermúdez

Identifying the Mind
Selected Papers of U. T. Place
Edited by George Graham and
Elizabeth R. Valentine

A Place for Consciousness
Probing the Deep Structure of the Natural World
Gregg Rosenberg

Three Faces of Desire
Timothy Schroder

Gut Reactions
A Perceptual Theory of Emotion
Jesse J. Prinze

Ignorance and Imagination
On the Epistemic Origin of the Problem of Consciousness
Daniel Stoljar

Simulating Minds
The Philosophy, Psychology, and Neuroscience of Mindreading
Alvin I. Goldman

Simulating Minds

The Philosophy, Psychology, and Neuroscience of Mindreading

Alvin I. Goldman

OXFORD
UNIVERSITY PRESS

2006

OXFORD

UNIVERSITY PRESS

Oxford University Press, Inc., publishes works that further
Oxford University's objective of excellence
in research, scholarship, and education.

Oxford   New York
Auckland   Cape Town   Dar es Salaam   Hong Kong   Karachi
Kuala Lumpur   Madrid   Melbourne   Mexico City   Nairobi
New Delhi   Shanghai   Taipei   Toronto

With offices in
Argentina   Austria   Brazil   Chile   Czech Republic   France   Greece
Guatemala   Hungary   Italy   Japan   Poland   Portugal   Singapore
South Korea   Switzerland   Thailand   Turkey   Ukraine   Vietnam

Published by Oxford University Press, Inc.
198 Madison Avenue, New York, New York 10016

www.oup.com

Oxford is a registered trademark of Oxford University Press.

Library of Congress Cataloging-in-Publication Data
Goldman, Alvin I., 1938–
   Simulating minds : the philosophy, psychology, and neuroscience of mindreading /
Alvin I. Goldman.
      p. cm.—(Philosophy of mind series)
   Includes bibliographical references and index.
   ISBN-13 978-0-19-513892-4
   ISBN 0-19-513892-9
      1. Social perception.   2. Empathy.   I. Title.   II. Series.

BF323.S63G65 2006
128'.2—dc22   2006040043

9 8 7 6 5 4 3 2 1

Printed in the United States of America
on acid-free paper

For Fiona

Preface

A perennial problem in philosophy of mind is how we understand self and others, how we identify the feelings, thoughts, and designs that compose our own daily lives and those of our neighbors, lovers, and foes. Is there anything to be learned here from common lore? People often say that they understand others by empathizing with them, by putting themselves in others' shoes: "I feel your pain." Is there any truth to this expression? Contemporary neuroscience has determined that there is much truth to it. When people observe others in pain, part (though not all) of their own pain system is activated. This provides an initial piece of scientific support for the intuitive idea that understanding others is mediated by putting ourselves in their (mental) shoes. In its bare essentials, this is what the simulation theory holds. Simulation theory is one approach to how people "mindread," the general question we'll be tackling here from an interdisciplinary perspective.

I began publishing on mental simulation in the late 1980s (Goldman, 1989), in the wake of papers by Robert Gordon (1986) and Jane Heal (1986). Functionalist and "theory-theory" approaches to folk psychology, or "theory of mind," were ascendant at the time, in both philosophy and developmental psychology. The trio of papers by Gordon, Heal, and me created a critical mass that put simulation theory on the map as an interesting alternative. The two rivals were juxtaposed in a 1992 double issue of *Mind and Language*, in which philosophers Stephen Stich and Shaun Nichols and developmental psychologists Josef Perner, Alison Gopnik, and Henry Wellman sang the praises of theory-theory, while Gordon, I, and developmentalist Paul Harris defended simulation theory. The debate has continued ever since. In the early 1990s, I published several other papers on simulation theory, including ones related to ethics (Goldman, 1992, 1993c) and the foundations of economic theory (Goldman, 1995). Another paper (Goldman, 1993a) addressed the self-attribution of mental states, a distinct but critical part of the full mindreading story.

A new angle emerged in 1998, when I heard Vittorio Gallese talk about mirror neurons at a conference in Tucson. No one at the conference had heard of mirror neurons, but to my ears they struck a simulationist chord. The Italian neuroscientists who discovered mirror neurons, including Gallese, were unfamiliar with the general issue of mindreading and simulation theory in particular. I proposed a connection between them: Mirror neurons might be a mechanism of primitive mindreading of a simulationist variety. We published this idea in *Trends in Cognitive Sciences* (Gallese and Goldman, 1998), creating a new link between cognitive neuroscience and the theory of mindreading. The approach obviously needed refinement, however, to deal more carefully and systematically with philosophical issues, developmental findings, and other approaches in cognitive neuroscience. So, after finishing a book on another topic (social epistemology), I turned to the present project, which has absorbed my attention for more than five years.

There are many debts to acknowledge on this project, for early influences and collaborations, as well as comments on the manuscript. First, there is Robert Gordon, who kept the torch of simulationism burning through the 1990s. Second, Steve Stich and Shaun Nichols laid down significant challenges to simulation theory that forced simulationists to address tough questions yet also created excellent openings for our responses. Next, and of major importance, is Vittorio Gallese. During and after our collaboration in 1998, he kept me regularly updated on emerging work from the Parma laboratory, explained technical details, and pinpointed key issues on the mirror-neuron front. (This is by no means the only front of interest here, however.) Although we sometimes disagree on philosophical details, Vittorio's friendship and breadth of vision have been crucial. Giacomo Rizzolatti, the head of the Parma laboratory, led the way with ingenious experiments and insights that yielded revolutionary findings. He has graciously welcomed me to Parma and invited my participation in a major cognitive neuroscience institute. Thanks for recent collaboration go to Chandra Sripada, who brought great energy and a neuroscience background to our collaboration on emotion mindreading, which occupies a core part of chapter 6.

In terms of manuscript commentary, my greatest debt is to Kelby Mason, who served as research assistant on the project for two years. He focused his microscope on all aspects of the manuscript (through multiple drafts) and provided incisive comments both philosophical and psychological. A few of his points are recorded in footnotes, but in many more instances his comments saved me from errors or ambiguities and yielded improvements in clarity, organization, and presentation. I gratefully received briefer stints of research assistance from Karen Shanton, Kevan Edwards and Frédérique de

Vignemont. Among the manuscript readers for the press, Philip Robbins gave me unusually detailed and helpful comments. David Chalmers, as series editor, raised a number of insightful and important points, resulting in significant revisions.

Many other commentators provided valuable pointers, for which I am grateful. They include Ralph Adolphs, Paul Bloom, Roberto Casati, Greg Currie, Jean Decety, Ori Friedman, Josh Greene, Andrea Heberlein, Pierre Jacob, Marc Jeannerod, Andrew Lawrence, Alan Leslie, Brian Loar, George Loewenstein, Cynthia MacDonald, Andy Meltzoff, Jason Mitchell, Iris Oved, Elisabeth Pacherie, Gualtiero Piccinini, Joelle Proust, Eric Schwitzgebel, Natalie Sebanz, Holly Smith, and Leaf van Boven. I am also indebted to several graduate seminars, one at the University of Arizona and two at Rutgers, where early or late versions of manuscript material were critically discussed.

I am happy to acknowledge financial support from the National Endowment for the Humanities, which awarded me a fellowship for university teachers during the academic year 2000–2001. The project was then entitled "Mind Understanding Mind." My research was also supported by a research professorship from the Social and Behavioral Science Research Institute of the University of Arizona (2000).

Portions of the book draw on material from previous or concurrent publications, specifically Goldman and Sripada, "Simulationist Models of Face-Based Emotion Recognition," *Cognition* (2005); Sripada and Goldman, "Simulation and the Evolution of Mindreading," in A. Zilhao, ed., *Evolution, Rationality, and Cognition*, Routledge (2005); Goldman, "Conceptual Clarification and Empirical Defense of the Simulation Theory of Mindreading," in C. Kanzian, J. Quitterer, and E. Runggaldier, eds., *Persons: An Interdisciplinary Approach*, Obvahaupt (2003); Goldman, "Imitation, Mind Reading, and Simulation," in S. Hurley and N. Chater, eds., *Perspectives on Imitation*, vol. 2, MIT Press (2005); and Goldman, "Imagination and Simulation in Audience Response to Fiction" in S. Nichols, ed., *The Architecture of the Imagination* (2006).

Contents

Chapter 1: Philosophical and Scientific Perspectives on Mentalizing 3

Chapter 2: Conceptualizing Simulation Theory 23

Chapter 3: The Rationality Theory 53

Chapter 4: The Child-Scientist Theory 69

Chapter 5: The Modularity Theory 95

Chapter 6: Simulation in Low-Level Mindreading 113

Chapter 7: High-Level Simulational Mindreading 147

Chapter 8: Ontogeny, Autism, Empathy, and Evolution 192

Chapter 9: Self-Attribution 223

Chapter 10: Concepts of Mental States 258

Chapter 11: The Fabric of Social Life: Mimicry, Fantasy,
Fiction, and Morality 276

References 305

Author Index 341

Subject Index 353

Simulating Minds

1

Philosophical and Scientific Perspectives on Mentalizing

1.1 The Social Mind and the Mentalizing Mind

The animal kingdom abounds with social species. Insect species feature sharp divisions of economic labor and intricate mechanisms of communication. Primate colonies have social hierarchies and spend a lot of time in mutual grooming and maintenance of alliances. But *Homo sapiens* is a particularly social species, and one of its social characteristics is especially striking: reading one another's minds. People attribute to self and others a host of mental states, ranging from beliefs and aspirations to headaches, disappointments, and fits of anger. Other creatures undoubtedly have pains, expectations, and emotions. But *having* a mental state and *representing* another individual *as* having such a state are entirely different matters. The latter activity, *mentalizing* or *mindreading*, is a second-order activity: It is mind thinking about minds.[1] It is the activity of conceptualizing other creatures (and oneself) as loci of mental life.

Mentalizing may be the root of our elaborate social nature. Would there be language and discourse without mentalizing? Would the exquisitely coordinated enterprises of cultural life, the structures of love, politics, and games, be what they are without participants' attending to the mental states of others? Would there be a human sense of morality without an understanding of what others experience, of what their lives are or might be like? The notion that mentalizing anchors the fabric of social life partly accounts for the profusion of recent interest in the subject. A welter of fascinating empirical discoveries and theoretical alternatives has also kindled interest. It has not proved easy to understand how the mind mentalizes, but that is the challenge undertaken here.

So, how is mindreading accomplished? In broad strokes, there are three competing answers: by *theorizing*, by *rationalizing*, or by *simulating*. The first approach (*theory theory*) says that ordinary people construct, or are endowed with, a naïve psychological theory that guides their assignment of mental states. The second approach (*rationality theory*) says that the ordinary person is a rationalizer. She assumes that her friends are rational and seeks to map their thoughts and choices by means of this rationality postulate. The third approach (*simulation theory*) says that ordinary people fix their targets' mental states by trying to replicate or emulate them. It says that mindreading includes a crucial role for putting oneself in others' shoes. It may even be part of the brain's design to generate mental states that match, or resonate with, states of people one is observing. Thus, mindreading is an extended form of empathy (where this term's emotive and caring connotation is bracketed). The present book examines all of these approaches but specifically develops, refines, and defends simulation theory (at least a hybrid form of simulation theory), appealing to a wide range of evidence from philosophy, psychology, and cognitive neuroscience. I have no new experiments of my own to report, but I draw extensively on the empirical research of others, across a broad spectrum of methodologies. Philosophers of science, including philosophers of cognitive science, can contribute to a field by proposing, refining, and systematizing theories and by helping to analyze research findings across multiple disciplines. These are among the contributions to which the present work aspires.[2]

Mentalizing is a complex subject because it's the focus of so many disciplines. Serious students of the field cannot ignore any of these disciplines, because each contributes valuable insights. Methodologically speaking, the investigation can be divided into three sectors. The philosophical sector uses the armchair method. It formulates theories and "tests" them by nonexperimental observation and reflection on human behavior and discursive practices. The psychological sector uses the traditional experimental methods of cognitive psychology. For the subject of mindreading, psychology is represented by its social and developmental wings, the latter focusing on the emergence of mindreading in the preschool years. The neuroscience approach is an amalgam of several methods, including lesion studies, single-cell studies, and neuroimaging. My analysis draws on theories and findings from all of these methodologies. Recent cognitive neuroscience, with some truly landmark discoveries, is an especially salient source of evidence for simulation theory.

This first chapter reviews some history of the subject. The "modern" history goes back roughly 50 years. Philosophy of mind received a major push around 1950 from Gilbert Ryle (1949) and Ludwig Wittgenstein (1953), who set philosophers stewing about how we commonsensically grasp mental concepts and attribute mental states. Philosophers had the field to themselves for almost 30 years, during which they developed several of the principal theoretical options currently on the table. (Simulation theory has an even older provenance, to be addressed shortly.) In 1978, David Premack and Guy Woodruff published a paper on whether chimpanzees have a theory of mind, and this launched the experimental methodology and an enormous cottage industry. Cognitive neuroscience entered the fray in the mid-1990s and has significantly changed the landscape. Responsible conclusions about mentalizing cannot be drawn without taking the products of all three methodologies into account.

1.2 Mentalizing and Philosophy of Mind

Traditional philosophy of mind had two principal parts: metaphysics and epistemology. The epistemology part had, in turn, two components: (1) the problem of other minds and (2) the problem of self-knowledge. The other-minds problem is the question: How can one know that there are other minds? Only my own mental states are directly accessible to me; other people's mental states—if they have any—seem forever hidden from my view. The self-knowledge problem concerns the exact nature of knowledge of my own mental states. Is there really such a thing as direct access or direct acquaintance with mental states? How is such access possible, and if it isn't, how *do* I know about my own mental states?

In terms of the philosophical literature, mindreading is naturally understood as a descendant of these epistemological problems. However, the ways the issues were tackled had as much to do with the metaphysical branch of philosophy of mind as the epistemological branch. The metaphysical questions that dominate philosophy of mind are: What are minds and mental states? Are they fundamentally physical or nonphysical? How are they related to brain states? Descartes focused on the respective *essences* of mind and matter. The essence of mind, he said, is to be a thinking, unextended thing. The essence of matter is to be extended but unthinking. Hence, mind and matter cannot be identical. In the last century, philosophers also inquired into the essence, or nature, of mind, but in doing so they often looked at the *concepts* of mind and mental states. The working assumption here was that our concepts of mental states, or the meanings of mental-state terms, are clues to what mental states *necessarily* are, or place constraints on what they can be. Thus, attempts at specifying the intensions of mental-state terms ultimately aimed at answering metaphysical questions.

A classic statement of logical behaviorism, Gilbert Ryle's *The Concept of Mind* (1949), was a good case in point. Ryle held that "when we describe people as exercising qualities of mind, we are not referring to occult episodes of which their overt acts and utterances are effects; we are referring to those overt acts and utterances themselves" (1949: 25). States of mind, then, are either pieces of overt behavior or dispositions to behave in certain ways. Ryle purported to establish this conclusion by means of conceptual analysis, by elucidating the commonsense concepts associated with mental-state terms. The upshot of his conceptual analysis was an important metaphysical thesis: Minds are not separate substances, "ghosts in the machine," but merely dispositions to behave. The mental world was made safe for the metaphysical doctrine of physicalism.

A similar story can be told about the dominant philosophy of mind that replaced logical behaviorism: *analytical*, or *commonsense*, *functionalism*. David Lewis (1966) and David Armstrong (1968) proposed that mental-state concepts are concepts of causal roles that these states occupy within a causal network relating environmental stimuli, internal states, and behavior. Pain states are the occupants of one causal role, desire states the occupants of another causal role, and so on. However, according to Lewis and Armstrong, conceptual analysis cannot tell us everything relevant to the nature of mental states. It cannot identify the intrinsic nature of the occupants of those roles. For that we need empirical science, and empirical science tells us that brain states are what occupy those roles. So again we have a physicalist story, in this case one that identifies mental states with brain states. The story does not follow from conceptual analysis alone, but it is responsible for the first chapter of the story. Emphasis on conceptual considerations continues in more recent philosophy of mind, sometimes on behalf of the opposite metaphysical pole. David Chalmers (1996) appeals to conceptual considerations to defend metaphysical dualism.

Even philosophers of mind who are ardent defenders of empirical, as contrasted with conceptual, methodology find it necessary to do conceptual work to advance their theses. For example, Paul Churchland (1981) views our ordinary concepts of the propositional attitudes as ill founded or misguided. Contrary to the apparent implications of folk psychology, the mind/brain has no states that are propositional, or sentential, in nature. Churchland arrives at this eliminativist conclusion, however, partly by conceptual analysis. In defending the nonexistence of the attitudes, he relies on the premise that our grasp of attitude concepts is underpinned by a commonsense theory, for it is the alleged poverty of this folk theory that supports the argument for elimination. To secure his premise about our commonsense grasp of the attitudes, he executes a kind of conceptual analysis.

Providing an account of mental concepts is one task of a theory of mentalizing, and it will be addressed in chapter 10 of this book. But the purpose here is not metaphysical; I shall try to steer clear of metaphysics. Complete neutrality, however, isn't feasible. The very study of mentalizing assumes that people attribute mental states, and *attributing* mental states involves having beliefs about them. So our very project assumes intentional realism: There *are* beliefs.[3] This is only a default, which could be abandoned if a viable successor concept to belief were found. But I won't explore this scenario seriously. The integrity of the belief construct, and other folk categories of the mental, will be assumed.

Another reason to review twentieth-century philosophy of mind is to see how it has influenced the science of mentalizing. To tell this story, let us spell out the functionalist theory in a bit more detail, continuing our focus on commonsense functionalism rather than psychofunctionalism.[4] A central problem for logical behaviorism is that mental-state terms cannot be defined, as behaviorists had hoped, one term at a time. The logical behaviorist program might succeed if the truth conditions for a mental sentence like "X believes that it is raining" could be given in terms of a behavioral disposition sentence like "X is disposed to take an umbrella if he goes out." But this doesn't work. Rain believers might have no umbrella-taking dispositions if they don't mind getting wet. Belief that it's raining generates an umbrella-taking disposition only if one *wants* to avoid getting wet. Thus, mental state terms are not behaviorally definable in isolation from one another. How a person behaves depends not just on his beliefs, not just on his desires, but on a combination of the two.

To accommodate this, functionalism introduced more complex linkages between the mental and the behavioral, linkages modeled on the treatment of observable and nonobservable states of affairs in science. Frank Ramsey (1931) had pioneered a method for defining theoretical terms of science by reference to lawful relationships among observable and theoretical states, including lawful relations among the theoretical states themselves. Wilfrid Sellars (1955/1997) suggested that mental states could be viewed as theoretical states of a commonsense psychological theory, a "folk psychology." By incorporating interconnections among mental states, as well as the joint impact of theoretical states on observable behavior, the behaviorist picture could be substantially enriched. David Lewis (1972/1980) provided a more elaborated version of this approach. Mental-state terms, he said, should be viewed as theoretical terms definable with the help of three types of psychological laws: (1) laws relating observable inputs to mental states, (2) laws relating mental states to other mental states, and (3) laws relating mental states to observable outputs (behavior). An example of the first type of law might be "Persons denied fluids for some time tend to feel thirst," an example of the second might be "Persons in pain tend to want to relieve that pain," and an example of the third might be "Persons who are angry tend to frown" (Churchland, 1988: 58–59). Lewis formulated the idea of defining mental-state terms (or concepts) in terms of such laws as follows:

> Think of commonsense psychology as a term-introducing scientific theory, though one invented long before there was any institution as professional science.

Collect all the platitudes you can think of regarding the causal relations of mental states, sensory stimuli, and motor responses. . . . Include only platitudes which are common knowledge among us—everyone knows them, everyone knows that everyone else knows them, and so on. For the meanings of our words are common knowledge, and I am going to claim that the names of mental states derive their meaning from these platitudes. (1972/1980: 212)

So Lewis proposed that our mental-state terms, terms understood by naïve users of the language, are implicitly defined by a commonsense theory. This is the core idea behind the theory-theory approach that has dominated the empirical literature on mentalizing, especially in developmental psychology. The very label for the field of inquiry, "theory of mind," probably derives from this functionalist, or conceptual role, approach.

Philosophical functionalists say very little about how people go about the everyday task of imputing psychological states. But it is easy to extend their account of mental concepts to the task of mental attribution: An attributor simply makes pertinent theoretical inferences from the observables—that is, behavior and environmental conditions—to mental states. Although the specifics of such inferences have been a marginal issue for functionalists, other philosophers of mind have said quite a lot about it.

Both Donald Davidson (1984a) and Daniel Dennett (1987), for example, proposed methods by which propositional attitudes are attributed to others. Davidson's method is sometimes called "interpretivism," and Dennett's proposal is the "intentional stance" theory.[5] In both cases, elements of *rationality* figure prominently in the story. Davidson describes an attributor as trying to "make sense" of his target. In ascribing attitudes to someone, he says,

We must work out a theory of what he means, thus simultaneously giving content to his attitudes and to his words. In our need to make him make sense, we will try for a theory that finds him consistent, a believer of truths, and a lover of the good. (1970/1980: 253)

The "we" to whom Davidson refers are ordinary attributors of mental attitudes. Similarly, Dennett says that the activity of imputing propositional attitudes involves adopting an "intentional stance"—that is, approaching imputation in terms of precepts of rationality and normativity. Here is how the intentional stance works:

First you decide to treat the object whose behavior is to be predicted as a rational agent; then you figure out what beliefs that agent ought to have, given its place in the world and its purpose. Then you figure out what desires it ought to have, on the same considerations, and finally you predict that this rational agent will act to further its goals in the light of its beliefs. A little practical reasoning from the chosen set of beliefs and desires will in many—but not all—instances yield a decision about what the agent ought to do; that is what you predict the agent *will* do. (1987: 17)

Both Davidson and Dennett, then, address the central question of mentalizing—namely, how naïve folk engage in mental attribution. Perhaps the originating motive for their discussions is the ontological status of the propositional attitudes. Nonetheless, substantial chunks of their writings are devoted to the question of how people actually engage in attribution, in other words, how they mindread.

Is there a connection between the folk's concepts of mental states and the way they attribute them? Yes. How the folk conceptualize mental states places significant constraints on the methods and conditions of ascription, and the conditions of ascription should provide clues to how they conceptualize them. These connections are important but not always systematically pursued.

What type of methodology should be used to determine how the folk conceptualize and attribute mental states? Attributing mental states is forming beliefs about their tokenings. How are such beliefs formed? Well, how are any beliefs formed, and how should this question be investigated? By armchair methods or experimental methods? The specifics of natural belief-fixation processes are not ascertainable by purely a priori methods. Nor are methods of belief fixation generally introspectible. Whether it's a matter of perceptual beliefs, probabilistic beliefs, beliefs about logical relations, or beliefs about grammaticality, introspective dissection of how these beliefs are arrived at isn't feasible. This doesn't mean that armchair methods are valueless. General theoretical reasoning and even introspection (see chapter 9) have roles to play in the inquiry. But the reasoning should proceed in the light of experimental findings. Thus, as noted earlier, the methodology pursued here is heavily empirical.

As it goes with belief fixation, so it goes with mental concepts. If the contents of mental-state concepts were conscious and introspectible (and if introspection were fully reliable), empirical investigation might not be needed. But the contents of mentalistic concepts cannot be identified by mere introspection. Indeed, conceptual contents *in general* are not introspectively available. To get a fix on conceptual contents, we must look at how they are used, in particular, how beliefs in which those concepts figure are formed. To be sure, belief fixation is a separate question from concept possession, but the former is evidentially relevant to the latter.

A third type of investigation about mentalizing concerns its characteristic ontogeny and psychopathology. How do normal children develop mentalizing skills, and how are these skills impaired in clinical conditions that relate to mentalizing? Though never probed by philosophers, these matters are potentially relevant to the preceding questions about concepts and belief fixation.

Because the subject of mentalizing includes questions about concepts, concept acquisition, and belief formation, does this confirm our earlier claim that mentalizing belongs in the domain of epistemology? Perhaps, but this needs some qualification. If by *epistemology* we understand purely *descriptive* epistemology, the proposal is not uncongenial. However, the core of philosophical epistemology addresses distinctively *normative* questions, such as "What methods can yield *justified* or *rational* belief?" where justification and rationality are normative concepts. *Knowledge* is another partly normative concept of philosophical epistemology. The subject matter of mindreading, however, doesn't investigate issues of justification or knowledge; these topics are set aside in the field of mentalizing in general and in this book. The inquiry focuses on naïve processes that produce mental-state beliefs, whether or not these beliefs are justified, rational, or specimens of knowledge. Normative epistemic issues require separate treatment that would take us too far afield. It would also be wrong to impose epistemic constraints on candidate methods of mindreading, to exclude methods on the grounds that they couldn't yield justified beliefs. It should not be assumed that our natural mindreading processes suffice for justifiedness by philosophical standards. As indicated, *epistemology* is sometimes used in a purely descriptive sense, to refer to the study of belief-forming methods independent of normative status. If we adopted this terminology, our inquiry could fairly be located within epistemology. But philosophical readers will not find epistemology pursued here in its most typical and familiar forms.

1.3 Cognitive Science and the "Theory-Theory"

The scientific study of mentalizing was launched by David Premack and Guy Woodruff's (1978) paper, "Does the Chimpanzee Have a Theory of Mind?" Premack and Woodruff performed experiments in which a chimpanzee viewed videotapes of humans engaged in problem-solving tasks and was then given behavioral choices to test its comprehension. Its excellent performance on these tests was interpreted as evidence that the chimpanzee possessed a "theory of mind." Although Premack and Woodruff did not cite philosophers of mind, they were apparently familiar with the functionalist idea that a folk understanding of psychology is guided, or underpinned, by a "theory." Ever since Premack and Woodruff's paper, psychologists and primatologists have studied mindreading under the label "theory of mind." This label is somewhat unfortunate, because "theory-theory" designates one particular approach to the subject, not the subject itself. A neutral label is preferable. Fortunately, the neutral labels "mentalizing" and "mindreading" have both become quite common.

What did Premack and Woodruff mean by "theory"? They wrote:

> A system of inferences of this kind is properly viewed as a theory, first, because such states are not directly observable, and second, because the system can be used to make predictions, specifically about the behavior of other organisms. (1978: 515)

These features are clearly borrowed from the philosophical literature. Unobservability is a traditional mark of theoreticity in philosophy of science, where "theoretical terms" were standardly contrasted with "observation terms" (Carnap, 1956; Hempel, 1958). Philosophers of science also emphasize the special role of theory in making predictions, though predictive power does not *entail* theoreticity. Whether mental states are really unobservable is another issue I shall address as the discussion unfolds.

Premack and Woodruff considered two alternative interpretations of their chimpanzee's behavior: classical associationism and the empathy theory. Classical associationism would try to explain the chimpanzee's behavior without assuming that the creature mentalizes at all. In the intervening decades, there has been a lively debate over whether nonhuman primates mentalize. This particular debate, however, is one I shall (largely) duck. My interest in Premack and Woodruff's article is its impact on the study of human mentalizing, not primate mentalizing.

The empathy theory received short shrift at the hands of Premack and Woodruff. This is interesting for present purposes because the "empathy theory" is another label for the simulation theory. Premack and Woodruff mentioned this theory briefly but described it in a very idiosyncratic and restricted fashion:

> The empathy view starts by assuming that the animal imputes a purpose to the human actor, indeed understands the actor's predicament by imputing a purpose to him. The animal takes over the actor's purpose, as it were, and makes a choice in keeping with that assumed purpose. The empathy view diverges only in that it does not grant the animal any inferences about another's knowledge; it is a theory of mind restricted to purpose. (1978: 518)

This restriction of empathy to purposeful states has no clear rationale and unnecessarily hobbles empathy theory from the outset. This may help to explain the relative dearth of sympathetic consideration of the empathy approach in developmental psychology.

Premack and Woodruff's article set the stage for the next major episode in research on mentalizing, an episode facilitated by several philosophers. In their commentaries on Premack and Woodruff, philosophers Dennett (1978a), Jonathan Bennett (1978), and Gilbert Harman (1978) independently suggested that a proper test of a creature's possession of the belief concept would involve the determination of its ability to impute false belief. Harman wrote:

> Suppose that a subject chimpanzee sees a second chimpanzee watch a banana being placed into one of two opaque pots. The second chimpanzee is then distracted while the banana is removed from the first pot and placed in the second. If the subject chimpanzee expects the second chimpanzee to reach into the pot which originally contained the banana, that would seem to show that it has a conception of mere belief. (1978: 576–577)

Two developmental psychologists, Heinz Wimmer and Josef Perner (1983), adapted this suggestion to the question of when (human) children are able to impute false beliefs to others. They constructed stories with the following sort of plot: Maxi puts a chocolate of his in location A, and then goes out to play. In his absence, Maxi's mother displaces the chocolate from location A to location B. Where will Maxi look for the chocolate when he returns? Children heard such a plot described on audiotape while the experimenter carried out the stage instructions. The young subjects were then asked to point to the cupboard where Maxi will look. The major finding was that although 5- and 6-year-olds all correctly pointed to location A (at least when advised to "stop and think"), none of the 3- and 4-year-olds gave the correct answer.[6] Citing previous studies with related findings, Wimmer and Perner concluded that "a novel cognitive skill seems to emerge within the period of 4 to 6 years. Children acquire the ability to represent wrong beliefs" (1983: 126). In the wake of Wimmer and Perner's results, numerous other studies replicated the finding that 3-year-old children do not perform correctly on "false-belief tasks." This was not a uniform finding, as I shall point out in chapter 4, but it was robust under many experimental manipulations.

Wimmer and Perner's suggestion of a major change between 3 and 5 years of age was confirmed in other tasks. For example, Flavell, Flavell, and Green (1983) reported that young children have difficulty with the appearance-reality distinction. Children were shown a sponge painted to look like a rock, and on first seeing it, they said that it was a rock. Then they were allowed to touch it and determine that it was really a sponge. When next asked what it *looked* like, they said that it *looked* like a sponge. One possible explanation is that children have no conception of the representational capability of the mind, so that they don't really grasp how something can *be* one way but *appear* another way. Another finding consistent with this suggestion was reported by Gopnik and Astington (1988). Using a procedure developed by Perner, Leekam, and Wimmer (1987), they showed children a box of candy and asked them to state the contents. After saying "candy," the children were shown that the real contents were pencils. After replacing the pencils and closing the lid, the experimenter asked children what they had thought was in the box when they first saw it. A substantial majority of the 3-year-olds said, wrongly, that they had thought pencils were in the box.

The conclusion widely drawn from these findings was that 3-year-olds do not have a full-fledged grasp of the distinction between representation and reality. Although they have some comprehension of mental states—they distinguish between real things and desires, dreams, imaginings, and the like—they don't yet have a fully representational model of mental states. Here is how Forguson and Gopnik (1988) stated it:

> The difference between the 3-year-olds and the 4-year-olds might be summarized as follows: The 4-year-olds have developed a *representational model of the mind.*

This model construes the relation between the mind and external reality as mediated by mental representations: mental states with contents that have satisfaction conditions in the external world. Some of these states are satisfied (roughly: the world is as it is represented as being); some of them are not. The world is independent of our thought and experience; but it is *represented in* thought and experience. (1988: 236)

By contrast, 3-year-olds have not yet developed this representational model of the mind. That is why they fail when asked to report their own previous beliefs. They don't fully understand that one might have had false beliefs. In other words, 3-year-olds have a profound "conceptual" deficit as compared with 4-year-olds (Astington and Gopnik, 1988). Three-year-olds' grasp of mental states "does not ... allow them to understand cases of misrepresentation, such as false beliefs or misleading appearances" (Gopnik, 1993: 6; see Perner, 1991).

If 3-year-old children lack the concept of false belief but acquire it by age 4 or 5, what could explain this conceptual change? A natural move, especially to anyone familiar with discussions of conceptual change in philosophy of science, is to say that the child must have a *theory* of mind that changes in the interim. In other words, the 3-year-old has one theory of mind, and the 4-year-old (or 5-year-old) has a different theory of mind. The latter, but not the former, incorporates a full grasp of representation and the possibility of misrepresentation. Thus, mental-state concepts are essentially underpinned by theories; as a corollary, all inferences to mental states must be species of theoretical inference. This is the *theory-theory* of mentalizing: a theory that accounts for the phenomenon in terms of mentalizers' possessing a naïve psychological theory, which changes over time (at least in early childhood). How does the child revise its theory, or model, of the mind? According to one version of the theory-theory approach, the child proceeds in very much the way that scientists proceed, getting new evidence and revising her theory in light of it. This approach is therefore called the *child scientist* approach (Gopnik and Wellman, 1992, 1994; Gopnik and Meltzoff, 1997; Gopnik, Meltzoff, and Kuhl, 1999).

1.4 The Modularity Approach

In contrast to the child-scientist view stands the modular-nativist theory. This approach was partly spurred by findings about a connection between autism and mindreading deficits. Simon Baron-Cohen, Alan Leslie, and Uta Frith (1985) reported an experiment in which the false-belief task was administered to a group of autistic children, a group of children with Down syndrome, and a group of normal preschool children. All had a mental age of above 4 years. The experiment showed that 80 percent of the autistic children failed the false-belief task. By contrast, 86 percent of the Down syndrome children and 85 percent of the normal preschool children passed the test. In another experiment, Baron-Cohen, Leslie, and Frith (1986) gave subjects scrambled pictures from comic strips with the first picture already in place. They were supposed to put the strips in order to make a coherent story and also tell the story in their own words. There were three types of stories: mechanical, behavioral, and mentalistic. All the autistic children ordered the pictures in the mechanical script correctly and used the right kind of language when telling the story; for instance, "The balloon burst because it was pricked by the branch." They also dealt adequately with the behavioral script, which could be told without reference to mental states. But the vast majority of the autistic children could not understand the mentalistic stories. They put the pictures in jumbled order and told their stories without the attribution of mental states.

The conclusion these researchers drew is that autism impairs a domain-specific capacity. In the 1986 study, the autistic subjects were not deficient on either mechanical or behavioral tasks. They did not have a generalized intellectual deficiency; they were deficient only at mentalizing. So there appears to be a special module or mechanism dedicated to mentalizing, which is impaired in autism. This represents a *modularity* approach to mentalizing, an approach that was immediately extended by Alan Leslie (1987, 1988) to the interpretation of pretend play. Let us introduce this topic with the help of some background.

As philosophers have pointed out, reports about mental states have a peculiar set of properties as compared with normal declarative reports. For example, given that Ronald Reagan was the president of the United States in 1984, the sentence "Ronald Reagan was once a movie star" will be true only if it is also true that "The president of the United States in 1984 was once a movie star." But when the same sentences are embedded in a belief context, this no longer holds. "John believes that Ronald Reagan was once a movie star" can be true without it being true that "John believes that the president of the United States in 1984 was once a movie star." Similarly, "John picked up the cat, which was ill" can be true only if the cat was really ill, but "John believed that the cat was ill" can be true even though the cat was not ill. So normal truth implications are suspended in mental-state contexts. Like mental-state reports, pretense seems to distort the normal reference, truth, and existence relations. In both domains, there is what Leslie (1987) called a "decoupling" of the "primary" representations—for example, "the cat was ill"—so that its normal reference links to the outside world are suspended. Philosophers call this "referential opacity."

Leslie pointed out that there is a striking isomorphism between the semantics of mental-state reports and pretense. Just as mental-state reports distort normal reference and truth relations, so does the activity of pretense. One can pretend that one object—for example, a banana—is a telephone, although it isn't really a telephone, and one can pretend that a doll's face is dirty, even though it is really clean. Leslie proceeded to argue that the ability to engage in pretense, and to understand pretense in others, draws on the same cognitive resources that are implicated in mentalizing. Next he speculated that the ability to engage in both pretense and folk-psychologizing depends on possession of a domain-specific mentalizing module or mechanism, which he dubbed ToMM ("theory of mind mechanism"). Finally, he argued that ToMM is an innate mechanism that normally matures between 18 and 24 months. That is why children begin to engage in pretense—and simultaneously to understand pretense in others—at this age. Autistic children, however, have an impaired ToMM; that explains why they are deficient in pretend play. Thus, Leslie extended the modular-nativist idea with his hypothesis of a ToMM.

Baron-Cohen (1995) elaborated the modularity idea by postulating four distinct but interrelated mentalizing modules. He advanced his version of modularism as part of a general evolutionary psychology approach. Evolutionary psychology looks at the brain as an organ that has evolved specific mechanisms to solve particular adaptive problems, just as a Swiss Army knife has different blades for different specific purposes (Cosmides, Tooby, and Barkow, 1992). In the case of folk psychology, the adaptive problem is to understand the minds of conspecifics.

Baron-Cohen hypothesized the existence of four separate components of the mindreading system. The first of these is an "intentionality detector" (ID). ID is a perceptual device that interprets motion stimuli in terms of primitive volitional mental states such as "goal" and "desire." These are "primitive" states in that they are responsible for the universal movements of all animals: approach and avoidance. The ID device is activated whenever there is any perceptual input that might identify an object as an agent, such as self-propelled motion.[7] The visual input can range from something as shapeless as an amoeba or as minimal as a stick insect, as long as it suggests self-propulsion. Also the stimulus can be tactile rather than visual. If something gently pushes you from behind, it is instantly interpretable in terms of an agent with a goal of doing something to you (Baron-Cohen, 1995: 33–34). In an early and now classic study, Heider and Simmel (1944) found that when subjects watched a silent film in which geometric shapes moved around, they usually used a vocabulary of volitional mental-state terms to describe the goings-on. The fact that similar results have been obtained with children as viewers (Dasser, Ulbaek, and Premack, 1989) suggests that we spontaneously interpret a wide variety of moving shapes as agents driven by mental states. Experiments by Gergely, Nadasdy, Csibra, and Biro (1995) also suggest that infants perceive geometric shapes in this way.

Baron-Cohen's second mechanism is an "eye-direction detector" (EDD). It is a specialized part of the human visual system, which (a) detects the presence of eyes (or eyelike stimuli), (b) computes whether eyes are directed toward it or toward something else, and (c) infers that if another organism's eyes are directed at something, then that organism sees that thing. The presence of EDD in the human neonate is inferred from studies by Daphne Maurer and her colleagues, who found that 2-month-old infants looked almost as long at the eyes as at a whole face but looked significantly less at other parts of the face (Maurer, 1985). EDD's ability to detect eye direction is supported by several lines of evidence. Papousek and Papousek (1979), for example, found that 6-month-olds look two to three times longer at a face looking at them than at a face looking away. Detecting a pair of eyes in mutual contact with one's own also seems to trigger pleasurable physiological arousal. Galvanic skin responses increase with mutual eye contact (K. Nichols and Champness, 1971), and eye contact reliably triggers smiling in human infants (Stern, 1977; Schaffer, 1977). EDD's third alleged function, of interpreting gaze as "seeing," presumes that the infant already knows that eyes can see. Baron-Cohen did not adduce specific empirical evidence for this hypothesis.

A third module that Baron-Cohen postulated is the shared-attention mechanism (SAM). Shared, or joint, attention is a phenomenon in early childhood identified by several developmentalists, especially George Butterworth (1991). By 9 months of age, infants begin to follow the gaze of others and to point objects out to them. Baron-Cohen drew the following contrast between EDD and SAM. EDD, he proposed, builds only dyadic (two-place) representations. An example would be a representation of "seeing" that might hold between the target Agent and the Self ("he sees me"). SAM, by contrast, is said to be capable of building triadic (three-place) representations. Included in a triadic representation is an embedded element that specifies that Agent and Self are both attending to the same object. One of his examples is "Mummy-sees-[I-see-the bus]" (1995: 45).

Finally, to complete his approach, Baron-Cohen endorsed Leslie's hypothesis of ToMM. Unlike the preceding modules, ToMM has the capacity to represent "epistemic" mental states, such as pretending, thinking, knowing, believing, imagining, dreaming, and guessing. It also has the function of tying together the three types of mental-state concepts (the volitional, the perceptual, and the epistemic) into a coherent theory. Baron-Cohen seconded Leslie's idea that ToMM processes representations of propositional attitudes of the form Agent-Attitude-Proposition, for example, John-believes-"it is raining," or Mary-thinks-"my marble is in the basket." Leslie calls these "M-representations" and argues that they are crucial to the representation of epistemic mental states. It is this ability that allegedly comes on line around the age of 18 to 24 months and is associated with the advent of pretend play and the understanding of pretense in others. Baron-Cohen supported his suggestion of four mechanisms because, as he argued from evidence about autism, the abilities that they respectively subserve come apart or "fractionate" in certain pathologies.

1.5 The Simulation Theory

Both the child-scientist approach and the modularity approach are usually classified as forms of theory-theory.[8] Whether they are really theory-theories in exactly the same sense will be explored in later chapters, but for the moment I take this classification for granted. In this section, I turn to a principal rival of theory-theory, namely, simulation (or empathy) theory.

Some of the general ideas behind simulation theory can be found in historical philosophers, though they were not always applied specifically to mindreading. David Hume displayed keen interest in mental mimicry or simulation, using the term *sympathy* (in the sense of "empathy"). Here is a sampling of Hume's musings on the topic.

> No quality of human nature is more remarkable . . . than that propensity we have to sympathize with others, and to receive by communication their inclinations and sentiments. (1739/1958: 316)
>
> In general we may remark that the minds of men are mirrors to one another. (1739/1958: 365)
>
> When I see the *effects* of passion in the voice and gesture of any person, my mind immediately passes from these effects to their causes, and forms such a lively idea of the passion as is presently converted into the passion itself.[9] (1739/1958: 576)

Hume's contemporary and fellow Scotsman Adam Smith also detected simulational phenomena in both motor and affective domains. Here are his comments on motor mimicry.

> When we see a stroke aimed, and just ready to fall upon the leg or arm of another person, we naturally shrink and draw back on our leg or our own arm. . . . The mob, when they are gazing at a dancer on the slack rope, naturally writhe and twist and balance their own bodies, as they see him do. (1759/1976: 10)

And here is one of Smith's observations on affective simulation.

> When we have read a book or poem so often that we can no longer find any amusement in reading it by ourselves, we can still take pleasure in reading it to a companion. To him it has all the graces of novelty; we enter into the surprise and admiration which it naturally excites in him, but which it is no longer capable of exciting in us; we consider all the ideas which it presents rather in the light in which they appear to him, than in that in which they appear to ourselves, and we are amused by sympathy with his amusement which thus enlivens our own. (1759/1976: 14)

Appreciation of bodily and affective mimicry is also found in nineteenth-century writers such as Edgar Allan Poe and Friedrich Nietzsche. In *The Purloined Letter*, Poe writes as follows:

> When I wish to find out how wise, or how stupid, or how good, or how wicked is any one, or what are his thoughts at the moment, I fashion the expression of my face, as accurately as possible, in accordance with the expression of his, and then

wait to see what thoughts or sentiments arise in my mind or heart, as if to match or correspond with the expression. (1845/1990)

A similar idea is found in Nietzsche.

To understand another person, that is to *imitate his feelings in ourselves*, we ... produce the feeling in ourselves after the *effects* it exerts and displays on the other person by imitating with our own body the expression of his eyes, his voice, his bearing. ... Then a similar feeling arises in us in consequence of an ancient association between movement and sensation. (1881/1977: 156–157)

These ideas of motor, postural, and affective mimicry anticipate, and are substantially confirmed by, today's scientific research, which will be reviewed in chapters 6 and 11.

Immanuel Kant expressed the kernel of simulation theory in this passage from his first *Critique*.

It is obvious that, if one wants to have an idea of a thinking being, one must put oneself in its place and thus substitute one's own subjectivity for the object which one wanted to consider (which is not the case in any other kind of investigation). (1781/1953: A 353).

Moving to the twentieth century, simulationist themes are found in scattered philosophical writings before the current surge of interest in simulationism. Theodore Lipps, who introduced the term *empathy* (in German, Einfühlung), used the same example as did Smith of watching an acrobat on the high wire, but Lipps spoke of internal mimicry rather than motor mimicry. Lipps (1903) commented: "I feel myself inside of him" ("Ich fühle mich so in ihm"). Some sort of simulationist idea was common among defenders of the Verstehen approach to understanding in the social sciences, such as Wilhelm Dilthey (1977) and R. G. Collingwood (1946).[10] Collingwood argued that a historian can know that Caesar enacted a certain thought only if the historian can reconstruct that thought in his own mind (thereby reenacting it).

Starting in 1960, W. V. Quine applied the simulation/empathy idea to radical translation and intentional-state attribution. Here is a typical passage from his *Pursuit of Truth*.

Practical psychology is what sustains our radical translator all along the way, and the method of his psychology is empathy: he imagines himself in the native's situation as best he can. (1990: 46)

This feature of Quine's writing received little attention at the time. It had no direct influence on philosophers who developed the simulation approach in the 1980s.

The first clear and sustained statement of simulationism applied to folk psychology, using the term *simulation*, was Robert Gordon's article "Folk

Psychology as Simulation" (Gordon, 1986). This was a pivotal paper in the development of modern simulation theory. Gordon not only proposed simulation as a replacement for functionalism in the story of folk psychology but also adduced evidence for simulation from empirical sources, in particular, from the early Wimmer-Perner experiments and the early Baron-Cohen and colleagues study of autistic children's problems with false-belief tasks. This inaugurated the interplay between philosophy and developmental psychology on the subject of mindreading.

Roughly contemporaneous with Gordon's article was Jane Heal's somewhat similar development of the theme, using the term *replication* (Heal, 1986). Heal, however, did not highlight scientific studies as bringing relevant evidence to the table. In the same year, the psychologist Nicholas Humphrey (1986) published an essay with a clear, if abbreviated, formulation of simulationism. Humphrey's version was explicitly first-person based.

> We could . . . imagine what it's like to be [others], because we know what it's like to be ourselves. . . . [I] make sense of [others'] behavior by projecting what I know about *my* mind into *them*. (1986: 71–72)

I pursued the theme a few years later (Goldman, 1989), and this flurry of activity led to a double issue of the journal *Mind and Language* (1992) on the debate between simulating and theorizing.[11] There the developmental psychologist Paul Harris (1992) added his voice to the defense of simulation theory, as he had previously (Harris, 1991). Although there are nonnegligible differences among simulation theorists, here I highlight some principal points of agreement.

Like theory-theory (TT), simulation theory (ST) hopes to account for a wide range of third-person mental attributions. Predicting another's decision is a stock example that ST aims to explain. It says that an attributor goes about this task by imaginatively putting herself into the target's shoes. She pretends to have the same initial states—for example, the same desires and beliefs—and then makes a decision given those initial, pretend states. Having made a decision in the pretend mode, the attributor predicts that this is the decision the target will make. An example is a chess player, Black, trying to predict her opponent's next move. Black would project herself into White's shoes by pretending to desire white to win and pretending to have the chess beliefs she takes White to have. Starting with this pretense, and looking at the board from White's "perspective," Black works out a decision and predicts that this will (probably) be White's decision.

Notice that the ST account imputes to the attributor no knowledge of psychological laws. The attributor is not portrayed as deploying any want-belief-decision generalization, such as "People always choose a course of action with the highest expected desirability given their goals and beliefs." This kind of folk-psychological law (or "platitude") is what attributors deploy according to orthodox versions of TT. Proponents of ST find it doubtful that the folk mentally possess or deploy such a law or generalization.

A fundamental idea of ST is that mindreaders capitalize on the fact that they themselves are decision makers, hence possessors of decision-making capacities. To read the minds of others, they need not consult a special chapter on human psychology, containing a theory about the human decision-making mechanism. Because they have one of those mechanisms themselves, they can simply *run* their mechanism on the pretend input appropriate to the target's initial position. When the mechanism spits out a decisional output, they can use the output to predict the target's decision. In other words, mindreaders use their own minds to "mirror" or "mimic" the minds of others. This resembles what an aeronautical engineer might do to predict how a newly designed airplane will behave under specified aerodynamic conditions. He might first build a model of the plane and then let it fly in aerodynamically similar conditions, such as in a wind tunnel. The results of the simulation are taken as a predictor of what the real plane would do under the targeted conditions.

Essential to ST, of course, is that attributors who run a decision-making task on their own decision-making mechanisms do not *act* on the decisional outputs. Clearly, attributors do not generally perform the actions they predict of their targets. Simulation theorists commonly accommodate this by saying that when people run simulation routines for purposes of attribution, they take their own system "off-line." Hence, the approach is sometimes called the "off-line simulation theory." Certain proponents of ST, like Jane Heal (1996, 1998), dislike this characterization because it adds to the scientific, or information-processing, construal of ST, which these proponents disfavor. Heal wants to cast ST as a sort of a priori thesis, not a hypothesis that stands or falls on scientific grounds. By contrast, I want to consider ST as a scientific hypothesis, intended to compete on empirical terms with other cognitive scientific theories of mentalizing. So although I won't typically include the phrase "off-line" in my label for ST, I am comfortable with whatever cognitive-scientific aura it lends.

In the early stages of discussion, propositional attitudes were the principal type of mental states examined and theorized about. This jibed with philosophy's original label for the subject matter, "folk psychology," which originally was dedicated exclusively to the attitudes. A comprehensive account of mindreading, however, should equally deal with other kinds of mental states: sensations, like feelings and pain, and emotions, like disgust and anger. Rival theories should be tested by their ability to account for the mindreading of all categories of mental states. This immediately poses difficulties for certain contenders, such as the rationality theory, that are ostensibly directed exclusively to the attitudes. It is also relevant to ST, because the evidence for ST is particularly strong for the reading of emotions and feelings, at least certain modes of reading them (see chapter 6). There seem to be different mechanisms for mindreading these states than for mindreading the attitudes, more primitive and automatic mechanisms. Simulational properties can be common to the multiple mechanisms, but we should be prepared for the prospect that mindreading is not a seamless affair. With this in mind, my treatment of ST will be divided into two categories: low-level mindreading (chapter 6) and high-level mindreading (chapter 7).

1.6 Central Questions of the Field

A more complete formulation of the questions on our agenda is now in order. Four questions are of prime interest to us.

(1) How do people mindread others—that is, attribute mental states to them?
(2) How do people mindread themselves?
(3) How is the mindreading capacity, or skill, acquired?
(4) What are the contents of people's concepts of mental states? How do they conceive the difference between belief and desire, anger and disgust?

Additional questions lying in wait include the following:

(5) How does the story of mentalizing fit into the larger story of human cognition? What is the cognitive architecture of mentalizing, and how is it related to the architectures of other cognitive domains?
(6) What is the relationship between mentalizing and other forms of social cognition? For example, how is it related to empathy and imitation? What is its relationship to clinical problems such as autism and psychopathy?
(7) What is the evolutionary story behind human mentalizing?

The relative priority of these questions has varied from discipline to discipline. Questions (2) and (4) figure more prominently in philosophy than in developmental psychology. Question (7) occupies cognitive neuroscientists more than philosophers. This book attempts to address all of these questions, at least to a limited extent. Our central questions, however, are (1) through (4), whereas (5) through (7) receive more abbreviated attention.

In organizational terms, the book proceeds as follows. After additional stage setting in chapter 2, ST's three principal rivals receive critical treatment in chapters 3 through 5. The adequacy of those rivals is tested by their answers to questions (1) through (4) and, to a limited extent, (5). Significant defects in the rivals are identified, so we turn to ST in chapters 6, 7, and 8. (More precisely, we advance an ST-TT hybrid, with emphasis on the simulation component.) Chapters 6 and 7 present evidence for simulational mindreading.[12] Chapter 8 deals with acquisition and autism from a simulationist perspective, as well as selected connections with empathy and evolution. Chapter 9 deals with question (2), reading one's own mind, and chapter 10 with question (4), the contents of mental concepts. Finally, chapter 11 seeks to illuminate various categories of social life. As suggested earlier, mentalizing may well be the keystone of the social brain, which is responsible for the warp and woof of human life. The final chapter explores applications of the simulational character of the mind to patterns of human affiliation, roots of narrative and fiction, and moral sensitivity.

Notes

1. The terms *mentalizing* and *mindreading* are used interchangeably.

2. On my preferred analogy, philosopher cognitive scientists are related to empirical cognitive scientists in the way that theoretical physicists are related to experimental physicists. Theorists specialize in creating and tweaking theoretical structures that comport with experimental data, whereas experimentalists have the primary job of generating the data. Of course, many individuals pursue both types of investigation in tandem.

3. What do I mean in endorsing realism about belief? All I mean is that there "are" beliefs as judged by the commonsense understanding of what belief is—*whatever* that commonsense understanding is. For most of the book, I shall remain noncommittal about this understanding, hence about the commitments of realism. I will propose a specific position on this question (admittedly a somewhat sketchy one) only in chapter 10.

4. On this distinction, see Block (1978).

5. Wittgenstein is easily read, in many passages, as focusing on the ways people attribute mental states to others, but any particular reading of Wittgenstein is bound to be controversial, so I shall not make any foray in that direction. The roots of Davidson's interpretivist theory are to be found in Quine's (1960) principle of "charity" for translating the utterances of an alien's speech.

6. These are the results in experiment 2 of Wimmer and Perner (1983); see table 4, p. 114.

7. Subsequent work by Woodward and coworkers (Woodward, 1999; Woodward, Sommerville, and Guajardo, 2001) undermines the notion that self-propelled motion is sufficient to elicit an interpretation of an object as an intentional agent.

8. Leslie has recently abandoned this label as applied to his approach. We shall return to the reasons for this in chapter 5.

9. Hume's view of the process of passion simulation, or transmission, is a bit different from the ones we shall examine later (chapter 6); in fact, it reverses the causal order between the receiver's passion and idea. The process he describes is sufficiently similar to modern ones, however, for purposes of historical comparison.

10. For comparisons of Continental, *Verstehende* approaches and contemporary simulationist approaches, see Kögler and Stueber (2000).

11. Other philosophers who expressed a favorable attitude toward the *Verstehen/* simulation idea in the same period include Putnam (1978, lecture 6), Nozick (1981: 637–638), Ripstein (1987), and Montgomery (1987).

12. Also included is first-person mindreading in *future* or *hypothetical* mode.

2

Conceptualizing Simulation Theory

2.1 Variations on the Standard Themes

Building on the historical overview of the preceding chapter, this one looks more closely at the theories in the field, with detailed attention to simulation theory (ST). The material on simulation is crucial for the rest of the book. I begin by first emphasizing the desirability of a comprehensive theory, one that plausibly answers each of the four central questions about mentalizing (section 1.6). A theory tailored to one of these questions may have difficulties with others. Second, how exactly should each theory be formulated? Choice of formulation can make a big difference when confronting the evidence. Third, many current researchers are attracted by hybrids of the basic approaches, and I, too, shall advocate a hybrid: a blend of ST and TT, with emphasis on simulation. More will be said about the kinds of ST-TT hybrids on offer. Fourth, because simulation is the linchpin of our theory, we shall consider carefully how simulation should be understood for present purposes.

Any comprehensive theory must proffer answers to all four questions on our list, and such a complete or comprehensive theory is what we ultimately want. But completeness isn't everything. We also want a coherent or cohesive theory, one whose parts hang together. In a preliminary pass at the rival approaches, let us examine their prospects for completeness and coherence.

The rationality/charity theory, like many of its cousins, focuses on third-person attribution. Attributors decide what attitudes to ascribe to others by crediting them with rationality and determining what rationality dictates in their circumstances. How, then, do they ascertain their own attitudes? Also by dictates of rationality? Rationality theorists commonly stick to their guns, applying the theory to the first-person case as well (see Dennett, 1987: 91), but consider the difficulties for this extension.

Suppose I try to recall the name of a visitor I met at lunch last week. Suddenly it occurs to me, "Garcia." I reflect on this act of recall and self-attribute a memory with the content, "The visitor's name was 'Garcia.'" Can this self-attribution, or metarepresentation, be explained by the rationality theory? What might be the rational relationships in virtue of which the memory episode is assigned *this* content (the Garcia content) rather than another? Wouldn't it be equally rational for the memory episode to contain a different name instead? (Suppose there isn't anything else I believe about the visitor with which "Garcia" distinctively coheres, nothing distinctively Hispanic, for example. The name "Garcia" just comes to mind.) How could rationality considerations dictate this particular content of my recall? Rationality/charity theorists obviously hope for a unified, streamlined theory, but does this have any plausibility?

Another completeness challenge to the rationality theory concerns the range of mental-state types it encompasses. The approach is designed to handle the attitudes, but the attitudes don't exhaust the mental states. We also attribute feelings such as pain and emotions like disgust. Are such attributions guided by considerations of rationality? When someone's scream leads me to ascribe pain to him, do I appeal to the "rationality" of screaming when in pain? When someone's facial expression tells me he is disgusted (see chapter 6), is it the "rationality" of displaying this facial configuration when disgusted that prompts my interpretation? No. It is not links of rationality that guide me. Nor have rationality theorists explicitly claimed that their theory applies to feelings or emotions. But, then, some other type of explanation is needed. The rationality story must be supplemented with an entirely different theme for sensation and emotion attribution. This need not impugn the rationality approach to the attitudes, but more work is needed to turn the theory into a full-fledged competitor with suitable breadth.

Issues of completeness and coherence can equally be raised for other candidate theories. Consider ST. No simulation theorist claims that the simulation routine is used in self-ascribing *current* mental states. (But it might be used for self-ascriptions of future, past, or hypothetical states.) So despite the labeling, no comprehensive theory will be simulationist through and through. At best, simulation will be only a partial story of mentalizing. What story should ST tell about first-person current attribution? For the sake of coherence, the story should mesh with the simulation element in third-person attribution. If a (pure) ST story denies that theoretical inference plays any role in other-attribution, it would be surprising if it invoked theoretical inference for self-attribution.[1] Still, this leaves many options from which ST can choose.

Both the rationality theory and ST are primarily driven by their stories of third-person attribution. Does the same hold of TT? And does this mean that TT requires all third-person attributions to involve inference from folk-psychological laws or generalizations? There are two reasons to hesitate here. One reason is that some (erstwhile) proponents of TT offer a looser or more liberal version of TT. Stephen Stich and Shaun Nichols (1992: 46–47) consider any "internally stored body of information" about a given domain an internally represented "theory" of that domain, whether or not laws are included. This specification of a theory, however, is questionable. Is *any* body of information a theory? Is the information contained in a telephone directory a "theory"? That would be a very loose use of the term indeed!

A second reason to hesitate is that TT might sometimes allow simulation to be used as a shortcut in third-person ascription, as an "epistemological tool" (Fuller, 1995). This seems right as a logical possibility. However, no working theory-theorists make much room for simulation. They typically emphasize putative problems for the simulation routine. So I shall proceed on the assumption that evidence for simulation-based attribution would be evidence against TT, certainly a pure form of TT.

What about TT and the question of first-person attribution? Is there a particular stance on self-attribution that must be taken to qualify as a specimen of TT? As we have seen, some theory-theorists (Gopnik, 1993) maintain that self-attribution also employs theoretical inference, in complete symmetry with other-attribution. This represents the purest form of TT. A more diluted form of TT might combine theoretical inference in the third-person case with self-monitoring in the first-person case. This was, arguably, the view of TT's founder, Wilfrid Sellars. Sellars says that mentalistic language begins as a theory but can subsequently acquire, in the first-person case, a nontheorizing role. "What began as a language with a purely theoretical role has gained a reporting role" (1955/1997: 107).

Attempts to reconcile functionalism with special first-person access can also be found in other formulations of philosophical functionalism. Putnam (1960) and Shoemaker (1975, 1996) hold that an essential feature of being in a mental state is being disposed to believe one is in that state. Being in pain automatically causes one to believe one is in pain, at least if one possesses a concept of that type of state. Under this approach, believing one is (currently) in pain requires no theoretical inference to the presence of pain, nor is introspection, self-monitoring, or any other form of "recognition" required. It is debatable whether these philosophers mean to offer a theory of mentalizing, as opposed to a theory of the *nature* of mental states. But if so, they advocate functionalism while rejecting theoretical inference for self-attribution. Two other philosophers, David Armstrong (1980) and William Lycan (1996), also combine functionalism with a special, noninferential approach to self-knowledge. Indeed, both identify consciousness with a perception-like awareness of first-order psychological states. So one can be a theory-theorist of sorts (assuming functionalists are theory-theorists) and not take a theoretical-inference view of self-attribution.

Another way of mixing special self-knowledge with theoretical inference is suggested by the following passage from the psychologist Paul Harris.

Provided [that children] have some awareness of their own mental states, and of the conditions they face, they can arrive at a set of generalizations about the links between situations, mental states, and actions. For example, they can notice the pain that ensues after a fall, or the way in which visual experience changes with direction of gaze. These regularities allow the child to make predictions about other people, by a process of analogy. (1991: 300)

This view looks like a TT view (although Harris usually defends ST) because it embraces the idea that third-person attribution relies on laws or generalizations. But how are these generalizations learned? Harris's story assumes that children "notice" their own mental states, which enables them to identify regularities in which those states figure. Then they apply these regularities to others. The "awareness" or "noticing" of which Harris writes ostensibly involves quasi-perceptual monitoring of some features of the mental states. Although this is an unorthodox form of TT, it plausibly belongs on the chart of possible versions of TT.[2]

What about the question of mental-state concepts? Arguably, an approach deserves the TT label only if its account of mental-state concepts is of the functionalist- or conceptual-role variety, requiring mental states to be conceptualized in terms of a functional-role theory. Not all descriptive content is here considered to be theoretical; descriptivity is not equivalent to theoreticity. What is special to TT, as regards the contents of mental concepts, is a specific form of descriptive contents, one that highlights causal-functional relatedness to external stimuli, overt behavior, and other internal states. Does TT have to take the canonical line on both third-person attribution and mental-state concepts, or can it take the canonical line only on third-person attribution and still be a form of TT? I am inclined to take the latter position.[3]

So, there are numerous ways to develop and refine the TT idea. But it is useful to have a single, default way to think of the TT approach. In the rest of the book, I'll often associate TT with what we may call *paradigm TT*. This view embodies three theses: (1) Mental-state concepts are conceptualized in terms of causal laws relating mental states to peripheral events (behavior and external stimuli) and other mental states. (2) Both third-person and first-person attribution proceed by way of law-guided inference from observed peripheral events. (3) Putative laws are acquired "empirically," by means of general-purpose scientizing procedures. When I speak of TT without qualification, I shall generally mean paradigm TT.

2.2 Contrasting ST and TT

The rivalry between TT and ST will engage much of our discussion, so let us clarify and highlight the chief differences between them with the help of some diagrams. The example I'll choose is a prototypical example from the

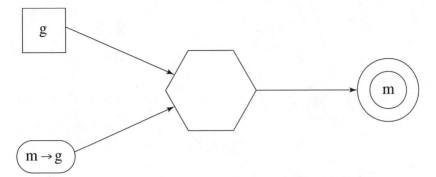

Figure 2.1.   Decision (by target) to do m. (Adapted from Gallese and Goldman, 1998, with permission from Elsevier.)

mindreading literature, especially the philosophical literature. Let me emphasize, however, that it does not typify all forms of mindreading. In developing ST, we shall encounter types of simulational mindreading with somewhat different features from this example. More general properties of simulational mindreading will be presented in section 2.5.

Suppose agent T makes a decision, depicted diagrammatically in figure 2.1. Shapes in figure 2.1 represent either mental states or cognitive mechanisms (operations) according to the following key:

Ovals (rounded rectangles): Beliefs
Squares: Desires
Double circles: Decisions
Hexagon: Decision-making mechanism
Diamond: Factual reasoning mechanism

The contents of mental states are indicated by text or abbreviated text inside the corresponding shapes. Thus, in figure 2.1, agent T is depicted as having a desire for goal g and a belief that action m would be an effective means to achieve g. This desire and belief are fed into T's decision-making system, which outputs a decision to perform action m.

Now let us suppose that an attributor sets out to predict T's decision and does so correctly. How could his accurate prediction be arrived at, according to the two rival theories? Figures 2.2–2.4 depict events in an attributor's head. Figure 2.2 depicts the TT story of how the attributor arrives at his decision prediction, and figures 2.3 and 2.4 depict the ST story. As TT tells it, the story begins with the attributor's beliefs about the prior mental states of T, namely, a desire for g and a belief that m would be an effective means to g. Notation within each oval conveys the contents of the attributor's belief. According to TT, another kind of belief plays a pivotal role in mindreading routines: belief in folk-psychological

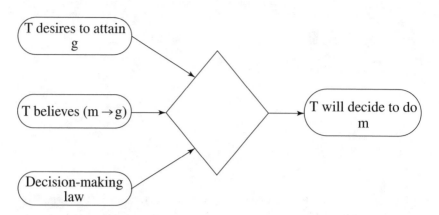

Figure 2.2.   Decision attribution reached by theory-based inference. (Adapted from Gallese and Goldman, 1998, with permission from Elsevier.)

laws. In this case, it's a belief in a decision-making law, which would run roughly as follows: "Whenever an agent wants a certain outcome (more than any competing outcome) and believes that a certain action is the best means to that outcome, the agent decides to perform that action." The attributor's belief in this law is depicted in the bottom-left oval of figure 2.2.[4]

Thus far, we have described the initial states that fuel the attributor's mindreading process. The next item is a cognitive mechanism into which these states are fed. This is a factual reasoning mechanism, the mechanism regularly employed in TT-style mindreading. TT assumes that arriving at a mental attribution (belief) is just a special case of factual reasoning, analogous to reasoning about physical states and occurrences.[5] The only difference is that reasoning about mental states involves a distinctive subject matter. The factual reasoning mechanism is represented by a diamond. It takes beliefs as inputs and generates further beliefs as outputs. In the present case, the mechanism's output is a new belief about the target's decision. This is shown in the oval at the right, with the content "T will decide to do m." Notice that the output of the factual reasoning process is a belief about a decision, not a decision (genuine or pretend).

Figures 2.3 and 2.4 depict a simulation routine[6] for the same mindreading task, where figure 2.4 is simply an elaboration of figure 2.3. The initial states of the attributor are the same belief states shown in figure 2.2, but the attributor uses these states differently. As shown in figure 2.3, information that T desires g is used to create a pretend desire. Desires are represented by squares and pretend desires by shaded squares; shading in general represents pretense. Thus, the attributor creates a pretend desire for g, represented by the shaded square with the content g. This pretend desire is tagged with a "T" to indicate that it's mentally associated with the target. Similarly, the attributor creates a pretend belief that m is an effective means to g, represented by the shaded oval with the content, m → g. The pretend desire and belief express the idea that the attributor puts himself in the target's (presumed) "mental shoes." These states are then fed as inputs into a decision-making, or practical reasoning, mechanism, depicted by the hexagon. A decision-making mechanism normally takes genuine (nonpretend) desires and beliefs as inputs and then outputs a genuine (nonpretend) decision. In simulation exercises, the decision-making mechanism is applied to pretend desires and beliefs and outputs pretend decisions. The shaded double-circle shape with the content "m" depicts the pretend decision.

The final step of the decision-prediction routine is to use the pretend decision to form a (genuine, not merely pretend) belief about the target, namely, that the target will make that decision. With this final belief, the sequence of states constitutes a process of mental attribution. The belief is represented by the rightmost shape, the oval with the content "T will decide to do m." Being a genuine belief, it is unshaded. Thus, the final stage of the simulation process coincides with the final stage of the theory-based process: a belief that the target will make a certain decision. Notice that figure 2.3, unlike figure 2.2, contains no belief in a folk-psychological law. According to (pure) ST, no such belief plays a causal role in generating the prediction that T will decide to do m.

Though not depicted in figure 2.3, it is often important to the success of a simulation for the attributor to *quarantine* his own idiosyncratic desires and beliefs (etc.) from the simulation routine. If the attributor has desires or beliefs that aren't shared by the target, allowing them to seep into the routine could contaminate it. Such seepage can occur even when the attributor is cognizant of self-other discrepancies, as we shall see. The inaccurate simulation that results, however, would still qualify as *attempted simulation* under the ST construal (see section 2.4). Figure 2.4 is simply an elaboration of figure 2.3, which adds at the bottom a depiction of certain genuine desires and beliefs of the attributor that are successfully quarantined.

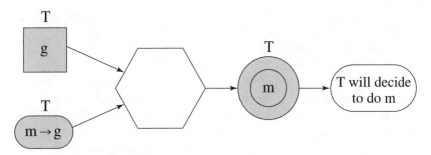

Figure 2.3. Decision attribution reached by simulation. (Adapted from Gallese and Goldman, 1998, with permission from Elsevier.)

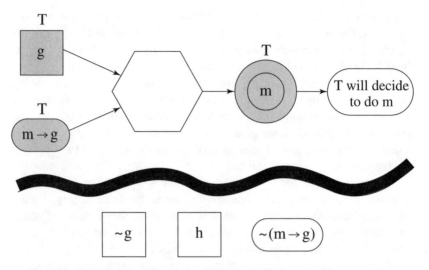

Figure 2.4.   Decision attribution reached by simulation, showing quarantine.

2.3 Threats of Collapse

A theory-theorist might criticize ST by arguing that the simulation routine really does require belief in a psychological law, contrary to ST's claims. In proceeding from a pretend decision to do m to a prediction that T will decide to do m, an attributor must assume (believe) that T is relevantly like himself. Moreover, because mindreaders take all sorts of people as targets, the working assumption must be quite general; for example, "In general, other people are like me," in particular, "psychologically like me." This is a believed psychological law or generalization, which means that simulational mindreading rests on a tacit psychological theory. Thus, contrary to its advertisement, ST is merely a special brand of TT. This point is urged by Frank Jackson (1999), among others.

ST has several available responses to this argument. For starters, note that the threatened "collapse" of ST into TT is not a total collapse. Even if the final stage of a simulation routine involves an inferential step utilizing a theoretical premise, this would not eliminate the distinctively simulational character of the earlier stages. In other words, even if a "theoretical" box or two is added at either end of figure 2.3, the model is still importantly different from figure 2.2. We would be left with a simulation-theory hybrid, which is the general type of approach I advocate in any case.

Second, the critic's argument seems to rest on the idea that the attributor wouldn't be *justified* in imputing to the target a decision to do m unless he believed that the target is relevantly like him. But justification conditions aren't relevant to the question of how a simulation routine actually works. Recall my distinction, at the end of section 1.2, between descriptive and normative epistemology. Jackson and others who invoke the foregoing argument seem to draw a descriptive conclusion from an (epistemologically) normative assumption, a type of move I have disavowed.[7]

It is true, of course, that there must be some delimited class of objects to which attributors apply the simulation heuristic. They don't apply it to rocks, for example. Mustn't the chosen targets have some properties or other, on the basis of which attributors decide to treat them as minded, more specifically, as objects to which the simulation heuristic is applicable? Yes, this seems right. But it isn't clear a priori that the characteristic in question is resemblance-to-self. Moreover, resemblance-to-self doesn't seem to be a characteristic that invokes any psychological *law*. The critic seeks to show that the simulation heuristic, when fully described, requires a tacit belief by the attributor in a folk-psychological law. But what is the believed law? Presumably, it is "All objects of such-and-such a sort [that is, the ones to which I apply the simulation heuristic] are similar to me." But this isn't a folk-psychological law of the sort TT posits. Laws in the TT mold are intrapersonal, diachronic laws, describing mental state transitions *within* an individual (or perhaps between an individual and her environment). The supposed law under discussion is some sort of interpersonal law, specifying similarities *across* individuals. So even if simulators believed such a law, this would not make the simulation heuristic collapse into a theorizing heuristic of the sort theory-theorists endorse.

Part of the foregoing argument is that one cannot use a priori considerations to establish that simulating mindreaders must utilize a resemblance-to-self premise. But this doesn't exclude the possibility of an empirical discovery that such a premise is in fact used. Indeed, we shall later encounter a bit of such empirical evidence.[8] The precise import of that evidence, however, is debatable. Moreover, the notion that mentalizers systematically employ a resemblance-to-self premise is very tenuous, because mentalizing is not always directed at similar targets. People anthropomorphize; they ascribe propositional attitudes and feelings to nonhuman objects such as animals, cartoon characters, and even moving geometrical shapes (as illustrated by the Heider and Simmel study reported in section 1.4). Do people really believe these targets to be similar to themselves?

We have just looked at one of several arguments attempting to show that ST collapses into TT. It's time now to examine two others. Daniel Dennett (1987) was perhaps the first to advance a collapse argument against ST.

An interesting idea ... is that when we interpret others we do so not so much by *theorizing* about them as by *using ourselves as analog computers* that produce a result. Wanting to know more about your frame of mind, I somehow put myself in it, or as close to being in it as I can muster, and see what I thereupon think (want, do...). There is much that is puzzling about such an idea. How can it work without being a kind of theorizing in the end? For the state I put myself in is not belief but make-believe belief. If I make believe I am a suspension bridge and wonder what I will do when the wind blows, what "comes to me" in my make-believe state depends on how sophisticated my knowledge is of the physics and engineering of suspension bridges. Why should my making believe I have your beliefs be any different? In both cases, knowledge of the imitated object is needed to drive the make-believe "simulation," and the knowledge must be organized into something rather like a theory. (1987: 100–101)

A response to Dennett's collapse argument was not long in coming (Goldman, 1989). There are two ways a simulation might be successfully executed. If a computer or a person seeks to simulate a system fundamentally different from itself (e.g., a weather system or an economy), it must be driven by a good theory of that target. Let us call this *theory-driven* simulation. Not all simulation need be like this, however. If a simulating system resembles the target, it might succeed by engaging some of the processes or operations that it shares with the target. It won't need a theory to do this, neither a theory of the target nor a theory of itself. This form of simulation was called *process-driven* simulation (Goldman, 1989). In the mindreading case, process-driven simulation can succeed in producing a final state that is identical or isomorphic to that of the target as long as (1) the process or mechanism driving the simulation is identical, or relevantly similar, to the process or mechanism that drives the target and (2) the initial states of the simulating system (the attributor) are the same as, or relevantly similar to, those of the target. Process-driven simulation does not collapse into theorizing.

Critics may argue that this response to the collapse argument is too quick. They will remind us that the postulated theorizing does not consist of explicit beliefs, beliefs explicitly represented in the cognitive system. Theory-theorists commonly claim that each cognitive system should be understood in terms of a tacit theory, a theory that isn't represented in the system but that underlies the system's operations. When the notion of a tacit theory is properly understood, they contend, all interesting cognitive activity turns out to be subserved by theorizing. Once it is appreciated that theorizing may be tacit and subpersonal, we see that any simulation process can and should be reinterpreted in terms of tacit theorizing. This is the third type of collapse argument to be discussed.

A central question, then, is: When is it appropriate to credit a system with possession of a tacit theory? Drawing on a suggestion of Gareth Evans (1981), Martin Davies (1987) proposed that a person be credited with a tacit theory (or tacit knowledge of a theory), provided that, for each separate proposition in the theory, there is a corresponding separate element inside the person that causally mediates between premises and conclusions that the person explicitly represents. It is further required that the overall causal pattern in the structure should duplicate the logical pattern of the relations within the theory. Now consider the case of a hypothetical attributor using a simulation routine to draw a conclusion about a target's mental state. Doesn't the simulation routine guarantee that some elements inside the attributor causally mediate between his explicit premises and conclusions, and that the causal structure of these elements mirrors the logical structure of a psychological theory (set of laws)? Jane Heal argues that, on the foregoing account of tacit theory possession, it follows that a simulating attributor uses a tacit theory (Heal, 1994: 131). Similarly, argues Heal, if I use my own heart as an instrument of simulation to make predictions about another person's heart, it will turn out, according to this account, that I possess a tacit theory of the heart.

In revisiting this topic, Davies and Stone (2001) now concede the inadequacy of Davies's earlier account of tacit theory possession. They produce an example of using one gas cylinder as an instrument of simulation to make predictions about the pressure in a second gas cylinder. They show how Davies's earlier account of tacit theory possession wrongly permits the conclusion that the user thereby counts as having tacit knowledge of Boyle's law. I certainly agree with the general drift of Davies and Stone's conclusion. An excessively permissive account of tacit theory possession must be avoided. When it is avoided, moreover, the threat of collapse against ST itself seems to collapse. But might there not be a sufficiently stringent account of tacit knowledge that still allows the threat of collapse to go forward? Can I guarantee that no such threat can be constructed?

I offer no definitive guarantee, but here are some guidelines that should mitigate the prospects for such a collapse. On the surface, there is a tolerably clear contrast between (mere) theory and simulation. In light of the contrast, it is prima facie implausible that evidence for a simulation routine should *also and equally* be evidence for a theory routine. Thus, any account of tacit knowledge that implies that the occurrence of a simulation entails the possession of a tacitly known theory is prima facie implausible and should be resisted.

An even more important point is that although there is a prima facie conflict between simulation and theory at the personal level, there is no conflict between them at different levels. There is nothing wrong in supposing that mindreading is executed at the personal level by simulation, which is in turn implemented at the subpersonal level by an underlying theory.[9] Indeed, some might say, how could simulation be executed unless an algorithm for its execution is tacitly represented at some level in the brain? Isn't such an algorithm a sort of theory?

To the last suggestion, I answer as follows. First, an algorithm isn't a theory in the sense of a set of laws or generalizations. An algorithm is a set of (conditional) instructions, and instructions are not laws. More specifically, an algorithm for doing and interpreting simulations is not a set of *folk-psychological* laws. This point will be elaborated in the following section. Even if all operations of the mind-brain are guided at the neural level by neural algorithms or computations, this does not mean that no distinctions can be drawn at higher levels of description between types of psychological activity. Even if all neural activity involves a fundamentally homogeneous set of computations, this does not imply that there is no cognitive-level distinction between factual reasoning and practical reasoning (from goals to subgoals to decisions). It would be foolish to suppose that because all molecules and all cells are ultimately composed of the same fundamental particles, therefore no distinction can be drawn between different types of cells or molecules. Similarly, the fact that all thought is implemented by neural computations does not obliterate the cognitive-level distinction between learning regularities and applying them, on the one hand, and executing simulation routines, on the other. These differences in psychological activities should not be obscured by the fact that all brain operations are computational.

Stepping back from this debate, we should take notice of two different approaches for defining ST: a *negative* and a *positive* approach. A negative approach focuses on what is *denied* by ST. Figure 2.3 (and 2.4) omits any belief by the attributor in a folk-psychological law. This omission is deliberate, in that defenders of ST typically deny that such laws are used in simulation. This denial has been an important part of the traditional characterization of ST and comprises what I am calling the "negative approach." A positive approach focuses on what ST *asserts*. The two critical positive features of (standard) ST are (1) the hypothesized role of pretend states and (2) the hypothesized use of mechanisms or processes of the same kind employed by the target. These are clearly depicted in figure 2.3 but absent in figure 2.2. For example, the ST story shown in figure 2.3 involves the use of a decision-making mechanism, the same mechanism a target would use to make a decision. The TT story shown in figure 2.2 instead involves a factual reasoning mechanism, which no target would use in decision making.

Under the negative approach to ST, any hint that mindreading is subserved by theorizing would be a threat, because (process-driven) simulation is supposed to be free of theorizing. Under the positive approach, by contrast, a hint that mindreading is subserved by theorizing would not necessarily be a threat. Simulation could be causally responsible for mindreading even if theorizing is also at work, because theorizing might simply *implement* simulation rather than replace it. Under the positive approach, simulation and theory are compatible. Thus, the threatened collapse need not be a collapse at all when ST receives a purely positive characterization. This is not to say that ST must endorse the presence of theorizing, even tacit theorizing, but it need not fear or resist tacit theorizing to preserve its integrity.

2.4 Reconfiguring Simulation Theory

To strengthen the positive version of ST, more should be said about the nature of simulation. What is a pretend state, for example, and does pretense constitute the be-all and end-all of simulation? Looking ahead to evidence of low-level mindreading (chapter 6), we need to cast our net more widely than the standard version of ST. We also need to meet the complaint of some writers that simulation theory has been understood in excessively heterogeneous ways. Stich and Nichols (1997) challenge the naturalness or utility of the term *simulation* and urge that it be retired. This campaign is continued in Nichols and Stich (2003), where they quote their 1997 paper with approval:

> In reaction to the apparently irresistible tendency to use the word "simulation" as a label for almost *anything*, we have for some years been arguing that the term "simulation" needs to be retired, because "the diversity among the theories, processes and mechanisms to which advocates of simulation theory have attached the label "simulation" is so great that the term itself has become quite useless. It picks out no natural or theoretically interesting category." (Stich and Nichols, 1997); (Nichols and Stich, 2003: 134)

Now I am not hesitant to acknowledge a diversity of processes or mechanisms that fall under the heading of simulation. But there is still unity amid this diversity; simulation is still a natural and theoretically interesting category. Analogously, although there are many different atomic elements, the category "atomic element" is a natural and theoretically interesting category. There are many types of cells and types of physical forces, but this doesn't mean that "cell" and "force" have no natural unity or are lacking in theoretical interest. We have to show, of course, that there is a suitable unity in the category of simulation by providing an appropriate definition or family of definitions. This is what I undertake in the remainder of this section.

The term *simulation* is open to different interpretations, one associated with the phrase *computer simulation*. What does it mean for a computer, or other computational system, to simulate a target system? It means that the computer "models" the target system, that is, generates correct symbolic descriptions of its outputs from descriptions of its inputs by means of descriptions of its intervening states. Scientists routinely use computers to generate simulations of all sorts of things—hurricanes, economies, and protein synthesis. *Simulation* in this sense does not require the simulating system to work according to the same principles, or undergo the same (or even similar) states, as the simulated system. Hurricanes are governed by laws of aerodynamics and hydrodynamics, but the computers (and computer programs) that model them are not so governed (Haugeland, 1985). Computers work symbolically, often numerically, carrying out calculations. Hurricanes do not carry out such calculations.

This sense of *simulation* has little to do with ST as understood in the mindreading literature. On the contrary, computational modeling is more like using a theory to predict and/or explain a system's behavior. Thus, computational simulation should not be confused with simulation in the sense intended by simulationists of mindreading. They (we) understand simulation in the sense of duplication or replication. Indeed, Jane Heal (1986) used the term *replication* in her first article on the subject, and in some ways that's a better term because it avoids connotations associated with computer simulation. However, *simulation* is the entrenched term in the mindreading literature, and there is little point in forswearing it. Let us simply mark the vital distinction between the two senses of *simulation*: *computational modeling* simulation and *replication* simulation. For purposes of the theory of mindreading, only the latter interests us.[10]

The last remark is not meant to exclude the possibility that mental processes are computational processes. Both first-order mental processes and second-order, metarepresentational processes might be computational processes. All I am saying here is that being computational does not make a mental process a simulation in the sense relevant to ST. We need a different meaning to attach to ST. The meaning I shall introduce is plainly inspired by the term's etymology.

The English verb *simulate* is derived from the Latin *simulare*, which means "imitate" or "feign." This in turn is derived from the adjective *similis*, which means "similar" or "like." So a generic notion of simulation is best approached in terms of similarity, likeness, or (approximate) copying or duplication. Let us proceed by constructing a more precise definition of simulation from this starting-point. From there, we can move to *mental* simulation as a special case and to mental simulation *for mindreading* as a special case of that.

The first two definitions I offer are definitions of *successful* simulation. These are followed by a definition of *attempted* simulation. Attempted simulations and successful simulations will count equally as simulations for purposes of mindreading, but successful simulation is the logically prior concept. Here is a first pass at defining generic simulation.

Generic Simulation (initial): Process P is a simulation of another process $P' =_{df.}$
P duplicates, replicates, or resembles P' in some significant respects (significant relative to the purposes of the task).

P and P' are token processes or episodes, rather than process types. An example of generic simulation is flight-training simulation. A flight simulator is a system or device that duplicates the actual situation of a pilot in significant respects, but not all respects. A flight simulator is not a real airplane and does not become airborne. However, it comprises an environment that resembles a genuine airplane cockpit, with the same instruments. Instrument readings resemble readings occurring in actual flight and respond in similar ways to actions performed on the controls. Thus, a token process that transpires in the flight simulator resembles in significant respects what occurs, or would occur, during a real flight. In general, a simulating activity can have any temporal relation to an activity it simulates: earlier, later, or contemporaneous. Furthermore, a simulated (target) activity P′ can be merely hypothetical rather than actual. For example, a particular flight simulation that eventuates in a (simulated) crash might not correspond to any real crash. The simulation could still be accurate in the sense that it corresponds to what would happen to a real airplane if a pilot performed the maneuvers actually performed in the simulation.

This initial definition of generic simulation needs refinement. One problem is that duplication, or resemblance, is symmetrical, whereas simulation is not. It is not generally the case that when P simulates P′, P′ also simulates P. In cases of mindreading, we want to be able to say that the attributor's mental activity simulates that of the target, but we don't want to say the converse. A patch to the definition might seem straightforward. Simply require that the simulating process occur out of the *purpose*, or *intention*, to replicate the simulated process. That won't hold in the reverse direction. This won't quite work, however, because it is doubtful that all simulation is purposeful. Some simulation may be automatic and nonpurposeful. Even without purposefulness, however, a phenomenon intuitively counts as a simulation of another if it is the *function* of the former to duplicate or resemble the other. I lack a theory of functions to provide backing for this approach, but I shall nonetheless avail myself of this notion. This enables us to revise the definition of generic simulation as follows:

Generic Simulation (revised): Process P simulates process $P' =_{df.}$
(1) P duplicates, replicates, or resembles P′ in some significant respects (significant relative to the purposes or function of the task), and
(2) in its (significant) duplication of P′, P fulfills one of its purposes or functions.[11]

Generic simulation is a notion that applies to all sorts of processes, mental and nonmental. Let us next introduce the notion of *mental simulation*, the simulation of one mental process by another mental process.[12] Mental simulation comes in two varieties: intrapersonal and interpersonal. Intrapersonal mental simulation occurs when P and P′ are mental processes in the same individual mind, and interpersonal mental simulation occurs when P and P′ are in different minds.

Mental Simulation: Process P is a mental simulation of target process $P' =_{df.}$

Both P and P′ are mental processes (though P′ might be merely hypothetical), and P and P′ exemplify the relation of generic simulation as previously defined.

A possible example of mental simulation is visualization. In visualizing something, the mind seems to undergo a process *somewhat* similar to seeing the thing. If it's a familiar object, the specific content of the visualization might resemble the content of the seeing, at least in significant respects. At a minimum, one has the introspective impression that visualization approximates seeing. Whether this introspective impression is confirmed by cognitive science is addressed in chapter 7. Evidence will be presented that supports this introspective feeling.

The resemblance claim made here must not be confused with another resemblance claim sometimes made by imagery theorists. The second resemblance claim, emphatically rejected here, is that visual images resemble *objects* or *scenes* visualized. By contrast, the resemblance claim endorsed here is not a mind-world resemblance. What transpires in the mind when one visualizes the sea presumably bears little interesting resemblance to the sea. The mind isn't blue, it isn't a body of water, and so forth. But visualizing the ocean might substantially resemble an episode of *seeing* the ocean, either an actual seeing or a hypothetical one.[13] This is the relationship between visualizing and seeing that might exemplify mental simulation.

Our current definitions of simulation require simulation to be a successful[14] process; P must duplicate, in significant respects, process P′. However, a reasonable version of ST would not hold that the mental processes of mindreaders always match, or even approximately match, those of their targets. ST, like any plausible theory of mindreading, should tolerate highly inaccurate specimens of mindreading. For example, a mindreader badly misinformed about her target might construct inaccurate pretend states, with minimal correspondence to those of her target. What ST essentially maintains is that mindreading (substantially) consists of either *successful or attempted* mental simulations. To accommodate this idea, we first need a definition of attempted mental simulation. So let us offer the following two definitions.

Attempted Generic Simulation: Process P is an attempted generic simulation of process P′ = df.
P is executed with the *aim* of duplicating or matching P′ in some significant respects.

Attempted Mental Simulation: Process P is an attempted mental simulation of process P′ = df.
P and P′ are both mental processes, and P is executed with the *aim* of duplicating or matching P′ in some significant respects.

The term *aim* in these definitions includes covert or implicit aims, not consciously available to the simulator.

Let us now consider the following factual thesis (not a definition).

Mental Simulations Are Used for Question Answering: People sometimes use successful or attempted mental simulations when answering a question (or forming a belief).

The use of mental simulation for question answering can also be illustrated by visualization. People often visualize things in order to answer questions about them (either self-generated or other-generated questions). A classic cognitive science example comes from Roger Shepard's study of "image rotation" (Shepard and Cooper, 1982). In so-called image-rotation tasks, subjects were shown pairs of line drawings portraying three-dimensional objects in space, and they were asked to determine, as rapidly as possible, whether the two depicted objects were the same or different, that is, whether they were congruent. Subjects' reaction time to pairs of congruent shapes was a remarkably linear function of the angular difference in their portrayed orientation. This led experimenters to conclude that subjects tried to answer the question by mentally rotating images of the objects in their heads. Of course, we needn't suppose that any mental entities (e.g., "sense-data") were literally being rotated. Rather, on each trial subjects engaged in a process of visualizing one of the objects being rotated in space. Talk of a visualizing process is noncommittal vis-à-vis the architecture of the process, whether, for example, it is fundamentally "pictorial" or "discursive." Whatever the architecture of visualization, the tacit aim of the subjects' visualization was to undergo a vision-like process, a process of *seeing* one of the portrayed objects rotated in space. Of course, the subjects didn't see any three-dimensional shapes being rotated; there were no three-dimensional shapes to be seen. The simulated seeing processes were purely hypothetical. However, our definitions allow simulations of hypothetical processes, and it is highly plausible that subjects (tacitly) tried to produce such simulations. The simulations were undertaken, moreover, to answer the question posed, namely, whether the portrayed shapes were congruent.

We turn next to the central notion here, that of mental simulation *to answer a mindreading question*. Again we advance a factual thesis.

Mental Simulations Are Used to Answer Third-Person Mindreading Questions: People often use mental simulations or attempted mental simulations to answer questions (form beliefs) about other people's mental states.

This says not only that people execute mental simulations and attempted mental simulations but also that some of these simulations are used to answer third-person mindreading questions, that is, to generate beliefs about third-person mental states. Notice that the thesis does not imply that all simulational mindreading is purposeful or intentional. Mental simulations might occur automatically, without intent, and then get used to form beliefs about mind-reading questions. So it is left open whether token simulations are purposeful or nonpurposeful, but cases of purposeful simulations that misfire are clearly allowed.

2.5 Simulation and Projection

In this section, I elaborate and extend my interpretation of ST to accommodate a pattern of empirical findings that will occupy us in later chapters. These empirical findings concern "egocentric" mindreading tendencies found in both children and adults. I shall tweak my interpretation of ST a bit (as compared with traditional interpretations) to help it explain these tendencies.

An allegedly distinguishing feature of ST is that a simulating mindreader makes special use of her own mind in assigning mental states to others. This simple statement, however, calls for more specifics. After all, a theorizing mindreader would also use her own mind in selecting mental states to assign to others. What is the "special" use of one's own mind under simulation? Consider our contrast between TT and ST accounts of the decision prediction example. According to ST the mindreader takes her *own* m-decision—a decision that occurs in simulation mode, to be sure—and ascribes that type of state to the target. Under the TT account, the mindreader never ascribes one of her own decisions to the target; no such decision is part of the theorizing routine. In the theorizing routine, all states of the mindreader are (third-person) *metarepresentations*—that is, beliefs about mental states of the target. This is depicted diagrammatically by the fact that all state-representing shapes in figure 2.2 are ovals. None of these metarepresentational states, however, is ascribed to the target. Only their *contents* are so ascribed, including the content of the final state, namely, that T decides to do m. Thus, ST is indeed distinctive in holding that a mindreader commonly takes one of her own first-order (pretend) states and imputes it (as a genuine state) to the target.

I shall call the act of assigning a state of one's own to someone else *projection*. As we have just seen, projection is a standard part of the ST story of mindreading. It is the final stage of each mindreading act, a stage that involves no (further) simulation or pretense. Indeed, it typically involves an "exit" from the simulation mode that occupies the first stage of a two-stage routine. The simulation stage is followed by a projection stage. Thus, a more complete label for the so-called simulation routine might be "simulation-plus-projection." I shall not adopt this cumbersome label for the duration of our discussion; it would add an extra weight to an already heavy terminological load. Note, however, that this is a more complete and informative label, which will be significant in some later chapters (especially chapters 4 and 7).

Having highlighted the projection feature of simulation routines, we are ready to see how such routines would be prone to generate egocentric biases. As noted in section 2.2, a requirement for successful simulation is *quarantining* one's own genuine states that don't correspond to states of the target, that is, keeping such states from intruding into the simulation. If one's own genuine (noncorresponding) states creep into simulations, inaccuracies or biases are likely to result. If leakage or quarantine failure is rampant, egocentric biases will also be rampant. In fact, there is extensive empirical evidence of precisely such biases across a wide range of mental subdomains (chapter 7). It is therefore an asset of ST, under the present configuration, that it's well positioned to explain these biases.

The notion of a simulation routine is thus mildly expanded by allowing *some* (input) states that are genuine (as opposed to pretend) states of the mindreader. These genuine states are initially assumed to be cases of quarantine failure. Now, however, an additional expansion can be considered. A mindreader might take a genuine state of her own and project it onto a target without otherwise constructing a simulation routine with pretend inputs and without feeding any such states into a cognitive mechanism. For example, the mindreader simply assumes that certain things she believes are also believed by the target. Should this be considered an instance of simulation, or simulation-plus-projection? Given our definition of projection, taking a genuine state of one's own and ascribing that state to another is clearly a case of projection. Is it a case of simulation-plus-projection? We might consider it a "limiting case" of simulation-plus-projection, a case in which the simulation element is null but the projection element is robust. This is what I propose for the sequel. This departs a bit from ST as classically understood. But we have no interest in retaining a familiar theory merely for the sake of familiarity; we want the best theory we can get. Given the mass of relevant empirical evidence, the proposed reconfiguration of the simulation-plus-projection theory should be helpful.

Let me briefly mention the kinds of evidence the present reconfiguration is intended to cover; details will be supplied later. One body of evidence is subsumed under the heading "the curse of knowledge." Psychological studies show that knowledge possessors tend to assume that others possess the same knowledge. In other words, knowledge attributions to others tend to be "biased" by one's own knowledge (Camerer, Loewenstein, and Weber, 1989; Nickerson, 1999, 2001; Keysar, 1994; Keysar and Bly, 1995; Keysar, Lin, and Barr, 2003; Birch and Bloom, 2003, 2004).[15] Egocentric tendencies aren't restricted to knowledge or belief. They crop up in connection with valuations, attitudes, somatic states, feelings, and so forth. Thus, projecting the self onto others is a well-supported phenomenon. Because ST traditionally highlights such projection—focusing on the projection of pretend states (projected as genuine)—it makes sense to expand the theory as indicated. This will enhance its empirical power.

2.6 Varieties of Simulationist Theses

At the end of section 2.4, we presented the core factual thesis about the use of simulation in mindreading. This thesis says that people "often" use mental simulations to answer (third-person) mindreading questions. The obvious question arises: How often is often? Whenever they mindread others? Every Tuesday, Thursday, and Saturday? Precisely what claim does ST mean to make? It is unreasonable to demand a precise answer at this time. Simulationist theses can vary in strength, and it is too early to decide which is right. The point of the inquiry is to explore the possibilities. Based on present evidence, a reasonable endorsement of ST would be the joint claim that at least one of the theses is very likely to be true, and there is a substantial probability that one of the stronger theses is true.

What are the dimensions of strength along which versions of ST might vary? Here are three such dimensions (see Goldman, 2002a; Jeannerod and Pacherie, 2004). The first dimension is *frequency of use*. The strongest version would say that simulation is always used for third-person mindreading; the weakest version would say that it is occasionally used; an intermediate version would say that it's the default method that can be overridden in various circumstances. A second dimension of variation is the *source of simulation*. A strong version would say that simulation is the primary, root form of interpersonal mentalization. A weaker version would say that simulation is merely a shortcut mode of mindreading, ultimately derived from theorizing. A third dimension of variation is the *range of mental-state types* susceptible of simulational mindreading. A strong version would say that all mental-state types are so susceptible, whereas weaker versions would restrict simulation to a proper subset of types. For example, perhaps only propositional attitudes can be mindread by simulation, or perhaps only occurrent, transient mental states can be mindread by simulation, not persisting mental traits or dispositions.[16]

Simulationist theses can also vary along dimensions other than strength. There is, for example, the dimension of system unity versus system multiplicity. One possible thesis is that a single simulation system, or operation, is used for all cases of mindreading-directed simulation. A different thesis is that multiple simulational systems or operations are used in mindreading. The latter sort of thesis will make a prominent appearance in this book. Chapter 6 identifies "low-level" mindreading processes associated with detecting emotions and pain in others. Chapter 7 identifies "high-level" mindreading processes associated with detecting propositional attitudes. Both types of processes qualify as simulationist, but they don't share all their interesting architectural properties. Low-level processes might be somewhat modular, whereas high-level processes seem to be nonmodular (see chapters 5 and 6). In any case, ST should not be required to identify a single paradigm of simulation that fits all cases. This is one reason that my definition of simulation is deliberately abstract.

2.7 ST-TT Hybrids

I have already announced my endorsement of a hybrid overall theory, a theory that combines elements of simulation, projection, and theorizing. This section formulates a number of ways to blend simulation and theorizing elements into a mosaic of mindreading possibilities. We have already seen that, contrary to traditional wisdom, simulation and theory need not compete with one another. Theorizing might implement simulation, implying that simulating and theorizing jointly execute mindreading. Other relationships are also possible.

2.7.1 Implementation

There are two ways whereby theorizing might implement simulation. This is because simulation for mindreading is (arguably) a "control" operation that *directs* a variety of processes or operations.[17] When one simulates a decision process, for example, the control operation directs the creation of pretend desires and beliefs and, once these are created, selects the decision-making system as the system into which to feed these pretend desires and beliefs as inputs. So there is a higher-order process—the simulation control process—and a number of lower-order processes, such as the decision-making process. Either of these types of processes might be implemented by a tacit theory. That is, theorizing could implement the control process, could implement the processes directed by the control process, or both. In none of these cases would simulation be threatened by theorizing.

This general idea is anticipated by Stich and Nichols (1992):

> There are some theorists—Fodor assures us that he is one—who believe that the practical reasoning system goes about its business by exploiting an internally represented decision theory. If this is right, then we exploit a tacit theory each time we make a decision based on our beliefs and desires. But now if we make predictions about other people's behavior by taking our own practical reasoning system off-line, then we also exploit a tacit theory when we make these predictions. Thus, contrary to the [earlier] suggestion ... off-line simulation

processes and processes exploiting an internally represented theory are not mutually exclusive, since some off-line simulation processes may also exploit a tacit theory. (1992: 47, n. 7)

This denial of mutual exclusivity is exactly right and illustrates one way in which simulating *might* be implemented by theorizing. Another way is for the "control" process of simulation itself to exploit a tacit theory, for example, a theory describing how pretend states are to be selected, how a suitable psychological mechanism is to be chosen, and how the selected pretend states are to be fed into the psychological mechanism.

I do not myself endorse either of these implementation theses. In the case of a decision-making mechanism, it is vastly more plausible to hold that the mechanism *conforms* to certain psychological laws but doesn't *represent* or otherwise *possess* them. This parallels the case of rocks, which obey the dynamic laws of physics without representing them. Similarly, a decision-making mechanism makes decisions as a function of the desire and belief inputs it receives, and this function is describable by psychological laws. But the mechanism does not itself describe those laws; it merely instantiates them. Although this view strikes me as eminently more sensible than its rival, the matter cannot be settled without a satisfactory theory of tacit knowledge or representation. As we saw in section 2.3, such a theory is not easy to come by. So all I am saying here is that it isn't essential to ST's viability that the theory-implementation story be false. I believe it is false, but I don't have to defend that view in detail.

2.7.2 Cooperation

If all third-person mindreading used simulation, then even if simulation were implemented by theory, there would be a sense in which pure simulationism would be vindicated: No mindreading would occur without simulation. But suppose that many token mindreading routines combine simulation elements with theorizing elements, where the latter are not simply simulation implementations. Then pure simulationism certainly would not be correct. A hybrid approach would be called for. I call this scenario "cooperation," and it seems to me highly probable.

For the sake of concreteness, two plausible examples of cooperation may be sketched. First, theory may be used to select pretend inputs. In a decision-prediction task, an attributor would use theoretical reasoning to infer the target's initial states (desires and beliefs), for which corresponding pretend states are constructed. The pretend states are then fed into the decision-making mechanism, which outputs a decision. The first step of this sequence features theorizing, whereas the remaining steps feature simulating.

A second example introduces a different pattern of mindreading, probably as common as the pattern of decision-making prediction. In decision prediction, the target's initially specified states are presumptive *causes* of a subsequent effect or outcome, which is to be calculated. The mindreader moves "forward" from the prior evidence events to their effect. Many mental attributions, however, must fit a second pattern, in which a sought-after mental state is the cause of some known (or believed) *effects*. Here the attributor moves "backward" from evidence states (observed behavior, facial expressions, etc.) to the mental cause of interest. How might the second pattern involve simulation? The difficulty is that psychological mechanisms probably do not run backward, only forward.[18] If mechanisms are restricted to forward directionality, how can simulation be employed in an evidence-posterior pattern?

This type of mindreading might be approached via a *generate-and-test* strategy. The attributor begins with a known effect of a sought-after state, often an observable piece of behavior. He generates one or more hypotheses about the prior mental state or combination of states that might be responsible for this effect. He then "tests" (one or more of) these hypotheses by pretending to be in these states, feeding them into an appropriate psychological mechanism, and seeing whether the output matches the observed evidence. When a match is found (perhaps the first match, or the "best" match), he attributes the hypothesized state or combination of states to the target.

The generate-and-test strategy employs simulation at a crucial juncture but also relies on theorizing. Theorizing seems necessary to generate hypotheses about states responsible for the observed effects, hypotheses presumably prompted by background information. Thus, pure simulationism is inapplicable here. The generate-and-test strategy requires cooperation between simulating and theorizing. This is another major reason that a hybrid approach seems compelling.

2.7.3 Independence

A final type of relationship between simulating and theorizing is independence. This means that some instances of mindreading—possibly entire categories of mindreading—are executed wholly by simulation or wholly by theorizing. *Independence* refers to cases in which neither method implements the other or cooperates with the other within a single token of mindreading. Perhaps certain types of mental states are always mindread wholly by theorizing, and other types are always mindread wholly by simulating (plus projecting). Or perhaps certain types of evidence are always exploited via theory, and other types are always exploited via simulation. If either of these scenarios is correct, it provides yet another reason that an overall approach must be a theory-simulation blend.

A reader familiar with the traditional configuration of the ST-TT debate may feel a bit perplexed at this juncture. If simulating and theorizing are compatible, especially via the implementation relationship, what happens to the old opposition between theorizing and simulating? It seems to evaporate. True, I still insist on the possibilities of cooperation and independence, in which theorizing and simulating retain their distinctive identities. I am not declaring that simulation "reduces" to theorizing or vice versa. But the moderate rapprochement between theorizing and simulating that I admit as a possibility seems to blur the old contrast, and that seems unsettling. What are the new terms of debate?

A helpful way to frame the new debate is in terms of ST versus *simulation-neglecting TT*. Under these terms of debate, it's no longer enough for TT to show that theorizing somehow takes place in mindreading; it must also show that this theorizing isn't merely an implementation of simulation.[19] Orthodox TT has usually denied or minimized the role of simulation. So it seems fair to reconstruct the debate so that TT has the burden of making good on its neglect of simulation. TT must show that theorizing isn't merely scaffolding for simulational processes. By the same token, proponents of ST (or a simulation-centered hybrid) can no longer earn victory over TT simply by showing that theorizing is not the standard method of mindreading. To gain victory over its rivals, ST must establish the intensive use of simulation as defined by the *positive* characteristics we have described. The major change in our new delineation of ST is that its defenders are no longer required to demonstrate the absence of theorizing. Demonstrating such an absence has long been regarded as a core burden of ST (avoiding "collapse" into TT). This is an obscure task, given the opacity of the notion of "tacit" theory. The new terms of the debate free ST from this old, misplaced burden.

If the test of ST is a positive one, however, more must be said about the positive characteristics of simulational mindreading. One point in need of clarification is the connection between our resemblance definition of simulation and the standard ST story about mental pretense, highlighted in figure 2.3. So I end this chapter with an explanation of what I mean by mental pretense and how it fits with the resemblance, or duplication, account of simulation.

2.8 Pretense and Imagination

There are two ways to conceptualize mental pretense.[20] First, *pretense* may refer to a distinctive type of propositional attitude, on a par with other attitudes like belief, desire, and intention. This is how Alan Leslie treats it: "My assumption is that there is a small set of primitive informational relations available early on, among them BELIEVE and PRETEND" (1994: 218). For Leslie, PRETEND is a state that can fill the attitude slot in a metarepresentational relation (Leslie 1994: 217). Nichols and Stich (2003) favor a similar notion (though they criticize Leslie's theory in other respects). They introduce a psychological construct called a "possible world box," and mental pretense is described as putting representations into one's possible world box. Although the possible world box is analogous to their belief box, they say that the functional role of representations in the possible world box is quite different from the functional role of either beliefs or desires. This confirms the impression that mental pretense is understood as a distinct type of propositional attitude.

This approach does not suit ST. If pretense is a distinct attitude, how can we intelligibly talk about pretend-belief, pretend-desire, pretend-hope, and so forth, as simulationists are wont to do? If pretense is a separate attitude, each hyphenated phrase would designate a compound attitude, and it's unclear what such a compound would be.

A second way to conceptualize mental pretense is to conceptualize it, in the first instance, as an operation or process. The outputs of the process can be called pretend states. This is my preferred way to conceptualize mental pretense. Moreover, I want to identify the operation of mental pretense with a species of imagination. Imagination is an operation or process that scientific psychology should take seriously, something to which it should be ontologically committed. However, there are different possible approaches to imagination and perhaps different types of imagination.[21]

In ordinary language, the verb *imagine* sometimes takes a *that*-clause complement, and in this construction, imagining that p is roughly equivalent to *supposing* that p. If I imagine that the United States lacked the atomic bomb in 1945, what I do is *suppose, assume,* or *hypothesize* that the United States lacked the bomb in 1945. Exclusive focus on this construction might lead to the view that imagination is always supposition. The trouble with this, as a full account of imagination, is that imagining sometimes generates different mental products. Imagining can create imagery of various kinds, as when one imagines seeing certain sights or hearing certain tunes run through one's head. Notice that in these uses, there is a different syntactic construction: "imagine M-ing" or "imagine feeling M," where *M* can designate any of a number of mental states, not just suppositions. For example, I can imagine seeing a yellow parrot, feeling sad, feeling outraged, or feeling elated. It is also possible, no doubt, to imagine *that* one feels elated, which is equivalent to assuming the truth of the proposition "I am elated." But there is another way to imagine feeling elated, namely, to conjure up a state that feels, phenomenologically, rather like a trace or tincture of elation. Our ability to do this is not confined to sensations, perceptions, or emotions. One can also imagine having attitudes such as desire, hope, doubt, and ambivalence. The range of states that can be imagined suggests that imagining, in a more inclusive sense, is an operation or process capable of creating a wide variety of mental states. Imagination's output, so understood, is not a single type of state but any one of a number of mental-state types, most of which are not suppositions. When I imagine feeling elated, I do not merely suppose *that* I am elated; rather, I *enact,* or *try* to enact, elation itself. Thus, we might call this type of imagination *"enactment imagination."*

Another mental verb that displays a similar range of interpretations and grammatical complements is *remember*. A person can remember *that* she was drunk, *that* she felt elated, or *that* she saw a tortoise cross the road. But she can also remember *being* drunk, *feeling* elated, or *seeing* a tortoise cross the road. These syntactic constructions for describing memory correspond roughly to what psychologists call "semantic" memory and "episodic" memory. It is debatable whether episodic memory requires reenactment of a remembered episode. But, I submit, imagining being in M does require at least partial enactment, or attempted enactment, of being in M.

I propose that pretend states—in the sense intended by ST—are states produced by enactment imagination (E-imagination). A pretend desire is the product of enacting, or attempting to enact, desire; a pretend state of fear is the product of enacting, or attempting to enact, fear; and so on. Pretend desire is quasi desire produced by E-imagination, pretend fear is quasi fear produced by E-imagination, and so forth. All of these proposals have at least some intuitive appeal, but I do not rest my proposals on intuitive considerations. In chapter 7, we'll explore empirical evidence to see whether this entire idea of construing imagination and pretense in enactment terms is viable.

What's the connection between imagination in the suppositional sense (S-imagination) and E-imagination? One possibility is that S-imagination is a species of E-imagination. Supposing that p may be equivalent to E-imagining *believing* that p. In other words, a supposition might be a pretend-belief, where this is understood in the enactment sense of pretense or imagination. An alternative possibility is that S-imagination is a sui generis form of imagination, irreducible to E-imagination. I am attracted by the reductive proposal but won't insist on it.[22]

We speak colloquially of "make believe." To make believe that p is to make oneself have a certain belief or belieflike state. Analogously, there are states of "make desire," "make hope," and so on. A process-product distinction is appropriate here. In the process sense, "making" believe is the activity of *endogenously* producing token states that resemble beliefs, that is, states that are normally produced in an *exogenous*, nonpretend fashion. In the product sense, make-believe is a state produced in this endogenous or top-down fashion. What simulationists call "pretend states" are states like make-believe, make-desire, and so forth. They are states produced by an operation of mental pretense, or E-imagination.

Of course, pretend states constructed for mindreading purposes may not match the intended states of the target even approximately because they may have been chosen badly out of ignorance. But what kinds of matching, or resemblance, are pretend states capable of, in the best of conditions—when the propositional content is aptly chosen? How closely can a pretend-desire for p resemble a genuine, nonpretend desire that p? Moreover, what are the pertinent respects of resemblance?

At least three categories of resemblance are eligible: introspectible, functional, and neural respects of resemblance. For some categories of imagination-created states, especially visual and auditory imagery, there seem to be substantial introspectible points of resemblance. For other categories of pretend states, introspectible resemblances are more problematic. Can one tell introspectively how similar a state of pretending-to-hope-that-p is to a genuine hope-that-p? In any event, cognitive scientists will place little credence in introspectible resemblances. These are not measurable facts. Another reason to place minimal weight on introspectible respects of resemblance is that their comparative paucity probably understates the overall resemblance between states. Pairs of states quite similar in functional and/or neurological respects may be quite different in terms of introspective accessibility. Many illustrations of this will be encountered in chapters 6 and 7.

When we turn to the functional and neural categories, promising dimensions of resemblance are revealed by empirical research. A pretend desire with a given content might share important functional properties with a non-pretend desire of the same content, and "endogenously" generated fear might share important neural properties with normal, "exogenously" generated fear. Initially, the prospect of functional and neurological similarities may seem dim. Surprising as it may sound, though, research supports such theses. These are the kinds of similarities I consider most relevant to ST.

ST orthodoxy assigns a pivotal role to the creation and deployment of pretend states. Given their prominence in the present treatment, including the diagrammatic presentation in figure 2.3, the reader might assume that pretense and pretend states are essential parts of *my* ST story as well. This is not so. Pretense and pretend states are one possible realization of the resemblance-related features crucial to simulation, but not the only possible realization. The constructs of imagination and pretense have connotations associated with higher (and more "central") cognitive activity than some of the activities we'll be dealing with here. As chapter 6 will indicate, recent cognitive science and cognitive neuroscience disclose striking instances of mental simulation that are largely automatic and unconscious. These cases are ones to which terms like *imagine, imagination, pretend*, and *pretense* do not naturally apply. These cases are probably underpinned by a very different neurocognitive architecture. By disengaging our account of simulation from pretense or imagination, we leave room for this important class of cases. At the same time, cases that comfortably fit under the rubrics of pretense and imagination can also fit under the heading of simulation, given our resemblance explication of that notion. Thus, our treatment of low-level simulational mindreading in chapter 6 makes no reference to E-imagination or pretense, whereas the treatment of high-level simulational mindreading in chapter 7 makes extensive reference to E-imagination and pretend states.

This completes my conceptual overview of the mentalizing controversy, as well as my articulation of the theoretical construct of simulation. The foundation is now laid for the empirical evidence of simulation to be assembled in chapters 6, 7, and 8. We shall show, first, that mental simulation, both intrapersonal and interpersonal, is a robust phenomenon of the human mind. This includes interpersonal mental mirroring, or resonance (chapter 6), as well as visual and motor imagery (chapter 7). Second, a wide range of evidence will be presented that supports the thesis that mental simulation is intensively used for mindreading. Well-replicated findings, such as deficits in face-based emotion recognition (chapter 6) and rampant egocentrism (chapter 7), are most naturally and plausibly explained by simulational methods of attribution. Before turning to this evidence, however, we use the next three chapters to pinpoint problems with ST's principal rivals: rationality theory, child-scientist theory, and modularity theory. Readers mainly interested in ST could proceed directly to chapter 6.

Notes

1. As we shall see, however, it isn't necessary for ST to deny that theoretical inference plays some kind of role in mentalizing; it might even implement a simulation routine.

2. As we shall see in chapter 4, there is at least one proponent of TT, namely, Andrew Meltzoff, who subscribes to this variant. In general, however, special first-person knowledge is anathema to psychologist proponents of TT.

3. Thus, in chapter 5, Alan Leslie's view is classified as a specimen of TT because he maintains a theoretical-inference view of third-person attribution, though he rejects a functionalist, or conceptual-role, account of mental-state concepts. As a somewhat distinct matter, notice the importance of distinguishing between functionalism as a theory of folk mental-state *concepts* and functionalism as a *factual*, or *metaphysical*, matter (psychofunctionalism). It is one thing to say that tokens of mental-state types *in fact* have patterns of causal interaction with external stimuli, peripheral behavior, and other mental-state tokens or even to say that tokens of mental-state types are (metaphysically) *constituted* by such interactions. Either of these theses is a far cry from the thesis that the folk naïvely *represent*, or *conceptualize*, mental-state types in terms of such causal interaction patterns. The question of contents for mental-state concepts concerns only the latter issue, the "conceptualization" issue, not the factual or metaphysical issue.

4. An alternative, modular approach to TT might say that the psychological law does not get deployed in the form of a premise belief that is inputted into the inferential process. Rather, a module specialized for decision prediction incorporates such a law in its inferential architecture and processes belief and desire inputs in accordance with it. Although this approach is possible, I know of nobody who has explicitly embraced it, so it will be ignored in future discussion.

5. A modular form of TT would hold that the reasoning is executed by a dedicated theory-of-mind module rather than by a general-purpose reasoning mechanism.

However, a factual reasoning mechanism would still do the essential work. That much is common to all forms of TT and stands in contrast with the (pure) ST approach.

6. The term *routine* is used here and throughout in a loose and nontechnical sense.

7. Thanks to Kelby Mason for this point.

8. I refer here to a finding of Mitchell, Banaji, and Macrae (2005), to be discussed in section 7.5. In addition, one prominent theory-theorist, Andrew Meltzoff, has frequently proposed that infants make "like me" (mental) inferences based on imitation (see section 4.8).

9. There is a close parallel here with the classicism-connectionism debate in cognitive science. Classicists often point out that classical computation might be implemented by connectionist networks, yet this is perfectly compatible with the truth of classicism, properly understood.

10. To increase confusion, there is a third sense of *simulation* positioned halfway between the computational modeling sense and the replication sense intended here. In cognitive science, the phrase *mental simulation* is sometimes used for the kind of cognitive activity posited by the *mental models* approach (Craik, 1943; Johnson-Laird, 1983; Johnson-Laird and Byrne, 1991; Hegarty, 2004). According to this approach, the mind constructs small-scale models of reality that are used (in working memory) to represent and reason about the world. Mental models are often said to be "isomorphic" to the physical situations they represent or to exhibit "analog" properties. This appears to combine the replication or resemblance theme with the modeling theme and is therefore easily confused with either the computational modeling sense, on the one hand, or the replication sense, on the other. A point to be emphasized is that when I speak of "mental simulation," I shall mean a replication or duplication of another *mental* state. A mental simulation is a simulation *of* a mental state *by* a mental state. By contrast, the mental models approach regards mental simulations as simulations of, and hence isomorphic to, *external* or *physical* states of affairs. This application is one I reject, or have strong doubts about, at least if "isomorphism" implies any simple, commonsense form of resemblance.

11. It is probably inappropriate to regard a token process P as having the function of duplicating a particular process P′. A more careful formulation would say that the token process P is of a type whose function is to duplicate another type (of which P′ is a token).

12. Perhaps a better label would be "mental-mental" simulation, as suggested by Justin Fisher. But I'll stick with the shorter form.

13. The exact spatiotemporal contours of seeing the ocean are a delicate matter. Some might want to include in this process the light waves that travel from the ocean to the perceiver's retinas. For present purposes, however, the only relevant part of seeing is the part that takes place in the perceiver's mind. In this context, that is the intended referent of the term *seeing*.

14. The term *successful* is not intended here to imply purposefulness or intentionality. I don't wish to claim that all simulation is purposeful. In calling a simulation successful, I merely mean that it involves genuine duplication, at least approximate duplication, whether intended or unintended.

15. Without mentioning this body of experimental evidence, Nichols and Stich (2003) also observe that people tend to impute their own beliefs to others. They accordingly posit a special method of mindreading they call "default belief attribution."

16. Jeannerod and Pacherie (2004) also list explicitness as a dimension of variability. I don't follow suit here because I don't regard explicitness or implicitness (consciousness or nonconsciousness) as a dimension of *strength*. An implicit simulational process is still fully simulational. The mindreading processes discussed in chapter 6 are almost all thoroughly implicit, but this doesn't make them weaker instances of simulation than explicit examples.

17. Thanks to Robert M. Harnish (personal communication) for suggesting that simulation involves a control process, as well as embedded processes of other kinds.

18. Facial expression of emotion is a possible exception, to be explored in chapter 6.

19. This new framing of the TT-ST debate—in which theory-theorists must show that theorizing isn't merely an implementation of simulation—nicely resembles the standard framing of the dispute between classicist and (radical) connectionist views of cognitive architecture. Thanks here to Philip Robbins.

20. Mental pretense stands in contrast to behavioral pretense. It does not involve any outward behavior, just mental states. Pretend play, being a behavioral matter, is not included under the heading of mental pretense, though mental pretense would, presumably, be the internal guide to outward pretend play.

21. Currie and Ravenscroft (2002) have independently developed a similar treatment of imagination and mental pretense.

22. For further discussion, see chapter 7.

3

The Rationality Theory

3.1 Mindreading as Rationalizing

The rationality (or rationality/charity) theory was briefly examined in chapter 2, but now we make a more thorough inspection of it. First, however, some readers might object to even including this theory in a list of mindreading theories. Isn't rationality theory, especially in the hands of philosophers like Dennett and Davidson, really a theory of the metaphysical status of propositional attitudes rather than a theory of mental attribution? Doesn't it aim to specify possession conditions for attitudinal states rather than how attributors go about their business of mindreading? (These possession conditions allegedly involve normative features, not purely descriptive ones.)

Undoubtedly, philosophical interest in rationality theory centers heavily on its metaphysical ramifications. But these are of interest only on the assumption that rationality theory gives a reasonably accurate account of how the attitudes are deployed, that is, deployed in folk psychologizing. That Dennett intends his intentional-stance theory as an account of mindreading is amply clear in his writing.[1] Here are two unambiguous statements to this effect: "Consider first how we go about populating each other's heads with beliefs" (1987: 17). To populate people's heads with beliefs, of course, is to mindread. "Do people actually use this strategy? Yes, all the time. There may someday be other strategies for attributing belief and desire and for predicting behavior, but this is the only one we all know now" (1987: 21). Finally, there are psychologists who follow Dennett's intentional-stance theory, and they clearly embrace it *as* a theory of mindreading (or a theory of action prediction). Specifically, Gergeley et al. (1995) argue that the intentional stance is adopted by 12-month-old infants.

Let us turn, then, to an assessment of the theory. An immediate obstacle, however, is the difficulty of identifying a clear formulation of it. Formulations by leading proponents such as Dennett and Davidson are rather elusive and have mutated in response to criticism. We also need to determine whether the rationality approach offers a complete, integrated theory of the kind we want, offering answers to all four questions on our primary list. The most prominent writings in this tradition do not squarely address all the questions, and it's an open question whether the approach can answer them. Another issue is scope. As indicated earlier, the rationality theory (RT) does not purport to explain the mindreading of all types of mental states; it is restricted to the propositional attitudes. What does this imply for a general theory of mentalizing? Finally, the fundamental question is whether the theory proves tenable even for the domain it purports to handle.

The basic idea behind RT (or intentional stance theory) is quite simple. To mindread a target is to rationalize her, to assign a set of states that make her come out (as much as possible) as a rational agent and thinker. Beyond this simple formula, however, the going gets tough. RT faces a dilemma. According to strong versions of it, attributors make strong assumptions of logicality, rationality, and truth-proneness. It is hard to sustain such strong versions as descriptively, or "empirically," correct. Weak versions of RT, on the other hand, are prone to underspecification: They fail to have clear implications about how attributors go about their mentalizing tasks. Dennett vacillates between these alternatives and never resolves the tension. Let us see how this plays out for the case of belief.

3.2 Rationality and Belief Attribution

According to Dennett, the assumption—or "myth"—of rationality lies at the core of folk psychology:

> However rational we are, it is the myth of our rational agenthood that structures and organizes our attributions of belief and desire to others and that regulates our own deliberations and investigations. We aspire to rationality, and without the myth of our rationality the concepts of belief and desire would be uprooted. Folk psychology, then, is *idealized* in that it produces its predictions and explanations by calculating in a normative system; it predicts what we will believe, desire, and do, by determining what we ought to believe, desire, and do. (1987: 52)

This points to a strong version of RT, which might be formulated as follows:

(SRT) Attributors always interpret targets, insofar as possible, as conforming with all normative principles of reasoning and choice.

In his early writing on intentional systems, Dennett applied something like (SRT) to belief and logical deduction. Proceeding on the widely held assumption that it is a normative principle of reasoning that you should believe whatever follows by rules of logic from anything else you believe, he wrote:

> The assumption that something is an intentional system is the assumption that it is rational; that is, one gets nowhere with the assumption that entity x has beliefs p, q, r ... unless one also supposes that x believes what follows from p, q, r. ... So whether or not the animal [who is interpreted as an intentional system] is said to *believe* the *truths* of logic, it must be supposed to *follow* the *rules* of logic. (1978b: 10–11)

Is it true that whenever attributors assign some belief P to a target, they also assign to her beliefs in all the logical consequences of P? This is palpably false. Attributors clearly allow for the possibility that people forget or ignore many of their prior beliefs and fail to draw all the logical consequences that might be warranted (Stich, 1981). In any case, the logical consequences of any prior set of beliefs are infinite, and it is doubtful that naïve attributors impute infinitely many beliefs to their targets.

The problem isn't confined to deductive closure; it applies equally to inconsistency avoidance. A putative norm of rationality is to avoid believing all members of any inconsistent set of propositions. The question for (SRT) is whether attributors try to interpret their targets' beliefs so as to "protect" them from violating this norm. Do attributors really proceed in this protectionist spirit? Absent relevant empirical work,[2] I appeal to a thought experiment (the same methodology used by Dennett).

Here is a variant of the paradox of the preface. George publishes a book in which he modestly concedes (asserts) in the preface that the book surely contains some falsehood, although he has been very careful and believes each thing asserted in the text. The resulting set of assertions by George is inconsistent. (If all propositions in the text are true, then the proposition in the preface is false, etc.) If attributors conformed to (SRT), no attributor would attribute to George *belief* in all these propositions. Instead, an attributor would find some different pattern of beliefs to assign to George. But—here comes the thought experiment—as one everyday interpreter, I would certainly not desist from attributing to George belief in all the asserted propositions. On the contrary, I would assume that George simply didn't notice the inconsistency and went ahead and believed all the propositions. So the norm of inconsistency avoidance does not guide belief attribution as (SRT) claims (Goldman, 1989).

Responding to worries of this type lodged by Stich (1981), Dennett grants that he has "hedged and hinted and entertained claims that [he has] later qualified or retracted" (1987: 94). So he proceeds once again to issue some retractions:

[A] few words on what rationality is *not*. It is not deductive closure. . . . Nor is rationality perfect logical consistency. (1987: 94–95)

If rationality of belief isn't determined by these logical relations, what does determine it?

The problem is more acute than Dennett realizes. In denying that rationality is governed by deductive closure, he means that rationality doesn't require agents to infer *all* logical consequences of their prior belief sets. But what about inferring a single proposition that logically follows from one's prior belief set? Is that always rationally permissible? Not so. Sometimes it is more rational to retract prior beliefs than to add new consequences of those beliefs. If you suddenly notice that one logical implication of your prior beliefs is a bizarre proposition, it is more rational to retract some prior beliefs than to accept that bizarre proposition. Unfortunately, unambiguous advice about rational belief formation cannot be obtained from principles of logic (Harman, 1973; Goldman, 1986). But if logic doesn't generate rules of rational belief, what does? Epistemological theorists, I fear, have no satisfactory answer. Although epistemologists lack such a theory, ordinary belief attributors might somehow manage to attribute beliefs in accord with the right rules of some still unknown theory of rationality. But what reason is there to suppose this?

Even if epistemology (by my lights) has no satisfactory theory of rationality, plenty of workers in related disciplines think they know what rationality consists in. Many researchers think that Bayesianism supplies principles of rational probabilistic judgment; others think that the transitivity of preference and the sure-thing principle constitute principles of rational preference or choice. Suppose some of these theories are right. How does the rationality approach to attitude attribution fare if these are the right principles? Do folk attributors use them in imputing attitudes to others? When it comes to the probability judgments, preferences, and choices of naïve agents, a large body of empirical literature suggests that people don't themselves conform to these precepts. They *could*, of course, violate these precepts in their own cognitive life but assume that others conform to them. But what reason is there to suppose this? On the contrary, the empirical literature strongly suggests that naïve agents have no clear grasp, even a tacit grasp, of these principles (Kahneman, Slovic, and Tversky, 1982; Kahneman and Tversky, 2000; Gilovich, Griffin, and Kahneman, 2002). If so, how could it be that they employ them in attributing attitudes to others?

Finally, attributors almost certainly impute to targets some clear cases of *irrational* belief-forming transitions. Leaping to conclusions and engaging in wishful thinking are foibles most people exemplify at least occasionally. Presumably, they are examples of epistemic irrationality. Are we to suppose that attributors never appreciate these foibles and never impute beliefs to others arising from them? That is precisely what (SRT) implies. It says that attributors always interpret targets as conforming to all normative principles of reasoning, so they must not interpret them as making mistakes like leaping to conclusions or engaging in wishful thinking. Surely, such a strong version of the rationality approach isn't right.

Weaker formulations of the rationality approach are obviously possible. Dennett sometimes seems attracted to this line.

> *Of course* we don't all sit in the dark in our studies like mad Leibnizians rationalistically excogitating behavioral predictions from pure, idealized concepts of our neighbors, nor do we derive all our readiness to attribute desires to a careful generation of them from the ultimate goal of survival. We may observe that some folks seem to desire cigarettes, or pain, or notoriety (we observe this by hearing them tell us, seeing what they choose, etc.) and without any conviction that these people, given their circumstances, ought to have these desires, we attribute them anyway. So rationalistic generation of attributions is augmented and even corrected on occasion by empirical generalizations about belief and desire that guide our attributions and are learned more or less inductively.... I would insist, however, that all this empirically obtained lore is laid over a fundamental generative and normative framework that has the features I have described. (Dennett, 1987: 53–54)

Here Dennett substantially qualifies his rationality theory by introducing an admixture of theory-theory. Suddenly we are told that people don't make attributions based solely on the "oughts" of rationality theory but (to a large extent) on empirically derived generalizations. Although this may be a sensible move toward greater accuracy, it also means the devolution of a once clear theory into a highly inchoate one. How, exactly, are rational *oughts* mixed with empirical *iss*? It's anybody's guess.

Elsewhere, Dennett proposes yet another variation on RT (1987: 98–101). First, he says, one may decline to identify rationality with the features of any formal system. But if formal systems don't disclose the content of rationality, where should we look? He answers:

> When considering what we *ought to do*, our reflections lead us eventually to a consideration of what we *in fact do*. (1987: 98)

This makes it appear, as Dennett concedes, that he is turning to (what is now called) simulation theory, or something rather similar to it.

> Now it will appear that I am backing into ... the view that when we attribute beliefs and other intentional states to others, we do this by comparing them to ourselves, by projecting ourselves into their states of mind. (1987: 98–99)

In terms of our classification of theories, of course, this would be an abandonment of RT and a substitution of ST instead. Although Dennett doesn't adopt this maneuver, his constant shifting makes for a blurry target.

Dennett aside, other theorists attracted to RT have suggested different weakenings of the position. Edward Stein (1996: 133–134) proposes weaker formulations along the following lines:

> (WRT′) Attributors interpret targets as always conforming to *some* normative principles of reasoning.
> (WRT″) Attributors interpret targets as *sometimes* conforming to *some* normative principles of reasoning.

These proposals follow Christopher Cherniak's (1986) conception of "minimal rationality." According to Cherniak, a minimally rational agent would satisfy the condition that if inconsistencies arise in his belief set, he will sometimes eliminate some of them (Cherniak 1986: 16). Adapting this idea to the practice of attribution, a proponent of RT might say that attributors interpret their targets as minimally rational, that is, as sometimes conforming to some normative principles of reasoning. Wouldn't the plausibility of RT be enhanced if we replaced the claim that attributors impute ideal rationality with the claim that they impute minimal rationality?

Granted, this would improve RT's plausibility, but at the cost of extreme vagueness or underspecification. The new theory leaves vast areas of indeterminacy as to how attributors proceed. To say that attributors expect targets *sometimes* to conform to *some* normative principles of belief formation leaves it entirely open which beliefs an attributor will attribute on specific occasions. If a theory of attribution seeks to identify the principles that generate the specific ascriptions that attributors make, this weakened theory hardly gets to first base.

3.3 The Role of Truth

Next let us examine another strand of rationality/charity theories, in application to belief ascription, and see how similar problems materialize. As we saw in chapter 2, charity theorists commonly suggest that attributors seek to ascribe *true* beliefs to their targets, at any rate, beliefs that are true by their own (the attributors') lights. Davidson writes in one place:

> The general policy . . . is to choose truth conditions that do as well as possible in making speakers hold sentences true when (according to the theory and the theory builder's view of the facts) those sentences are true. (1984a: 152)

And elsewhere he writes:

> A theory of interpretation cannot be correct that makes a man assent to very many false sentences; it must generally be the case that a sentence is true when a

speaker holds it to be. ... The basic methodological precept is, therefore, that a good theory of interpretation maximizes agreement. Or, given that sentences are infinite in number, and given further considerations to come, a better word might be *optimize*. (1984a: 169)

Thus, Davidson's theory of interpretation seems to say that attributors so impute beliefs to a target as to maximize (or optimize) the number of truths the target believes. Is this strong version of the charity approach correct? Here is one putative counterexample from the literature:

Suppose Paul has just arrived at a party and asserts: "The man with a martini is a philosopher." And suppose that the facts are that there is a man in plain view who is drinking water from a martini glass and that he is not a philosopher. Suppose also that in fact there is only one man at the party drinking a martini, that he is a philosopher, and that he is out of sight. (Grandy, 1973: 445)

What belief does Paul express with his assertion? Is it a belief that the first man, the one in plain view, is a martini-drinking philosopher? Or is it a belief that the second man, the one out of sight, is a martini-drinking philosopher? More relevant to our discussion, which of these beliefs would an interpreter, in possession of these facts, impute to Paul? The charity approach ostensibly implies that an interpreter will impute to Paul the belief that the second man is a martini-drinking philosopher, because that belief is true, and hence imputing it would maximize truth. But what an interpreter would actually do is impute to Paul the belief that the first man is a martini-drinking philosopher, even though this belief is false. So the charity approach gets things wrong.

A charity theorist might reply that the goal of maximizing truth is well served by imputing to Paul a true belief like "A man in plain view is holding a martini glass." Once this belief is imputed, and given what Paul uttered, shouldn't the attributor also impute to him the belief "The man in plain view is a martini-drinking philosopher"? So he need not impute the belief "The man out of sight is a martini-drinking philosopher." Is this proposal warranted by the principle of truth maximization? No. If truth maximization were the dominant principle, there would be no reason for the attributor to impute the belief "The man in plain view is a martini-drinking philosopher," but there would be ample reason to impute "The man out of sight is a martini-drinking philosopher." So the proposed account must really be appealing to another strand of the charity approach, for example, the rationality strand. If Paul already believes "A man in plain view is holding a martini glass," then it would be rational of him to believe "The man in plain view is drinking a martini," and so forth. So the rationality component is what must take over here if we are to get a plausible account of an attributor's pattern of interpretation.

Unfortunately, neither Davidson nor any other rationality/charity theorist provides a clear account of the priorities used in moving between truth and rationality considerations. As a stand-alone principle, truth maximization does not work. If truth maximization is simply one factor in a priority ranking, this ranking should be specified. Instead, Davidson typically takes recourse in a much weaker principle about truth. For example, "We can, however, take it as given that *most* beliefs are correct" (1984a: 169), and "A theory of interpretation cannot be correct that makes a man assent to very many false sentences: it must generally be the case that a sentence is true when a speaker holds it to be" (1984a: 169). What Davidson really means, of course, is that most of the beliefs imputed by an attributor must be *taken* by the attributor to be true (not that they *are* true). But is this correct? If truth maximization is assigned a lower priority than rationality, this does not follow. If a target is interpreted as holding a very general theory that happens to be false, such as a whole Aristotelian cosmology and metaphysics, he might rationally believe many theoretical consequences that are also false. Similarly, an attributor guided by charity considerations, where the highest-ranked factor is rationality, might well impute to the target a majority of false beliefs. These kinds of problematic cases have been discussed in the critical literature (e.g., McGinn, 1977). So it is hard to assemble a coherent charity/rationality story that comports both with things Davidson actually says and what seems called for by a correct account of attributive practice.

3.4 Desires and Other Mental States

Beliefs are not the only mental states attributed. What story does RT tell about other states, for example, desire? Some desires result from practical reasoning from more basic desires, and the ascription of the former would be handled under the heading of rationality. This would raise problems similar to those encountered with belief. Let us instead look at what RT says about ascribing "basic" desires. Dennett tells us the following: "A system's desires are those it *ought to have*, given its biological needs. . . . 'Ought to have' means 'would have if it were *ideally* ensconced in its environmental niche'" (1987: 49, emphasis in the original).

What shall we make of this? The *oughts* of which Dennett speaks here are extremely elusive. It is doubtful that there is any clear meaning to a statement about what desires an organism *ought* to have, given its ecological niche (see Stich, 1981). But, assuming the meaning is clear, Dennett's account just seems wrong. Consider, for example, ascribing a desire for pain. This is certainly ascribed on occasion, when dealing with masochists. But is a desire for pain something a system "ought" to have, given its biological needs, or if it were ideally ensconced in its environmental niche? Presumably not. So Dennett's account can't make sense of our actual attributional practice in this territory.

There is another worry about Dennett's proposal here. The proposal intimates that attributors appeal to evolutionary principles about what would be good for a type of organism to have, given its environmental niche. But is it plausible that naïve attributors use information about environmental niches, or any other notions from evolutionary theory, to attribute basic desires? Some people reject evolutionary theory but engage in mental-state ascription in the same fashion as everybody else. Some attributors lived long before the advent of evolutionary theory and lacked any concept of an environmental niche. Humans attributed mental states to one another long before evolutionary theory appeared on the scene, and the notion that they appealed to any such theory, or to related concepts, is fanciful. There is every reason to suspect, though, that modern people use the same basic operations for mind-reading as did their ancestors.

Finally, turn to other categories of mental states, such as sensations. I suggested in chapter 2 that RT has dim prospects for handling the ascription of sensations, but perhaps that conclusion was premature. Consider sensations like hunger, thirst, and itchiness. Don't these states participate in rational relationships? Isn't it (prudentially) rational to eat when you're hungry, to drink when you're thirsty, to scratch when you itch? Can't an attributor use rationality principles to reason backward from scratching to itchiness, from voracious eating to hunger, from beer swilling to thirst? But, I reply, rationality alone doesn't do the job. Rationality principles might entitle an attributor to reason backward from an act of scratching to a desire to scratch, from an act of eating to a desire to eat, from an act of swilling to a desire to drink. It is also true that a desire to scratch can be explained by itchiness, a desire to eat by hunger, and a desire to drink by thirst. But these last three relationships are not governed by rationality. The links may be governed by functional accounts of itchiness, hunger, and thirst, respectively, but this is different from rationality principles. So RT cannot really handle these cases of sensation ascription on its own. It must be supplemented by an additional kind of theory. By contrast, each of the major rivals to the rationality theory, TT and ST, has the prospect of giving a single story for attributing both attitudes and sensations, so they enjoy a prima facie advantage over RT.

3.5 Self-Attribution

What should RT say about self-attribution of the attitudes? There are two options: a symmetric approach and an asymmetric approach. The former says that people read their own minds in the same way they read the minds of others, via rationality principles. The latter says that there is an asymmetry between first- and third-person attributions; self-ascription is done one way, and other-ascription in another. Dennett takes the first option, and Davidson the second.

Dennett says that each of us is "a sort of inveterate auto-psychologist, effortlessly inventing intentional interpretations of our own actions in an inseparable mix of confabulation, retrospective self-justification, and . . . good theorizing" (1987: 91). How would this inventive intentional self-interpretation work in the case of my own plans and intentions? Do I infer such plans and intentions from information about my other states or from circumstances that make it rational for me to have a particular plan or intention? Suppose I am deciding whom to vote for among candidates to chair my department. *Before* deciding how to vote, I may consider how it would be rational to vote. Which one of the candidates would do the best job, in terms of either the department's interests or my own? But once I make up my mind, I no longer have to engage in rational calculation to determine how I intend to vote. Once the plan is in place, I know it directly and noninferentially, without asking anew what it would be rational to do. So the strict symmetry account has little appeal.[3]

In contrast with Dennett, Davidson (2001) admits the asymmetry of the first-person case. At any rate, he admits that there is special first-person "authority," although he denies that it derives from any sort of introspection or acquaintance with inner objects. He denies that there are any entities that the mind can "entertain," "grasp," "have before it," or be "acquainted" with (2001: 35). Among the things denied are propositions, tokens of propositions, representations, or fragments of "mentalese." Does he also mean to reject instantiations of attitude types? When an attributor seeks to classify one of his current attitudinal states, he must determine not only its content but also its type. Is it a desire, a belief, a hope, a fear? Isn't there anything "inner" he has to go on here, whether object, state, or event? Apparently not, according to Davidson. At any rate, he does not suggest that any "inner" sort of thing plays a role in conferring special access. So Davidson's account of self-knowledge is quite a "deflationary one" (as Boghossian, 1989, puts it). Perhaps this isn't surprising, because his view of the attitudes, like Dennett's, is essentially "third-personal," consisting in whatever warrants interpreters in creating sense-giving interpretations.

What positive account of self-ascription, then, does Davidson offer? All that he offers is an argument for the thesis that first-person psychological ascriptions have a *presumption* of correctness that third-person ascriptions lack. The reason for this presumption is connected with the role of language in the attitudes. For Davidson (1984b), thought presupposes language. To know what somebody believes, you must know which sentences she holds true. This requires you to know what her sentences mean. In the third-person case, knowing what a speaker's sentences mean is a hurdle. In the first-person case, however, Davidson holds that there's a presumption that she knows what she means. Hence, she has special authority, not only for what her utterances mean but also for what she believes. As Barry Smith (1998) points out, however, Davidson never explains *how* a speaker knows what she means.

He just gives a "transcendental argument" to the effect that she must (usually) know. He tells us neither how someone knows what she means nor how she knows (or believes) what mental state she currently is in. So, despite discussing and admitting special first-person authority, he gives us no insight into the answer to *our* question, namely, how do people go about self-attributing mental states?

The Davidsonian link between attitudes and language hints at a method of self-attribution in cases where a speaker utters an avowal of some propositional attitude. Perhaps she infers her mental state from her own verbal avowal. But this approach is clearly backward. Surely the avowal (if sincere) is the expression of a prior belief. Furthermore, how does a person arrive at a self-attribution when it isn't explicitly avowed in language? Many mental states are privately self-ascribed without being formulated in language. How this is done is our first-person attribution question. Davidson simply doesn't answer it. Nor is it clear how it could be answered, in any credible way, within the framework of rationality/charity theory.

3.6 Mental-State Concepts under Rationality Theory

How would RT answer our question about mental-state concepts? What do the folk understand by the terms *believe*, *want*, *hope*, and *fear*? What naïvely grasped concepts do these terms express? Consider what Dennett says when he poses the question: What is it for any object or system to be a believer? He replies: "*What it is* to be a true believer is to be an *intentional system*, a system whose behavior is reliably and voluminously predictable via the intentional strategy" (1987: 15).[4] This answer is not complete, of course, because one could equally well say that what it is to be a true *desirer* is to be an intentional system, so belief would not be distinguished from desire. Set this point aside. Can Dennett's answer be used to identify the folk's *concept* of belief (or desire)? Modifying the proposal slightly, do the folk understand by the term *belief* something like the following: "a type of state, the positing of which via the intentional strategy, yields reliable and voluminous predictions of behavior"?

There are problems of detail here. Does belief ascription via the intentional strategy really yield reliable predictions of behavior? That depends on how much information the intentional stance taker possesses about the target. If his information is scant, misattributions of belief are probable, and mispredictions of behavior will ensue. So, only when the intentional strategy is used with "full" information about the target might reliable prediction follow (see Webb, 1994). With this amendment in place, does the definition capture what an ordinary person understands about belief?

No. The very idea of the intentional strategy, or the intentional stance, is a philosopher's creation, a recent one at that. It is unlikely to be in the conceptual repertoire of philosophically (or psychologically) uneducated people. As indicated in chapter 2, any concept defined in terms of the intentional strategy is unlikely to be in the layperson's conceptual repertoire. Nor is it likely to have been in the conceptual repertoire of ordinary people in earlier eras, when the concept of belief was in place but long before this brand of philosophy of mind was introduced. It is equally unlikely that 5-, 6-, or 7-year-old children have the concept of "usable to make reliable predictions via the intentional strategy." Yet children of these ages have considerable mastery of the belief concept. What they understand by belief cannot presuppose the highly reflective notion of an intentional strategy.

Perhaps RT has other resources for attacking the mental-state concept question. Perhaps the specific norms governing the attitudes can be used to specify the concepts of the attitudes. Here is one possibility. Just as functionalism says that each mental state is associated with a distinctive syndrome of typical causes and effects, so RT might suggest that each attitude is associated with a distinctive syndrome of norms. Associated with belief is the norm that one ought to have that attitude with respect to p if one's perceptual environment features the fact that p, the norm that if one has that attitude toward p and toward q, one ought to have it toward p&q, and so forth.

Several questions arise about this proposal. First, it isn't clear that there is a distinctive set of norms for each distinct attitude concept. Second, we already raised serious worries about whether clear norms are known (even tacitly) by philosophically untutored people and young children. Third, RT seems committed to the idea—at least under the present proposal—that the contents of the attitude concepts are *exhausted* by the norms. *That's all there is* to our concepts of the attitudes, RT seems to say. As Dennett puts it, intentional attribution abstracts from the realization of belief, desire, and the other attitudes; it treats these realizations as "black boxes" (1987: 58). Subpersonal cognitive psychology is charged with the task of specifying the implementation mechanisms of belief, desire, and the other attitudes, but these matters are beyond the ken of the folk. Is it plausible that *all* we commonsensically know about desire and belief are the norms that govern them?

Objections can be raised from many directions. Some will complain that we have an "inward" awareness of intrinsic characteristics of desire and belief that isn't captured by the hypothesized norms. Others will complain that the folk know causal properties of desire and belief, not simply norms. A third, more general, worry is whether it would be possible for people untrained in abstract thought to represent a given act or state solely in terms of the norms associated with it without first understanding (in some terms or other) *which* act or state is governed by the norms. Philosophers are trained to understand abstract definite descriptions, so a definition of the form "The state-type governed by norms N1, N2, and N3" is not unfamiliar or forbidding. But even college students with no training in philosophy, I wager, might have difficulty grasping such a definition. People usually learn norms about a given type of activity only when they already have a prior grasp of the activity the norm governs. They easily grasp norms governing the return of borrowed library books because they have a prior understanding of what it is to return a book to a library. But the present proposal says that a prior grasp of norms is all people have at their disposal to comprehend what a belief is. They have no independent understanding of what it means to believe something. They are supposed to glean such an understanding from a specification of a list of norms (although the specific list of norms remains obscure). This proposal is hard to credit; but RT has no better one on offer.

3.7 Empirical Research on the Intentional Stance

The discussion has thus far been confined to philosophical treatments of RT. Let's now examine related empirical research by Gyorgy Gergely, Gergely Csibra, and colleagues, which is guided by the intentional-stance idea. Based on a series of experiments, this group claims to have evidence that 12-month-old infants take the intentional stance in interpreting an agent's goal-directed actions. Thus, they claim to find empirical support for the foundational role of rationality in the intentional analysis of behavior (Gergely et al., 1995; Csibra, Gergely, Biro, Koos, and Brockbank, 1999; Csibra, Biro, Koos, and Gergely, 2003; Gergely and Csibra, 2003).

The group's central hypothesis is that infants have a theory of agency that features, as its foundational component, an assumption of *rationality of action*. Thus, an infant who observes an equifinal approach behavior of an agent toward a given spatial location will attribute that location as the goal of the agent's actions. Furthermore, the infant will be able to generate an expectation as to the most likely future pathway through which the agent will approach its goal in a new situation. In particular, the infant will expect the agent to get to its spatial location through the shortest available pathway or the one requiring least effort.

To test these ideas, the investigators conducted an experiment in which 12-month old infants were habituated to a computer-animated goal-directed event in which a small circle approached and contacted a large circle by jumping over a rectangular obstacle separating them. During the test phase, the rectangular obstacle was removed. Infants then saw two test displays: the same jumping goal-approach as before (though there was nothing to jump *over*) or a perceptually novel straight-line goal-approach. They looked longer at the old jumping action and showed no dishabituation to the novel straight-line approach. This suggests that the jumping action violated their expectation for the agent's action once the obstacle was removed. Apparently, they appreciated the fact that the new rational route to the goal would be the straight-line approach (although they had not previously seen it employed), and they expected the agent to choose that rational route.

Gergely, Csibra, and collaborators viewed this evidence, plus similar experimental demonstrations, as support for the intentional stance theory. However, it can be explained just as easily by the simulationist approach. Proponents of ST can say that the infants formed an expectation by "putting themselves into the agent's place" and deciding what they would do. They expected the agent to behave likewise. That's why they were surprised by the agent's selection of the jumping action.

In a later article, Gergely and Csibra (2003) address the possibility of a simulationist explanation. In doing so, however, they clarify exactly what their intentional-stance model of the 12-month-old purports to say. Because it is widely thought that 12-month-old infants are not able to attribute beliefs, Gergeley and Csibra do not mean to impute a *mentalistic* action interpretation system to 12-month-olds.[5] Instead, 1-year-olds represent, explain, and predict goal-directed actions by applying a nonmentalistic, reality-based system, which they call the "teleological stance." One-year-olds, they suggest, interpret goal-directed actions without attributing intentional mental states to the actor's mind. The teleological stance makes reference only to the relevant aspects of reality—action, goal-state, and situational constraints—as those are represented by the interpreting infant herself (Gergely and Csibra, 2003: 289). Gergely and Csibra contrast the nonmentalistic character of their own approach with that of the simulationist approach, evidently assuming that a nonmentalistic approach is preferable when it comes to 1-year-olds.

It is obvious, however, that simulationism can equally take this route. Using a modified simulationalist routine, the infant could put herself in the actor's place, decide what to do, and form an expectation that the actor will do likewise, all without imputing any mental states to the actor. This alternative theory is readily available to ST, if one is persuaded that 12-month-olds do not impute attitudes (especially beliefs). So Gergely and colleagues' experiments establish no superiority of RT over ST.

One might also wonder whether a switch from the intentional stance to the teleological stance, with the latter's nonmentalism, would be welcomed by the likes of Dennett. The entire rationale for the original intentional-stance theory was to shed light on intentional mental states and their ascription, and the Gergely et al. approach seems to abandon that mission. A related shortcoming of this approach is that it provides no hint of how to deal with mental-state attribution in nonactional contexts. Dennett, it will be recalled, aspired for his intentional stance theory to explain belief attribution based on rational inferences from other beliefs. Teleological stance theory is wholly silent on this topic and other topics linking mental states with other mental states. In the end, then, this empirical work on 12-month-old infants provides little help or succor to RT.

3.8 Conclusion

To sum up, RT stumbles badly in its attempts to answer the three main questions it purports to answer: the question of third-person attribution, the question of first-person attribution, and the question of mental-state concepts. Nor does it get much help, if any, from the small amount of empirical research inspired by its core idea. I conclude that RT is no longer a serious rival to TT and ST, so it will receive limited attention in the remainder of our discussion.

Notes

1. The very label "intentional stance" signals that the topic is the stance, or strategy, taken by *attributors* for the purpose of making attitude ascriptions.

2. Older literature in social psychology might suggest evidence of a consistency principle that governs the interpretation of others. For example, the literature on "impression formation" (Asch, 1946) talks a good deal about "consistency" and "coherence" as assumptions people make in trying to understand others. What is meant by consistency in this literature, however, is not logical consistency in *beliefs* (at a given time) but consistency in a looser sense pertaining to personality traits and behavior. In particular, consistency as discussed in this literature often means stability of behavior and traits over time. In reviewing the principles of impression formation, Hamilton and Sherman (1996) include the following two principles related to consistency: First, the perceiver (interpreter) expects consistency in the target person's traits and behaviors, specifically, temporal stability of attitudes and attributes. Second, the perceiver strives to resolve inconsistencies in the information acquired about the target person. When a person whom you know to be friendly and considerate suddenly bursts into rude criticism of another person, it captures your attention. You stop and think, "Hey, what's going on here? Why did she do that? That doesn't fit with my impression of her." Obviously, neither of these two consistency themes bears on logical consistency of beliefs as a constraint in mindreading. A different body of literature in social psychology, cognitive dissonance theory, *is* aimed at people's efforts to maintain consistency in beliefs (Festinger, 1957). But cognitive dissonance theory addresses only people's attempts to constrain their *own* belief systems. It does not speak to the question of mindreading others. Notice this possibility, moreover. If people do constrain their own belief systems in terms of consistency, they might also *project* this tendency onto others. If so, their mindreading would be guided by considerations of consistency. However, if this account were correct, a consistency principle of mindreading would not be a stand-alone principle that supports RT but a product of projection and hence support for ST. (See sections 7.5–7.8 for the central role of projection in mindreading.)

3. First-person attribution will be treated in detail in chapter 9.

4. Here is another passage with the same idea: "*all there is* to being a true believer is being a system whose behavior is reliably predictable via the intentional strategy, and hence *all there is* to really and truly believing that p . . . is being an intentional system for which p occurs as a belief in the best (most predictive) interpretation" (1987: 29, emphases in the original).

5. This was already adumbrated in Gergely et al. (1995), but it is highlighted in Gergely and Csibra (2003).

4

The Child-Scientist Theory

4.1 Elements of Theory-Theory

As emphasized throughout, a comprehensive account of mentalizing should tackle at least four topics: (1) third-person attribution, (2) first-person attribution, (3) the contents of mental concepts, and (4) the acquisition or development of mentalizing skills. The purest form of theory-theory (TT) would adopt the following positions on these topics: (1) Third-person attribution is executed by theoretical reasoning, the premises of which are observed features of the target's environment and behavior, plus causal laws or principles of folk psychology. (2) First-person attribution is executed by the same theory-guided method as third-person attribution. (3) Mental-state concepts are understood in terms of theoretically specified causal relations between behavior, environment, and other mental states.[1] In other words, mental-state concepts are understood in terms of causal or functional roles. (4) Mentalizing skills develop in step with, and as a consequence of, changes in a mentalizer's folk-psychological theory. Theory change in infants and children is generated by the same learning or acquisition methods used by adult scientists.

The child-scientist version of TT embraces all four of these views and therein contrasts in various ways with its competitors. Unlike the rationality/charity theory, it places no special weight on rationality, either in the account of attribution or the account of mental-state concepts. Unlike simulation theory (ST), it says that third-person attribution proceeds wholly via inferences that are guided by causal principles of folk psychology. No steps of mental pretense, or "putting oneself in the target's shoes," are postulated, or at most they are deemed incidental. On the topic of first-person (current) attribution, it contrasts with introspectionist ST in rejecting a distinctive introspective method of determination. Finally, in contrast with the nativist-modularity theory (MT), the child-scientist theory views the acquisition of mental-state concepts and folk principles as (primarily) a matter of theory construction and revision, a process that mimics, or is closely analogous to, the construction and revision of scientific theories in adult science. The acquisition process is supposedly underpinned by domain-general learning mechanisms, not by modules devoted to mentalizing. This last, architectural dispute is not on our list of four primary questions, but it addresses question (5), one of our secondary questions (section 1.6).

The bulk of the developmental literature is devoted to question (4) (including its architectural cousin). From the vantage point of ST, however, the crucial issue concerns topic (1), third-person attribution, where the child-scientist approach is purely inferentialist, whereas ST is simulationist. A secondary point of contention centers on (2), first-person attribution, where pure TT is inferentialist and ST (at least in its introspectionist variant) is not. As it happens, however, proponents of the child-scientist theory offer little *direct* evidence for pure inferentialism. Their line of argument is more indirect, drawing heavily on their account of development. Though not usually spelled out in detail, here is how that chain of argument seems to run.

(i)   Young children's performance on mentalizing tasks changes over time as a function of changes in their grasp, or understanding, of mental concepts.
(ii)   These changes in concepts, or conceptual understanding, reflect successive stages in children's theories of the mental.
(iii) Therefore, mental concepts must be theoretical concepts.
(iv)   Hence, all determinations of the instantiation of mental concepts, in both self and others, must be inferential in character.

The best illustration of this line of argument is found in Gopnik (1993), which is devoted to first-person attribution. That article cites the usual evidence of changes in performance on belief tasks (inter alia), which is interpreted as evidence of a conceptual change (between 3 and 4 years) from a concept that excludes the possibility of false belief to one that admits the possibility. This conceptual change is supposedly responsible for the child's improvement from a pattern of systematically incorrect belief attributions to a pattern of correct attributions. Because the change is said to derive from a theory change, Gopnik concludes that all attributions, including self-attributions, are executed by theoretical reasoning.

Clearly, step (i) in the foregoing argument is crucial. The key evidence in support of (i) is that normal children's transition from failure to success on false-belief tasks hinges on a transition from a nonrepresentational to a representational conception of belief. The 3-year-old conception of belief is said to be nonrepresentational because it makes no allowance, in conceptual terms, for *mis*representation. The 4-year-old conception incorporates the possibility of error and therein coincides with that of the adult. In other words, younger children have a *conceptual deficit* in their understanding of belief, a deficit that is responsible for early false-belief task failure. This claim has become a lightning rod for controversy in the field, so much of this chapter is devoted to findings that bear on it.

Before turning to this empirical literature, however, we should examine the rest of the foregoing argument, which purports to link conceptual change to methods of attribution. A first worry concerns the truth of (ii). Contrary to a widely shared assumption, *conceptual* change is not necessarily *theoretical* change, in the sense that matters here. The kind of theory in question here is a sciencelike theory, which posits causal relationships between observable and unobservable states. Not all concepts, or conceptual changes, involve this kind of theory or theoretical change. For example, someone's concept of a bachelor might change from the concept of an unmarried male of any age to the concept of an unmarried male of marriageable age. Such a change would lead to different decisions about whom to classify as bachelors. But this does not show that "bachelor" is a theoretical concept of the sort found in science, a concept understood in terms of causal relations between observable and nonobservable events.

A second worry concerns the putative link between (iii) and (iv). Even if a concept is a theoretical one, in the sense relevant here, it doesn't follow that determinations of its instances must proceed wholly by theoretical inference. If the user of the concept can instantiate it herself, or instantiate pretend surrogates of it, simulation can be used as a shortcut procedure to determine its instantiation in others or in one's future or past self (section 2.1). So purely inferential methods of attribution are not a necessary consequence of the theoreticity of mental-state concepts.

Worries of these kinds could derail a march to the TT conclusion about third- and first-person attribution, even if the developmental story told by child-scientist theorists were correct. But there are also large questions about the correctness of the child-scientist developmental story. Its correctness or incorrectness therefore deserves a central place on our agenda.

4.2 Early Conceptual Deficit Concerning Belief?

Again, a principal claim of the child-scientist approach is that poor performance by "younger" children (e.g., younger than 4 years) on false-belief tasks and appearance-reality tasks is the result of a conceptual deficit. In endorsing this thesis in 1991, Josef Perner wrote:

Young children fail to understand belief because they have difficulty understanding that something represents; that is, they cannot *represent* that something
is a *representation*. (Perner, 1991: 186)

Nine years later, the controversy swirling around this thesis led Perner to
write:

There has been a veritable onslaught on the finding that children below a certain
age of about 4 years do not understand false belief. (Perner, 2000: 368)

The critique of the alleged conceptual deficit finding comes from studies that
seem to show, in one way or another, that 3-year-olds suffer from *performance*,
or *information-processing*, difficulties rather than *conceptual* deficiencies.
Even if children understand that beliefs can be false, the so-called Sally-Anne
task is still difficult. In this task (essentially the same as the Maxi task of
chapter 1), a character named Sally leaves a desirable object such as a chocolate in her basket and then departs the scene. In her absence, Anne removes
the object and places it in a box. Children who witness this scene are asked to
predict, on Sally's return to the room, where she will look for the object or
where she thinks the object is. As Bloom and German (2000) indicate,

To solve [the problem], the child has to follow the actions of two characters in a
narrative, has to appreciate that Sally could not have observed the switching of
the chocolate, has to remember both where the chocolate used to be and where it
is at the time of the test, and has to appreciate the precise meaning of the question
(for instance, that it means where will Sally look not where she *should* look).
(2000: B27)

Several investigators have modified the false-belief task to make it simpler,
and this often results in the tasks being passed by 3-year-olds. This supports
the view that younger children have a sophisticated enough concept of belief
but lack efficient processing capacities. Let us review some of these modifi-
cations and their upshots, in the context of various hypothesized processing
deficiencies that offer alternative explanations of performance failure.

4.3 Salience, Inhibitory Control, and Success

One stock version of a false-belief task is the deceptive container task (reviewed in chapter 1). Children are shown a familiar type of candy container
and asked to state its contents; the reply is always "candy." Then they are
shown that the box really contains something else, such as pencils. Finally
they are asked a further question: what did they originally think was inside
the box when they first saw it, before it was opened? Typically, a majority of
3-year-olds say that they originally thought pencils were in the box. That this
is a simple problem of memory is claimed to be implausible, because in

general they have no difficulty recalling their own past psychological states. Conceptual deficit theorists explain this 3-year-old failure as a failure to grasp the possibility of false belief. As they now know, the box really contained pencils, so they cannot impute to themselves a past belief that it contained candy.

Subsequent experiments, however, suggest that memory, or information processing, may indeed be the root of the problem. Mitchell and Lacohee (1991) gave children a memory aid for the false-belief content by asking children, when they first answered the content question, to "post" a picture of what they thought the content was into a special postbox. After revealing that the tube contained pencils, the children received the test question: "When you posted your picture in the postbox, what did you think was inside this tube?" In this condition, 3-year-olds often judged correctly that they had (mistakenly) thought the tube contained Smarties (candy). Thus, these 3-year-olds apparently understood that their old representation was false. Lewis, Freeman, Hagestadt, and Douglas (1994) also suspected that memory was the culprit. They hypothesized that a young child needs time to integrate the discrete episodes that make up the Sally-Anne story. They gave their subjects more chance to absorb the required information by exposing some of them to the story *twice*. Children who made two runs through the story were twice as likely to pass the test as children who made only one run. German and Leslie (2000) also report memory manipulations that facilitate false-belief attribution.[2]

Several investigators have obtained results in modified false-belief tasks that suggest salience is a key variable in creating problems for 3-year-olds. Zaitchik (1991) did a study that manipulated two new conditions: Seen and Unseen. In the Seen condition, Big Bird shows the child the location of a toy in a box and tells her that he will trick a frog by telling him that the toy is in another box. The child is asked where the frog will then think the toy is located. Three-year-olds respond incorrectly. In contrast, in the Unseen condition 3-year-olds tend to answer correctly. In this condition, the child does not initially see the toy's true location. She is only told where the toy is. Zaitchik's explanation focused on whether the child herself saw the fact that made the belief true, that is, the actual location of the object. When 3-year-olds see the actual fact, suggests Zaitchik, it is very salient to them, and they cannot override this salient reality with a false-belief attribution. When they do not see the actual fact, as in the Unseen condition, it is less salient, and they can override it with a false-belief attribution.

Saltmarsh, Mitchell, and Robinson (1995) used a Smarties (candy) tube that at first did contain Smarties, and this was shown both to the child and to the puppet Daffy. When asked what it contained, both the child and Daffy answered, "Smarties." Daffy then left the room and, as the child watched, the Smarties were removed and replaced by a pencil. Daffy then returned, and the child was asked what Daffy thinks is in the tube now. Three-year-olds correctly answered Smarties, attributing a false belief to Daffy. Here, in contrast to Zaitchik's finding, the child did see the actual fact but succeeded in attributing a false belief anyway.

This finding needn't undercut a salience-style explanation, however. Robinson (1994) pointed out that the two explanations can be combined into a single saliency rule, one that predicts success when either true belief is attenuated in the child's mind or false belief is elevated (for a summary, see Fabricius and Imbens-Bailey, 2000). If the child does not see the actual fact, reality will be less salient, and she will more easily attribute the false belief; if she does see the actual fact, it will help to have seen the now false situation as well (the tube's containing Smarties) in order to attribute it, because that will make this content more salient. In other words, diminishing the salience of conflicting reality (as in Zaitchik's Unseen condition) or elevating the salience of the now false situation (as in Saltmarsh et al.) facilitates the 3-year-old's attribution of false belief.

A theoretical perspective related to salience is a popular explanation of false-belief task failure. To answer a false-belief question correctly, a child must be able to juggle two competing representations of reality: the true state of affairs (by the mentalizer's lights) and the state of affairs represented in the head of the target. The child has to *inhibit* an incorrect but compelling answer: the true location of the object. Inhibitory control is a facet of general executive functioning and is thought to be weak in younger children. As the capacity for greater inhibitory control increases with maturity, the child is better able to handle the challenges of false-belief tasks. When the true location of an object is the wrong but salient answer, a young child with poor inhibitory control finds it difficult to inhibit that "prepotent" response. If the salience of the true location is reduced (as in Zaitchik, 1991), the amount of needed inhibition is reduced, and the child finds it easier to answer correctly. If poor inhibitory control is the proper explanation of young children's failure on many false-belief tasks, the diagnosis of the problem is a general performance or information-processing deficiency rather than a conceptual deficit in the belief concept (Frye, Zelazo, and Palfai, 1995; Carlson, Moses, and Hix, 1998; Carlson and Moses, 2001; Hughes and Russell, 1993; Russell, Mauthner, Sharpe, and Tidswell, 1991).[3]

If inhibitory control can be shown to arise for younger children in tasks other than false-belief tasks, that would further support this approach. This has been demonstrated by several studies. Moore et al. (1995) arranged a desire task that closely matched the structure of the false-belief task. A child played a game with a competitor, and initially both required a certain event to occur, so each wanted to get a red card. Once this interim goal was achieved, the child could progress in the game only if the next card was blue, whereas the competitor was left requiring a red card. So the child's own desire (now a desire for a blue card) has changed, but the competitor's desire (for a red card) has stayed the same. The child was then asked what color card the competitor wanted next. This is analogous to a false-belief task where the child and the protagonist both start out with one belief (marble in the basket) and then the child's belief but not the protagonist's is updated (marble in the box). In the Moore et al. study, 3-year-olds failed this task just as they do in analogous false-belief tasks, and their task is readily amenable to an inhibitory control explanation. Leslie and Polizzi (1998) also created an inhibitory control problem that included desire reasoning. They increased inhibitory demands in false-belief tasks by changing the protagonist's motivation to a negative desire; the protagonist's desire was not to find but to *avoid* a target object. Under this increased inhibitory demand, even 4-year-old and 6-year-old children consistently failed to answer correctly.

Consistent with the spirit of the inhibitory control approach, Birch and Bloom (2003) report findings that they interpret under the "curse of knowledge" label (borrowed from Camerer et al., 1989). They presented 3-, 4-, and 5-year-olds with two sets of toys, one described as being familiar to a puppet friend, Percy, and one described as being unfamiliar to Percy. Each toy was said to have an object inside, and the children were asked to judge whether Percy would know what was inside the toys. Half of the time, the children were shown the toys' contents; the other half of the time, they were not. Birch and Bloom found that there was a significant difference between the child-knowledgeable and child-ignorant conditions for the 3- and 4-year-olds but not for the 5-year-olds. Thus, the younger children suffered from the curse-of-knowledge, that is, a bias toward what they themselves knew, but the older children didn't. Birch and Bloom propose that inhibiting one's own knowledge requires inhibitory control, something lacking in younger children. They did not find any curse-of-ignorance effect in the younger children. This is explained by saying that when one is ignorant, there is nothing to inhibit. So they offer another processing account of young children's failure, this time where the target is ignorant (rather than possesses a false belief).[4]

Nonetheless, child-scientist theorists have not abandoned their view. In an extensive meta-analysis, Wellman, Cross, and Watson (2001) note that improvement in 3-year-olds' performance from salience manipulations reflects only a change from below-chance to chance performance and therefore does not implicate a fully operational concept of belief. They argue that the correlation between inhibitory control and false-belief performance does not demonstrate masking of a preexisting competence. Instead, inhibitory control might facilitate conceptual change, because a child who can disengage from prepotent representations of reality may be better able to learn about mental representations. Perner and Lang (2000) also raise questions about what exactly is proved by the correlation between executive function and performance on false-belief tasks. More generally, Wellman et al. contend that their meta-analysis supports the conceptual deficit thesis, that an important conceptual change takes place between the ages of 2½ and 5 years. Scholl and

Leslie (2001) disagree, saying that the meta-analysis merely demonstrates what everyone concedes, namely, that *some* important change that influences performance occurs between these ages, but it sheds no light on what drives that change. In particular, Scholl and Leslie challenge the conclusion that it supports a conceptual deficit diagnosis.

4.4 Early Success on False-Belief Tasks

Although it is generally claimed that 3-year-olds fail false-belief tasks, it has been known for some time that they sometimes succeed in such tasks. Oddly, this sort of finding is partly due to Wellman and Bartsch, leading proponents of the conceptual deficit approach (or close variants thereof). In the "Not Own" belief task of Wellman and Bartsch (1988), children were told about two possible locations for an object but not told which one was correct. They were told, however, that a protagonist believes it to be in the other location and asked where the protagonist will look. Three-year-olds passed this test, although it presupposed attribution of a false belief. In Bartsch and Wellman (1995), young children (age 3 plus various months) successfully used false-belief "contrastives." Here are three examples of such contrastives:

> *ADULT:* Let me see if I can use your scissors. They're not too small.
> *ABE (3, 1):* I thought so 'cept they weren't.

> *ADULT:* I thought it was a bus.
> *ADAM (3, 3):* It's a bus. I thought a taxi.

> *ABE (3, 6):* The people thought Dracula was mean. But he was nice.

As these examples make plain, 3-year-olds are quite capable of recognizing false beliefs.

Indeed, Bartsch and Wellman (1995) go on to concede that Wellman's (1990) earlier "copy" theory of belief does not comport with their subsequent findings. They write as follows:

> Our new view is required by, and also helps to account for, the fact that 3-year-olds at times appreciate full-blown representational—and thereby interpretive, misrepresentational—notions of belief and false belief. A "copy" view, which limits children to a consideration of only true beliefs, for some period of time, cannot encompass this finding. At the same time, however, 3-year-olds largely and insistently talk about true beliefs rather than false ones, and they fail to normally use beliefs in explanations. (1995: 203)

It is difficult, however, to reconcile this passage with the apparent retention of the conceptual deficit, or conceptual change, position in Wellman et al. (2001).

Other research indicates an understanding of false belief among children even younger than 3. One finding of this sort is Clements and Perner (1994). They used an implicit measure of understanding as contrasted with the explicit measure of children's verbal answer to the question of where a protagonist would look for an object. The implicit measure was where the child *looked*. Children from 2 years, 5 months to 2 years, 10 months erroneously looked at the object's real location (which they also gave as their verbal answer). But in the group ranging from 2 years, 11 months to 3 years, 2 months, 80 percent looked at the empty location where the protagonist thought the object was. This location, of course, is the correct "answer."

A very recent study moves children's competence in understanding false belief dramatically earlier than 2 years, 11 months. Onishi and Baillargeon (2005), using a new paradigm with reduced task demands to test for false-belief understanding, found evidence of such understanding even in 15-month-old infants. If this finding holds up, it will totally undercut the conceptual deficit hypothesis (at least with anything like the traditional time line). Onishi and Baillargeon employed the violation-of-expectation method patterned after Woodward (1998). In the main experiment, the infants first watched an actor hide a toy in one of two locations. Next, the toy moved to the other location. Finally, the experiment asked whether the infants would expect the actor to seek her toy in its new hiding place when she had or had not witnessed—and hence did or did not know about—the toy's change of location.

The infants were assigned to a true-belief or a false-belief condition. Infants in both conditions received familiarization trials, in which an actor, appearing through opened doors in the back wall of the apparatus, played with a toy watermelon slice and then hid it inside a green box. Next, the infants received a belief-inducing trial, in which they saw the toy slide out of the green box and move across the apparatus floor (by means of a magnet under the floor) into a yellow box, where it remained hidden. In the true-belief condition, the upper halves of the doors in the back of the apparatus were open, and the actor could be seen leaning into the opening and watching the toy's change of location. In the false-belief condition, the doors in the back wall remained shut; thus, only the infant saw the toy's change of location. Following these trials, infants in the two belief conditions received a single test trial. For half of the infants in each belief condition, the actor opened the doors, reached into the green box, and paused until the trial ended (green-box condition). In the other condition, infants saw the same event except that the actor reached into the yellow box (yellow-box condition). Onishi and Baillargeon predicted that in the true-belief condition the infants should expect the actor to reach into the yellow box (where she had seen the toy disappear) and should respond with increased attention when the actor reached into the green box instead. In the false-belief condition, if the infants understood that the actor had a false belief about the toy's location, infants should expect her to reach into the green box (where she falsely believed the toy to be), and they should respond with increased attention when she reached into the yellow box. Thus, infants in the yellow-box condition should look reliably longer than those in the green-box condition. These predictions were confirmed, thereby supporting the thesis that these 15-month-old infants had a grasp of false belief. This result disconfirms a core thesis of the child-scientist approach, that young children's mental-state theory either omits belief entirely or construes it as a nonrepresentational state (which cannot be false).

4.5 Conceptual Change concerning Desire?

The idea of conceptual change in the mental domain is certainly not restricted to belief. Indeed, it is somewhat adventitious that belief has occupied such a pivotal role in the debate. Another strand of the child-scientist idea has been articulated with respect to desire, where Bartsch and Wellman (1995), in particular, have argued for a succession of different understandings of this concept.

Bartsch and Wellman hold that when children first grasp the concept of desire, around 2 years of age, they have a "connectionist" concept of desire.[5] What is a "connectionist" concept of a mental state? To think of desiring in connectionist terms is to think of it as a subjective state with a certain relation to an external object. As Bartsch and Wellman explain it, this

> requires no conception of a represented state of affairs, in the target person's head...as it were. Whatever contents are involved are out there, in the world, rather than in the person's mind. The mental state being attributed here is intentional in the minimal sense of being about something; it is about the apple. But the object of the desire, what it is about, is a real apple in the world. (1995: 151)

The objects of desires, under the 2-year-old's connectionist conception, are not restricted to physical items such as apples, toys, and tools. Objects of desire include actions and states of affairs (1995: 152). One desired state of affairs might be having a full cup of milk.

The obvious and oft-raised problem with this conceptualization of desire is how it deals with nonexistent objects of desire (Perner, 1991: 278–279). Suppose somebody (another child, for example) wants a dragon. Unfortunately, there are no dragons, so what object or state of affairs in the world is the desire "connected" to? Similarly, suppose a child wants a full cup of milk to drink (right now), but there is no full cup of milk, and no milk in the refrigerator. There seems to be no state of affairs for the desire to be connected with. These would not be problem cases if the 2-year-old had no grasp of unfulfilled or unsatisfied desires. But Bartsch and Wellman make it perfectly clear that 2-year-olds *do* understand the notion of unfulfilled desire. So what real-world things are the objects of these unfulfilled (and sometimes unfulfillable) desires?

Granting that the connectionist conception of desire is problematic, does that prove that the 2-year-old doesn't have it? Many adults have weird beliefs and even incoherent concepts. So perhaps 2-year-olds have a fundamentally deficient conception of intentional states. Why is that hypothesis obviously untenable? Fair enough. We should not assume that every conception of 2-year-olds is adequate to the "facts." On the other hand, exactly what is Bartsch and Wellman's evidence for imputing this inadequate, nonrepresentational conception of desire to 2-year-olds? Why not impute to them a representational concept of desire?

Imputing a representational concept of desire seems especially appropriate when it is granted that 2-year-olds understand unfulfilled or unsatisfied desires. An unfulfilled desire is precisely analogous to a false belief. Desires have a world-to-mind direction of fit, whereas beliefs have a mind-to-world direction of fit. A belief is false when it fails to fit the world. A desire is unfulfilled when the world fails to realize the desire. In both cases, what counts as fitting or nonfitting is the representational, or propositional, content of the state. Without such representational content, one cannot grasp what it means for there to be a failure of fit. Beliefs can qualify as false only if they have representational content. But the same should hold for desire. Desires can qualify as unfulfilled only if they have representational content. Since Bartsch and Wellman acknowledge that 2-year-olds' conception of desire incorporates the idea of nonfulfillment, they should also acknowledge that this conception of desire is a representational conception.[6]

What reasons are offered for imputing to 2-year-olds the connectionist, nonrepresentational concept of desire? This is what they say:

> In our data, 2-year-olds talk about desires and not beliefs, thoughts, or imaginings. If 2-year-olds are construing people's mental states in representational fashions, why do they not make reference to such representational mental states? It is important to recall here that 2-year-olds have the words and the syntactic wherewithal to talk about such states and that they hear about these states from their parents. It is not that they fail to talk about some one or two representational mental states, say, beliefs alone or dreams; they do not talk of any of them, as far as we can tell from our data—not beliefs, thoughts, imaginings, dreams, knowledge, what have you. If children attribute representations to people, why would that attribution appear in desires alone? (1995: 155)

To understand this argument, we should clarify the phrase "representational mental states" as used in this passage. In its first occurrence, the phrase refers to states like beliefs and thoughts, which have a depictive, mind-to-world direction of fit. Bartsch and Wellman allude to the fact that their corpus of 2-year-olds' mentalistic utterances discloses very few uses of the language of "think," "know," or the like (especially as genuine references to mental states as opposed to conversational turns of phrase). This suggests to them that 2-year-olds simply don't conceive of *any* mental states as representational.

Here "representational state" is not confined to depictive states but has the broader sense of a state with propositional content. What Bartsch and Wellman conclude, then, is that 2-year-olds have no conception of representational mental states at all, that is, states with propositional content, whether depictive or nondepictive. In particular, the 2-year-old conception of desire is a nonrepresentational conception.

This argument is unpersuasive for many reasons. As the study of Onishi and Baillargeon (2005) indicates, children of even 15 months appear to have a representational conception of belief. They appear capable of understanding that others have false beliefs. In the light of this, why should 2-year-olds not have a representational (rather than connectionist) conception of desire? The further fact that remains to be explained is why 2-year-olds make intensive use of the language of "wanting" and hardly any use of the language of "thinking" or "believing." There are many possible explanations of this finding. For example, children have an obvious pragmatic reason to master first-person talk of desire. "I want X" (and its cognates) is an utterance by which children cause adults to give them what they want. This highly convenient piece of language might then be extended to third-person uses. Whether or not this explanation is right, we need to separate questions about the frequencies of occurrence of certain terms, including terms that don't occur at all, from questions about how they understand or conceptualize the terms they do use.

There are other changes in young children's performance on desire tasks that also fail to testify to a *conceptual* change rather than a change in *processing* ability. For example, Repacholi and Gopnik (1997) had children observe an experimenter expressing disgust while tasting one type of food and happiness while tasting another. They were then invited to offer food to the experimenter, either the first type or the second. In effect, this was a task to predict which type of food the experimenter wanted. The 14-month-old children responded egocentrically, offering whichever food they themselves preferred, whereas the 18-month-olds responded "correctly," offering the food associated with the experimenter's positive affect rather than the child's own preference. Repacholi and Gopnik suggest (or at least hint) that this change should be explained as a shift in the child's ("theoretical") concept of desire, but this explanation is not compelling. The shift is more readily explained in terms of processing ability, perhaps associated, once again, with an increase in the ability to inhibit attribution of one's own state.

4.6 Inference Neglect

I have emphasized the argument from conceptual change as the primary argument in the child-scientist theory's arsenal. It isn't the only one, however. Another argument focuses on learning a specific class of laws, namely, laws about mental states that lead to knowledge, often called "sources" of knowledge. By about 4 years of age, it appears, children learn to link seeing with knowing but until much later don't link being verbally informed with knowing (Wimmer, Hogrefe, and Sodian, 1988; Ruffman and Olson, 1989). If a 4-year-old child sees another child or an adult gain visual access to a box's contents, the child will conclude that the target *knows* what's in the box. But if the target is merely verbally informed of what's in the box, although he could come to know what's in the box by inference, the child won't credit him with knowing. Wimmer, Hogrefe, and Perner (1988) and Perner (1991) argued that children at this age seem to possess a rule, law, or generalization, which they call a seeing = knowing rule. They interpret this as support for the TT position. Use of the seeing = knowing rule implies "inference neglect": children don't appreciate inference as a source of knowledge. Stich and Nichols (1992) argued that inference neglect cannot be explained by ST. To secure this latter point, Ruffman (1996) performed a series of experiments designed to test whether ST might accommodate children's patterns of success and failure on tasks concerning knowledge or belief (along lines sketched by Harris, 1991). Ruffman concluded that ST is unable to accommodate his experimental findings. TT, on the other hand, explains them by exactly the kind of folk-psychological law that TT generally postulates (Ruffman, 1996: 389). Saxe (2005) endorses Ruffman's work as demonstrating ST's limits.

Some of the questions in Ruffman's experiments included questions about what a target *knows*. He says that children's knowledge attributions were determined by two rules: "doesn't see ⇒ doesn't know" and "doesn't know ⇒ gets it wrong/holds a false belief." These rules are obviously mistakes; the second is a mistake because not knowing might arise from ignorance rather than false belief. But do these mistakes tell us something about *mental-state* generalizations that children believe? Are they generalizations that genuinely fit TT? That is questionable.

The verb 'know' is not a pure mental-state verb. The standard epistemological story says that knowing p entails the truth of p; a variant of the standard story adds that the belief must be acquired by a reliable method (Goldman, 1986). If this is correct, children who possess a seeing = knowing rule do not possess a purely psychological generalization, which links pairs of pure mental states. More than recognition of mental state-transitions is involved. This is supported by a brief comment by Wimmer, Hogrefe and Sodian (1988: 180). They say that even when a target gave evidence of his or her knowledge of an inferred conclusion by explicitly stating it, 4-year-olds disregarded this and judged the conclusion to be a guess. In other words, the 4-year-olds didn't doubt that the target had the relevant belief or belief-like state, arrived at (apparently) by inference. Nonetheless, they judged that this belief didn't rise to the level of "knowledge." Perhaps they judged it to be a mere guess because the method used wasn't sufficiently reliable, by their lights. So the reason they make different assessments of knowledge may not be failure to recognize certain mental-state transitions, but failure to recognize certain *epistemic* qualifications. In addition to their failure to appreciate that some inferences are reliable enough for knowledge, the second rule signals children's tendency to confuse ignorance, i.e., lack of true belief, with false belief. This is certainly an error, but not an error involving mental-state generalizations. It's more like a logical error. So none of this fits the canonical kind of generalization posited by TT.

However, some of Ruffman's findings concern *belief* ascriptions rather than *knowledge* ascriptions, and he also takes these findings to undercut ST. In Ruffman's "two colors" task (the closest one—though not identical—to the example given by Saxe), a dish with two differently colored sweets, red and green, is shown both to a child subject and to a doll. The child hears the doll being told that 'a sweet', color unspecified, will be moved from the dish to a box. The doll leaves ('goes out to play'), and the child observes the experimenter move a red sweet from the dish to the box. The doll then returns, and the child is asked several questions, including 'What color does the doll *think* is in the box?' Ruffman's finding was that a large majority of children, between roughly 5 and 8 years of age, ascribed a false belief to the doll, i.e., answered the 'think' question with 'green'. Ruffman continues:

> This result is inconsistent with ST. The message made it equally possible that the sweet could be red or green and hence that the doll could form either belief. If placed in the doll's situation children themselves should have chosen randomly between red and green. Children's failure to do this when assessing the doll's belief suggests that they were not simulating (i.e., using their own experience as an analogy). (1996: 399)

In other words, Ruffman argues that if the children used their own experience of ignorance to create their pretend inputs, they would have chosen the 'think' color randomly, which is not borne out by the findings.

Ruffman is assuming, however, that ST must impute 'proper' pretend inputs to the children, and this isn't right. As we have explained, ST allows attributors to make mistakes in their construction of inputs. In the present case a mistake is almost necessitated by the task demands. The 'think' question asked of the children virtually required them to choose either red or green as the color believed by the doll. Strictly, they could reject these alternatives and say that the doll has no definite belief. But such a rejection of the question is a lot to expect of young children. They probably felt required to specify a color. Hence, if they were simulating, they would feel impelled to construct a pretend belief that best accords with their information. A vivid component of their information was the doll's ignorance of the true color, and this could easily steer them toward an opposite pretense, viz., green rather than red. Gordon (2005) offers a similar story on behalf of ST. For children of the relevant age, he says, the only way to hide or withhold a fact from one's vicarious decision-making is to negate it. Because they can hide a fact only by negating it, they collapse ignorance into being wrong. So ST is not inconsistent with Ruffman's results on the 'think' question.

The results discussed here are only a portion of Ruffman's total findings, however, and I do not claim that all of them can be explained in simulation-friendly terms. It must be recalled, though, that the overall theory I endorse is a simulation-theory hybrid. It is no embarrassment to such a theory that *some* mindreading is done by theorizing.

4.7 Causal Learning in Children

Domain generality is a major facet of the child-scientist theory of development. The theory holds that children go about forming and changing their theories of mind in the same way scientists go about forming and changing their theories, by general-purpose causal reasoning. What exactly is that method of causal reasoning, and do children really have the capacity to employ it? Until recently, child-scientist theorists had no specific account to offer, but now work by Alison Gopnik, Clark Glymour, and colleagues aims to fill this void (Gopnik et al., 2004; Gopnik and Glymour, 2002; Gopnik, Sobel, Schulz, and Glymour, 2001). They propose a computational framework using the formalism of directed graphical causal models, known as "Bayes nets" (Pearl, 2000; Spirtes, Glymour, and Scheines, 2001), and hypothesize that children employ specialized cognitive systems facilitating the construction of causal maps and use these maps for prediction. They report experimental results suggesting that 2- to 4-year-old children engage in causal learning in a manner consistent with the Bayes net formalism.

Cognitive maps of the *spatial* environment were first proposed by the psychologist Tolman (1932), but Gopnik and Glymour talk about cognitive maps of the *causal* environment. The Bayes net idea has its roots in philosophy of science. Suppose we observe that event A is correlated with event B; that is, the occurrence of A changes the probability that B will occur. Can we infer that instances of A cause the occurrence of instances of B? The problem is that other events might also be causally related to B. For example, some other event C might be a common cause of both A and B. A does not cause B, but whenever C occurs, both A and B occur together. What is needed is a way to consider the probability of A and B relative to the probability of C. The philosopher of science Hans Reichenbach (1956) proposed the idea of "screening off" to capture this matter. If A, B, and C are the only variables and A is only correlated with B conditional on C, then C screens off A as a cause of B; event C rather than A is the cause of B. On the other hand, if A is correlated with B independent of C, then C does not screen off A, and A causes B. Bayes nets are directed-graph formalisms intended to capture and generalize the idea of "screening off" reasoning. The arrows of their directed graphs depict probabilistic causal relationships between variables and can be used to enable predictions. Moreover, given certain assumptions (the Markov and Faithfulness assumptions), a system can construct algorithms to arrive at a correct Bayes net causal structure if it is given information about the contingencies or correlations among the target events. Thus, these systems can learn about causal structure from observations and behavioral interventions.

Bayes net representations are not restricted to observable variables. They can also involve unobservable variables, and there are procedures for learning about such variables from the data. These are particularly important for TT purposes, because desires, beliefs, and other psychological states are assumed to be unobservable. How can children infer unobserved variables from patterns of data? How is such learning possible? Gopnik et al. (2004) contend that constraint-based procedures can sometimes identify the presence of unobserved common causes. However, they concede, there are no Bayesian methods that do a general search for the presence of unobserved variables.

Gopnik et al. hypothesize that people—and children, in particular—represent causal relationships in ways that can be described as causal Bayes nets. Moreover, children use learning procedures to construct new causal representations from observations of correlations and interventions. Gopnik et al. (2004) present experimental evidence that young children can make causal inferences that require such powerful learning mechanisms. One study, they contend, shows that children as young as 30 months can implicitly use conditional dependence information to learn a causal map. Other studies show that competing accounts of causal learning in the psychological literature cannot handle children's causal learning as well as theirs.

Gopnik et al. (2004) concede some significant lacunae in their account. For example, they have no story to tell about how a subject chooses or constructs her variables from which causal hypotheses may be constructed. That is an important issue in theory formation, of course, and a major bone of contention between child-scientist and modularity theorists. The latter hold that the variables of propositional attitude psychology are (or are represented by) distinctive data structures of a specialized, domain-specific module. To show the applicability of their general causal learning framework to mentalizing, Gopnik and colleagues need to make a persuasive case that propositional-attitude variables could be produced by general-purpose concept-forming abilities.[7] This has not been done.

Many problems and concerns face this general theoretical approach to mentalizing. A central theoretical issue in contemporary discussions of learning is whether there is a *single* learning process in cognition. C. R. Gallistel (1990, 2000) argues to the contrary.[8] Rather than a single learning process, there are many different learning mechanisms adaptively specialized for the solution of different kinds of problems. "We should no more expect to find a general-purpose learning mechanism than we should expect to find a general-purpose sensory organ" (Gallistel, 2000: 1190). Chomsky's (1975) idea that the language acquisition device embodies a very special type of learning mechanism is a classical instance of this. Thus, even if Gopnik and colleagues could persuade us that children use their favored causal learning procedure for some domains, it is highly speculative to infer that the same procedure is used in learning mentalizing skills. This is especially pertinent because Gopnik et al. (2004) report no experiments with specifically psychological, that is, *mentalizing*, subject matter. Their experiments were done with entirely different subject matters. One cannot assume that if children have the capacity to use learning mechanisms like the Bayes net, they will surely apply them to the problem of mentalizing. That simply begs the question against the multiple-learning-mechanisms approach of Gallistel and others.

Moreover, their discussion ignores evidence from psychopathology that is often urged as damaging to the child-scientist approach. It is well established that mentalizing competence is not well correlated with general reasoning ability. Autistic children are impaired on (some) mentalizing tasks but skilled in general mechanical reasoning (Baron-Cohen, Leslie, and Frith, 1986). Sufferers from Williams syndrome have a complex pattern of deficits and skills. Although they suffer from general retardation, they achieve at least a 4-year-old level of mentalizing (Carey and Johnson, 2000).[9] It is difficult to reconcile these findings with an approach that views mentalizing as just a special case of domain-general causal reasoning. The findings argue strongly for something distinctive about mentalizing.

It bears emphasis that the problem facing children in the mentalizing domain is a problem with unobservable states (at least according to theory-theorists). When we look closely at the experimental evidence supporting children's learning in such matters, what Gopnik et al. provide is very sparse indeed.[10] They present exactly one experiment (Experiment 3) that involves the postulation of unobserved entities. Moreover, the sorts of unobserved causes the children postulate in this experiment are causes that are unobserved but observ*able*. Asked to explain why a pair of puppets move together, 9 of 16 children appealed to such causes as "your hands," "you behind there," or "something else." These are kinds of causes that have previously been observed on many occasions; they are not unobserv*ables*. By contrast, desires and beliefs are supposedly unobservable states, according to the pure TT account. Gopnik et al. offer no experimental evidence of children learning to postulate such states.

Another problem facing the account is one that many critics of the child-scientist approach have lodged. In real adult science, there is no evidence that individual scientists independently come up with the same theoretical posits.

There may be convergence among scientists after long periods of experimentation and debate, but different scientists pursue lengthy careers in disagreement with others in such matters. By contrast, children come to essentially the same (allegedly) theoretical posits concerning mental states, and they do so in pretty short order. Thus, the parallel with genuine science isn't very close, giving rise to skepticism about the claimed parallelism. What seems particularly miraculous is that normal children acquire competence with respect to the same assortment of mental-state concepts and in exactly the same order. They acquire the same concept of belief (not schmelief), and they acquire it *after* they acquire the concept of desire. Can this matched order be explained by the Bayes net learning mechanism? We are given no reason to think so. According to the canonical story, 2-year-olds understand that a desire can go unfulfilled but do not understand false belief (or even belief). Why? Desire and belief are symmetric in terms of position in a causal network of the mind, so belief's causal role should be as accessible as desire's causal role to a general causal learning mechanism. How, then, does a general Bayes net mechanism explain the indicated differences in the pace of acquisition?

Might Gopnik, perhaps, abandon the traditional milestones in light of recent results like that of Onishi and Baillargeon (and a somewhat similar finding of early sensitivity to knowledge reported by O'Neill in 1996)? Onishi and Baillargeon's study involved 15-month-old children. The experimental work reported by Gopnik et al. (2004) does not claim to find causal learning abilities of the indicated sort before 30 months of age. So this later-developing causal learning process could not explain the earlier acquisition of false-belief skills.

A different kind of problem facing the Gopnik et al. framework concerns the complex "values" of the propositional-attitude variables that mentalizers invoke. Theorists often oversimplify the matter by depicting attitude variables as simply belief, desire, intention, and so forth. But the causal variables invoked in any particular case have an additional value or parameter, namely, the content of each attitude. An inferred causal state is not simply belief, but belief-that-p or belief-that-q, not simply desire but desire-that-u or desire-that-v. The question then arises: By what method do mentalizers construct a content clause to embed into an attitude (thereby yielding a two-part combination of attitude-plus-content)? Is the method used part of a general scientific hypothesis-forming mechanism? That is dubious. As I shall argue more fully in section 7.10, when imputing contents to others, mentalizers standardly make special use of (a) the concepts they themselves deploy in their own first-order cognition and (b) the combinatorial techniques they themselves deploy in constructing propositions out of concepts. In other words, people tacitly impute to their targets the same conceptual repertoire and the same conceptual combinatorics they find in themselves. This kind of "projection" fits the simulationist theme; it's a bad fit with a story of domain-general causal theorizing. Nowhere else does scientific theorizing impute conceptual contents as elements of the causal states it posits; this is unique to the mentalizing domain. Nowhere else does science operate by projecting or bootstrapping from one's own case, by using oneself as a (tacit) model. Nothing in the causal learning framework endorsed by Gopnik et al. predicts the deployment of this projective method, which apparently *is* the method in use.[11]

Finally, the story of causal learning before us does not sit well with the striking evidence of the influence of language understanding on mentalizing skill. I turn to this evidence in the next section.

4.8 Language and the Development of Mentalizing

Recent studies by Jill de Villiers and colleagues have shown that a child's grasp of pertinent linguistic features, especially the syntax of sentential complementation, is a strong predictor of successful performance on false-belief tasks (de Villiers, 2000; de Villiers and de Villiers, 2000). De Villiers and colleagues studied deaf children of nonsigning parents, who have markedly reduced access to the spoken language of their caregivers. The deaf children who were studied also attended oral schools for the deaf, where they did not learn conventional sign language. The average deaf child in such a setting is significantly delayed, both in lexical knowledge and in grammar. On tests of vocabulary and syntax, their performance is about 3 to 4 years delayed compared with hearing children. In particular, they are delayed in their acquisition of sentence complemention, in which embedded sentential complements contain either mental state verbs or communication verbs (e.g., "Fran thought that the toy was under the couch," or "the butcher said that he had no lamb"). These deaf children were tested on false-belief reasoning tasks using nonverbal techniques. The average age of passing was 7,3 years, compared with 4,4 years for the hearing control subjects (Gale, de Villiers, de Villiers, and Pyers, 1996). In separate studies of normally developing hearing preschoolers, a predictive relationship over time was found between grasp of complement syntax and performance on standard false-belief tasks, with syntax predicting subsequent mentalizing performance (but not vice versa).

These studies ostensibly pose problems for the domain-general causal learning approach of the child-scientist theory. Unlike children with autism, deaf children do not have other associated handicaps such as socioemotional disabilities, social withdrawal, or low intelligence. Because they have no handicap in general intelligence, they should possess the same domain-general causal reasoning powers as children who are not hearing impaired. There is no straightforward reason, then, why the child-scientist theory should predict delay in their mentalizing development. They ought to do as well in the mentalizing sphere as their normal hearing peers, because both groups share the same causal reasoning powers, and these powers are responsible for mentalizing, according to the child-scientist approach.

In response, child-scientist theorists might make a major adjustment in their position. Instead of depicting causal learning as proceeding entirely on the basis of observed correlations and contingencies, they might allow causal theories to be influenced by other theories, including theories about other domains. This clearly happens in science. Bohr's theory of the atom was developed by analogy with the theory of the solar system, and Darwin arrived at his theory of natural selection after reading Malthus's tract on human population growth. Why shouldn't a child's theory of syntactic complementation influence her theory of mental states, as de Villiers's evidence suggests? That still fits with the indicated variant of a domain-general theory of causal learning.

Does it fit? First of all, the syntax of English is not a *causal* domain, and a theory of syntax possessed by a child (if "theory" is an appropriate label) is not a *causal* theory. It does not treat any states that causally interact or influence one another. Second, few psycholinguists, if any, will agree that syntax is learned by means of a domain-general learning process of the kind Gopnik and colleagues sketch. Thus, if the development of mindreading is decomposed into two or more stages, one of which is the learning of syntax, then not all of the learning process has a domain-general character, as child-scientist theorists postulate.

The precise relationship between the de Villiers's syntactic influence theory and the child-scientist theory hinges on the strength of the interpretation of the influence theory. De Villiers seems to prefer an extremely strong interpretation: One cannot have the *concept* of belief without competence in sentence complement syntax. In one place, she contends that "language is the only representational system" that can support the concept of (false) belief, because language is "propositional, and can therefore capture falsity and embeddedness of propositions" (2000: 84). This might be seen as congenial to the general spirit of the child-scientist view because it is one possible way of defending a version of the conceptual deficit approach to false-belief performance. But this strong interpretation seems excessive. Saxe, Carey, and Kanwisher (2004) take de Villiers's suggestion that one cannot represent false belief without mastery of embedded sentence complements and derive the following prediction: Belief attribution and sentence-level syntax should recruit the same neural structures. This prediction, however, does not hold up. Studies that vary the syntactic complexity of sentences often find brain activation in and around Broca's area in the left inferior frontal cortex, but this is not in close proximity to any of the regions implicated in belief attribution.[12]

In addition, if Onishi and Baillargeon's results are sustained, false-belief understanding cannot depend on the grasp of sentence complement syntax. According to Onishi and Baillargeon, 15-month-old children understand false belief, but they certainly have no grasp of sentence complement syntax. In any case, a tight connection between syntax and false-belief understanding seems dubious on other grounds. As was argued in section 4.5, there is an excellent analogy between unfulfilled desire and false belief. Each involves a "mismatch" between mind and world, though the mismatches go in opposite directions. It is undisputed that 2-year-olds have an understanding of unful-filled desire and do not have a grasp of sentence complement syntax. So grasping the full concept of desire does not depend on mastery of sentence complement syntax. Why should this conceptual dependence hold for belief?

To summarize the main conclusion of the last two sections, many problems confront the sole attempt by child-scientist theorists to flesh out a specific model of domain-general learning. Even if Gopnik et al. are right that causal learning via Bayes nets is a general capacity of the human mind (and the child's mind in particular), there is no evidence that this capacity is what enables the acquisition of mentalizing skills in particular.

Notice that a rejection of the domain-general learning story of acquisition is perfectly compatible with the view that people sometimes use inductive reasoning to make third-person mental attributions. As a proponent of a hybrid approach to third-person attribution, I have no hesitation in agreeing that inductively based attributions sometimes occur, with no simulation in-gredient at all. Here is an example.

Suppose that Maria is a frequent luncheon companion of mine. Expecting to be late today, she asks me to order drinks before she arrives. I easily predict her beverage preference because I know that Maria always wanted iced tea as her luncheon beverage in the past. I don't perform a simulation to predict her beverage desire on this occasion. I simply extrapolate from the past pattern. Now although this case is better classified as theorizing than simulating, "theorizing" isn't a very apt description. My extrapolation from past cases is not based on anything like a psychological "law." It is a good example of what Gopnik and Meltzoff (1997) call an "empirical generalization" as opposed to a psycho-logical law. Empirical generalizations are associated with "scripts" or "narra-tives" rather than theories. Nonetheless, the example illustrates the obvious need to refrain from claiming that simulation is involved in *all* cases of third-person attribution. It is one of several considerations that motivate a hybrid approach.

4.9 TT, ST, and the Priority
of First-Person Attribution

Now let us be a little more explicit about the commitments of the child-scientist viewpoint, especially in its pure form. Gopnik, Glymour, and their colleagues (2004) talk of a learner "observing" correlations or contingencies, and by "observation" they presumably mean ordinary perceptual observation. Their model is supposed to describe what child scientists do, and surely scientists gather evidence by perceptual observation. They do not use "introspective" or other first-person privileged methods; at least this is the standard view. Defenders of TT typically greet appeals to any sort of introspective method with scorn and regard it as the ill-advised property of simulationism (in its Cartesian variant). However, if one peels away the covers, it is not hard to find special first-person methods being invoked even by leading exponents of the child-scientist approach. I defend special first-person methods (chapter 9), so this invocation is not something I mean to criticize. My point, rather, is to show how hard it is to uphold a pure TT position in which first-person attribution is systematically treated as parallel to third-person attribution.

The clearest example of what I am talking about is Andrew Meltzoff. When Meltzoff writes with Gopnik (e.g., Gopnik and Meltzoff, 1994, 1997), they endorse a pure TT position in which special first-person methods have no place. But Meltzoff has also written many articles that endorse a unique role for special first-person access to mental life. Meltzoff does not fully acknowledge this, but its presence is unmistakable.

Meltzoff frequently argues that infants use imitation as a "discovery procedure" in mentalizing. When a child observes a creature that imitates the self and hence is behaviorally "like me," this prompts an inference to the conclusion that the other is also *mentally* "like me," using an analogical argument from one's own mental states to those of the other. Because the infant knows what she is mentally like in specific circumstances, this can help her identify the mental states of others under similar circumstances. Here are passages from three papers of Meltzoff that articulate these ideas.

[1] Through experience [infants] may learn that when they act in particular ways, they themselves have certain concomitant internal states (proprioceptions, emotions, intentions, etc.). Having detected this regularity, infants have grounds for making the inference that when they see another person act in the same way that they do, the person has internal states similar to their own. (Metzoff, 1999: 390)

[2] This grasp of the other as like oneself . . . allows the infant to use the self as a framework for enriching its understanding of the other. Having done an action itself, the infant has subjective, experiential knowledge of that act. When the infant sees another perform an act that he knows is like his own, the infant can interpret the seen act in terms of this subjective experience. (Meltzoff and Moore, 1995: 65)

[3] We are now in a position to see how the imitative mind and brain may contribute to the development of mentalizing. We offer a three-step developmental sequence as follows.

    (i) Innate equipment. Newborns can recognize equivalences between perceived and executed acts. This is that starting state, as documented by newborn imitation. . . .

(ii) Constructing first-person experience. Through everyday experience infants map the relation between their own bodily acts and their mental experiences. For example, there is an intimate relation between "striving to achieve a goal" and the concomitant facial expression and effortful bodily acts. Infants experience their own unfulfilled desires and their own concomitant facial/postural/vocal reactions. They experience their own inner feelings and outward facial expressions and construct a detailed bidirectional map linking mental experiences and behavior.

(iii) Inferences about the experiences of others. When infants see others acting "like me," they project that others have the same mental experience that is mapped to those behavioral states in the self. (Meltzoff and Decety, 2003: 497)

In all three of these passages, Meltzoff relies on the idea that one can have direct knowledge through "experience" of one's own inner feelings, desires, and other mental occurrences. The term *experience* seems to refer both to a mental occurrence per se and to direct knowledge of that occurrence. The passages imply, or presuppose, that when such mental events occur, the subject has direct knowledge of them at the time of their occurrence, knowledge that serves as the basis for inference to the mental events of others. This is an unacknowledged privileged-access doctrine. Moreover, it conflicts with things Meltzoff said earlier in collaboration with Gopnik. For example, they wrote: "Even though we seem to perceive our own mental states directly, this direct perception is an illusion. In fact, our knowledge of ourselves, like our knowledge of others, is the result of a theory" (Gopnik and Meltzoff, 1994: 168).

Meltzoff's position is partly aimed at warding off nativism about mentalizing. Once we see how the child acquires the adult theory of mind by general-purpose reasoning, including reasoning by analogy, we will feel no need to postulate innate specification of the adult theory of mind. In this respect, Meltzoff's views remain fully in the spirit of child-scientist TT. But to sustain this doctrine, Meltzoff assumes that the infant has special access to her own inner life. Here he departs from "paradigm" TT, in particular, its characteristic stance against special methods of first-person attribution or knowledge. Although I do not criticize the privileged access view, Meltzoff's tacit endorsement of it shows the tensions that arise in trying to defend a pure, child-scientist TT in all of its facets. Moreover, Meltzoff offers us no *account* of special first-person access; he simply presupposes it. It is unclear that TT, in any of its versions advanced by psychologists, has the resources to account for special first-person access.

Many TT proponents criticize ST for its reliance on first-person knowledge. Wellman, Cross, and Watson (2001), for example, contrast the "special primacy" that ST assigns to knowing one's own mental states with TT's "interrelated body of knowledge" approach, which applies to "all persons generically, that is, to both self and others" (2001: 678). Wellman et al. go on to extract a prediction from ST and to claim that this prediction is falsified. The ST approach, they say, predicts that self-understanding should develop before other-understanding. That is presumably because in using simulation to mindread others, the attributor must mindread her own states. Wellman et al. then claim that, empirically, self-understanding does not precede other-understanding. The specific evidence cited in support of this claim concerns false-belief tasks. Performance on such tasks for self and for others, they say, is virtually identical at all ages, thereby undercutting the ST position.

But this parallelism between self and other didn't hold in a study by German and Leslie (2000). They explored performance on self- and other-versions of a false-belief task and found that if memory enhancements are provided, performance on self-versions improves and performance on other-versions stays about the same. In German and Leslie's variant of the Sally-Anne task, children played the part of Sally and searched for an object in the wrong place. Each child was videotaped while doing this and subsequently was shown a video recording of either herself or another child going through this procedure. At the critical moment when the incorrect search took place, the video recording was paused, and the child was asked to explain her own (or the other child's) action and questioned about her belief at the time of the search. Children asked about self were more likely to offer false belief-based explanations (46 percent) and more likely to attribute to themselves a false belief (88 percent) than were children asked about the beliefs of another (12 percent and 42 percent, respectively).

This is only one of many pieces of evidence that undercut the oft-repeated claim of parallelism in first- and third-person mental knowledge. Extensive evidence contrary to the parallelism claim is reviewed in Nichols and Stich (2003: 167–178), and we shall report samples of such findings in chapter 9. In addition, an unpublished study by Imbens-Bailey, Prost, and Fabricius (1997) (cited by Fabricius and Imbens-Bailey, 2000) found that typically there is a year's delay between the onset of self versus other reference in the use of verbs of desire and belief. Children used the first-person forms earlier, despite the fact that they heard both forms from their parents. These findings are quite consistent with a privileged access approach to first-person knowledge and inconsistent with the parallelism approach.

4.10 Conclusion

Our discussion has revealed serious weaknesses in all of the main arguments that child-scientist theorists advance for their view. Their conceptual deficit diagnosis of early performance on false-belief tasks has crumbled in the face of accumulating evidence, and new studies suggest quite a different time line for the understanding of false belief. Appeal to other mental states (e.g., desire) to support the child-scientist story is unpersuasive, and the proposed domain-general causal learning mechanism as an explanation of mentalizing development is open to many serious critiques. Finally, the rejection of ST by child-scientist theorists because of its appeal to privileged access is unwarranted. Indeed, one of their own number has found it helpful to appeal to such privileged access in his somewhat heterodox variant of the child-scientist view. For all these reasons, the child-scientist version of TT is on shaky grounds.

Notes

1. Actually, theory-theorists often characterize mental-state concepts in terms of abstract properties not fully explained by means of causal relations. For example, users' mental concepts are said to be either "representational" or "nonrepresentational," where the notion of representationality is not spelled out in terms of causal relations.

2. These results are presented in section 4.8.

3. Related to the inhibitory control diagnosis of poor false-belief task performance is the reality-bias explanation proposed by Peter Mitchell and colleagues. Riggs, Peterson, Robinson, and Mitchell (1998) designed two types of questions in an unexpected transfer test. The first was a familiar false-belief question: "Where does John think the chocolate is?" The second was a counterfactual reasoning question: "If mother had not baked a cake, where would the chocolate be?" The second question didn't concern belief at all. Intriguingly, the children who wrongly answered the counterfactual reasoning question tended to be the same as those who wrongly answered the false-belief question. Of a sample of 32 subjects, only 4 answered differently across conditions. This invited the conclusion that the reigning difficulty is not with false belief specifically but with going against reality. This, of course, would totally scotch the notion that a deficit in grasping the belief concept is the culprit in poor false-belief task performance. However, other studies of counterfactual reasoning have not supported such a strong correlation (Harris, German, and Mills, 1996; Harris and Leevers, 2000). And, of course, young children's skill at pretense seems to involve precisely the ability to contemplate and navigate counterfactual scenarios.

4. We shall revisit findings on inhibitory control, curse of knowledge, and related phenomena in chapters 7 and 8. There they will be interpreted in ST-friendly terms.

5. This use of the term *connectionist* has nothing to do with parallel distributed processing.

6. For further critique of Bartsch and Wellman on this point, see Nichols and Stich (2003: 113–115).

7. Moreover, this should be achievable without any form of direct access, including introspective access, to states that instantiate these variables. This is part of the TT credo, which standardly insists that the variables of folk psychology are "abstract" and "unobservable."

8. Also see Chomsky (1975), Gould and Marler (1987), and Gelman and Williams (1998).

9. For a more pessimistic assessment of mindreading competence in Williams syndrome, see Tager-Flusberg and Sullivan (2000). Thanks here to Philip Robbins.

10. Thanks to Kelby Mason for help on this point.

11. This might be regarded as a restatement of Quine's point that the imputation of propositional attitudes is a "dramatic" act rather than an act of scientific reasoning. This is among Quine's reasons for being suspicious of the propositional attitudes and not viewing them as bona fide posits of science.

12. Other possible regions are also associated with syntax in some studies, but Saxe et al. do not find persuasive evidence of the predicted pairing of syntax and belief attribution.

5

The Modularity Theory

5.1 A Modular Form of Theory-Theory

Chapter 4 uncovered an array of serious problems for the child-scientist theory. Does the modularity theory (MT) fare better? After expounding the main themes of its principal proponents, I shall focus on two questions. First, is there good evidence for the view that the posited core system of mindreading (ToMM) is really modular, under the intended conception of modularity? Second, do the modularists make a better case than the child-scientist theorists for the view that mental-state attribution is executed by theoretical reasoning or inference, as contrasted with simulation? We shall also discuss the possible modularity of mindreading systems other than the most familiar one (ToMM), but the first two questions are the main ones on our agenda.

Alan Leslie, Jerry Fodor, and Simon Baron-Cohen have been the leading proponents of MT. Fodor gave it a theoretical formulation in the late 1980s and early 1990s. Leslie has contributed the richest theoretical characterization, including specific proposals about cognitive architecture and the generation of supportive empirical research. Although Leslie is the most visible and sustained champion of the view, it is appropriate to begin with Fodor's formulations (with which Leslie largely agrees, it would appear).

Fodor begins his book *Psychosemantics* (1987) with an interpretation of a passage in Shakespeare's *A Midsummer Night's Dream*. He interprets Hermia as doing a bit of folk psychology, which Fodor characterizes as "implicit, nondemonstrative, theoretical inference" (1987: 1). He continues:

> When such [commonsense psychological] explanations are made explicit, they
> are frequently seen to exhibit the "deductive structure" that is so characteristic of

explanation in real science. There are two parts to this: the theory's underlying generalizations are defined over unobservables, and they lead to its predictions by iterating and interacting rather than by being directly instantiated. (1987: 7)

As these passages make clear, Fodor's account of commonsense psychology posits an implicit, sciencelike theory featuring generalizations over unobservables (in this case, mental states). People are said to arrive at commonsense mental attributions by using the theory to guide their inferences.

Where does our naïve psychological theory come from? Fodor addresses this in his epilogue:

Here is what I would have done if I had been faced with this problem in designing *Homo sapiens*. I would have made a knowledge of commonsense *Homo sapiens* psychology *innate*; that way nobody would have to spend time learning it. . . . The empirical evidence that God did it the way I would have isn't, in fact, unimpressive. . . . There is, so far as I know, no human group that doesn't explain behavior by imputing beliefs and desires to the behavior. . . . At least in our culture, much of the apparatus of mentalistic explanation is apparently operative quite early. (1987: 132)

In a subsequent paper on the child's theory of mind, Fodor elaborates his nativist, modularist, theory-theorist hypothesis. In discussing false-belief phenomena, he says that 3-year-olds and 4-year-olds share the same "primitive theory" (1987: 285) and offers an account of the changes between 3- and 4-year-olds that he regards as "compatible with . . . an extreme Cartesianism, according to which intentional folk psychology is, essentially, an innate, modularized database" (1987: 284).

Leslie's approach is very similar. Here is a position statement from the same period that includes the theorizing feature:

We believe that having access to such data structures [namely, three-place relational structures involving an agent slot, an anchor slot, and a proposition slot], together with the system of inferences they support, constitutes a tacit and intuitive *theory of mind*, or, if you like constitutes a *theory* of the specific "representational relations" (like *pretends*, *believes*, *wants*) that enter into the causation of agents' behavior. (Leslie and Roth 1993: 91, emphasis added)

Elsewhere Leslie and German again highlight a commitment to theory-theory: "We make no bones about the fact that we are on the side of theory-theory and that we are skeptical about at least *radical* simulationism" (Leslie and German, 1995: 123).

There are other places in Leslie's writing, however, especially recent writings, where the "TT" label is spurned. For example, "here I shall confine myself to examining the deeper motivations for theory-theory in order to say why I believe the entire enterprise is mistaken" (Leslie, 2000: 198). Such disavowals of the "TT" label, I suspect, do not constitute a major change in his position. Instead, they emphasize a point on which he has always taken issue with child-scientist theorists. This concerns acquisition of the implicit, intuitive theory. Leslie takes strong exception to the notion that the theory is acquired in the same way that adult scientists acquire their theories (whatever way that may be). This component of *paradigm* TT, then, Leslie does not embrace (on "paradigm" TT, see section 2.1). So he isn't a paradigm theory-theorist, but I would count him as a kind of theory-theorist nonetheless.

Leslie's maneuvers to distance himself from the child-scientist position sometimes take a slightly odd form. For example, he claims that children have only "theory-like" knowledge structures, not "real" theories of the sort scientists have (Leslie, 2000). What is the difference between a "real" theory as opposed to mere "theory-like" knowledge? It sometimes seems to reside, for Leslie, in the difference between explicit versus implicit knowledge: explicit in the case of scientists, implicit in the case of children. But isn't the theory-theory position usually explained in terms of an implicit theory? That is certainly the language used by Fodor and often Leslie himself. Why can't implicit knowledge of a theory still be knowledge of a *real* theory rather than something merely theory*like* (whatever the latter difference is)?

Another way Leslie sometimes distances himself from TT is in his depiction of children's grasp of mental-state concepts. Leslie, Friedman, and German (2004) reject the child-scientist idea that "we are born as 'little scientists' who discover belief and desire through experimentation, observation and theory-building" (p. 528). But Leslie et al. still depict desires and beliefs as theoretical entities—"abstract" entities, in their terminology—on a par with electrons and genes. They contrast the concepts of belief and desire with the concepts of electron and gene insofar as the former are innate and the latter aren't. But their insistence on the "abstractness" of desire and belief bears testimony to the continuing hold of the theorizing theme, in which the posited states are unobservable in the manner of classical scientific theorizing.

Like Fodor, Leslie does not maintain that users of naïve psychology merely *possess* a theory; he holds that they *deploy* that theory to make inferences leading to mental-state attributions. Invocation of theory-guided inference appears in the previously quoted passage from Leslie and Roth (1993), which speaks of the "system of inferences" that the proprietary data structures of the theory support. Talk of inference—presumably, theory-guided inference—can also be found in this passage describing mental attributions:

> These results support a number of features of the metarepresentational model of pretence. They demonstrate counterfactual causal reasoning in 2-year-olds based on imaginary suppositions. For example, in the CUP EMPTY/FULL scenario the child works from the supposition **the empty cups "they contain juice"** and upon seeing the experimenter upturn one of the cups, the child applies a "real world" *inference* concerning the upturning of cups. . . . In the experiment, the children correctly *inferred* what the experimenter was pretending. The very

possibility of "correctness" depends upon some definite pretend situation being communicated. The child calculates a construal of the agent's behavior—a construal which relates the agent to the imaginary situation. The child is not simply socially excited into producing otherwise solitary pretend; the child can answer questions by making definite *inferences* about a definite imaginary situation communicated to him by the behavior of the agent. (Leslie, 1994: 224–225; emphasis added)

The phrasing here refers repeatedly to the child's "causal reasoning," "inferences," and "calculations," reinforcing the inferentialist and hence theorizing nature of the model. The commitment to TT is further elaborated in the following passage:

On the other hand, you may ask, why call a [mentalizing mechanism] a "theory-theory"? The minimal answer is that, as we saw in the case of language, systems of representation themselves constitute bodies of knowledge. To fully deploy such systems, additional abilities are required (e.g., inferencing that is sensitive to the structure of the representations). For this entirely general reason, theory-theories embrace both knowledge and ability. (Leslie and German, 1995: 128)

On the question of modularism, Leslie's position departs a bit from Fodor's in rejecting thoroughgoing modularism. His position is best characterized as semimodularist. It begins by postulating the "theory of mind" mechanism (ToMM), regarded as part of the core architecture of the human brain. ToMM is specialized for learning about mental states. It kick-starts belief-desire attribution, but effective reasoning about belief contents also depends on a process of content selection by inhibition. This process is executed by the selection processor (SP), a second mechanism that develops slowly through the preschool period and beyond and is not regarded as modular.

5.2 The Attribution Question

It is clear that Leslie has a continuing commitment to some central features of TT, though not all features of "paradigm" TT. What is questionable is whether he presents any evidence that favors the theoretical reasoning account of attribution over the simulationist account. It is hard to pinpoint any such evidence. Take the discussion of the cup example, for instance, which is addressed to the attribution process. In the two sentences preceding the quoted cup passage, Leslie and German seem to acknowledge that the example provides no clear-cut advantage to the theoretical inference account as contrasted with a simulational account.

If the child can infer that a cup containing water will, if upturned over a table, disgorge its contents and make the table wet, then the same child can also elaborate his own pretence or follow another person's pretence using the same inference: if x pretends of the cup that "it contains water," and if x upturns the cup, then x pretends of the cup "the water will come out of it" and "will make the table wet." Now, if someone wants to call the above "simulation," then they can; but it adds little or nothing to the account to do so. (1995: 128)

The final sentence appears to concede that the cup example is compatible with a simulationist treatment. Leslie and German try to downplay this compatibility by saying it would "add nothing" to their account to call the child's mindreading a simulation. But this isn't right; it would add something definite, though admittedly subtle. As simulational mindreading has been explained (chapter 2), it involves *enactively* imagining (E-imagining) what another person is thinking or feeling. In the cup scenario, the child may E-imagine the experimenter supposing the cup to contain water. Elaborating this bit of E-imagination, the child proceeds to E-imagine the experimenter also supposing the cup to contain juice and to pour liquid out and make the table wet. In other words, the child tracks the experimenter's thinking in "enactment" mode, which is not part of a TT account. The difference may be subtle, but it's a difference. The ST account does not say that the child merely generates metarepresentations of the experimenter's mental states. Rather, she tries to reenact them. Perhaps Leslie's talk of mental "pretence" is alternative terminology for the reenactment idea. If so, his theory becomes a disguised version of ST. In any case, there is nothing in the evidence that excludes or even disfavors the ST interpretation. So in one of the few examples where Leslie juxtaposes TT and ST, the evidence by no means supports TT over ST.

A similar point holds of Leslie's inhibitory-control diagnosis of the childhood development of belief-desire reasoning (Leslie and Polizzi, 1998; Leslie, German, and Polizzi, 2005). As indicated in section 4.3, Leslie and collaborators have intriguing findings about 4-year-olds' difficulties and successes on various avoidance-desire tasks, and they construct models of these 4-year-old successes and difficulties by using the apparatus of ToMM and SP. Their chief aim is to demonstrate that patterns of success and failure are a result of *performance* factors involving inhibitory control rather than *conceptual* factors (as claimed by child-scientist theorists). I am entirely on their side in this dispute. In particular, I find the inhibitory-control style of explanation very appealing. An inhibitory control explanation, however, is not the exclusive property of TT (nor does Leslie tout this approach *as* an application of TT). Indeed, I'll later suggest that the problem of inhibiting one's self-perspective or failure to inhibit it fits better with ST than TT (sections 7.7–7.8).

To illustrate Leslie's findings, consider an avoidance-desire task used by Leslie, German, and Polizzi (2005). Subjects are told of a girl who is to place some food in one of two boxes, and they are asked to predict which box she will choose. A complicating factor is that there is a kitten in one of the boxes. In a true-belief version of the task, the girl watches the kitten move from box

A to box B. In the false-belief version, she observes the kitten in box A but is absent when it moves to box B. A second complicating factor is that the girl's behavior is motivated by an avoidance desire: She wants to avoid putting the food in the box with the kitten, because the kitten is sick and might eat the food and become worse. The finding was that 94 percent of the 4-year-old subjects passed the prediction task in the true-belief version but only 12 percent passed it in the false-belief version (Leslie, German, and Polizzi, 2005). This is despite the fact that 4-year-olds have no difficulty in correctly attributing a false belief to the protagonist when answering a "think" question ("where does she think the food is?"). In other words, a problem requiring two applications of inhibitory control (one for false belief and one for outcome avoidance) is much more difficult for 4-year-olds than a single application of inhibitory control. Leslie, German, and Polizzi proceed to construct and test models of why this might be so.

As indicated before, my response to this work is to ask why ST shouldn't also be able to accommodate the findings in this area. ST's basic strategy is to say that a subject tries to solve the tasks by simulating the protagonist's thought processes. In the false-belief version of the avoidance-desire task, she must simulate (E-imagine) a belief that is contrary to her own knowledge (or belief) and a desire that is contrary to a standard desire. Such a combined simulation, apparently, is difficult for 4-year-olds. For both belief and desire, the subject must inhibit a *prepotent* tendency. Although 4-year-olds exhibit inhibition quite well when only one tendency requires inhibition, they have difficulty when two tendencies (of the indicated sorts) require inhibition. An ST-based approach should be able to accommodate a precise model of how this works as well as a ToMM-SP approach can accommodate it. Of course, the two models would not be identical—one would involve E-imagination and the other wouldn't—but the two might be structurally isomorphic. Intriguingly, Leslie et al. concede that they have no story about what *triggers* inhibition in these cases: "What *triggers* the inhibition is an interesting question but not one we will address here." Perhaps it's the act of E-imagining.

On other topics, too, ST and MT might not conflict. A nonradical version of ST, the kind I favor, cheerfully grants that mindreading involves metarepresentations, that is, descriptive representations of mental states. Certainly a mental attribution is itself a metarepresentational state. So the metarepresentational emphasis of MT is something ST can embrace. This is to agree with Leslie and German's comment that "simulation needs metarepresentation" (1995: 133), at least where "metarepresentation" is not understood to involve any particular architectural implications. The possibility of even greater rapprochement between MT and ST will also be considered (section 5.8).

In sum, MT is best understood as a form of TT, despite Leslie's periodic protestations to the contrary. However, there isn't any evidence that supports

MT over ST on the most salient topic that concerns us, third-person attribution. It is time now to evaluate MT on its own terms. Does MT have the right story on the architectural question, and is it a genuinely modular story (as its moniker suggests)?

5.3 Modularity and the Current Dialectic

Before proceeding, I want to comment on the dialectical situation in the mentalizing debate. People often come to the topic of mentalizing with prior theoretical commitments. Some are convinced that nativist-modular theories *in general* are right and that modularity should *especially* inhabit a domain like mentalizing. Perhaps they think that mentalizing is an obvious paradigm of domain specificity and hence of modularity. These same people conclude that because modularism is right for mentalizing, simulationism *can't* be right, because it's a platitude that modularism (a form of TT) and simulationism are rivals and hence incompatible.

In dialectic with people of this persuasion, I want to make several points. First, it is difficult to sustain the modularity of mentalizing in undiluted form because mentalizing has several traits inconsistent with the most important features of (Fodorian) modularity. This may be why Leslie's carefully honed form of modularism about mentalizing is only *minimally* modular. However, the alleged incompatibility between MT and ST is less obvious and clear-cut than is widely supposed. In fact, in one subdomain of mind-reading, the processes at work have several hallmarks of modularity. So if you have a hankering for modularity, you shouldn't turn a blind eye to ST (see section 5.8).

In defending the modularity of mentalizing, Leslie clearly has Jerry Fodor's (1983) conception of modularity in mind. Fodor listed a number of fairly specific criteria for modularity and claimed that something is a module to the extent that it satisfies those criteria. His nine criteria are (1) domain specificity, (2) mandatoriness of operation, (3) limited access by other systems to intermediate representations within the module ("interlevels" of processing), (4) speed, (5) informational encapsulation, that is, lack of access (by the module) to information outside the module, (6) shallowness of outputs, (7) susceptibility to characteristic breakdowns, (8) a characteristic pace and sequencing of ontogeny, and (9) instantiation in specific, hardwired neural structures. In different discussions of the principal mentalizing mechanism, ToMM, Leslie emphasizes different criteria and their importance to what he calls "theory of mind."[1] In Leslie (1994), four characteristics of ToMM are emphasized: (a) It is domain specific, (b) it employs a proprietary representational system that describes propositional attitudes, (c) it forms the innate basis for our capacity to acquire theory of mind, and (d) it is damaged in childhood autism, resulting in impairments in the capacity to acquire theory of mind. In Scholl and Leslie (1999), the initial emphasis concerns restrictions on information flow. This includes the claim that some of the information outside a module (especially information in "central systems") is not accessible inside the module. Scholl and Leslie further claim that the normal acquisition of theory of mind is at least partly due to the operation of a theory-of-mind-specific "architectural" module, which is domain specific, that is, involves specialized sorts of representations and computations, and is also fast and mandatory (Scholl and Leslie, 1999: 133–135).

A number of problems arise about these theses, which I shall address under several headings. First, is mentalizing genuinely domain specific (section 5.3)? Second, is mentalizing informationally encapsulated (section 5.4)? Third, does the evidence support a *computational* (Fodorian) module rather than a *Chomskian* module (section 5.5)?

5.4 Is Mentalizing Domain Specific?

The domain-specificity test for modularity is perhaps the most commonly invoked, and it looks like the easiest one for mentalizing to pass. Isn't it obvious that mentalizing deals with a distinctive domain, namely, psychological states? How could the ability to cognize this domain fail to satisfy the domain-specificity test? So if there is some mechanism distinctively dedicated to this topic, mustn't it satisfy the domain-specificity test?

One problem here concerns the precise domain in question. Talk of a "psychology module" makes it sound as if the entire range of psychological states should be its domain. Modularists, however, have not come close to defending modularity for this entire domain. The argument for domain specificity typically focuses on a proper subset of psychological states, namely, the propositional attitudes. Modularists (including Leslie) commonly argue that the psychology module, ToMM, features a distinctive type of data structure—a metarepresentation, or M-representation—for representing mental states. But this type of data structure is inapplicable to many psychological states, including sensations (pain, itch) and emotions (fear, disgust, anger). These kinds of psychological states are usually ignored in the modularist literature. Are we to infer that the domain of the posited module(s) is much narrower than the term *psychology module* suggests? I shall argue, ironically, that the case for modularity is hard to make for the attitudes but somewhat easier for emotions or sensations.

In the rest of this section, I concentrate on conceptual problems associated with the notion of domain specificity. Fodor (1983) recognized from the start that domain specificity is a tricky construct. The fact that cows are different from telephones does not guarantee that there are different mechanisms for cow perception and telephone perception. Cow recognition might be medi-ated by some sort of prototype-plus-similarity metric. That is, perceptual recognition of cows might be produced by a mechanism that provides solu-tions for computational problems of the form: how similar—how "close"—is the current stimulus to a prototypical cow? If so, then cow perception would be mediated by much the same mechanisms that operate for many other domains (1983: 49). In that case, it would be wrong to say that there is a cow-cognizing module. The mere distinctiveness of a subject-matter "cows" isn't enough to pass a plausible domain-specificity test for modularity. What else is necessary?

Fodor approaches the matter in terms of distinct *stimulus* domains (1983: 48). The proposal is that each distinct module has its own distinctive stimulus domain. Perceptual systems that effect the phonetic analysis of speech differ from ones that effect the perceptual analysis of auditory nonspeech. Speech-analyzing perceptual systems are distinctive in that they operate only upon a particular set of stimuli, namely, acoustic signals taken to be utterances.

> Only a restricted class of stimulations can throw the switch that turns [the system] on. (Fodor, 1983: 49)

Generalizing, we might say that there is a module for domain D only if there is a psychological system that operates only on *stimuli in domain D*.

Now Fodor's proposal about triggering stimuli was intended specifically for *input* systems, as contrasted with *central* systems and *output* systems. For the most part, the only modules he discusses are input systems, and he regards central systems as nonmodular, in light of their nonencapsulation. But how are we supposed to apply his proposal about domain specificity when we move to mentalizing? Mentalizing, at least most types of mentalizing, is surely not an input process. To see this, consider the case of predicting Maria's beverage desire (section 4.8). At the time I predict her desire, she has not yet arrived at the restaurant or formed any beverage desire for today's lunch. Even if she has formed such a desire, it does not impinge on my mindreading activity. No "stimulus" from her behavior or facial expression throws a switch that turns on my (tea-prediction) mindreading process. A similar point applies to the mindreading of fictional characters, as when one mindreads a character in a novel. The only *stimuli* that elicit this mindreading activity are bits of print on paper (or light waves reflected from the print). Are these to be counted as part of the mentalizing domain?

An obvious move is to permit some central systems to qualify as modules. The domains of such central modules would be defined by outputs from input systems that are inputs to these central systems. Something like this is sug-gested by Botterill and Carruthers (1999: 66–67). However, there is still an intractable problem of how the module's domain is to be defined via these inputs. There are two ways to proceed here. First, the domain might include all cognitive (mental) events that turn on the candidate module. That entire class would comprise the system's domain. Second, instead of counting the cognitive events themselves, one might count their *intentional objects* as comprising the system's domain. The obvious problem with the first proposal is that *every* central system would turn out to be a mentalizing module, because the inputs to every such system would be mental or cognitive events. That is ridiculous. We want to allow for the possibility of central modules that aren't mentalizing modules (e.g., we want to allow modules for number or logic). The trouble with the second proposal is that it is far too permissive. Consider, for example, the imagination. An incredibly diverse range of cognitive events can trigger the imagination. If one takes the intentional objects of all of those events and makes a "domain" out of them, it will be a radically heterogeneous, disconnected lot. Intuitively, it would not constitute a unified "domain" at all, which is certainly what modularists intend to capture. If we adopt the second proposal, what precludes such a weird domain, and what precludes the implication that imagination is modular (or satisfies the domain-specificity test for modularity)?

My conclusion is that the theoretical construct of domain specificity is difficult to pinpoint.[2] It is doubtful that mentalizing passes the domain-specificity test for modularity unless the test is so trivial as to allow many systems or cognitive activities to qualify as modular that should not qualify.

5.5 Informational Encapsulation

Fodor has always regarded informational encapsulation as the heart of modularity (Fodor, 2000: 63). A system is informationally encapsulated if it has only limited access to information contained in other mental systems. In particular, restricting attention to input modules, a module does not have access to, and hence is not influenced by, information contained in central systems, such as beliefs, desires, and expectations. For example, the visual system does not have access to central system information about the relative lengths of lines in a stimulus. Hence, when viewing a Müller-Lyer drawing, the visual system generates a percept of one line being longer than the other, even though the central system possesses the knowledge that they are actually of equal length. Is there comparable informational encapsulation in the case of core mentalizing mechanisms, especially ToMM? Is information in central systems "screened off" from the mentalizing operation?

Consider the inferential processes of ToMM. Leslie says that ToMM operates on certain types of data structures, namely, metarepresentations. What operations on M-representations does ToMM employ? This is often left unclear, but Leslie and German (1995) provide insight into this matter in the following passage (partly quoted earlier):

One key part of Leslie's (1987) account of early pretense postulated that infants used the "primary" knowledge they had acquired about the physical world to elaborate their own pretend scenarios and to understand the pretend scenarios communicated to them in the action, gesture, and speech of other people.... Some simple, general assumptions about how processes of inference operate over the internal structure of metarepresentations shows how *the child can employ his primary knowledge in pretend scenarios.* For example, if the child can infer that a cup containing water will, if upturned over a table, disgorge its contents and make the table wet, then the same child can also elaborate his own pretend or follow another person's pretence using the same inference: if x upturns the cup, then x pretends of the cup that "the water will come out of it" and "will make the table wet." (1995: 127–128, emphasis added)

This proposal makes ToMM violate the encapsulation criterion. The emphasized clause indicates that ToMM uses *primary* knowledge of the physical world to construct inferences suitable to mental attribution, in particular, attribution of pretend states. Primary knowledge of the physical world would be located somewhere in the central system. To use this knowledge for mind-reading, ToMM must have access to it, which violates informational encapsulation.

This point complements one made by Nichols and Stich (2003: 120–121). They note that mindreaders typically attribute many of their own beliefs to targets (a phenomenon they call "default attribution"), and Leslie, too, acknowledges this. But a mindreader's own beliefs, generally speaking, are lodged in a central system, not in ToMM. If ToMM has access to these beliefs, it must not be a module, at least if informational encapsulation is a critical condition for modularity, which it surely is.

To deal with these problems, a mentalizing modularist might revisit the previous section's proposal that ToMM be viewed as a central system rather than an input system. However, we shall then need a different characterization of encapsulation.[3] Botterill and Carruthers try to provide one with their proposed notion of *processing* encapsulation, intended to contrast with the notion of *information* encapsulation. Information encapsulation is determined by the extent to which information from elsewhere enters a modular processor to be operated upon by it, whereas processing encapsulation is determined by the extent to which the processing of the module can be influenced or affected by other parts of the system (Botterill and Carruthers, 1999: 69). As Nichols and Stich (2003: 121) point out, however, processing encapsulation is an exceedingly weak constraint to place on a component of the mind. It is so weak that it is hard to think of any interesting systems that violate it. For example, practical reasoning—one of Fodor's favorite examples of a nonmodular process—is not likely to have its processing (or program) influenced by other systems. So this and other stock examples of nonmodular processes will pass the encapsulation test for modularity. If the only type of encapsulation demanded of modularity is processing encapsulation, the test will be far too easy to satisfy. Obviously, modularity theory needs something like the original test of informational encapsulation, but, as we have seen, mentalizing fails that test.[4]

5.6 Computational versus Chomskian Modularity

Samuels (2000) introduces a distinction between two conceptions of modularity: computational (roughly, Fodorian) modularity and Chomskian modularity. Computational modules are symbol-manipulating devices that receive representations as inputs and manipulate them according to formally specifiable rules in order to generate representations (or actions) as outputs. Chomskian modules, by contrast, are just systems of representations. Unlike computational modules, they are "inert." They eventuate in behavior only when manipulated by various cognitive mechanisms. Chomskian modules, being bodies of information, can be manipulated by computational modules. For instance, a parser might be a computational module that deploys the contents of a Chomskian module devoted to linguistic information in order to generate syntactic and semantic representations of sentence forms (Samuels, 2000: 18–19). It is entirely possible, says Samuels, for the mind to contain Chomskian modules while not containing any computational modules. Although humans may have domain-specific systems of knowledge for physics or geometry, we may not possess any domain-specific computational mechanisms for processing information about physical objects or geometrical properties. Such domain-specific knowledge may be utilized only by *domain-general*, and hence nonmodular, computational mechanisms (Samuels, 2000: 19).

Samuels goes on to argue that Leslie has not provided convincing evidence that theory of mind is subserved by one or more *computational* modules as opposed to mere *Chomskian* modules (yet Leslie clearly intends to argue for the former). The main source of evidence for a theory-of-mind computational module comes from dissociative studies, demonstrating that in one group of subjects, theory of mind capacities are selectively impaired, whereas in another group they are selectively spared. A relevant case concerns two groups of subjects with mental disabilities: autistics and people with Williams syndrome. Autistics, even autistics within the normal IQ range, have trouble passing false-beliefs tasks. By contrast, Williams syndrome subjects, with very low IQs, routinely pass standard false-belief tasks. Such data are taken to provide evidence for a computational module for theory of mind. The proffered explanatory hypothesis is the existence of a theory-of-mind computational module (in normals) that is selectively impaired in autistics but selectively spared in Williams syndrome subjects.

Samuels argues, however, that this explanatory strategy can be mimicked by one that invokes only a specialized body of *knowledge* for theory of mind. Perhaps autistics fail the false-belief task because their specialized body of theory-of-mind knowledge is impaired, whereas that body of knowledge is intact in Williams syndrome subjects. Although it is plausible to explain the data by positing *some* kind of modular cognitive structure, why prefer the computational module account to the Chomskian module alternative? (Samuels, 2000: 39).

5.7 A Minimally Modular Theory

In this section I elaborate my contention that Leslie's theory assigns much less importance to modularity than is generally appreciated. When examined carefully, the modular component of the theory plays a much smaller role in the fully evolved theory than has been widely advertised. This doesn't show the theory is wrong, but its popularity among modularists might be somewhat misplaced.

Leslie has always maintained that ToMM is a modular mechanism. What does it do? Most distinctive to ToMM, according to Leslie (1994), is its deployment of a special type of data structure: the *metarepresentation* (or *M-representation*). Metarepresentations are data structures that make explicit four kinds of information: (i) an agent, (ii) an informational relation (an attitude), (iii) an aspect of a real situation (an "anchor"), and (iv) a possibly imaginary situation. For example, ToMM might construct a representation of a mother's believing a banana to be a telephone. Here the mother is the agent, belief is the attitude, a banana is a component of the real situation, and "it is a telephone" is the imaginary situation. An important facet of Leslie's conception of ToMM is that it constructs these distinctive relational data structures from more primitive types of representations, namely, the four types of representations indicated. Also crucial to his conception is that metarepresentations are *opaque* representations, "decoupled" from primary, *transparent* representations that purport to describe the world as it actually is. The decoupling operation, which is supposedly distinctive to ToMM, provides the best example of a proprietary feature of ToMM as a representational system.

It is crucial, of course, to distinguish between the *representational* powers of a mentalizing mechanism and its *attributional*, or belief-forming, powers. Let me illustrate this distinction in the domain of the physical. The mind clearly has powers to create representations of physical entities, properties, and systems, such as electrons, forces, and sets of interacting particles. But the power to create a certain representation is different from the power to generate a *belief* in the realization of the representation. Imagination can construct a representation of a unicorn, but constructing a unicorn representation is quite different from constructing, or generating, a *belief* that unicorns exist (or that unicorns don't exist). Similarly, it is one thing for a system to create representations of (possible) psychological states and quite another thing for a system to generate a belief—or attribution—that a particular person actually occupies, or exemplifies, a certain state at a given time. Belief-generating operations are distinct from representation-generating operations.

Suppose we grant Leslie the thesis that a particular class of representations, namely, metarepresentations, are generated by modular operations, operations of ToMM. It doesn't follow that a mentalizer's *beliefs* concerning who has which mental states are also the products of ToMM. In fact, it is not clear that Leslie *means* to claim that ToMM is responsible for generating mentalizing beliefs. That seems to be the job of the selection processor, which has the responsibility of choosing a specific attitudinal content to be ascribed to a given target on a given occasion. Leslie does not claim that the selection processor is modular or even that it is theory-of-mind specific (see Scholl and Leslie, 1999: 147)! As to the question of belief fixation, Leslie has remarked (personal communication) that modules do not have the job of fixing belief. That job belongs to a nonmodular central system.[5] This implies that the entire attributional dimension of mindreading—that is, forming beliefs about mental states—is a nonmodular activity, which takes a big bite out of the theory's modular facade.

I do not suggest that Leslie has been obscure on this point. Scholl and Leslie (1999), for example, make extremely modest or weak claims about the role of modularity in "theory of mind" (ToM).

> Our claim is not that the entirety of theory of mind is modular, but only that theory of mind has a specific innate *basis*. (1999: 134)

> When we talk about ToM in the context of the modularity theory, we intend to capture only the origin of the basic ToM abilities, and not the full range of mature activities which may employ such abilities. It is certainly the case that these basic ToM abilities may eventually be recruited by higher cognitive processes for more complex tasks, and the resulting higher-order ToM activities may well interact (in a nonmodular way) with other cognitive processes.... *The interesting question is whether there's any significant part of the capacity that is modular.* (1999: 140)

> Again, the interesting question is whether *any* significant part of ToM is modular. (1999: 141)

Focus on the final passage. It implies that the interesting question is whether there is even *one* part of ToM that is modular. The clear inference is that Scholl and Leslie don't wish to defend any stronger thesis than the existence of a single modular component for the mentalizing system. This is a very minimally modular theory indeed.

Let us now return to ToMM as a representation-forming device, surely the core of Leslie's theory. As noted earlier, however, it cannot even be viewed as a theory of all mental-state representation. The metarepresentations generated by ToMM are representations of propositional attitudes, which do not exhaust all mental states or all mental states people routinely represent. Scholl and Leslie (1999) begin their paper by saying, "The currency of our mental lives consists largely of propositional attitudes," and they quickly identify "theory of mind" with the capacity to interpret behavior in terms of such attitudes (1999: 131). But people impute many other types of mental states in addition to the attitudes: somatic states such as aches, itches, tickles, and hunger, as well as emotions such as joy, sadness, fear, disgust, and anger.

According to the usual philosophical taxonomy, these are not propositional attitudes. To be sure, verbs associated with some of these nouns can take propositional clauses as complements: "Jones fears that p," or "Roberto is angry about y." But there are other linguistic constructions involving these terms that omit propositional objects. One can say, "Jones is happy," without saying what he is happy *about*, and one can say, "Roberto is hungry," without specifying what he is hungry *for*. Some philosophers (Tye, Lycan, Dretske) try to reduce all mental states to *representational* mental states, but even if all mental states really are, at bottom, representational, it doesn't follow that the folk think of matters this way. Suppose, then, that many of the folk's mental-state representations are not representations of propositional attitudes. Then the data structures they use to represent the other mental states presumably don't involve the proprietary type of data structure associated with ToMM. It is an open question, then, whether the mechanisms involved in representing the other types of states are modular.

In short, the attitudes do not seem to exhaust the mental categories with which the folk mentalize. Hence, even if theory of mind—understood as the capacity to cognize the attitudes—were underpinned by a module, it wouldn't follow that the capacity to cognize mental states in general is underpinned by modules. A system like ToMM would subserve only a fraction of mentalizing activity. Although Leslie's modularity thesis is restricted to the attitudes, I shall now argue, perhaps ironically, that the strongest case for modularity lies in another (more primitive) subdomain of mentalizing.

5.8 Modularity and Simulation

There are multiple subdomains of mindreading and possibly different processes associated with them. As I have emphasized, Leslie focuses on the attitudes and builds a case for MT by reference to them. But there may be more primitive, low-level types of mindreading that pass some of the modularity tests that ToMM fails. Baron-Cohen's (1995) approach already provides an illustration of this. Baron-Cohen himself does not draw fundamental architectural distinctions among his four mechanisms, but others might look at ID and EDD, the two earlier maturing mechanisms, and view them as better candidates for modules than SAM or ToMM (for the case of ID, see Scholl and Tremoulet, 2000). In the next chapter, we shall examine processes involved in the recognition of emotion in facial expressions. "Recognition" is here understood as attribution. The main conclusion to be drawn in chapter 6 is that neuropsychological evidence about emotion recognition supports a simulationist account of these processes. In this section, I call attention to the fact that these processes may also pass some of the Fodorian tests for modularity. I don't say they pass *all* the tests, but they arguably pass quite a few. This raises the intriguing prospect of "limited compatibility" between ST and MT.

To preview chapter 6, substantial evidence suggests that the neural substrates of several basic emotions—fear, disgust, and anger—are crucially involved in the process of recognizing those same emotions in others via their facial expressions. Impairment in experiencing fear is associated with a selective impairment in recognizing fear, impairment in experiencing disgust is associated with a selective impairment in recognizing disgust, and the same for anger. This evidence can be best explained by positing that normal recognition of a given emotion is executed by a simulational process, one that exploits the same neural machinery used in undergoing the same emotion. What I shall now point out is that these emotion-recognition processes may have some of the (Fodorian) features of modules. It would be rash to conclude that they *are* modules, but they are (in some respects) modulelike.

Let me briefly list some criteria of modularity that the (face-based) emotion-recognition processes have a good prospect of satisfying. First, they seem to be extremely fast, satisfying the speed criterion. Second, they seem to be mandatory, or automatic. They do not require effortful processing and are outside voluntary control. Third, emotion-recognition processes are susceptible to characteristic breakdowns, as indicated by the neuropsychological evidence sketched previously. Fourth, each emotion-recognition process seems to be instantiated by specific neural structures that are presumably hardwired. More precisely, at least one part or stage of each process utilizes these distinctive neural structures, though other parts or stages may use shared methods.

Next consider informational encapsulation. Do face-based emotion-recognition processes have access to information contained elsewhere in the organism, especially general world knowledge lodged in the central system? Plausibly, they do not. Emotion-recognition processes may not require access to any information except what is proprietary to faces and emotions. So prospects look fairly bright for the encapsulation test to be met.

What about domain specificity? Here we begin to see serious problems for low-level mindreading modularity. The issues relate to the murkiness of module individuation, a nagging problem in the theory of modularity. If low-level mindreading is a candidate for modularity, what exactly is its domain? Does one mindreading module have all feelings in its domain? Or are there distinct modules for each separate basic emotion and sensation?

Another problem concerns the criterion of proprietary data-structures and principles of operation. Is there a distinctive principle of operation for each separate emotion? At some levels of abstraction, surely, that cannot be right. The emotion recognition studies suggest that the same type of face-based mindreading operation is in place for fear, disgust, and anger. This supports the idea of homogeneous principles of operation and hence a unified module for (at least) those three emotions.

I shall not try to resolve all of these issues. In the end, I do not endorse the idea that low-level mindreading is subserved by modules in a strict Fodorian sense of modularity. Nonetheless, I call attention to the fact that, unlike high-level mindreading (the domain of ToMM), low-level mindreading seems to have some of the features that interest modularists. This is intended to dislodge the preconception that the simulation approach and the modularity approach are "worlds apart."

5.9 Conclusions about TT

Where do chapters 4 and 5 leave us with respect to TT? There are only two substantially worked-out versions of TT, and each of them, as we have seen, has its distinctive problems. The child-scientist approach holds that children's grasp and deployment of mental concepts depends on a series of scientific "revolutions," including "conceptual" revolutions. But a wide range of evidence suggests that the most intensively studied phenomenon in the domain, namely, false-belief task performance, is better explained by processing factors than by conceptual factors. In addition, it is unclear that young children have the capacity to engage in sciencelike revolutions and particularly puzzling why all (normal) children would undergo the same (allegedly) revolutionary course on the same schedule. The nativist-modularist approach has difficulty showing that the central characteristics of modularity really apply to commonsense psychology, at least the core part of naïve psychology (propositional-attitude psychology) allegedly executed by ToMM. Information encapsulation, in particular, does not seem to hold of ToMM. When it comes to particular mindreading tasks, neither version of TT has demonstrated that they are generally executed by theoretical inference rather than simulation. Thus, TT has not made the case that simulation "neglect" is the proper stance for a theory of mindreading to take (see section 2.8).

Finally, two of our principal knocks against TT are yet to be presented. First, virtually all proponents of TT hold that mental states are unobservables, and they usually conclude that there is no privileged access to our own mental states or any special method of first-person mindreading.[6] I shall argue to the contrary in chapter 9. Second, all brands of TT present our grasp of mental-state concepts as suited, in some fashion, to the unobservability status of mental states. By contrast, in chapter 10, I shall sketch a view of our grasp of mental-state concepts that is aligned with the special, first-person mode of access to these states.

Notes

1. Theory of Mind (ToM) should be distinguished from ToMM (theory of mind mechanism). The former refers to the fundamental *capacity* for mindreading, whatever structure or mechanism implements it. The latter refers to a specific *mechanism* postulated to account for the fundamental mentalizing capacity.

2. Fodor seems to be aware of the inadequacies of his earlier characterization of domain specificity, because he revisits the problem and sketches a new approach in *The Mind Doesn't Work That Way* (Fodor, 2000: 58–61). Unfortunately, it is very difficult to grasp exactly what his new proposal is or how it applies to domain specificity for a mentalizing system.

3. Fodor (2000) offers a different characterization of encapsulation as follows: "To a first approximation, each module is supposed to have access to its current input, and to its proprietary database, and to nothing else" (2000: 91). In saying that a module has access only to its *current* input, how is "access" used, in a dispositional or a nondispositional sense? If the sense is nondispositional—that is, it says that a module operates at a given time only on inputs at that time and its data-base—then this looks to be trivially true of all systems, modular or nonmodular. If the sense is dispositional, then the restriction seems intolerable. Any system, even a modular system, has *potential* access to more than its actual, current input.

4. For further discussion of the modularity of mindreading, see Currie and Sterelny (2000).

5. I do not quite see how to reconcile this with other things Leslie has said about ToMM, for example, that ToMM executes *inferences*. Inferences are processes whose outputs are beliefs (or, if not full beliefs, at least doxastic states of some sort). Perhaps Leslie means that ToMM merely supports inferences but doesn't execute them.

6. As noted in chapter 4, Meltzoff is a theory-theorist who relies on special first-person access. In so doing, however, he clearly departs from the TT mainstream, and he hardly acknowledges that his moves rest on such an assumption.

6

Simulation in Low-Level Mindreading

6.1 Face-Based Emotion Recognition

This chapter begins our defense of the (hybrid) simulation approach.[1] It looks at evidence for simulation in relatively primitive, "low-level" mindreading. Simulation in more advanced, high-level mindreading will be examined in chapter 7, and developmental (and other) issues concerning simulation will be treated in chapter 8. By contrast with preceding chapters, this one draws extensively on evidence from cognitive neuroscience.

The chapter starts by examining a special class of mindreading tasks: attributing emotions to others based (mainly) on their facial expressions. This task is chosen as our ST starting point both because emotion reading is a fundamental kind of mindreading and because the case for simulation here is very substantial. Face-based emotion recognition (FaBER) is "low-level" mindreading because it is comparatively simple, primitive, automatic, and largely below the level of consciousness. The comparative simplicity of FaBER consists in recognizing emotion types (e.g., fear, disgust, and anger) without identifying any propositional contents, presumably a simpler task than identifying desires or beliefs with specific contents. The process may be primitive in two senses: Reading basic emotions has special survival value, so specialized programs may have evolved for emotion recognition that don't operate in other mindreading domains. In addition, emotion reading may be based on a type of process—a mirroring process—that is cognitively fairly primitive, whether or not it is innate and whether or not it evolved for emotion detection.

Emotions are routinely attributed to others in daily life, and facial expressions are a prime basis for such attribution, originally discussed by

Darwin (1872/1965). In keeping with the existing literature, I here talk of emotion "recognition" instead of "attribution." To recognize someone's face as expressive of a certain emotion is to judge the person to be in that state and to categorize the emotion as being of the specified type.

Our discussion will focus heavily on the striking empirical findings about emotion recognition that were sketched in chapter 5. Before turning to those findings, let us ask what our two main theoretical competitors would predict about the effects of brain damage on emotion recognition capacities. Suppose a patient suffers substantial damage in a brain region responsible for the production, or undergoing, of a specific emotion E. What would be the expected effect on that patient's ability to recognize emotion E and other emotions through facial expressions, according to ST and to TT?

Starting with ST, what is its story for the normal execution of a FaBER task with respect to E? ST would say that normal people use the same mental equipment in mindreading E as they use when undergoing, or experiencing, E. This is analogous to ST's account of decision prediction, in which the mindreader deploys her own decision-making system. Now, if an E-damaged mindreader tries to mindread emotion E in someone else, ST predicts that the damage will impair her ability to mindread E accurately. On the other hand, as long as the damage doesn't extend to brain regions responsible for other emotions, E', E'', and so on, ST predicts that FaBER performance with respect to those emotions would not be impaired.

Turning to TT, what would it predict for the same scenarios? A modular form of TT could say that there is a dedicated module for mindreading, conceivably a dedicated module for emotion mindreading specifically (though no modularist, to my knowledge, has made the latter proposal). It would not be part of a standard modularity approach, however, to say that an emotion-mindreading module would exploit emotion-bearing neural machinery to execute the mindreading. According to all forms of TT, including MT, mindreading is a thoroughly *metarepresentational* activity. It exploits data structures and computational procedures *about* first-order mental states, here emotions. It would not, however, use the first-order states themselves as data structures or as computational procedures to mindread those states, any more than people use their livers to represent or reason about livers. Of course, it could happen that a dual-function or multifunction neural region is coincidentally used both as a substrate for some mental state M and as a substrate for representing and/or reasoning about M. But there is no reason for TT to predict such a coincidence in the case of emotions (especially if one assumes that theorizing and emoting occur in different neural regions). For argument's sake, however, suppose there is a dedicated emotion-reading module with this coincidental property and it is damaged in a particular patient. An emotion-mindreading impairment would then be predictable. But such impairment would apply to *all* emotion types (all types that the module reads); one would not predict a selective impairment for a single emotion type. The same reasoning holds for a domain-general form of TT. If a domain-general reasoning system is damaged, it might be impaired for mindreading emotion states in general (as well as other mental states), but there is no reason to expect it to be impaired for just a single emotion. Precisely such *selective* impairments patterns are found, however, for several emotions. There is a deficit both in *experiencing* a given emotion and a selective deficit in *recognizing* that very emotion. Such a paired deficit is not easily explained by TT.[2] But it is predicted straightforwardly by ST.

I proceed now to review a set of findings that display this systematic pattern of paired deficits. The first case pertains to fear. The amygdala is known to have a prominent role in mediating fear, including a role in fear conditioning and the storage of fear-related emotional memories. Accordingly, Ralph Adolphs and colleagues investigated whether damage to the amygdala might also affect face-based recognition of fear (Adolphs, Tranel, Damasio, and Damasio, 1994; Adolphs, 1995). One patient they studied was SM, a 30-year-old woman with Urbach-Wiethe disease, a rare metabolic disorder that resulted in bilateral destruction of her amygdalae. SM was quite abnormal in her experience of fear. Antonio Damasio, a co-investigator in the Adolphs et al. studies, notes that SM "approaches people and situations with a predominantly, indeed excessively, positive attitude."

> S[M] does not experience fear in the same way you or I would in a situation that would normally induce it. At a purely intellectual level she knows what fear is supposed to be, what should cause it, and even what one may do in situations of fear, but little or none of that intellectual baggage, so to speak, is of any use to her in the real world. The fearlessness of her nature, which is the result of the bilateral damage to her amygdalae, has prevented her from learning, throughout her young life, the significance of the unpleasant situations that all of us have lived through. (Damasio, 1999: 66)

Other evidence also indicates abnormality in SM's fear experience. For example, she reports not feeling afraid when shown film clips that normally elicit fear, such as *The Shining* and *The Silence of the Lambs*, but she does seem to experience other emotions strongly (Adolphs and Tranel, 2000). In addition, she was tested with a conditioned stimulus repeatedly paired with a startle-inducing unconditioned stimulus, namely, a boat horn delivered at 100 decibels. She failed to demonstrate a conditioned autonomic reaction to the conditioned stimulus, indicating an abnormality in acquiring or expressing a conditioned fear response (Bechara et al., 1995).[3]

SM was then tested on various FaBER tasks (Adolphs et al., 1994). In these tasks, photographs or video slides are presented that depict facial expressions, and patients are asked to identify the emotion states to which the expressions correspond. SM was abnormal in face-based recognition of fear.

Her ratings of fearful faces correlated less with normal ratings than did those of any of 12 brain-damaged control subjects, and fell 2 to 5 standard deviations below the mean of the controls when the data were converted to a normal distribution. She was also abnormal, to a lesser extent, in recognizing expressions for anger and surprise.

Another group of investigators studied patient NM, who also had bilateral amygdala damage (Sprengelmeyer et al., 1999). Like SM, NM was abnormal in his experience of fear. He was prone to dangerous activities, such as jaguar hunting and deer hunting in Siberia while hanging on a rope under a helicopter! In these situations, he said that he always experienced excitement but never fear. On a self-assessment questionnaire that measured experience of the emotion fear, he tested as abnormal, though he scored normally for experience of anger and disgust. NM also exhibited a severe and selective impairment in face-based recognition of fear. He was asked to decide which of six emotion names (happiness, surprise, fear, sadness, disgust, or anger) best described the emotions shown in photographs of faces from the Ekman and Friesen (1976) series. NM performed significantly less well than controls in recognition of fear ($p < .01$) and of sadness ($p < .05$). NM was also tested for his ability to recognize emotional body postures. Actors produced several postures expressing different emotions, and their faces were masked so that facial cues could not be used. When NM's recognition performance was compared with that of 10 control subjects, he was found to be significantly impaired ($p < .01$) *only* for fear. Similarly, when tested for the ability to recognize emotional sounds, such as screams for fear, laughter for happiness, sobbing for sadness, and retching for disgust, NM was again significantly impaired *only* in fear recognition ($p < .01$). Other neuropsychological studies, involving additional patients, are broadly consistent with these findings (see Adolphs et al., 1999; Adolphs, 2002; Lawrence and Calder, 2004; see section 6.2 for some qualifications).

A similar pattern of paired deficit for fear was found in a group of psychopathic individuals (Blair et al., 2004). Impairment of fear experience in psychopaths is suggested by neuroimaging, neuropsychological, and functional data. Psychopathic individuals have reduced amygdaloid volume relative to comparison individuals and reduced amygdala activation during emotional memory tasks. Functionally, psychopathic individuals show impairments in aversive conditioning and reduced startle reflex potentiation (Blair, 2002). In the Blair et al. (2004) experiment involving facial emotion recognition, there were significant group differences between psychopathic and nonpsychopathic subjects only for sensitivity to fearful faces. In another study, Blair et al. (2002) found that psychopaths were severely impaired in recognizing fearful vocal affect relative to comparison individuals.

The pattern found here, a paired deficit in experiencing and recognizing the same emotion in faces (or vocal expressions), is also found in two other basic emotions, disgust and anger, as well as the secondary emotion of guilt. We next examine disgust, an even clearer case than fear. Scientists conceptualize disgust as an elaboration of a phylogenetically more primitive distaste response (Rozin, Haidt, and McCauley, 2000). Many aspects of taste processing are known from animal studies to be localized primarily in the anterior insula region, a region also known as the "gustatory cortex" (Rolls, 1994). Functional neuroimaging studies confirm that the anterior insula plays a similar role in taste processing in humans (Small et al., 1999, 2003). The question arises as to which neural structures are implicated in recognizing facial expressions of disgust. Phillips et al. (1997) undertook an fMRI study to see which brain areas are activated when subjects observe facial expressions of disgust. The most striking finding for perception of facial expressions of disgust was activation of the right insula; adjacent regions such as the amygdala were not activated. Phillips et al. concluded that "appreciation of visual stimuli depicting others' disgust is closely linked to the perception [i.e., experience] of unpleasant tastes and smells" (Phillips et al., 1997: 496).

Paired deficits in the experience and facial recognition of disgust were also found with lesion studies. Calder, Keane, Manes, Antoun, and Young (2000) found such a pairing for patient NK, who suffered insula and basal ganglia damage. On a questionnaire for probing the experience of disgust, NK's overall score was significantly lower than the controls, whereas his scores for anger and fear did not significantly differ from the mean scores of controls. In tests of his ability to recognize emotions in faces, NK also showed significant and selective impairment in disgust recognition (see also Adolphs, 2002). That is, his recognition of disgust, and disgust only, was significantly impaired. NK was also tested on nonverbal emotional sounds and emotional prosody. NK showed a marked deficit in recognizing disgust in response to nonverbal sounds and a mild deficit in recognizing surprise. On the emotional prosody cues, he showed significant recognition impairment only in disgust. Adolphs, Tranel, and Damasio (2003) made a similar finding for their patient B, who suffered extensive damage to the anterior insula (among other regions). B was able to recognize all six basic emotions *except disgust* when shown dynamic displays of facial expressions or told stories about actions.

Wicker et al. (2003) used functional imaging to explore the relationship between experiencing and observing disgust in normal subjects. The aim was to see whether the same neural regions are activated both during the experience of disgust and during the observation of disgust-expressive faces. In two "visual" runs, participants passively viewed movies of individuals smelling the contents of a glass (disgusting, pleasant, or neutral) and spontaneously expressing the facial expressions of the respective emotions. In two "olfactory" runs, the same participants inhaled disgusting or pleasant odorants through a mask on the nose and mouth. The core finding was that the left anterior insula and the right anterior cingulate cortex are preferentially activated during the experience evoked by inhaling disgusting odorants (compared with activation levels during pleasant and neutral odors), and this same region is preferentially activated during the observation of disgust facial expressions (compared with activation levels during pleasure-expressive and neutral faces). In other words, observing disgust-expressive faces activates the same neural substrates implicated in experiencing disgust.

I turn now to a third primary emotion system, anger, for which a paired deficit in emotion production and face-based recognition is also found. Various lines of evidence (Lawrence, Calder, McGowan, and Grasby, 2002) indicate that the neurotransmitter dopamine is involved in the processing of aggression in social-agonistic encounters in a wide variety of species and plays an important role in mediating the experience of anger. For example, dopamine levels in rats are elevated during social-agonistic encounters, and increased dopamine levels can lead to enhanced appetitive aggression and agonistic dominance.[4] Conversely, administration of an acute dopamine antagonist (a drug), which reduces the level of dopamine, selectively impairs responses to agonistic encounters.

Given the paired deficits found in the experience and facial recognition of fear and disgust, Lawrence et al. (2002) hypothesized that dopaminergic blockade via the drug sulpiride would lead to selective disruption of face-based recognition of anger while sparing the recognition of other emotions. This is indeed what they found. Sulpiride was administered to normal subjects, producing, in effect, a temporary "impairment" in their dopamine system. Sure enough, these subjects performed significantly worse than controls at recognizing angry faces but displayed no such impairments in recognizing facial expressions of other emotions.

A fourth paired deficit in experience and recognition concerns guilt. This example does not perfectly fit the mold of the other three, because guilt is a secondary emotion and the recognition test used was story understanding rather than facial (or vocal) observation. These and other features may place this phenomenon outside the category of low-level mindreading. Still, the findings about guilt provide helpful ancillary evidence.

Blair et al. (1995) reviewed the evidence and theory behind the notion that psychopaths lack the emotion of guilt. According to Hare's (1991) revised psychopathy checklist (PCL-R), the psychopath lacks remorse or guilt (item 6). In the empirical literature, psychopaths show reduced arousal responses to the distress of others (Aniskiewicz, 1979; Blair, Jones, Clark, and Smith, 1997). Blair et al. (1995) examined the ability of psychopaths and non-psychopathic controls to attribute emotions to others by using two primary emotions, happiness and sadness, and two secondary emotions, embarrassment and guilt. Emotion stories were read out to subjects, and after each story the subject was asked, "How do you think that person [the protagonist of the story] would feel in that situation?" Responses of psychopaths and non-psychopathic controls to the happiness, sadness, and embarrassment stories did not significantly differ. But psychopaths were significantly less likely than controls to attribute guilt to others. Here again is a deficit in experiencing an emotion paired with a selective deficit in attributing that emotion.

6.2. Explaining Emotion Recognition by Simulation versus Theory

There is thus substantial evidence from several emotions that deficits in the experience of an emotion and selective deficits in the face-based recognition of the same emotion reliably co-occur.[5] With the specific data before us, let us now return to the question discussed hypothetically in section 6.1: How might TT explain the paired-deficit data? One possibility floated in section 6.1 is that there might be an accidental colocalization of the neural machinery that undergoes the emotion and the theorizing machinery that executes emotion mindreading for that emotion. Is such colocalization plausible, given current knowledge? Analogous colocalizations exist in other cognitive domains. For example, lesions to the fusiform gyrus of the right occipital cortex produce both prosopagnosia (impaired ability to recognize faces; Kanwisher, 2000) and achromatopsia (impaired perception of color; Bartels and Zeki, 2000). These two deficits have no interesting functional relationship to one another. It just so happens that the impaired capacities are at least partially colocalized in the fusiform gyrus, leading to the paired deficit. Could such a happenstance also be the story of the paired deficits found in fear, disgust, anger, and guilt?

In theory, this is possible. But the occurrence of paired deficits in production and recognition for four distinct emotions and several classes of stimuli makes this unlikely. The pairings seem to reflect a systematic, functional relationship between emotion experience and emotion attribution, as ST postulates. Four "accidental" pairings of this one type is highly improbable.

Additional data emerging from paired-deficit studies also create at least initial difficulties for a TT explanation. Let's be more specific about how a TT explanation of the paired deficits might go. Three types of declarative knowledge might be used in the normal execution of FaBER according to TT: (1) visually obtained knowledge of the facial configuration of the target; (2) semantic knowledge concerning these configurations, such as knowledge that facial configuration C is paired with emotion label 'E'; and (3) general knowledge concerning a given emotion, that is, its typical elicitors or behavioral effects. To account for a paired deficit in one emotion, TT must say that one or more of these types of knowledge about that emotion are selectively damaged, while similar knowledge is preserved for other emotions. Let's take these in reverse order.

An informational deficit of type (3) is strongly disconfirmed by existing evidence. In several of the cited studies, FaBER deficits are accompanied by preserved general declarative knowledge about the relevant emotion. Subjects can readily cite situations in which a person might experience the emotion whose face-based recognition is impaired. For example, the fear-impaired patient SM can provide entirely normal descriptions of situations and behaviors associated with fear when asked to do so (Adolphs and Tranel, 2000; Adolphs, Tranel, Damasio, and Damasio, 1995), and the same is true of the fear-impaired patient NM (Sprengelmeyer et al., 1999). Similarly, Calder, Keane, Manes, Antoun and Young write that their patient NK's deficit in recognizing disgust "did not reflect impaired knowledge of the concept of disgust" (2000: 1078). Again, the subjects in Lawrence and Calder's anger-recognition study were normal subjects with only transient recognition impairments; they would not have lost their grip on the functional properties of anger.[6] Finally, in most cases subjects' lesions occurred relatively late in life. Thus, it cannot be plausibly argued that they lacked declarative knowledge about emotions because of deficits in their own emotional experience. Although they had experience deficits at the time of examination, most had had ample opportunities in earlier life to undergo relevant experiences and to build normal declarative knowledge of the emotions' functional properties from those experiences.

What about deficits in information of type (2), information consisting of semantic labels paired with representations of facial configurations? In taking this option, a theory-theorist must propose that labeling information for fear, disgust, anger, and guilt depends on the integrity of the amygdala, anterior insula, dopaminergic system, and guilt system, respectively. Moreover, she must claim that it is possible to damage this labeling information quite selectively, in two ways. First, it must be possible to damage the labeling information for one emotion while leaving it preserved for others. Second, in the three FaBER cases, it must be possible to so damage the labeling information that the label is inaccessible exclusively for visual representations of faces, because impaired subjects have command of the label when verbally discussing the impaired emotion type. Such postulations are not a priori impossible, but absent any positive reason to think that naming information is stored in this way, the postulations seem ad hoc. Thus, this kind of deficit also seems ad hoc and unlikely.

Finally, what about an explanation that appeals to a deficit in the first kind of knowledge: knowledge of facial configurations? This type of explanation was initially excluded by tests accompanying the original FaBER studies. FaBER studies have typically included standard tests for visual processing of faces, and brain-damaged subjects performed normally on measures designed to identify processing impairments. The most commonly used measure was the Benton Face Matching Task, in which different views of unfamiliar faces must be categorized as belonging to the same face (Benton, Hamsher, Varney, and Spreen, 1983). Subjects were also able to recognize high-level properties of faces, including age, gender, and identity. SM's ability to recognize facial identity, for example, was fully preserved. However, a recent study by Adolphs et al. (2005) indicates that SM has a visual-processing deficiency that appears to explain her selective deficit for recognizing fear from faces.

Adolphs et al. (2005) first explain that the amygdala is thought to do other important things in addition to those reported previously. In fact, the amygdala is a very complex structure, with different sectors serving different functions. In particular, the amygdala plays a role in controlling the direction of gaze vis-à-vis emotional faces (Anderson and Phelps, 2001; Vuilleumier, Richardson, Armony, Driver, and Dolan, 2004). Bearing this in mind, Adolphs et al. monitored SM's eye movements when she was judging emotions from faces and compared them with the eye movements of normal controls. Their finding was that SM does not look at a target's eye region as much or as carefully as normal controls. Normal subjects make use of high spatial frequency information from the target's eyes, especially when discriminating fear. SM did not do this; she did not spontaneously fixate on the eye region. Of course, her failure to fixate on the eye region occurs not only when she looks at fearful faces but also when she views expressions of other emotions. However, eyes are the most important diagnostic feature for identifying fear. Her inadequate scanning of the eye region accounts for her selective impairment in fear recognition. Notably, SM's recognition of fearful faces became entirely normal when she was instructed explicitly to look at the eyes. Thus, a proponent of TT could argue that there is an explanation of SM's paired deficit involving no simulational element. SM's deficit, one might say, is a deficit in evidence gathering. She doesn't gather visual evidence about emotional faces in the same fashion normal people do, and this seems to result from her amygdala damage—not because the amygdala is the fear substrate (if it is) but because it has another function, namely, controlling eye gaze when processing emotional faces.

Does this new finding tilt the argument in favor of TT over ST as a general account of the paired deficits? First, SM is obviously just one subject. One needs to see whether other patients with amygdala deficits have similar visual processing deficiencies. Second, the special features of SM's case have no straightforward bearing on disgust or anger, where there are FaBER deficits but no amygdala damage. If the amygdala's only function in FaBER is to direct eye gaze, what causes selective recognition deficits for disgust and anger? Could a lowered dopamine level create a visual processing deficiency, thereby explaining Lawrence and Calder's (2004) findings of an anger-recognition deficit in their dopamine-lowered subjects?

Third, not all the recognition impairments reviewed earlier involve facial cues or even the visual modality. Recall that Sprengelmeyer et al.'s (1999) amygdala-damaged patient NM showed selective fear-recognition impairment for postural and vocal emotional stimuli. Clearly, those recognition impairments cannot be explained by failure of his damaged amygdala to guide eye fixation properly toward the region of the target's eyes. The target's eyes were not visible in the bodily posture task, neither to NM nor to the controls, and eye fixation played no role at all in the vocal expression task. Similarly, Calder et al.'s (2000) patient NK displayed selective recognition impairment for disgust via the auditory as well as the visual modality. Was there an auditory processing deficiency there? Finally, the Blair et al. (1995) finding of an experience/recognition deficit for guilt in psychopaths had nothing to do with visual processing. So the SM case is special for several reasons. There are numerous cases of experience/recognition deficits to which the proposed visual-processing explanation of SM's paired deficit cannot be extended.

Fourth, the new SM findings cannot undermine the fMRI-established matching of emotion production and observation in *normal* subjects. Wicker et al. (2003) demonstrated that normal subjects undergo matching disgust experiences (at least matching neural activations) when they inhale foul odors and when they make facial observations of others who are inhaling foul odors. Many additional simulational matches, in other domains, will be reported later. To be sure, establishing the occurrence of such simulational event pairings does not establish their causal role in emotion *reading* or *recognition*. But the independent establishment of simulations via fMRI studies makes the simulation story of emotion recognition eminently "eligible" at a minimum.[7]

Returning to SM, what might explain her improvement in fear recognition under instructed viewing of the eye region? SM must use an alternative cognitive strategy for trying to read fear in faces, what may be termed a "theorizing" method. This is entirely compatible with our general hybrid position, which allows that theorizing is a sometimes-used method of mindreading. SM may try to map fear, as she understands it functionally, with relevant facial configurations. Until instructed to focus on the eye region, however, SM does a poor job of identifying diagnostic facial features for fear. With instruction, she improves dramatically.[8]

If that's how SM succeeds under suitable instruction, a theory-theorist might respond, maybe that's how normals succeed, too. Indeed, doesn't the normal person's fixation on a region that provides excellent diagnostic evidence for fear eliminate the hypothesis that the normal's own fear system plays a role in fear recognition? No. Normals may succeed not only because they intensively monitor the eye region but also because the detection of the crucial facial features produces activation in their own fear system (the amygdala), which in turn generates a fear attribution to the target. How, exactly, this process goes will be addressed in section 6.3. If this hypothesis is right, the normal method used in FaBER tasks is based on simulation.

The plausibility of this explanation may be enhanced by reflecting on a study by Buccino et al. (2004) in which subjects observed mouth actions performed by humans, by monkeys, and by dogs. Actions that were in the motor repertoire of the observer—such as biting, silent speech reading, and even monkey lip smacking—were mapped onto the observer's own motor system. Actions not belonging to the observer's repertoire—for example, barking—were mapped by purely visual properties. These results suggest that actions made by other individuals may be recognized through different mechanisms. Actions belonging to the motor repertoire of the observer are understood from a motor perspective; actions not belonging to this repertoire are recognized differently. Analogously, there may be two ways of understanding and recognizing emotions: a way that maps them onto visceromotor structures used in our own experience of those emotions and another that maps them onto visual properties. How is this relevant to SM? Perhaps the normal, simulation method of emotion recognition exploits a visceromotor representation of emotions. Someone lacking in the visceromotor representations associated with an emotion, like SM for fear, must try to exploit purely visual properties to solve the recognition task. SM tried to do that before receiving face-scanning instructions but didn't do it very well. After instructions, she used the same method but used it more effectively. That she succeeded via that method, however, doesn't show that normals use the same method.

Aside from the topic of eye-fixation deficiency, other complications facing a simulation approach to emotion recognition should be mentioned. Heberlein and Adolphs (in press) review several classes of data that pose challenges to what they call "simple shared-substrate" models—that is, simple simulation models—of emotion recognition. Their main thesis is that no single brain "organ," such as the amygdala, is wholly "dedicated" to, or is the unique and total substrate of, any given emotional state or its recognition. For example, some people have bilateral amygdala damage and still recognize expressions of fear, and fear isn't the only emotion that can suffer impaired recognition as a result of bilateral amygdala damage. So, very simple simulation stories of the kind just sketched are likely to be inadequate.

The first point to emphasize is that Heberlein and Adolphs do not take this evidence to cut against the simulation approach to emotion recognition in general. It leads them to resist only certain *versions* of shared-substrate models, while they continue to endorse the approach more globally. What theoretical points should be made, then, to accommodate the "recalcitrant" data that they review? Several comments are in order, many suggested by their discussion.

First, it should be granted from the outset that important cognitive phenomena are typically underpinned not by a single brain structure, or a small group of nuclei, but by a circuit of activity involving multiple loci and structures. Although our discussion of simulational phenomena often pinpoints a pivotal region or locus, it should be understood that activation in these loci is invariably part of a larger circuit. Second, a conventionally labeled structure, like the amygdala, may not be a unitary structure (as already noted in our discussion of eye fixation). Indeed, it has been suggested that the amygdala is a complex collection of nuclei with quite diverse connectivities. Thus, fear-related phenomena may be associated with only a subset of the amygdala's nuclei, not all of them. This makes it unproblematic if other amygdaloid nuclei are involved with other emotions, such as sadness or even negative affect more diffusely. Similarly, in the case of disgust, the substrate of disgust is not the entire insula. As Wicker et al. (2003) note, activations elicited by aversive stimuli occur in the anterior portion of the insula, whereas pleasant stimuli elicit activations in the posterior portion of the insula. Third, cognitive neuroscience and neuropsychology regularly encounter inconsistent data across studies for several familiar reasons. Lesion patients have different specific areas of damage, and such differences may be crucial. There are also differences in individual (undamaged) brains that generate differences in empirical findings. Next, there are limitations in imaging techniques, such as limitations of temporal resolution inherent in BOLD fMRI, which undoubtedly account for certain discrepancies across experiments. Finally, different individuals with brain lesions may compensate in different ways (as we speculated in the case of SM) and thus may show different patterns of impairment and "preserved" function. So we should not hastily abandon the general regularities identified in this area simply because some discrepancies remain to be accounted for. No doubt, greater complexity will have to enter the picture in future theorizing, but the general outlines of a simulation story are still well supported by the evidence we have highlighted.

Until now, I have provided only a bare sketch of how a simulation routine might execute FaBER tasks. An ST account of FaBER will not be wholly compelling, however, unless and until a detailed simulational method of FaBER execution is presented. Is there such a method, and is it compatible with existing evidence? This is the topic of the next section.

6.3. Possible Simulationist Processes

Four possible kinds of processes, or computational models, will be considered.

6.3.1 Model 1: Generate and Test

In this model, depicted in figure 6.1, a certain emotion is first hypothesized as the possible cause of the target's facial display. A facsimile of the hypothesized emotion is then generated in the attributor's own system. The facsimile emotion runs its typical course, which includes production of its natural facial expression, or at least a neural instruction to the facial musculature to construct the relevant expression. If the resulting facial expression, or an

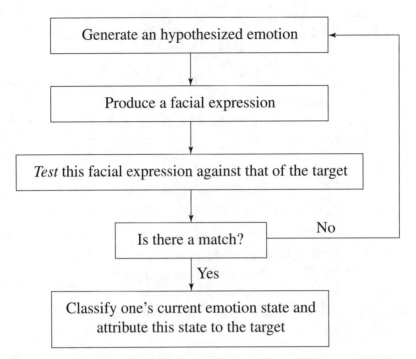

Figure 6.1.   Generate-and-test simulation. (Reprinted from Goldman and Sripada, 2005, with permission from Elsevier.)

instruction to construct such an expression, matches the expression observed in the target, then the hypothesized emotion is confirmed and imputed to the target. According to Model 1, this scenario is what transpires in a normal emotion interpreter. When the relevant emotion area is damaged, however, a facsimile of the emotion cannot be produced. The face-related downstream activity needed to recognize the emotion isn't generated. This results in recognition impairment specific to that emotion.

6.3.2 Model 2: Reverse Simulation

The idea here is that an attributor runs a standard emotional process in the reverse direction.[9] In most cognitive processes, reverse simulation is not an option: The standard forward directionality of mental processes precludes the possibility that these processes can be utilized in the opposite direction. However, FaBER may be an important exception.

Under conditions of normal operation, an emotion episode causes a co-ordinated suite of cognitive and physiological changes, including, at least in the case of the so-called basic emotions, a characteristic facial expression (Ekman, 1992). This causal relationship appears to be bidirectional. There is

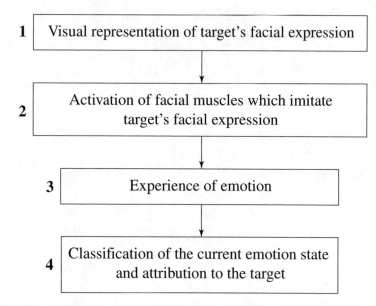

Figure 6.2.   Reverse simulation. (Adapted from Goldman and Sripada, 2005, with permission from Elsevier.)

substantial evidence that manipulation of the facial musculature, either voluntarily or involuntarily, has a causal effect in generating, at least in attenuated form, the corresponding emotional state and its cognitive and physiological correlates. Changes in a person's facial musculature can produce corresponding emotions, even when he is unaware that the musculature has any emotion-linked properties (Ekman, Levenson, and Friesen, 1983). Techniques have been used to induce smiles or frowns without subjects' awareness that they were smiling or frowning. For example, simply holding a pen in one's teeth eases the facial muscles into a smile, whereas holding a pen in one's lips eases the muscles into a frown. Corresponding types of emotional experiences can be induced by such unconscious tilts of the face. Strack, Martin, and Stepper (1988) had students look at Gary Larson cartoons while holding a pen either in their teeth or in their lips. Students found the cartoons funnier when they held the pen in their teeth (and smiled) than when they held it in their lips (and frowned). Cacioppo, Klein, Berntson, and Hatfield (1993) found that a similar manipulation of bodily postures had an effect on liking or disliking attitudes. When we like a stimulus, we tend to bring it toward us, but when we dislike something, we tend to push it away. Cacioppo et al. (1993) found that manipulating people's posture into one of these contrasting poses subtly influences their attitude.

Because the relationship between basic emotion states and their facial expressions exhibits a kind of rough one-to-one correspondence in both directions, a characteristic facial expression could potentially be used in a backward direction for the purpose of attribution by simulation.[10] As shown in figure 6.2, a potential attributor who sees a target's emotion-expressive face [1] proceeds to imitate the observed facial expression in an attenuated and largely covert manner [2]. These facial exertions produce traces of the relevant emotion [3]. These emotion traces in the attributor are classified for their emotion type and finally, in keeping with the common core of all simulational heuristics, produce a corresponding attribution to the target whose face is being observed [4]. All this would happen at a preconscious level.

The reverse simulation model would explain the paired deficits as follows: Someone impaired in experiencing a certain emotion would be unable to produce that emotion, or even significant traces thereof, in her own system. The requisite facial exertions [2] would occur, but they would not arouse the appropriate neural activity that constitutes an experience of the emotion [3]. Such a person would not have a matching emotion in herself to classify and hence would not reliably attribute that emotion to the target [4].

6.3.3 Model 3: Reverse Simulation with as-if Loop

Adolphs, Damasio, Tranel, Cooper, and Damasio (2000) did a quantitative study of 108 subjects with focal brain lesions and concluded that recognition of facial emotion requires the integrity of right somatosensory cortices. They hypothesized that emotion recognition engages somatosensory representations that may simulate "how one would feel if making the facial expression shown in the stimulus." This suggests a variant of the reverse simulation model, using Damasio's (1994) idea of an "as if" loop (see figure 6.3). Perhaps there is a link between a visual representation of a facial expression [1] and a somatosensory representation of what it would feel like to make that expression [2]. This visual/somatosensory pathway bypasses the facial musculature, hence the phrase "as-if" loop. Activation of the appropriate somatosensory representation in turn leads to (subthreshold) activation of an emotion [3] appropriate to the facial expression of the target. Finally, this emotion activated in the self is classified and imputed to the target. Explanation of the paired deficits by Model 3 would follow the explanation by Model 2.

6.3.4 Model 4: Unmediated Resonance (Mirroring)

According to this model, perception of the target's face "directly" triggers (subthreshold) activation of the same neural substrate of the emotion in question. "Directly" here implies some form of mediation different from any of those postulated by the other models. A detailed positive account of the resonance, or mirroring, process is not presently available.[11] The proposal of

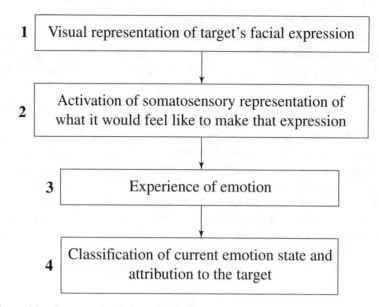

Figure 6.3.   Reverse simulation with as-if loop. (Adapted from Goldman and Sripada, 2005, with permission from Elsevier.)

unmediated matching, or mirroring, is made for the case of disgust by Wicker et al. (2003: 661) and echoes a hypothesis of Vittorio Gallese, a co-investigator in the Wicker et al. study, of widespread sharing of mental states by targets and observers, which Gallese (2001, 2003) calls the "shared manifold hypothesis." This hypothesis, in turn, is a generalization of the notion of mirror systems in monkeys and humans (Rizzolatti, Fadiga, Gallese, and Fogassi, 1996; Gallese, Fadiga, Fogassi, and Rizzolatti, 1996; Rizzolatti, Fogassi, and Gallese, 2001). Mirror systems provide one paradigm of mental simulation and hence *potentially* a method of simulation-based mindreading. Model 4 would explain the paired-deficit data in the same familiar way as Models 2 and 3. Someone impaired in the capacity to experience a particular emotion won't undergo a recognizable occurrence of that emotion, so the cognitive center will not reliably classify and attribute that emotion to the target.

Let us be clear why these four models are all descriptions of *simulation* processes, and why the processes might generally yield accurate attributions. Models 2, 3, and 4 share the following characteristic. Some process in the observer responds to the facial cues of the target by generating an (attenuated) emotion in the observer. This emotion is classified and then projected onto the target. Recall that projection (section 2.6) is a core part of a simulational mindreading routine. Now if the first stage of the process is sufficiently sensitive to the target's facial cues and if the observer's emotion equipment is intact, the emotion produced in the observer will match the triggering emotion in the target. Such matching implies that interpersonal mental simulation has occurred. If, in addition, the observer's classification of his own emotion is accurate,[12] his attribution of that same emotion to the target will also be accurate. So, there will be accurate, simulation-based mindreading. Model 1 differs slightly from 2, 3, and 4, because in Model 1 the hypothesized emotion must first pass the facial-match test before it is accepted and projected onto the target. But otherwise the process is similar. So all four processes share core simulational properties, certainly in cases where the observer's emotion is sufficiently similar to that of the target.

6.3.5 Assessing the Four Models

Let us now assess the strengths and weaknesses of the four models from an evidential standpoint. Model 1, the generate-and-test model, raises several questions. One centers on the phase of the process in which the observer's system tries to match his own facial expression to that of the target. One's own facial expression is represented proprioceptively, whereas the target's expression is represented visually. How can these representations "match"? One possibility is that the system has acquired an association between proprioceptive and visual representations of the same facial configuration, through some type of learning. Alternatively, there might be an innate cross-modal matching of the sort postulated by Meltzoff and Moore (1997) to account for neonate facial imitation. This postulate has struck researchers as quite plausible.

A second question is how the hypothesis-generation process works. If candidate emotions are generated serially and randomly, say, from the six basic emotions, the observer must covertly generate on average three facial expressions before hitting on the right one. This might be too slow to account for actual covert mimicry of displayed facial expressions, which occur as early as 300 milliseconds after stimulus onset (Dimberg and Thunberg, 1998). One alternative is parallel rather than serial testing of hypotheses, which might solve the timing problem, but it's not clear that this is feasible. A second alternative is to say that "theoretical" information guides and narrows the generation process—though it isn't clear what theoretical information it would be. The latter proposal would turn the generate-and-test model into more of a theory-simulation hybrid rather than a pure simulation model. In any case, unless parallel testing of hypotheses is plausible, the timing problem makes the generate-and-test model the least promising of the four on offer, and the other three are all more purely simulational in character. Moreover, all three of the other models have more evidential support than generate-and-test, so the latter should be relegated to the bottom of the stack.

What can be said for Model 2, the reverse simulation model? Its plausibility crucially depends on speedy facial imitation. That such imitation capacities exist, apparently innately, is well established. Meltzoff and Moore (1983) found that infants as young as 1 hour old imitate tongue protrusion and other facial displays modeled before them. In addition to a capacity for facial mimicry, there is evidence that adult humans spontaneously and rapidly activate facial musculature corresponding to visually presented facial expressions. Dimberg and colleagues (Dimberg and Thunberg, 1998; Dimberg, Thunberg, and Elmehed, 2000; Lundquist and Dimberg, 1995) have found that the presentation of pictures of facial expressions produces covert activation of one's own facial musculature, which mimics the presented faces. Such muscular activation is often subtle but electromyographically detectable. It occurs extremely rapidly, as noted previously, as early as 300 milliseconds after stimulus onset.

However, spontaneous, rapid, and covert facial imitation is also consistent with a model in which self-generated facial expressions are the *consequences* rather than the *causes* of emotion states. Is there any support for the claim that facial muscle movements come first and produce subsequent emotion states? Yes. The first line of evidence is based on the rapidity of the covert muscular movements. The early onset of these movements suggests that they arise because of direct imitation of the target, rather than a presumably slower process in which the facial expression of the target is deciphered, the corresponding emotion state is induced, and the facial expression is then produced. This direct imitation of the target may be part of an action-mirroring system, which is known to generate covert activation of distal musculature. In an early experiment that helped establish an action-mirroring system in humans, Fadiga, Fogassi, Pavesi, and Rizzolatti (1995) found that observation of actions (e.g., grasping an object, tracing a figure in the air) modeled by a target reliably produced electromyographically detectable activation in the corresponding muscle groups of the observer. Other evidence indicates that the action-mirroring system may also operate during the observation of facial expressions. An fMRI study by Carr, Iacoboni, Dubeau, Mazziotta, and Lenzi (2003) found that subjects passively observing emotion-expressive faces display neural activation in the premotor cortex and neighboring regions, which are normally activated in the production of facial movements and which are in one of the regions thought to house the action-mirroring system (to be explored later).

Some important data, however, are inconsistent with the reverse simulation model. Hess and Blairy (2001) used a more challenging FaBER task and found that although spontaneous facial mimicry did occur, successful mimicry did not correlate with accuracy in facial recognition, suggesting that facial mimicry may accompany but not actually facilitate recognition. More pointedly, Calder, Keane, Cole, Campbell, and Young (2000) found that three patients with Mobius syndrome, a congenital syndrome whose most prominent symptom is complete *facial paralysis*, performed normally on FaBER tasks. Keillor, Barrett, Crucian, Kortenkamp, and Heilman (2002) reported a similar finding in which a patient with bilateral facial paralysis performed normally on FaBER tasks. These findings need to be interpreted with caution; given the long-standing nature of these patients' impairments, they may have found a compensatory (TT) strategy for executing FaBER, so their normal level of performance may not have utilized typical pathways. Nonetheless, these findings constitute grounds for skepticism about the reverse simulation model.

The problem of facial paralysis with spared FaBER performance is a problem attending Model 2 but not Model 3, the as-if loop variant of reverse simulation. Model 3 explicitly postulates a pathway that bypasses facial musculature, so it is unthreatened by the findings cited in the preceding paragraph. This is a signal advantage. Recall that the postulated pathway engages somatosensory cortices. A role for right somatosensory cortices in emotion recognition is confirmed in a study by Heberlein, Adolphs, Tranel, and Damasio (2004), who found that lesion patients with impairments in judging emotions from point-light walkers had the most reliable focus of lesion overlap in right somatosensory cortices.[13]

The trouble with Model 3 is that it isn't wholly clear how it explains the selectivity of emotion-recognition impairments. Take the just-cited study of point-light walkers. This study found that the region in which lesions were most consistently associated with impairments in emotion judgment was right somatosensory cortices. But there were no clear differences in the regions of lesion overlap associated with impaired judgment of specific individual emotions. So it is not clear that activation in this region is specific enough to recognize one emotion as contrasted with others, which is what a model of (accurate) emotion recognition must explain, of course. A second concern with Model 3 is whether it accounts for the anger-recognition findings by Lawrence et al. (2002). Would lowering of dopamine levels have an association with impairment in right somatosensory cortices? Would such a lowering have such a specific impact on right somatosensory cortices as to significantly affect only anger recognition, not recognition of the other basic emotions? These are dubious prospects.

Let us turn, then, to Model 4, the unmediated resonance, or mirroring, model. A deeper examination of empirical evidence that bears on this model is deferred to later sections (6.4 and 6.7). Here I merely pose a theoretical question: Does the model fit our proposed pattern of ST? Because the model posits unmediated resonance, it does not fit the traditional form of simulation in which pretend states are fed into an attributor's own cognitive equipment (e.g., a decision-making mechanism) to produce a further state. However, I do not regard the creation of pretend states, or the deployment of cognitive equipment to operate on such states, as essential to simulation. I associate that form of simulation only with high-level mindreading. First, pretense or imagination is a high-level activity. Second, it is an activity that is potentially and intermittently under intentional guidance or control, whereas low-level mindreading is fully automatic. As articulated in chapter 2, the generic idea of simulation is the idea of a process that is similar, in relevant respects, to a second process. (Alternatively, it can be undertaken with the *aim* of being similar, or have the *function* of being similar to the simulated process.) Such process similarity is what we have here, at a minimum, a similarity between the pair of emotion events in target and observer.

But, the reader may object, doesn't a simulating *process* have to consist of multiple steps or stages, multiple steps that match those of a target process? I shall take a relaxed stance here: A simulating process can consist, minimally, of a single matching (or semimatching) state or event. This minimal condition for simulation is satisfied in Model 4. The model says that in successful FaBER by normal people, an attributor's attribution is based on a (sub-threshold) tokening of the same emotion experienced in the target. The observer's emotional system "resonates" with that of the target, and this is the matching event on which the attribution is based. So Model 4 fits the ST pattern as I characterize it.[14]

A defense of ST, even for the restricted category of FaBER, does not require a firm decision about which of the four models is correct.[15] Each of them, after all, is a simulational account. (Well, Model 1 is a *hybrid* account, so its correctness would lend the weakest support to ST, but it's the least plausible model of the four.) In fact, I think that a good case can be made for Model 4, the resonance or mirroring model. To make this case, we must inspect evidence for resonance, or mirroring, in related areas of cognition. This is the principal topic of the next section.

6.4 Mirroring as Interpersonal Mental Simulation

In a major series of discoveries, neuroscientists have established the existence of a wide range of interpersonal mirroring mechanisms, in which cognitive states of one organism are matched or mirrored by similar cognitive states in an observing organism. Given our definition of "mental simulation," these qualify as instances of interpersonal mental simulation. The example of disgust, described in Wicker et al. (2003), is a recent finding of this kind, but analogous simulational phenomena abound. What is less clear is whether these simulational, mirroring processes are used to *mindread* others, that is, attribute mental states to them. In chapter 2, we distinguished mental simulation *full stop* from mental simulation *for mindreading*. In the emotion cases discussed earlier, the presence of mindreading is uncontroversial; that's why I began the chapter with these cases and have analyzed them at length. What needs to be argued, given the goals of this chapter, is that these acts of emotion *mindreading* have a simulational basis. In cases I describe later, it is uncontroversial that mirroring takes place, but only in a fraction of them is it established that there is mindreading. A mirroring event is a *potential* launching pad for an act of (accurate) mindreading, but it's an open question whether, and to what extent, such potential launching pads are actually exploited for mindreading. Wherever there is both mirroring and mindreading based on that mirroring, we have examples of low-level simulation-based mindreading.

A few words are in order about "mirroring" or "resonance," intended to indicate what mirroring is and isn't, at least in definitional terms. Mirroring is not the mere accidental sharing of a given mental state (type) by two individuals. Two people might token the same mental state quite independently of one another. If this occurs at a single time, it might be called mental "synchrony." Mental synchrony isn't necessarily mental mirroring. Imagine two people on separate ocean voyages, one in the Atlantic and one in the Pacific. Both undergo a bout of nausea at exactly the same time. Because nausea is a kind of sensation, they share a certain mental state and exemplify mental synchrony. But this coincidental sharing is not mirroring.

A more interesting type of sharing or synchrony obtains when there is a systematic, repeatable causal pathway, leading from one individual's mental state to a matching (or semimatching) state in an observer. When this sort of causal pathway exists—mediated by specific neural mechanisms, presumably—we have what I would call a mirroring system. A systematic causal pathway would have two components: (a) a subpath within the sender from his own mental state to a behavioral expression of that state and (b) a subpath within the receiver from an observation of the sender's behavior to a mental state that matches the sender's. By means of such a dual pathway, a receiver winds up "mirroring" a mental state of the sender. The receiving individual may or may not know (or believe) that such a mirroring event occurs. She may not know about her own mental event (such events need not be conscious), and even if she (or her system) is aware of it, she may not know that it matches an event occurring in a sender. She may not think about the sender or connect her own mental event with an event in the sender. However, when mental matching occurs by means of a regular causal pathway, I will consider it an instance of mirroring—and an instance of mental simulation. But it isn't *yet*, from anything I have said, an instance of simulation-based *mindreading*.

What more is required for there to be *mindreading*? As indicated from the start, mindreading involves mental attribution to a target. This requires two mental acts by the attributor: selecting a mental-state category, or classification, and imputing an instance of that classification to the pertinent target. Let's call these acts *M-classification* and *imputation*. Given our definition of mirroring, mirroring per se entails neither M-classification nor imputation. It requires only that a receiver *undergo* a matching event, which doesn't guarantee that she has a repertoire of M-classifications. Even if she has such a repertoire, she may not deploy it on the present occasion. Moreover, mirroring doesn't entail mind-reading because the receiver may not impute anything to the sender. Although mirroring doesn't entail mindreading, as a matter of definition, it is entirely possible that mirroring *is* used as a basis of mindreading.

I now present a brief survey of mirroring research. The discovery of mirror neurons and mirroring systems is the product of Giacomo Rizzolatti's labo-ratory in Parma, Italy (Rizzolatti et al., 1996; Gallese et al., 1996).[16] They first discovered mirror neurons for action in the ventral premotor cortex (area F5) of macaque monkeys, using the technique of single-cell recording. Action mirror neurons are cells that discharge both when an acting monkey executes a goal-related action—the initial research dealt with hand actions—and also when an observing monkey watches the same type of hand action performed by someone else (a monkey or a human). Each of several types of goal-related hand actions—such as grasping, holding, or tearing an object—has a distinctive family of associated mirror neurons in the premotor cortex (and also the parietal cortex). Individual members (cells) of each neuron family fire at close to maximal rates not only when the animal executes the asso-ciated type of action but also when it merely observes another animal, or a human, execute the same type of action. Because the premotor cortex is mainly responsible for action planning, it was quite surprising that the mere observation of another's action should involve some of the same neuronal activity as the planning or representation of one's own action. These neu-rons seem to constitute an execution/observation "matching" system, or "resonance" system. Certain neural activity in an observer resonates with the neural activity in an observed actor. Each family of mirror neurons comprises the substrate of a distinctive type of (nonconscious) mental representation, something like a *plan* to achieve a certain behavioral goal (grasping or tearing, for example). In the case of the observer, however, the plan is not executed.

If the so-called plan isn't executed, is a neuron's firing in the observation mode really the same type of cognitive event as its firing in execution mode? Is it really a "plan" in both cases? For this to hold, arguably, the firings must share functional properties, and it appears that they do not. This final con-clusion, however, is premature. At least two findings indicate that an ob-server's mirroring-induced plan does have the usual functional property of "instructing" the motor system to act, but this instruction is inhibited, or countermanded. First, in Fadiga et al. (1995), which initially demonstrated the existence of mirror systems in humans, it was found that the same muscle groups are facilitated in the observer as in the acting agent. This muscular activation gets inhibited, so there is no overt action. But the matching muscular activity indicates that the same action instruction was initially sent. Second, there is clinical evidence of so-called imitation behavior (Lhermitte,

Pillon, and Serdaru, 1986). A group of patients with prefrontal lesions compulsively imitated gestures or even complex actions performed in front of them by an experimenter. Their compulsive behavior was explained as an impairment of the inhibitory control that normally governs motor schemas, or plans. It may be inferred from this that normal humans, when observing someone else perform an action, generate a plan to do the same action themselves. The plan is normally inhibited; but the neural activity in the observer—the mirror neuron activity—that sends an instruction to imitate is functionally similar to the neural activity in the acting agent.

The existence of mirror systems in humans has been established by an assortment of methodologies. The human mirror system is formed by a network composed of the rostral part of the inferior parietal lobule and by the caudal sector of the inferior frontal gyrus (*pars opercularis*), plus the adjacent part of the premotor cortex (see Rizzolatti et al., 2001). The human mirror system resonates in response to a wider range of actions than the monkey system. In monkeys, the presence of a goal object seems to be necessary, but it isn't necessary in the human system. Observation of nongoal-related ("intransitive") actions and merely mimed actions can activate the human system.

Early experiments on mirror neurons featured hand actions only. But an fMRI study by the Parma group extended their discoveries to the mouth and foot as well. Buccino et al. (2001) studied subjects who were shown not only hand actions but also actions made with the mouth or a foot, such as biting an apple or kicking a ball. There was matching neuronal activity in each case. In a further extension of the early results, mirror activity was found even when the critical final stage of an action—that is, interaction between hand and goal object—is not visible but is hidden behind a screen (Umilta et al., 2001). This implies that a motor representation of an action performed by others is internally generated in the observer's premotor cortex, even when a full visual description of the action is lacking. Yet another extension of these results involves auditory recognition of types of actions. Certain neurons in a monkey's premotor cortex discharge both when the animal performs a specific action and when it hears a sound related to that type of action (Kohler et al., 2002).

Another study by the Parma group lends additional weight to the "massive matchingness" picture of human intersubjectivity by adding *touch* to the familiar pattern of mirror matching. Keysers et al. (2004) wondered whether there is such a phenomenon as "tactile empathy." Introspectively, this seems plausible. Watching a movie scene in which a tarantula crawls on James Bond's chest can make you literally shiver—as if the spider were crawling on your own chest. If a mirroring mechanism applies to the sight of touch, then watching someone being touched should activate the same area(s) as getting touched oneself. That was indeed confirmed by Keysers et al. The secondary (but not the primary) somatosensory cortex was activated both when participants were themselves touched and when they observed someone else getting touched by objects.

Finally, a mirroring or resonance system has been established for *pain*. Mirror neurons for pain were first discovered serendipitously by Hutchison, Davis, Lozano, Tasker, and Dostrovsky (1999), while preparing a neurological patient for cingulotomy. They found that a single cell responded both to painful stimulation (a pinprick) and to the observation of the same stimulation applied to another person (the medical examiner). More recently, three fMRI studies—one by Singer et al. (2004), one by Jackson, Meltzoff, and Decety (2004), and one by Morrison, Lloyd, de Pellegrino, and Roberts (2004)—report findings of pain resonance or mirroring. Singer et al. (2004) assessed brain activity while volunteers experienced a painful stimulus and compared it with the activity elicited when a signal indicated that a partner, present in the same room, was receiving a similar pain stimulus. Several brain regions—bilateral anterior insula (AI), rostral anterior cingulate cortex (ACC), brain stem, and cerebellum—were activated both when subjects received pain and when they received a signal that a loved one experienced pain. These common areas do not exhaust the entire "pain matrix" but are restricted to that part of the pain network associated with its affective (rather than sensory) qualities. Extremely similar results were obtained by Jackson et al. Participants were shown photographs of hands and feet in situations that are likely to cause pain. Perceiving these third-person painful situations was associated with significant bilateral changes in activity in the ACC, the AI, the cerebellum, and the thalamus, regions known to play a significant role in one's own pain processing.

6.5 Mirroring and Mindreading

Because mirroring systems were initially discovered in monkeys, and mindreading ability in monkeys is questionable, researchers and theorists about mirroring have been cautious about claiming a link between mirroring and mindreading. Thus, in the first published suggestion of such a possible link, Gallese and Goldman (1998) entered the following caveat:

> It should be emphasized that the hypothesis being advanced here is not that MNs themselves constitute a full-scale realization of the simulation heuristic. In particular, we do not make this conjecture for MNs in monkeys. Our conjecture is only that MNs represent a primitive version, or possibly a precursor in phylogeny, of a simulation heuristic that might underlie mind-reading. (1998: 498)

Many writers speak of mirroring as giving rise to "empathy," a kind of state that has less association with mental classification or conceptualization (although it does connote a "directedness" of the self toward the other). In one

recent theoretical statement, Gallese, Keysers, and Rizzolatti (2004) characterize mirror systems as providing a distinctive kind of social "understanding"
that doesn't require "conceptual" elements. In that article, they restrict themselves to the question of how the meaning of an *action* is understood, not how
an agent's *intention* is captured (2004: 397).

Is there evidence, then, of mindreading based on mirroring? As indicated
earlier, the definition of mirroring (as I construe it) does not imply mindreading. This leaves open the possibility, however, that some mindreading is
based on mirroring.

Very few of the studies that establish mirroring phenomena outside the
emotion domain have included tests that provide evidence for or against
mindreading. As an example chosen at random, the vision-of-touch study by
Keysers et al. (2004) was a straightforward fMRI study that explored the
brain areas activated when one is being touched and when one watches others
being touched (more precisely, movies of other people or objects being
touched). The study did not ask participants to *judge* or *attribute* any mental
states to others, or seek to determine whether they spontaneously formed
mental-state *beliefs* about the people observed. There are good reasons for
this omission, no doubt. Questions of belief and ascription, especially mental-
state belief and ascription, are not trivial matters to test for experimentally,
and this research project had different fish to fry. Do other studies provide
good evidence for mirroring-based *mindreading*?

We needn't restrict the inquiry to evidence embedded in a single study; of
equal interest is evidence that might be assembled from multiple studies. The
Wicker et al. (2003) study of disgust plus lesion studies of selective impairment of disgust recognition jointly provide this type of evidence. The
Wicker et al. fMRI study (along with similar ones that preceded it) clearly
establishes a mirroring relationship between observing someone else exhibit
disgust and experiencing disgust oneself. That study did not employ any tasks
concerning mental-state judgments or attributions. But the lesion studies we
reviewed clearly indicate that there is an association between damage to
substrates for the experience of disgust and impaired interpersonal judgments
of disgust (through faces and sounds). This association speaks strongly to a
counterfactual relationship between the integrity of one's own disgust substrate and a facility for interpersonal disgust attribution: "If one didn't have
an intact disgust substrate, one wouldn't make disgust attributions normally."
This counterfactual, in turn, lends support to a causal connection between
experiencing disgust while observing a disgust expression and *attributing*
disgust to the person who makes that expression. Taken together, the evidence points toward the use of one's disgust experience as the causal basis for
third-person disgust attributions.[17]

For additional evidence, let us examine two of the pain studies reported
previously. Singer et al. (2004) used a conventional fMRI technique and did

not employ tasks requesting attributions or ascriptions to the "other." However, one important feature of their study provides evidence that the mirroring relationship is not, or need not be, a process of pure emotional contagion that entirely bypasses cognitive-level involvement. In their experimental setup, subjects being scanned did not see the face of their partner or perceive any other emotional cue (though they saw the partner's hand that would receive painful stimulations). The subject was shown an arbitrary cue on a large screen that signaled the partner's feeling state. Thus, the subject had to *infer* the partner's feeling state from the cue, a cognitive-level act that produced a resonant, or empathic, feeling of her own. Obviously, this doesn't speak to the question of whether a mindreading attribution might *result from* a resonant experience. But it does show an interaction between mirroring-type phenomena and cognitive-level judgments. The Singer et al. manipulation is also relevant to a different question, namely, which simulationist model of emotion attribution is most likely in FaBER tasks? The Singer et al. study shows that mirroring of feelings can occur without the sorts of intermediaries postulated by Models 1 and 2, such as cues from facial musculature. A scanned pain subject did not see the partner's face, so there was no stimulus that would prompt automatic facial mimicry that might launch a Model 2-like process.

More pertinent evidence for mindreading comes from the Jackson et al. (2004) pain study. Here, subjects watched depictions of hands and feet in painful or neutral conditions and were asked to rate the intensity of pain they thought the person shown in the picture would feel. This intensity rating is a kind of third-person attribution task. One result of this experiment was that watching others in pain-inducing situations triggered a part of the neural network known to be involved in self-pain processing. This confirms the mirroring process for pain. More important for the present point, there was a strong correlation between the ratings (attributions) of pain intensity and the level of activity within the posterior ACC, a crucial part of the network for self-pain processing. This definitely confirms the idea that a mirror-induced, or resonant, feeling can serve as the causal basis of a third-person mindreading.[18]

A more recent article by Iacoboni et al. (2005), including members of the Parma group, provides evidence that *intention* ascription sometimes involves the motor mirror system. Iacoboni et al. begin by acknowledging that the basic properties of motor mirror neurons could be interpreted as a mechanism for recognizing merely the motor acts of a target, such as grasping, holding, or bringing to the mouth, not as recognizing or imputing to the target a *mental* state like an intention. True, mirror theorists often *define* "action" as implying an embedded goal, but it isn't clear whether such goal-talk implies a mentalistic state. If this *is* implied by the definition, it is debatable whether mirror neurons recognize "actions" *so defined*. Iacoboni et al. therefore proceed as follows: If the mirror neuron system codes a goal beyond the action itself—something that explains why the agent is doing the action—that should support the idea that the mirror neuron system "codes" a global intention. Is Mary grasping an apple in order to eat it, to give it to her brother, or to throw it away?

Iacoboni et al. noted that the same action in two different contexts may reflect two different intentions. So they investigated whether observation of the same grasping action, embedded in different contexts, elicited the same or different activity in an observer's mirror neuron areas for grasping. If the mirror neuron system simply codes the type of observed action and its embedded goal, the neural activity in mirror neuron areas should not be influenced by the presence or absence of context. By contrast, if the mirror neuron system codes the global intentions associated with the observed action, then the presence of a context that cues the observer should modulate activity in mirror neuron areas. Thus, they had subjects watch three kinds of movie-clip stimuli: (1) grasping hand actions without any nearby objects ("Action" condition); (2) context only, that is, scenes containing still objects like teacups and saucers ("Context" condition); and (3) grasping actions performed in two different contexts, a during-tea scene and an after-tea scene ("Intention" condition). The third condition is called "Intention condition" because each context suggests a further intention associated with the hand grasping—either grasping a cup to drink or grasping it to clean up. In comparison with the other two conditions, the Intention condition yielded a significant signal increase in premotor areas already known to be mirror neuron areas. This increase suggests that this cortical area does not simply provide an action-recognition mechanism ("that's a grasp") but is critical for understanding the intentions behind others' actions.

A further manipulation in this study speaks even more directly to intention attribution being mediated by the mirror system. Participants in the study received two different kinds of instructions. Half were told simply to watch the movie clips (Implicit task). The other half were told to infer the intention of the grasping action according to the context in which it occurred in the Intention clips (Explicit task). After the imaging experiment, participants were debriefed. Notably, all of them had clearly attended to the stimuli and could answer appropriately. They all associated the intention of drinking to the grasping action in the "during tea" Intention clip and the intention of cleaning up to the grasping action in the "after tea" Intention clip. This was true regardless of the type of instruction received. Moreover, the two groups of participants receiving different instructions had similar patterns of increased neural signal as compared with rest. Critically, the right inferior frontal cortex—the grasping mirror neuron area that showed increased signal for Intention as compared with Action and Context—showed no differences between participants receiving Explicit instructions and those receiving Implicit instructions. Thus, the mirror neuron areas made the same contribution to interpreting intentions behind the grasping actions even when the participants were not explicitly instructed to infer intentions.

The foregoing discussion of intention attribution might make it sound as if the motor mirror system contributes to high-level, "propositionalized" intention states. Doesn't this belie our claim that mirror systems contribute to a more primitive, lower level of mindreading? Further details from the Iacoboni et al. study support our original low-level interpretation rather than a high-level one. Iacoboni et al. postulate that mirror systems learn which motor acts commonly follow other acts to achieve a characteristic goal. One chain of acts might include grasping followed by drinking (bringing the cup to the mouth), and another chain might include grasping followed by cleaning. Intention attribution, at the level of mirror systems, may consist of coding an action as part of a probable sequence of motor acts with a final upshot (goal). This isn't a terribly "high" level of cognitive functioning. When subjects are verbally debriefed, of course, higher cognitive centers are also brought into play, which characterize the behavior in fully propositionalized terms.

The Iacoboni et al. study of human intention understanding has been (more or less) duplicated by Fogassi et al. (2005) in the case of monkeys. This lends added support to the relative "primitiveness" of the cognitive level. It also introduces a topic we have thus far sidestepped: the question of mindreading in animals. Because of the massive literature on the subject, and the rapid changes it is undergoing, I have carefully avoided this terrain. But now, after a period of considerable skepticism about primate mindreading, there is new evidence—unrelated to mirror systems—that substantially supports nonhuman primate mindreading. Indeed, there is evidence of mindreading even among birds, some of which might point in a simulation theoretic direction.[19]

To summarize, the case for mirroring-based *attribution* of mental states is quite strong, at least in three categories: emotions, feelings, and intentions. Because mirroring is one species of interpersonal simulation, this lends weighty support to the thesis that low-level mindreading typically proceeds by simulation. I do not claim that whenever there is mirroring, there is also low-level mindreading. But wherever there is mirroring, the potential for simulation-based mindreading is there, and creatures with the requisite conceptual resources, especially humans, seem to exploit this potential extensively.

6.6 Neural Regions for Low- and High-Level Mindreading

How does our treatment of low-level mindreading comport with the many neuroimaging studies of so-called theory of mind? Haven't these studies identified rather different regions of the brain as the locus, or loci, of mindreading? Doesn't that undercut much of what we have been saying?

The distinction between high-level and low-level mindreading resolves this worry. The standard treatments of "theory of mind" have primarily studied the locus of *high-level* mindreading (as I would describe it), and it should not be assumed that *low-level* mindreading has the same locus. As we'll see, other investigators also propose different brain areas for more primitive versus sophisticated forms of mindreading. Before examining such a proposal, let us review and update the most familiar findings about "theory of mind" in the brain.

Beginning in 1995, four cortical regions have been consistently identified as possible candidates for a specialized neural substrate for theory of mind (Fletcher et al., 1995; Goel, Grafman, Sadato, and Hallett, 1995; Gallagher et al., 2000; Frith and Frith, 2003): the right and left temporoparietal junctions (RTPJ and LTPJ), posterior cingulate (PC), and medial prefrontal cortex (MPFC). MPFC is probably the most popular candidate. Recently, however, Saxe and collaborators have produced several strands of evidence pointing toward RTPJ rather than MPFC as the locus of theory of mind.

Saxe and Kanwisher (2003) found that the BOLD (blood oxygen level dependent) response in the TPJ area was higher when subjects read stories about a character's mental states, compared with stories that described people in physical detail. This area also did not respond to false representations (e.g., false photographs) in nonsocial control stories. Saxe and Wexler (2005) focus on RTPJ and argue that it alone among the four contenders fulfills each of the predictions they derive from theory of mind. For example, the BOLD response in RTPJ was low while subjects read descriptions of a protagonist's social background and increased only once the mental state of the protagonist was described. Moreover, they argue, several studies undercut the candidacy of MPFC. Bird, Castelli, Malik, Frith, and Husain (2004) studied a patient, GT, who suffered damage to most of the left and right anterior portions of her medial frontal lobes, including regions previously implicated in mentalizing by functional imaging. But GT showed normal ability in representing and understanding mental states of others.

However, other researchers are not persuaded by Saxe's evidence. (Here I follow the reply of Jason Mitchell, personal communication.) Many would argue, first, that the RTPJ region subserves the mentalizing only of beliefs, not all types of mental states. MPFC seems to participate in a wider array of mentalizing processes, so it should be considered primary. Moreover, as concerns patient GT, it could simply be the case that the damage to her MPFC simply isn't extensive enough to knock out the whole system. (For comparison, note that patients with sizable but incomplete lesions to the hippocampus show impaired memory performance but are still able to perform some very easy memory tasks.) Third, other neuropsychological studies do implicate MPFC in social cognition. Patients with the frontal variant of frontotemporal dementia (fvFTD)—which selectively impairs MPFC—typically present to neurologists with severe social disturbances. For purposes of this chapter, it is not essential to make a definitive choice between RTPJ and MPFC as the primary substrate of high-level mindreading. In the next chapter, however, a special role in high-level mindreading will be found for a certain part, the ventral part, of MPFC (see section 7.5).

Whether MPFC or RTPJ is highlighted, these regions are critical only to high-level, not low-level, mentalizing. High-level mentalizing might also be called a late-developing system, as contrasted with an early-developing system that targets different mental states and uses different substrates.[20] Saxe, Carey, and Kanwisher (2004) also find compelling reasons to distinguish early- and late-developing systems. They view the mindreading of goals, perceptions, and emotions—as contrasted with beliefs, for example—as the province of the early mindreading system. I could agree with their allocation of tasks to the more primitive and more sophisticated forms of mindreading, respectively, but I am leery of assigning low-level mindreading to a single system. As shown in this chapter, there are a multitude of low-level mindreading tasks and a multitude of different brain regions implicated in them. It is hard to see these as the joint province of a single mechanism, though they may share a single *type* of process, namely, mirroring.

In conclusion, nothing in our overall approach conflicts with existing neuroimaging or neuropsychological studies of mentalizing in the brain, especially with recent theorizing about the proper morals to be gleaned from these studies. Indeed, there is broad concurrence with all kinds of neuroscientific results.

6.7 Where Do Mirror Systems Come From?

Mirror neurons may strike people as mysterious. Where do they come from? Are they innate? If so, how or why did they evolve? If not, what in ontogeny could account for them? Hardwiring initially seems like the most plausible hypothesis; it is widely regarded as the default. However, it is not firmly established. No experiments on infant monkeys have been conducted, for example, because it isn't feasible. Moreover, a principled explanation in simple physiological terms has now been offered of how mirror properties could arise in ontogeny, specifically through Hebbian learning. Such an explanation is offered by Christian Keysers and David Perrett (2004). Although I do not endorse this explanation, it must be included as a serious possibility.

In his book *The Organization of Behavior*, D. O. Hebb (1949) offered the following postulate: "When an axon of cell A is near enough to excite cell B or repeatedly or consistently takes part in firing it, some growth or metabolic change takes place . . . such that A's efficiency, as one of the cells firing B, is increased." Put in a simple phrase, "neurons that fire together, wire together."

Modern neuroscience now strongly supports this speculation (Markram and Lubke, 1997).[21] Keysers and Perrett show how a circuit involving three areas in the brain of the macaque monkey can interact over time to acquire mirroring properties; a similar circuit appears to exist in humans.

The relevant anatomical circuit in the macaque involves the superior temporal sulcus (STS), area PF of the inferior parietal lobule, and the premotor cortex (F5). STS, F5, and PF all provide high-level visual descriptions of observed actions. F5 and PF also have motor properties (as we have seen earlier); their visual and motor properties are usually congruent, which is why they are called "mirror neurons." Here, according to Keysers and Perrett, is why the mirroring properties arise in this circuit.

Monkey (and human) infants observe their own actions carefully. During this process, some movements lead them to grasp objects in particular ways. Action potentials in STS neurons responding to the sight of this type of grasping overlap in time with activity in the PF and F5 neurons that *cause* the infant to grasp in that way, for example, precision grip. This creates the prerequisites for Hebbian associations: Neurons that fire together, wire together. For example, at first the STS → F5 connections are weak and unselective. But because the monkey is currently performing, say, a precision grip, the synaptic signal from the STS finds only the precision grip neurons to be active in F5. Hebbian learning will hence reinforce only the connections between precision grip in STS and precision grip in F5. Over time, neural associations strengthen to the point where neurons in F5 will respond to the visually driven synaptic input from STS. Many STS cells show viewpoint invariance, so the same STS neurons will respond both to the monkey's own actions and to those of others. After "learning" the association between F5 motor commands and visual STS descriptions of the monkey's own actions, the observation of someone else performing a similar action will also activate the neurons in F5, and mirror properties will have emerged.

This explanation is tendered for the emergence of *motor* mirroring properties, but the main ideas could apply to other cases where brain areas are involved in both observing and experiencing an event. Keysers and Perrett sketch such accounts for other mirroring examples reviewed in this chapter, such as touch and disgust. The social properties of these systems—for example, our ability to empathize with other people without confusing ourselves with others—arise from basic anatomical facts and physiological principles.

I have argued that low-level simulational mindreading rests substantially on mental mirroring, and mirroring may be underpinned by Hebbian learning. But isn't Hebbian learning a kind of "theorizing," at least a species of "inference"? If so, isn't there a new threat that simulation will collapse into theory? No. First, it is a dubious proposition that Hebbian association is a form of theorizing. Second, even if it is, we have already rejected the notion (chapter 2) that any grounding of simulation in theorizing is ipso facto a threat to simulation. Here we have another case in point, where grounding poses no threat. The mere fact (if it is a fact) that mirroring emerges *as a result* of Hebbian learning doesn't *eliminate* mirroring, doesn't show that it's a chimera. Moreover, mirroring is a clear form of mental simulation, under our definition, and it doesn't cease to be so because of its etiology.

Notes

1. The first three sections of this chapter are adapted from Goldman and Sripada (2005). Thanks to Chandra Sripada for substantial contributions to this material, both scientific and philosophical.

2. This claim needs qualification for one case to be discussed in section 6.2.

3. Additional evidence that the amygdala is intimately linked to fear experience is the finding that when the amygdala is stimulated during surgery, fear is commonly evoked (Halgren, 1992).

4. For further details, see section 8.9.

5. As the discussion continues, I sometimes focus on the evidence involving FaBER tasks and ignore the guilt example. I don't mean to discount the evidence in the guilt case, but the FaBER data facilitate a uniform treatment of the theoretical issues.

6. In the case of the psychopaths, it is less clear that they have a full grip on the concept of guilt. Their failure to attribute guilt correctly in *story* cases may indicate a deficient grasp of the concept.

7. In calling experience/observation matches "simulations," I have in mind the "success" sense of *simulation* explained in chapter 2, where "success" merely means actual (rough) duplication, whether or not there is voluntariness or intent.

8. This did not permanently rehabilitate SM's impaired recognition of fear, however. When subsequently shown face stimuli under unconstrained viewing conditions, she failed to fixate the eye region spontaneously and reverted to impaired fear recognition.

9. The "reverse simulation" idea is invoked by Blakemore and Decety (2001), in connection with their "forward-model" approach to intention attribution.

10. Robert Gordon (1995a) has discussed facial feedback as a mechanism of emotion contagion, citing early descriptions of the phenomenon by Hume.

11. However, section 6.7 sketches a possible story of the acquisition of mirroring properties, and this may contain hints about how mirror processes work.

12. The topic of classifying one's own mental states is explored in chapters 9 and 10.

13. The study of "point-light walkers" was introduced by Johansson (1973), who attached small lights to the major joints of actors and filmed them walking or running in a dark room. These moving lights are immediately recognizable as human motion (often called "biological" motion).

14. If the reader isn't prepared to concede that a *process* might consist in only one event, bear in mind that "simulation" didn't have to be defined in terms of processes. We might have defined simulation from the outset as a relation between either *single events* or *sequences of events*. Under this definition, the current matter wouldn't be an issue. So, if the reader prefers, let this be our original definition.

15. Goldman and Sripada (2005) took no stance on which of the four models is correct.

16. A related tradition that also studies automatic mappings between self and other goes under the heading of "common-coding theory" (Prinz, 1990, 1997; Viviani, 2002; Preston and de Waal, 2002; Knoblich and Flach; 2001; Barsalou, Niedenthal, Barbey, and Ruppert, 2003). Its core assumption is that actions are coded in terms of the perceivable effects they should generate, and that perception of the behavior of another individual automatically activates one's own representations of that behavior.

17. The existence of such a causal basis for attribution was already argued for, in effect, in sections 6.2 and 6.3. What is being added here is that the causal basis of attribution is associated with mirroring.

18. To be sure, the correlation doesn't *establish* the causal status of the mirrored feeling.

19. Skepticism about primate mindreading was dramatically sparked by findings of Povinelli and Eddy (1996) that chimpanzees were unable to take into account what different experimenters could or could not see when choosing whom to ask for food. Without training, they failed to distinguish between an experimenter whose head orientation was directed at them versus one directed away from them. Even after training, the apes continued to beg for food from experimenters unable to see them. This led the authors to conclude that chimpanzees possess little understanding of the nature of visual attention, let alone mental states such as beliefs or intentions. More recent work by Hare, Call, and Tomasello (2001; Hare, Call, Agnetta, and Tomasello, 2000) and by Santos and colleagues (Flombaum and Santos, 2005; Santos, Flombaum, and Webb, in press) has turned the field around by obtaining new results that run in the opposite direction. Flombaum and Santos (2005) investigated whether macaque monkeys spontaneously took into account the direction of an experimenter's gaze when attempting to steal food. By this technique, they probed monkeys' abilities in a more naturalistic setting, where there is an element of competition. In one study, monkeys were shown two experimenters with a grape nearby, one who was facing the grape and the other with his back turned on the grape. The monkeys approached the experimenter who had his back turned. They also were able to use subtler cues, for example, selectively retrieving the grape from someone whose head and eyes were oriented away, whose eyes alone were oriented away, or whose gaze was blocked by a small barrier. Flombaum and Santos also found evidence for monkeys' understanding that seeing leads to knowing (Santos et al., in press). Evidence for mindreading in birds has been obtained by Emery and Clayton (2001), who studied scrub jays. Scrub jays not only cache their food and remember where they cached it but also remember where conspecifics have cached and pilfer them when given an opportunity. Might they adjust their own caching strategies to minimize potential pilfering? Emery and Clayton found that jays with prior experience of pilfering another bird's caches subsequently recached food in new cache sites, but only when they themselves had previously been observed caching. Jays without pilfering experience did not adjust their own caching strategies, even though they had observed other jays caching. These results suggest that jays relate information about their previous experience as a pilferer to the possibility of future stealing by another bird. This supports the notion not only that scrub jays engage in mindreading but also that they employ a *simulation* heuristic, because they project their own experience onto intentions of conspecifics. (Thanks to Randy Gallistel for pointing me to this last wrinkle.)

20. Onishi and Baillargeon's (2005) work considerably advances the period of false-belief understanding. If they are right, false-belief understanding does not begin at the canonical age of 4, or even 3. So to speak of high-level mindreading as "late" may require some revision.

21. There are some skeptics about Hebbian learning. C. R. Gallistel, for example, questions the existence of this putative kind of learning, as well as associative learning in general. However, Gallistel has no quarrel with the neuroscientific evidence of changes in synaptic conductance more or less along the lines Hebb imagined; he questions only whether this constitutes *learning* (personal communication). However, for understanding the origins of mirroring properties, it doesn't matter whether the hypothesized synaptic-change story is classified as an instance of "learning." It still contrasts importantly with an innateness explanation.

7

High-Level Simulational Mindreading

7.1 Overview

This chapter develops the simulationist approach to high-level mindreading. "High-level" mindreading is mindreading with one or more of the following features: (a) it targets mental states of a relatively complex nature, such as propositional attitudes; (b) some components of the mindreading process are subject to voluntary control; and (c) the process has some degree of accessibility to consciousness. Later I shall add further characteristics of high-level mindreading, to help distinguish it from the low-level variety. These features, however, provide only a rough-and-ready characterization, not a strict definition. Although a strict definition of high- versus low-level mindreading processes is lacking, two fairly different prototypes are intended for high- versus low-level *simulational* mindreading. The low-level prototype is the mirroring type of simulation process. The high-level prototype is the kind that uses pretense or E-imagination, as presented in section 2.2.

The evidence for high-level simulational mindreading presented in this chapter comes from many sources, both experimental and theoretical. The first two thirds of the chapter looks at experimental evidence that bears on three aspects of ST. First, we address the basic capacity of high-level simulation to achieve attributional *accuracy*. Naïve mentalizing seems to attain at least a moderate level of accuracy. If this is accomplished largely through simulation, as ST postulates, pretend states must be sufficiently similar to their counterpart target states. In other words, accurate simulational mindreading requires substantial resemblance between the attributor's pretend states and the corresponding nonpretend states of the target. Are pretend states in general the kinds of states that can attain the required resemblance to their nonpretend counterparts? Does E-imagination have the capacity to generate pretend states with this property? Sections 7.3–7.5 adduce ample evidence to support this precondition for accurate simulational mindreading.

A second line of evidence points to a type of cognitive activity that is intimately involved in the simulation-projection method but quite dubious for theorizing. *Self-reflection,* or *self-reference,* is a natural subactivity of third-person mindreading according to ST. For one thing, simulational mindreading requires an attributor to monitor her own genuine states so as to identify those that should be inhibited and excluded from a simulation routine. In addition, a paradigm simulation routine, at its next-to-last step, involves detecting and classifying an output state of a cognitive mechanism (e.g., a decision). This detection-and-classification step requires self-reflection. So ST predicts the use of self-reflection in third-person mindreading, something not naturally predicted by TT. In section 7.6, we report evidence that subjects engaged in third-person mindreading in fact use a region of the brain that is used in self-reflection, or self-reference. This lends supports to ST.

Third, although third-person mindreading seems to achieve a tolerable level of overall accuracy, abundant evidence reported in section 7.7 attests to a specific pattern of error, a pervasive egocentric bias even among adults. How is this bias to be explained: by ST or by TT? I shall argue that the empirically observed errors are most naturally explained by ST. Accurate simulation requires the attributor to quarantine his genuine states that have no counterparts in the target. Because such quarantining appears to be difficult, ST readily predicts the experimentally observed errors. By contrast, TT does not naturally predict them.

The evidence for egocentric bias is drawn primarily from social psychological studies, as reviewed in section 7.7. Section 7.8 reports additional evidence from a neuropsychological patient that speaks directly to quarantine failure. This patient has clear-cut difficulty in inhibiting self-perspective, that is, inhibiting his own perspective in tasks requiring the adoption of another's perspective. This inhibitory failure is evidently responsible for his marked egocentric errors on several kinds of mindreading tasks, confirming the ST story.

The foregoing occupies the first two thirds of the chapter. The final third adopts a more speculative methodology and examines other issues in the ST-TT debate. I argue (section 7.10) that simulation offers a more promising account than theorizing of the assignment of *contents* to other people's thoughts and a more promising account of how they predict inferences and choices (section 7.11). Retrodictive mindreading can reasonably be handled by our hybrid approach (section 7.12), and, finally, our own brand of ST is preferable to a principal competitor (section 7.13).

7.2 Enactment Imagination

Given the centrality of mental pretense or E-imagination in ST, its properties require careful examination. Let us begin the discussion of E-imagination by reference to a nonmindreading task. I am planning tonight's dinner. I just purchased a white beans and artichoke salad, which might nicely combine with a bed of leafy greens already in the refrigerator. To test the appeal of this combination, I visualize the white beans and pale green artichoke hearts against the background of the dark green (and red) leafy ingredients. This act of visual imagination is an instance of E-imagination, involving deliberate construction of a mental state with (quasi-) visual character. The immediate output of the imaginative process is intended to resemble a *counterpart* state: a percept of the culinary creation I am considering. I do not merely *suppose* that this culinary creation is before me; I try to create a mental surrogate of seeing it. This illustrates what is meant by "enactment" imagination.

The indicated act of visualization has no attendant mindreading purposes. But ST contends that E-imagination is often employed for mindreading. To determine whether my wife, seated elsewhere in the room, can see the bird in the birdfeeder, I might visualize how things look from her perspective. Such perspective taking could lead me to mindread both her visual state and any consequent beliefs about the bird. Analogously, many nonvisual specimens of E-imagining might be utilized for mindreading purposes. In general, E-imagining isn't confined to the production of imagery, visual or otherwise.

Can E-imagining produce states that truly resemble their intended counterparts? For example, do outputs of visualizing resemble, to any substantial extent, their counterpart states of seeing? If E-imagining is utilized for mindreading, and if its mindreading applications are to be accurate (i.e., yield correct imputations), it seems necessary that outputs of E-imagination should resemble their counterparts in important respects. Is such resemblance psychologically feasible? Can "endogenously" produced mental states resemble those that are produced in a normal, "exogenous" fashion? This is a question for cognitive science; it isn't answerable from the philosopher's armchair.

E-imagination's accuracy does not depend entirely on the general capacity of E-imagination; it partly depends on task-specific knowledge. For example, my chances of producing an accurate visualization of Helen of Troy are minimal. Having never seen her in the flesh, or any reliable reproduction of her face, I have virtually no chance of visualizing her facial features accurately. This is not a flaw in my powers of visualization; it is simply lack of knowledge: I don't know what Helen looked like. By contrast, a contemporary of Helen who had seen her frequently might easily have produced an accurate visual image of her fabled beauty. Stored (visual) knowledge of her face could have been retrieved and used to construct a visual image of her even when she was absent. Thus, E-imagination can be guided by knowledge. In the same way, E-imagination-based mindreading can also be guided by knowledge (knowledge that isn't merely a design-feature of a module or special-purpose program). This is a fourth feature that may be distinctive to high-level simulational mindreading.

In the traditional ST-TT debate, the question arose whether image production really qualifies as simulation rather than theory (Nichols, Stich, Leslie, and Klein, 1996). Established accounts of visual imagery routinely say that image generation involves recourse to information stored in memory. If the contrast between simulation and theory is drawn in terms of knowledge-poor versus knowledge-rich processes, how could visualization or image generation qualify as simulation at all? However, we have rejected the notion that simulation is incompatible with using rich bodies of information (section 2.4). In particular, there is no reason that the creation of pretend states should not rely on information stored in memory. This does not prevent a cognitive operation from being a simulation. What makes it simulation is its top-down (as opposed to stimulus-driven) mode of producing the state in question, a mode of production with the ostensible purpose—or at least function—of replicating standardly produced states.

Recall that ST requires only attempted, not necessarily successful, simulation (chapter 2). Here we have another possible difference between high-level and low-level mindreading. Our case for low-level mindreading (chapter 6) was predicated on genuine resemblances between states of the attributor and the target. The case for high-level mindreading, by contrast, rests on the ostensible purpose or function of E-imagination, not on the regular achievement of faithful reproductions. However, if resemblance is rarely achieved, and if this entails highly inaccurate mindreading, how could a simulation routine have gained and maintained a foothold in our psychology? It seems unlikely that systematically poor mindreading routines would have persisted. So a defense of (hybrid) ST should include evidence that E-imaginative resemblance is feasible across a respectable spectrum of cases.

What kinds of resemblance are at issue here? One potential dimension of resemblance is phenomenology; a defense of ST might appeal to this category of resemblance. That is not the line of defense pursued here, however. First, phenomenology is elusive, incapable of supporting weighty theses. Second, claims of phenomenological similarity between E-imaginative products and their counterparts are hotly disputed, even when E-imaginative products are indisputably conscious. Hume famously defended the thesis that "ideas" of imagination generally have a "great resemblance" to the perceptual "impressions" from which they are derived. "When I shut my eyes and think of my chamber, the ideas I form are exact representations of the impressions I felt" (Hume 1739/1958: 3). Ideas of imagination differ from percepts, said Hume, only in their force and vivacity. But Hume's phenomenological resemblance thesis is hotly denied and debated by philosophers, and questions of phenomenological resemblance are difficult to resolve. Third, a great deal of mindreading, even high-level mindreading, is nonconscious or minimally conscious, so we should allow simulational processes to include E-imaginative states even when the latter are entirely nonconscious. This presumably excludes phenomenological respects of resemblance. So the respects of resemblance I shall highlight are functional or neural.

The term *E-imagination* is a term of art, not beholden to naïve conceptions of the imagination. Thus, even if the naïve conception of imagination restricts its province to the sphere of consciousness and the control of the will, our use of "E-imagination" is not so restricted.[1] E-imagination is introduced here as a psychological construct, the referents of which can either be conscious or covert, voluntary or automatic, and these properties can hold for both the generating process and the products so generated. (Well, the products are unlikely to be voluntary.)

If high-level mindreading is substantially simulationist, mentalizers must engage in a great deal of E-imagining. And if people use simulation across a wide spectrum of mindreading tasks, they must E-imagine many types of mental states, including beliefs, desires, plans, and hopes. To study these matters, it would help to have extant empirical research on the E-imagination of *all* these states, research exploring similarities between E-imagined tokens and their genuine counterparts. How similar is E-imagined desire-that-p to genuine desire-that-p? How similar is E-imagined belief-that-p to genuine belief-that-p? Detailed research on these topics, unfortunately, is sparse. But there's a wealth of research on two species of E-imagination, visual and motor E-imagination, usually studied under the headings of visual and motor "imagery." So they will be the primary focus of our attention, in the hope that what we learn is more widely applicable. We cannot currently prove that these two cases are representative, but there is some supportive evidence.

7.3 Visual Imagery

Research on resemblances between visual imagery and vision is heavily neuroscientific, but let me begin with behavioral research. My conception of E-imagining is a fairly demanding conception. To E-imagine Xing, where X is some kind of mental state, it does not in general suffice merely to suppose or hypothesize that Xing occurs in you. To enactively imagine seeing something, you must "try" to *undergo* the seeing—or some aspects of the seeing—despite the fact that no appropriate visual stimulus is present. When this is clearly understood, a wary reader might be skeptical of any substantial similarity between seeing and E-imagined seeing. "When one looks at an object attentively," a reader might reflect, "the experience of it is far from passive. The object is scanned or tracked with the eyes. Saccadic eye movements accompany and facilitate attentive seeing. Surely this doesn't happen when one merely visualizes an object. Visualizing does not consist in literally *enacting* the seeing in a full-blooded sense. So postulating something called 'enactment imagination' is misleading at best and positive nonsense at worst."

Wrong, wrong, wrong. Studies indicate that visualizing is, precisely, attempted *enactment* of seeing. Saccadic eye movements do occur during visual imagination (even when the eyes are closed), movements that approximate the ocular movements for corresponding acts of visual perception. Michael Spivey and collaborators (Spivey, Tyler, Richardson, and Young, 2000) had subjects listen to spoken scene descriptions while a remote eye-tracking camera recorded their eye movements (without their knowledge). Although their eyelids were down, their eyes could still be detected, and they tended to move in directions that accorded with the directionality of the scene being described. The subjects heard five stories, four with a preferred directionality (upward, downward, rightward, and leftward) plus a control story with no directionality. The downward story, for example, was a vignette in which someone is described as standing at the top of a canyon watching people rappel down to the canyon floor. The results of the study were that, in the four critical stories, the average proportion of eye movements in a preferred direction was significantly greater than the average proportion of eye movements in the unpreferred directions. It is noteworthy that this experiment featured no explicit instructions to imagine anything. Nonetheless, participants spontaneously made eye movements that mimicked the kinds of eye movements appropriate to viewing the actual scene. Thus, they imaginatively enacted seeing not only mentally but also in oculomotor terms.

In a slightly earlier study, Brandt and Stark (1997) also found that spontaneous eye movements during visual imagery reflected the content of the visualized scene. Experimenters studied their subjects' ocular scanpaths while the subjects viewed an irregularly checkered grid. This viewing pattern was then compared with the scanpaths produced while the subjects merely visualized the absent grid. The paths showed a high degree of similarity for the seeing period and the imaging period. This confirms that visual imagination is very much an enactment (simulation) of seeing in behavioral as well as purely cognitive terms.

Turn now to visual imagery itself and its relationship to visual percepts. If imagery is similar to perception, one should find interactions between them; visual imagery should interfere with visual perception, and people should sometimes confuse them. Perky (1910) found evidence for such interference and confusion, which has been confirmed by more recent experiments. Segal and Fusella (1970) found that maintaining a visual image impaired visual perception more than auditory perception, and Craver-Lemley and Reeves (1987) found that accuracy in a line-orientation detection task was impaired when a subject formed an image near the visual target but not when the image was moved. A possible example of confusing imagery with perception involved a patient with Anton's syndrome. Although completely cortically blind, she denied her blindness and claimed to have visual experiences (Goldenberg, Muellbacher, and Nowak, 1995). Goldenberg et al. tentatively concluded that the patient was able to generate mental visual images, and her blindness denial resulted from confusing images and percepts.[2]

Stephen Kosslyn has pioneered the study of visual imagery and its relationship to vision. One of his hypotheses is that the visual "buffer" is used in both perception and imagery. The visual buffer, he claims, evolved to process input from the eyes, which subtend only a limited visual angle. Hence the visual buffer should have a circumscribed spatial extent, which would constrain visual images as well as visual percepts (Kosslyn, 1994: 99). This hypothesis predicts that an imagined object will overflow the visual field of imagination at about the same imagined distance as it overflows the real visual field. Kosslyn (1978) tested this idea by having subjects actually walk to the "point of overflow" while viewing rectangles mounted on a wall. In another condition, subjects merely visualized the rectangles while imagining a similar walk. The results from the imagery and perception experiments were almost identical. We shall return to Kosslyn's investigations later.

Another famous example of evidence for a strong equivalence between visual perception and imagery concerns the clinical phenomenon of unilateral visual "neglect." Patients with damage to the posterior right parietal lobe sometimes "neglect" (i.e., ignore) the left (contralesional) half of the visual space they are looking at. Bisiach and Luzzatti (1978) famously found that their two patients with this syndrome also failed to "image" the left half of their visual field. These neglect patients were asked to imagine being in a familiar location, the Piazza del Duomo in Milan. When asked to describe the scene from vantage point A, they named only landmarks on the right side of the imagined scene. When asked to imagine the square from the opposite vantage point, B, they omitted landmarks mentioned previously and again named only landmarks that were now to the right of the newly imagined point of view. This suggests that visual imagery uses some of the same neural machinery as vision itself and hence should bear some substantial resemblance to vision. Additional clinical evidence indicates corresponding deficits in seeing and imaging. Levine, Warach, and Farah (1985) reported one patient who had trouble recognizing objects in both perception and imagery but could identify spatial relations in both cases, and vice versa for another patient. (As often occurs in neuropsychology, results from different patients are not always consistent. In some patients, for example, visual neglect and imaginal neglect were found to be dissociable. Some patients neglect one side of a visual scene but do not neglect one side of their image, and conversely for other patients; see Beschin, Basso, and Sala, 2000. It is possible that different types of impairment can lead to visual neglect, and some of these impairments overlap more with visual imagery centers than others.)

Neuroimaging studies show a notable overlap between parts of the brain active during vision and during imagery. A region of the occipitotemporal cortex called the fusiform gyrus is activated both when we see faces and when we imagine them (Kanwisher, McDermott, and Chun, 1997; O'Craven and Kanwisher, 2000). Lesions that include the fusiform face area impair both face recognition and the ability to imagine faces (Damasio, Tranel, and Damasio, 1990; Young et al., 1994). All this is significant evidence for shared neurological properties between vision and visual imagination. Especially convincing is evidence of the contribution of early visual cortex, specifically area 17, to visual mental imagery, as well as to vision itself. Area 17 is part of the medial occipital cortex and comprises a substrate of the visual buffer hypothesized by Kosslyn. Kosslyn, Pascual-Leone, Felician, and Camposano (1999) used two convergent techniques, both positron emission tomography (PET) and repetitive transcranial magnetic stimulation (rTMS). Subjects closed their eyes while they visualized and compared properties of sets of stripes (e.g., their relative length). PET scans showed that when people perform this task, area 17 is activated. Then rTMS was applied to the same area, which resulted in impaired performance of the same task. This technique essentially creates a temporary, reversible "lesion," demonstrating a causal link of the specific cortical region to task performance. The crucial point, for our purposes, is that parallel activation and impairment were found when the subjects performed the task by actually looking at the stimuli rather than visualizing them.

Kosslyn (1980) and Farah (1984) initially formulated a model of visual imagery involving a very strong equivalence between perception and imagery. In subsequent work, that thesis has been weakened, partly in response to evidence of dissociations between perception and imagery. Behrmann, Moscovitch, and Winocur (1992) and Jankowiak, Kinsbourne, Shalev, and Bachman (1992) described brain-damaged patients with preserved imagery in the face of impaired perception, and Chatterjee and Southwood (1995) found that imagery may persist even following cortical blindness. Kosslyn et al. (1997; Kosslyn, 1994: 329–334) concede that such findings demonstrate that only some processes used in vision are also used in visual imagery. This is not surprising, given that imagery relies on previously organized and stored information, whereas perception requires performance of all aspects of figure-ground segregation, recognition, and identification (1997: 320). We should not expect imagery to share low-level processes involved in organizing sensory input.[3] Kosslyn et al. (1997) set out to identify different subsystems that perform high-level visual processing tasks in the analysis of perceptual or imagistic materials. They found that two thirds of the activated areas were activated in common.

More troublesome for Kosslyn's approach are apparent findings of visual imagery in *congenitally* blind subjects. Bertolo et al. (2003) used an indirect method to assess whether dreams with visual content occur in the congenitally blind. They assumed that the pattern of cortical activation during dreams with visual content would be similar to that during visual imagery, and this pattern would be reflected in a change of the scalp EEG alpha rhythm. (In normal subjects, visual imagery is generally accompanied by a decrease of alpha activity recorded from the scalp.) They therefore recorded the EEG from the occipital and central scalp areas of congenitally blind subjects, who were awakened every 90 minutes to be questioned about their dream recall. The dream reports were vivid not only with tactile, auditory, and kinesthetic components but also with visual content. Among other measures, these subjects could make drawings of their content.

To explain this finding, Lopes da Silva (2003) proposes that visual perceptions can be considered an innate property of specific cortical areas, and, in the absence of visual stimulation in early life, these can be stimulated by sensory modalities other than vision (e.g., touch). Thus, the occipital area responsible for visual imagery can be brought into a visual mode of activation even in the congenitally blind. Buchel et al. (1998) demonstrated the existence of cross-modal activation by tactile stimulation in extrastriate visual cortical areas. In a parallel finding, Brugger et al. (2000) reported the case of a woman born without forearms and legs who nonetheless experiences phantom limb sensations in all four limbs. This, too, may be explained in terms of cross-modal interactions, here between visual perception and an innate body schema, as suggested (though not endorsed) by Funk, Brugger, and Shiffrar (2005). The upshot for the visual imagery issue is that neural correspondences between vision and visual imagery are not undercut by finding visual imagery in the congenitally blind.[4]

Kosslyn has focused much of his research and theorizing on a matter of cognitive *architecture* that is central to certain questions about visual imagery but tangential to our questions. Drawing on mental scanning experiments, Kosslyn concluded that greater distances on a physical map are represented by greater distances in some mental space. In other words, mental images have spatial properties or magnitudes; they are "depictive" in the sense of resembling the *objects they represent*. Representations of larger distances are themselves, in some sense, larger. Kosslyn's explanation of the timing results in his mental scanning experiments is that the cognitive architecture of visual images restricts or constrains the operations you can perform. These conclusions are strongly disputed by Zenon Pylyshyn (1981, 1994, 1999, 2003a, 2003b). Pylyshyn denies that visual representations resemble the objects represented and that timing results in image-scanning experiments are attributable to the fact that images are "laid out in space," even in "functional space."

My sympathies are entirely with Pylyshyn in his critique of Kosslyn's depictionalism and pictorialism (or "quasi pictorialism"). These issues, though, are irrelevant here. The simulation hypothesis does not say that either visual imagery or vision has a spatial architecture or spatial format. Simulationism is entirely neutral on the architecture or format of both vision and visual imagery. Simulation's resemblance thesis says only that visual imagery resembles visual experience (in some relevant respects), not that it resembles the *external* physical objects that are represented.

Pylyshyn himself sometimes grants that visual imagination resembles vision. He says that subjects, when engaged in visual scanning, "make the *same thing* happen in their imagining" as what happens in actual seeing (1999: 18, emphasis added). On other occasions, when discussing findings that support the kinds of resemblances highlighted here, Pylyshyn often switches the topic to the admittedly dubious architectural theses of Kosslyn and company. Here is an example:

> Farah, Soso, and Dasheiff (1992) report that a patient who developed tunnel vision after unilateral occipital lobectomy also developed a reduction in the maximum size of her images (as determined by asking how close an image of a familiar object, such as a chair or an automobile, could be before it overflowed the edge of her image). If the cortical display were involved in both vision and imagery, and if the peripheral parts of the display were damaged, then it might explain the parallel deficits. Although it is certainly possible that tunnel vision and tunnel imagery could have a common underlying neural basis, the Farah et al. finding does not show that this basis has anything to do with a *topographical mapping of the mental image onto spatial properties of a neural display.* (Pylyshyn, 2003b: 397, emphasis added)

I agree that the indicated finding shows nothing about a mapping of the mental image onto spatial properties of a neural display. But that point is irrelevant to the present issue. Pylyshyn himself concedes the relevant issue here in granting that tunnel vision and tunnel imagery have (or possibly have) a common neural basis.[5]

We have seen that Kosslyn recognizes differences between visual imagery and genuine vision.[6] Does this acknowledgment pose problems for the claim that visualization is an enactment of vision, a simulation of vision? Recall our definition of simulation from chapter 2. It says that process P is a simulation of another process P' only if P duplicates, replicates, or resembles P' *in some significant respects* (relative to the purposes or function of the task). The "significant respects" qualification allows the simulating process to be an imperfect match of the simulated process. In the case of visual images, they obviously do not share *all* properties with their counterpart percepts.[7] They are invariably less vivid and less detailed. So they differ from percepts at least phenomenologically, and one might expect related differences on functional and neural dimensions. Nonetheless, this leaves open the question of whether they resemble their counterparts in significant respects.

One primary use of visual images is to answer questions about states of affairs not currently observable, the sorts of questions visual percepts could help answer if the state of affairs were visible. So a reasonable interpretation of "significant respects" is whether visual images are capable of yielding the same answers vision itself would provide. Obviously, this varies with the question. But for some substantial range of questions, images appear to have such a capacity.

A stock example from the literature is visualizing one's previous living room in order to answer the question "How many windows did the living room of your previous domicile have?" One could answer accurately if the living room were currently visible, but one may also answer correctly by visualizing the living room. No doubt there would be differences of vividness and detail between an image generated from memory and an actual percept of the living room. But there would be sufficient resemblance that both image and percept could generate correct answers. Similarly, consider Shepard's famous "mental rotation" task (Shepard and Metzler, 1971; Shepard and Cooper, 1982). The task was to determine whether pairs of three-dimensional objects, shown in line drawings from different perspectives, were congruent or noncongruent with one another. Subjects' performances indicated that they visualized one object being rotated into correspondence with the second, so that they could then visualize congruence or noncongruence. No doubt these acts of visualization differed in numerous respects from perceptual states that would have occurred, had subjects actually observed a rotation and resultant juxtaposition. Nonetheless, the imagery states apparently resembled the hypothetical visual states in some significant respects, because the imagery states enabled subjects to answer the series of congruence questions with an accuracy rate of nearly 97 percent, an accuracy rate that must be very close to what would have been achieved if actual observations had been made.

We can now give tentative answers to our earlier questions about visual imagination's capacity to produce states that resemble their perceptual counterparts, sufficient resemblance to yield accurate mindreading attributions. Psychology and neuroscience have revealed extensive and often surprising correspondences between visual imagery and perception. This suggests that the power of E-imagination is very considerable, at least in the visual domain. It also suggests that if visualization were used for mindreading, it could indeed yield accurate attributions. Much depends, of course, on the specific attributions, but thus far it is quite credible that mindreading applications of visual E-imagination could attain high levels of accuracy.

7.4 Motor Imagery

The case for similarity between motor imagery and its counterpart is, if anything, stronger than the one for visual imagery, though less well known or introspectively compelling. What is meant by motor imagery? It is the representation or imagination of executing bodily movement, a representation *from the inside*. Unlike visualization, motor imagination is not a conspicuous part of consciousness. Nonetheless, it is very common, as we shall see.

What kinds of tasks involve motor imagination? Here is an example from the research literature. If someone is shown a hand and asked whether it is a left or a right hand, he will imagine his own hand moving from its current orientation into the stimulus orientation for comparison (Parsons, 1987, 1994). The trajectory imagined for the left hand is strongly influenced by the biomechanical constraints on actual left-hand movements, and likewise for imagined right-hand trajectories. Parsons, Gabrieli, Phelps, and Gazzaniga (1998) showed that imaginative processes for the two hands are controlled by their opposite (contralateral) hemispheres, just like ordinary manipulation. When patients with disconnected cerebral hemispheres judged the handedness of drawings of left and right hands in various positions, their accuracy was high when a hemisphere judged the handedness of a contralateral hand but not above chance when the judged hand was ipsilateral to the perceiving hemisphere. Thus, imagining a hand movement is apparently executed by the same cerebral mechanism that actually executes movements of that hand.

As this example illustrates, motor imagination occurs in tasks quite different from mindreading. However, at the moment our discussion is not directed at mindreading, though it will shortly turn to that. It is meant to show that E-imagination is a robust phenomenon, capable of producing outputs that correspond closely to counterpart states. What exactly are the counterpart states of the outputs of motor imagination? They are events of motor production, events occurring in the motor cortex that direct behavior. Such events have minimal levels of consciousness and little, if any, phenomenology, so it would be difficult to advance a thesis of phenomenological resemblance between motor imagination and genuine motor guidance. But lots of experimental research support a fairly strong neural resemblance thesis.

To avert possible confusion, motor imagination should be distinguished from mirror-neuron activity. Mirroring activity is an involuntary response to perceptual stimuli, whereas motor imagination is subject to voluntary control and not normally driven by any distinctive class of perceptual stimuli. Researchers assume voluntary control of motor imagination when they instruct subjects to imagine doing certain movements, and subjects routinely report complying with such instructions. Compliance seems to be genuine, because in many studies highly significant changes occur. A salient example is enhancement in athletic performance. In one dramatic demonstration, Yue and Cole (1992) compared the increase in muscular strength among subjects who actually trained with the increase in subjects who generated mere motor imagery. Actual training produced a 30 percent increase in maximal force; motor imagery produced a 22 percent increase. The effect is the product of cortical activity, not covert muscular activity, because subjects did not make covert muscular contractions during motor imagery.

Many studies of motor imagery have used chronometric methods. Mental simulation time mimicked real movement time, and many other kinematic properties were also preserved in the simulations. Decety, Jeannerod, and Preblanc (1989) measured the time it took subjects to walk to a target. When they were blindfolded and encouraged to imagine walking to the target, imagined walking times were very similar to actual walking times. Similarly, subjects either actually walked or imagined walking on beams with different widths. It was assumed that the narrower the width, the more difficult the task. A clear effect of task difficulty was found in both actual movement times and mental movement times. This suggests that mental simulations of action are supported by sensorimotor structures used for real action.

If common use of sensorimotor structures obtains, motor pathologies should affect motor imagery in the same ways they affect motor performance. This hunch is indeed borne out. Dominey, Decety, Brouselle, Chazot, and Jeannerod (1995) examined patients with Parkinson's disease who were significantly slower on a finger-sequencing task with one hand than with the other. In an imagined performance of the same task, this timing asymmetry between affected and unaffected hands was closely matched. Sirigu et al. (1995) tested a subject with motor cortex damage on finger, arm, and leg movements. A correlation was found between actual and imagined movement times. One test involved a finger movement task to keep up with a metronome. Doing the task in imagination, the patient kept up with the metronome to 95 beats per minute in the impaired hand and 160 beats with the intact hand. Her later actual performance was very close to this: maximum speeds were 90 and 170 beats.

Brain imaging studies provide additional evidence of shared motor representations as between motor execution and imagery of action. Experiments with patients who had impairments in motor imagery following lesions in the parietal area provide clear evidence of this sharing. Sirigu et al. (1996) studied mentally simulated hand movements in four patients with unilateral left or right parietal lobe lesions. All patients experienced movement difficulties restricted to the hand and fingers. Nine normal individuals showed excellent congruence between maximum imagined and executed movement speeds. In contrast, patients with parietal cortex lesions produced estimates that were systematically inaccurate or that were inconsistent from one trial to the next. Thus, the ability to estimate manual motor performance through mental imagery is disturbed after parietal lobe damage. For two patients with right parietal lesions, imagined movements of the intact hand accurately predicted actual motor performance, indicating that their deficit is a selective incapacity to generate a mental representation of the relevant hand's movements. Sirigu and colleagues concluded that mental rehearsal of a motor act involves internal simulation.

Marc Jeannerod (2001) reviews a large number of regions in which neural activity for executed action and neural activity for imagined action is very similar. With regard to primary motor cortex, for example, fMRI studies demonstrate that pixels activated during contraction of a group of muscles are also activated during imagery of a movement involving the same muscles (Roth et al., 1996). The level of activation during imagery is about 30 percent of the level observed during execution, which is still substantial. Lotze et al. (1999) did additional fMRI tests to study other motor-related subsystems, such as the premotor cortex and supplementary motor area (SMA). Both the premotor cortex and SMA were equally activated during both actual and imagined movement. They characterized their results as "support[ing] the hypothesis of functional equivalence of motor imagery and motor preparation" postulated by Jeannerod (Lotze et al., 1999: 494).

If motor imagery (in normal subjects) so closely resembles the "real thing," how does the system distinguish an imagined event from its genuine counterpart? Why doesn't motor imagery result in muscular responses? The same question arises equally for visual imagery. Why doesn't visualization produce hallucination (radically false belief about the environment)? In the case of motor imagery, the accepted wisdom is that motor imagery is like motor production except for an added inhibitory signal that prevents overt movement (Lotze et al., 1999). One study provides striking confirmation for this accepted wisdom. Schwoebel and colleagues (2002) report the case of C.W., a patient with bilateral parietal damage from two separate strokes. When C.W. imagines movements, he actually produces them, but without being aware of doing so. He gives every indication of understanding instructions to merely imagine certain hand movements, and he reports no awareness of overtly moving his hands when following the instructions. So it appears that the inhibitory signal has been selectively removed by his parietal damage. In his case, motor imagination has the unintended consequence of following through to execution (M. Wilson, 2003). This study lends further support to the case for close similarity between motor imagery and actual motor production.[8] It also alerts us to a phenomenon important for understanding simulational mindreading, namely, that simulations can "leak out" or "spill over" into genuine, nonsimulational activity.[9]

7.5 Conceptual Uses of E-Imagination

The previous two sections amply demonstrate that E-imagination can generate outputs with substantial neurological similarities to their naturally produced counterparts. The similarities thus far demonstrated, however, pertain only to visual and motor imagery, not purely conceptual, nonimagistic domains. Can E-imagination also operate in these domains and produce similar outputs?

To address the question of E-imagination in conceptual domains, we switch gears from neurological to functional similarities. A nice example from social psychology concerns the well-established *bystander apathy effect* (Darley and Latane, 1968; Latane and Darley, 1968). Someone facing a situation of another person in distress who knows that others are also present and available to help is slower and less likely to respond than someone who knows that he or she is the only helper available. In a permutation of this robust finding, Garcia, Weaver, Moskowitz, and Darley (2002) found that the same effect holds when the "bystander" merely *imagines* a group of others. Individuals who merely imagine being in a group exhibit less helping behavior on a subsequent, completely unrelated task, for example, contributing to charity. In one experiment, participants completed a two-page questionnaire. On the first page, each was asked to imagine winning a dinner for himself and 30 friends (or 10 friends, or 1 friend) at his favorite restaurant. On the second page, each was asked how much he would be willing to donate to charity. The results showed a linear pattern, in which participants in the group-of-30 condition were prepared to pledge less than those in the group-of-10 condition, who in turn were prepared to pledge less than those in the group-of-1 condition. Thus, people who merely imagined a group of potential helpers displayed a pattern of behavior similar to people who actually believed they were in a certain helping situation, a result that lends support to a functional similarity between belief and imagination.

In this Garcia et al. study, participants were specifically asked to imagine a certain situation. But if ST is a correct story about mindreading, E-imagination must be engaged both frequently and spontaneously, without external invitation. Third-person mindreading is a frequent mental activity, and if much of it is done by (high-level) simulation, E-imagination must be frequently engaged. Because a large portion of mindreading is either unconscious or marginally conscious, E-imagination would have to be engaged at an implicit level. Is this hypothesis plausible? A wide range of recent research meshes with this idea, research describing spontaneous covert enactment or reenactment that could be considered E-imagination.

The research I have in mind, primarily the work of John Bargh and Ap Dijksterhuis, documents striking cases in which verbal materials elicit incidental behavior that might be attributed to covert E-imagination. Bargh, Chen, and Burrows (1996) had subjects form sentences from short word lists. A subset of words was related to a social stereotype or trait; for example, *gray*, *Florida*, and *bingo* are related to the *elderly* stereotype. Once the experiment was over, subjects primed with the *elderly* stereotype took longer to walk from the lab to the elevator than did control subjects who were primed with neutral words. In another experiment reported in Bargh et al. (1996), some subjects were primed with words related to rudeness, others were primed with words related to politeness, and still others were in a neutral priming condition.

When the experiment was ostensibly over and subjects waited to talk with the preoccupied experimenter, those whose concept of rudeness had been primed interrupted the experimenter more quickly and frequently than those primed with polite-related stimuli. Similarly, Aarts and Dijksterhuis (2002) primed subjects with the names of either fast or slow animals (e.g., "cheetah" versus "snail"). Subjects primed with fast animals subsequently took less time walking to another room than subjects primed with slow animals. Dijksterhuis and van Knippenberg (1998) primed subjects with the stereotype of professors or secretaries and then had them perform an allegedly unrelated task of answering general knowledge questions taken from Trivial Pursuit. Participants primed with the stereotype of professors outperformed those who were primed with the stereotype of secretaries. Dijksterhuis and van Knippenberg (2000) primed subjects with words related to the politician stereotype, which presumably includes long-windedness. Those subjects wrote longer essays on nuclear testing than did subjects primed with neutral words.

Bargh and Chartrand (1999) interpret these studies as showing that behavior-relevant cognitions automatically create a behavioral tendency, a tendency to engage in that behavior. However, an interpretation in terms of covert E-imagination also fits with the findings. Mentally digesting the elderly stereotype might lead subjects to E-imagine being elderly, which would lead them to walk more slowly. Mentally digesting the professor stereotype might lead participants to E-imagine being scholarly, which might lead to superior performance on a quiz. These surprising findings need more investigation and theorizing. But it is possible that covert E-imagination is an appropriate explanatory construct to cover them.[10]

7.6 Self-Reflection and Third-Person Mindreading

This section turns to the use of self-reflective thought in third-person mindreading. Mitchell, Banaji, and Macrae (2005) suggest that ST's account of third-person mindreading posits a strategy of imagining one's own thoughts, feelings, or behaviors in a situation similar to the target, which involves using self-reflection as a tool to understand the mental states of others. Although this differs slightly from our account of ST, ours also assigns self-reflection an important role in a simulation routine (section 7.1). Mitchell et al. proceed to cite a number of fMRI studies in which medial prefrontal cortex (MPFC), especially the ventral sector thereof, was found to be selectively engaged during tasks requiring self-reflection, self-referencing, or introspection. Kelly et al. (2002) scanned participants while they made judgments about trait adjectives. Participants judged each trait adjective in one of three ways: "Does the adjective describe you?" "Does the adjective describe current U.S. President George Bush?" or "Is the adjective presented in uppercase letters?"

Self-judgments, when compared directly with other-judgments, revealed greater activation in the MPFC region. In another study, Johnson et al. (2002) had participants respond to statements requiring reflection on their own abilities, traits, and attitudes (e.g., "I forget important things," "I'm a good friend") or, in the control condition, to statements simply involving basic semantic knowledge (e.g., "Ten seconds is more than a minute," "You need water to live"). Consistent and robust MPFC activation during self-reflection was observed in all 11 participants. In a study by Schmitz et al. (2004), subjects were asked questions about presented adjectives that requested either self-evaluation, other-evaluation, or the valence of the adjective (the last being a control condition). Again, MPFC was strongly implicated. Similar or related results are reported in Gusnard, Akbudak, Shulman, and Raichle, 2001; Zysset, Huber, Ferstl, and von Cramon, 2002; Macrae, Moran, Heatherton, Banfield, and Kelley, 2004; and Vogeley et al., 2004.

Mitchell et al. take these findings to be congenial to ST, because MPFC has long been one of the regions thought to be associated with theory of mind (section 6.6). Mitchell et al. did a study in which participants underwent fMRI scanning while engaged in either a third-person mentalizing task or a nonmentalizing task, both involving displayed photographs. The mentalizing task was to judge how pleased a person shown in a photograph was to have his or her photograph taken. The nonmentalizing task was to judge how symmetrical the face in the photo was. After scanning, participants viewed each photograph again (30 minutes later) and were asked to indicate the degree to which they perceived the other person to be similar to themselves.[11]

Consistent with earlier research, the contrast of mentalizing versus non-mentalizing tasks yielded a set of loci of activation that have been associated with (third-person) mental-state attribution, including the dorsal aspect of MPFC. The relation between BOLD signal and similarity ratings was stronger for mentalizing than for nonmentalizing trials at a single locus in the ventral MPFC. No effect of similarity was observed on nonmentalizing trials. When the analyses were conditionalized on the basis of postscanning ratings of self-other similarity, a correlation between activity in ventral MPFC and rating of similarity was observed. The coordinates for the peak of this ventral MPFC activation were remarkably similar to (i.e., only 4 voxels away from) the average coordinates reported by the studies previously described that ex-amined self-referential processing. Mitchell et al. interpret these findings as conferring evidence on one important prediction of ST, namely, that under-standing the mental states of similar others draws on self-reflection.[12]

Some might view the role of similarity-to-self in the findings as under-cutting support for ST. As discussed in section 2.2, certain philosophers argue that if simulation is based on judgments of similarity to self, it becomes a piece of theorizing in which the attributor is guided by a "like-me" premise that resembles a psychological law. Two points may be made in response.

First, numerous responses were made to this argument in section 2.2, showing that use of a like-me premise wouldn't really undercut ST and, in particular, wouldn't undercut the hybrid approach endorsed here. Second, the Mitchell et al. data don't show conclusively that similarity beliefs guide, or influence, self-reflective activity in the ventral MPFC. The perceived similarity data are merely correlational and are consistent with the possibility that the judgments of similarity (elicited 30 minutes after scanning) were an *effect* rather than a *cause* of the earlier self-reflective activity. Adverting to their own mental states to judge certain targets may have caused participants later to judge the same targets as more similar to self. If so, perceived similarity cannot be invoked to explain *when* subjects used self-reflection, or simulation, to judge others' states.[13] The important issue for present purposes, though, is establishing that participants do engage in self-reflection in many third-person high-level mindreading tasks, and this appears to be shown in the Mitchell et al. study.[14] That the engagement doesn't occur in all instances of third-person mindreading is fully compatible with the hybrid approach favored here.

7.7 Egocentrism and Projection

I turn now to the third of the three types of experimental evidence mentioned in section 7.1. This evidence concerns what simulationists call "quarantine violation" and what is called in psychological literature either "projection" or "egocentrism."

There is an extensive literature on egocentric biases in mindreading, and this section and the next one argue that these egocentric biases are best explained by the simulation-plus-projection model. Most of the pertinent studies examine the mindreading of other people, but some concern future (or hypothetical) states of the self. For many purposes, attributing states to others (interpersonal attribution) and attributing future states to oneself (intertemporal attribution) are equivalent.[15] In speaking of "projection" here, I shall somewhat refine the characterization given in section 2.6.

In its most general sense, "projection" refers to ascribing one's own characteristics to others (Kawada, Oettingen, Gollwitzer, and Bargh, 2004). But in the psychological and psychoanalytic literature, "projection" usually refers to something suspect, untoward, or inappropriate. In Freud's case, it referred to a motivational process by which individuals ascribe their own negative characteristics to others while also denying these same characteristics in themselves (Freud, 1915/1953). Our characterization of projection in section 2.6 did not make out projection as a notably suspect or inappropriate process. To bring the notion of projection more in line with its current use in psychology (especially social psychology), perhaps we should understand it more narrowly. In terms of the ST framework, we can profitably understand projection in terms of a quarantine-violating simulation process in which the quarantine violation strongly affects, or contaminates, the resulting attribution. In other words, projection occurs when a genuine, nonpretend state of the attributor seeps into the simulation routine despite its inappropriateness (as judged by information the attributor possesses). This results in an attribution that is inappropriately influenced by the attributor's own current states (genuine, nonpretend states). I won't try to settle the question of when, exactly, being influenced by one's own genuine states is inappropriate. This description, however, helps convey the connotation of *projection* as the term is used in psychology, especially social psychology. The simulation approach makes sense of the projection findings reported here without having to settle the question of how, exactly, appropriateness and inappropriateness should be specified.

The most important point is that projection, in the sense of inappropriate quarantine violation, can account for egocentric bias. I review a body of work about egocentric bias that is readily interpretable within the projection framework. This evidence is divided into three sectors: knowledge, valuations, and feelings.

7.7.1 Knowledge

That young children suffer from egocentric biases is well known from the literature on false-belief tasks. But egocentric biases were demonstrated in other kinds of tasks long before developmentalists became interested in "theory of mind" as a well-defined field of inquiry. Krauss and Glucksberg (1969) had two children sit across from each other with a screen placed between them so they could not see one another. One child was designated the speaker, and the other the listener. The speaker's job was to communicate what objects he or she is selecting so the listener can choose the same objects. The speaker had to calculate the information needed by the listener to mentally pick out the desired object. In effect, this was a mindreading task for the speaker. Krauss and Glucksberg found that most 4- and 5-year-old children provide too little information for the listener to choose the correct object. This is presumably because they have an egocentric tendency to project onto the listener their own knowledge states that the listener lacks. Recent experimental findings on children by Birch and Bloom (2003) yielded very similar results, as reported in section 4.3.

Quite similar findings have been made even for adults. Camerer, Loewenstein, and Weber (1989) investigated situations in which well-informed people were required to predict corporate earnings forecasts by other, less-informed people. The better-informed people stood to gain if they completely discounted or neglected their own knowledge when making predictions about the less-informed people who they *knew* lacked the same knowledge. Nonetheless, the predictors failed to discount their own knowledge completely, so their predictions partly reflected their proprietary knowledge. The inability to purge this knowledge from their mindreading routine was called *the curse of knowledge*.

In a study of adults by Keysar et al. (2003), a "director" in a communication game instructed a participant to move certain objects around in a grid. Participants first hid an object in a bag, such as a roll of tape. The participant knew what was in the bag, but the director didn't know—and the participant knew that the director didn't know. When the director said, "Move the tape," there were (from the participant's perspective) two candidate tapes: a videotape that both participant and director could see and a secret roll of tape in the bag. Which tape should be moved? This was a mindreading task for the participant. If the participant read the director's mental state correctly, the matter was unambiguous. The director couldn't be referring to the tape in the bag, because he didn't know about it, so he must be referring to the videotape. Nonetheless, adult participants behaved "egocentrically," wrongly interpreting what was said in terms of their own knowledge rather than the (lesser) knowledge of the speaker.

A study by Newton (1990; described by Pronin, Puccio, and Ross, 2002) vividly illustrates how difficult it can be to divest oneself of privileged knowledge or experience. Participants were assigned to one of two roles: "tappers" or "listeners." Each tapper was given a list of 25 well-known songs and asked to choose a song, whose rhythm they then tapped out to a listener. The tapper was then asked to assess the likelihood that the listener would correctly identify the song and to estimate the proportion of listeners who would do so, given the same opportunity. Many of Newton's tappers reported hearing the full orchestration of the song while tapping, because they knew the song and how it sounded in all its richness. They were apparently unable to quarantine this knowledge when making their predictions. The tappers' average prediction of listener success was 50 percent, whereas the listeners' actual success rate was less than 3 percent. In trying to take the perspective of their listeners, it appears, tappers projected their own rich embellishment of a song and failed to construct the more impoverished experience of their listeners.

7.7.2 Valuations

Projecting one's own mental states onto others extends to valuations and preferences. Van Boven, Dunning, and Loewenstein (2000) did a study in which certain participants were given Cornell coffee mugs and asked to indicate the lowest price they would sell their mugs for, while other participants didn't receive mugs but were asked to indicate the highest price they would pay to purchase one. The first group, the mug owners, then estimated the highest purchase price of the average buyer, and buyers, the second group, estimated the lowest selling price of the average owner. Because prices reflect valuations, these price estimates were, in effect, mental-state estimates. As previous studies had shown, being endowed with a mug makes a big difference to one's valuation, but this difference—the so-called endowment effect—isn't adequately appreciated. Both owners and buyers underestimated the difference between themselves and their opposite numbers. They apparently projected their own valuations onto their opposite numbers and therefore misestimated how much these participants in opposite roles would set for their buying or selling price. Van Boven et al. called these differences "egocentric empathy gaps." The only manipulation by the investigators that substantially reduced these gaps was the creation of the role of "buyer's agent." Each buyer's agent represented buyers in transactions with owners. Participants assigned to this role who never owned a mug continued to make unduly low offers, whereas buyers' agents endowed with mugs made significantly higher offers. Van Boven, Dunning, and Loewenstein propose that buyers' agents who owned a mug were better able to imagine how they themselves would feel if they were in the other role; in other words, they could better simulate the sellers' valuations.

In this last experiment, attributors tended to assume that their targets shared their valuations. This suggests that default attribution is not confined to default *belief* attribution, as Nichols and Stich (2003) assume. Default attribution of preference was also studied by Ross, Greene, and House (1977). Subjects were asked to wear a large sandwich board reading "Eat at Joe's" while walking around campus for half an hour and later were asked how many of their peers would agree to the same request. Subjects who had agreed predicted that 62 percent of their peers would agree, whereas subjects who had refused predicted that only 33 percent of their peers would agree (and the rest would refuse). Thus, subjects tended to predict that others would feel the same way they did.

Projection of desire or aversion also occurs in intrapersonal mindreading (e.g., self-prediction). Loewenstein, Prelec, and Shatto (1998; cited in Read and Van Leeuwen, 1998) refer to people's inability when in a state of arousal to get into their own future shoes when unaroused, or vice versa. They call this perspective-taking deficiency an "intrapersonal empathy gap." A cold-to-hot empathy gap is the gap between a nonaroused (cold) self and an aroused (hot) self when the cold self is doing the predicting. A typical case occurs when, after a huge dinner, we believe we will never want to eat again and may even announce plans to skip breakfast. The next morning, of course, when hunger returns, our preference is different.

7.7.3 Feelings

Van Boven and Loewenstein (2003) studied the prediction of hypothetical drive states like hunger and thirst. Participants were asked to predict the feelings of a described group of hikers lost in the woods with neither food nor water. They made these predictions either before or after vigorous exercise, which presumably made them thirsty and warm. They were also asked how *they* would feel if they were in the hikers' situation. Participants who had just exercised were more likely to predict that they would be more bothered by thirst than by hunger than participants who had not yet exercised. Similarly, those who had just exercised were more likely to predict that the *hikers* would be more bothered by thirst than by hunger. Participants' combined feelings of thirst and warmth were positively associated with their self-predictions, and their self-predictions reliably indicated their predictions of the hikers' feelings. Van Boven and Loewenstein conclude that people predict how others feel by imagining how they themselves would feel in their situation. People experience empathy gaps in self-predictions; that is, they project their current drives onto the states they would have in the imagined hiking situation. Because this personal perspective taking is also used to predict the feelings of others (the described hikers), there is "social" projection of their own current feelings.

Most, if not all, of the foregoing studies report mindreading episodes that are readily understood in terms of the simulation-plus-projection model. The cases all seem amenable to treatment in terms of simulation that is inappropriately influenced by current states, which bleed into the process as unquarantined inputs. So all of the cases fit the ST story quite comfortably. But, it will be replied, can't they fit a TT story just as well?

Loewenstein and Schkade (1999) discuss different possible accounts of how people predict future feelings, including the use of intuitive theories. Intuitive theories of "hedonics," for example, are extremely common. People have theories about what types of activities make them happy or unhappy (good food, human relationships, money, intoxicants), about how their current experiences will affect their future tastes (satiation, addiction, taste formation), and about serial correlation between moods at different points in time (theories about mood swings and monthly and yearly cycles). Could intuitive theories account for all the egocentric biases reported in this section?

No, that is highly implausible. How could an intuitive theory account for the curse of knowledge? Does everyone afflicted with the curse of knowledge accept as a general proposition that "other people believe whatever I believe"? Do they go on accepting that theory even when specifically informed that others are ignorant of what they themselves know? In typical curse-of-knowledge cases, an attributor is apprised of the fact that certain information in his possession is proprietary, that is, unshared by the target. Does he cling to the indicated theoretical generalization in the face of that fact and innumerable other facts of divergent beliefs? Perhaps people don't accept such a broad and unqualified generalization. Maybe they accept only a qualified, ceteris paribus generalization, like "other things being equal, others believe what I do." When things aren't "equal," such as when somebody lacks epistemic access to facts to which I have access, then he or she may believe something different from what I believe (or lack a relevant belief altogether). The trouble with this approach is that attributors in curse-of-knowledge examples *are* informed that their target lacks epistemic access to the relevant facts. If they were using the qualified generalization, they should not ascribe their own belief to the target. But attributors *do* ascribe their own beliefs to the target, all too frequently. So reasoning from the qualified generalization as the operative intuitive theory does not explain the phenomenon. A better approach, clearly, is a nontheorizing, nonpurely inferential model of mindreading that somehow incorporates people's predilection to inject their own knowledge or other genuine first-order states into mindreading activity. That is the sort of model provided by the simulation-plus-projection theory.

A mixed-method approach that accommodates both simulation and theorizing is becoming increasingly popular. It borrows the idea of "anchoring and adjustment," originally described by Amos Tversky and Daniel Kahneman (1974). Subjects were asked to estimate various quantities stated in percentages, for example, the number of African countries in the United Nations. For each quantity, a number between 0 and 100 was determined by spinning a wheel of fortune in the subjects' presence. Subjects were instructed to estimate the value of the quantity by moving upward or downward from the given number. These arbitrary numbers had a marked effect on estimates. For example, the median estimates of the percentage of African countries in the United Nations were 25 and 45 for groups that received 10 and 65, respectively, as starting points. In recent work on perspective taking, a two-step procedure analogous to anchoring and adjustment has been suggested (Epley, Morewedge, and Keysar, 2004; Epley, Keysar, van Boven, and Gilovich, 2004; Gilovich, Savitzky, and Medvec, 1998). In a form I find particularly promising, a mindreading process might consist of a two- or three-step procedure in which an anchoring phase involves simulation-plus-projection and an adjustment phase uses general theoretical information to revise the initial, default attribution.

A clear example of this approach, applied to self-prediction, is found in Gilbert, Gill, and Wilson (2002). Although Gilbert et al. do not use the term *simulation*, they describe the first phase of their proposed model in the language of "mental proxies." This description corresponds closely to what I have been calling "E-imagination."

> If we wish to predict how we would feel upon finding our spouse in bed with the letter carrier on New Year's Eve, we might imagine the event and then take note of how we react to the mental image. Because real and imagined events activate many of the same neural and psychological processes . . . reactions to imaginary events can provide useful information about one's likely reaction to the events themselves. (2002: 431)

We can reformulate Gilbert et al.'s suggestion in ST terminology. A person E-imagines observing the hypothetical event, feeds this imagined observation into an affect-generating mechanism, and lets it operate on the input to produce affective outputs, for instance, waves of jealousy and anger. The affective reactions experienced are then used to predict how one would react in the hypothetical situation. So far, this sounds like a page out of an ST textbook.

Gilbert et al. call the output reactions "proxy reactions." They do not hold, however, that predictors make unmodified use of proxy reactions. When trying to predict real (as opposed to hypothetical) future events, people realize that the events to be predicted are temporally removed from the current situation, so they commonly use a more complex, three-step procedure. They first imagine events without temporal information ("atemporal representation"). Next they use their hedonic reactions to these mental images ("proxy reactions") as the basis for a preliminary prediction. Third, they correct or adjust their preliminary forecast by explicitly considering the target event's temporal location ("temporal correction"). The adjustment step, of course, introduces an element of theorizing, so the entire Gilbert et al. model is a simulation-theory blend. That is perfectly congenial to the hybrid approach endorsed here.

7.8 The Neuropsychology of Quarantine

The previous section reported studies of a behavioral nature; this section looks at neuropsychological evidence. According to ST, third-person mindreading involves taking (or trying to take) the target's perspective. Accuracy of perspective taking, however, involves two things: First, one must E-imagine states of the target that differ from one's own; second, one must quarantine states of one's own that differ from the target's. Section 7.7 explained many cases of erroneous mindreading in terms of quarantine failure, as befits ST. TT, however, might try to explain these errors in terms of bad or misapplied theories. Is there additional evidence to support ST over TT here?

At the level of the brain, what would quarantine consist in? Quarantine prevents something from happening that might otherwise occur; specifically, it prevents one's own states from being projected onto the target. In neural terms, such prevention is *inhibition*. It might be described as "inhibiting the self-perspective." If simulation is a major facet of third-person mindreading, successful mindreading should involve inhibition of the self-perspective. As a corollary, someone impaired in the ability to inhibit the self-perspective should have trouble producing accurate mindreading. This is what ST predicts, and this prediction is dramatically confirmed in the case of a particular stroke patient.

Samson, Apperly, Kathirgamanathan, and Humphreys (2005) report the case of patient WBA, who suffered a lesion to the right inferior and middle frontal gyri extending into the right superior temporal gyrus. WBA's brain lesion includes a region that Vogeley et al. (2001) highlighted as possibly sustaining the ability to inhibit one's own perspective. A neuropsychological assessment of WBA revealed continuing problems in executive control, especially inhibition. A series of tests Samson et al. did on WBA strongly indicate that the damage WBA suffered to the process of inhibiting self-perspective led to egocentric errors in many (third-person) mindreading tasks.

The first tests administered by Samson et al. concerned third-person belief attribution. They used two tasks based on nonverbal videos. In the first task, a participant had to work out which of two boxes contains a hidden green object. He is told that a woman in the video will help him find where the green object is. The video shows the woman watching as a man places the green object in one of the boxes. However, the camera doesn't show which box the green object is placed in. The woman then leaves the room and while she is away, the man swaps the boxes. When the woman returns, she points to one of the boxes. To find out in which box the green object is located, a viewer must infer that the woman has a false belief, and therefore the viewer must point to the box opposite to the one the woman points to. In this task, the participant has no idea where the green object is located before inferring that the woman has a false belief. The task generates a discrepant perspective between the participant and the woman similar to standard false-belief tasks, but the participant has no knowledge of where the object is to cause interference. So Samson et al. call this first task a "low inhibition" false-belief task. The second task given to WBA was a "high inhibition" false-belief task. Here the man in the video moves the green object from one box to the other in full view of the participant, ensuring that the participant knows the object's new location. When asked which box the woman will open first, the participant now has to inhibit his own knowledge of the object's new location. It was only the high-inhibition task that WBA failed, thereby pinpointing the nature of his problem.

WBA scored 11/12 on the low-inhibition false-belief trials, significantly above chance. By contrast, he scored only 1/12 on false-belief trials in the high-inhibition false-belief task, significantly below chance. This indicates that he was not guessing but, rather, was systematically predicting the woman's behavior on the basis of his own knowledge of reality rather than on the basis of her (false) belief. In the high-inhibition task, he dramatically failed to inhibit his knowledge.

Similar tests were administered to WBA to check his ability to attribute visual experiences, desires, and emotions to someone else. In a visual perspective-taking task (adapted from Langdon and Coltheart, 2001), WBA sat at a table, with four colored circles in the center and one person at each side, and was asked how someone around the table would see the circle display. Over 20 trials, WBA responded according to his own visual experience on all but one occasion, irrespective of the point of view he was asked to take; there were 70 percent egocentric errors. This was considerably worse than that of three age-matched control subjects, who made between 20 percent and 0 percent egocentric errors. In an analogous social perspective-taking task, WBA had to simulate four persons (including himself) watching a football match between WBA's favorite team and their local rivals. The three other persons were described as having preferences different from his own. As the match unfolded, WBA was asked questions about the various persons' emotions and desires. WBA's overall score was quite poor (21/40 correct). When attributing an emotion or desire to himself, he scored 8/10, but when he had to give a perspective other than his own, he made 15/27 errors (56 percent errors), 14 of which were egocentric responses. Thus, WBA clearly displayed a selective deficit in inhibiting his own perspective, supporting the hypothesis that the right frontal lobe (maybe especially the right inferior gyrus) is necessary for self-perspective inhibition.

Of crucial importance, the evidence from WBA appears to demonstrate that the root of at least *some* egocentric errors in mindreading is failure to inhibit, or quarantine, self-perspective. This, of course, is precisely ST's story. Because Samson et al.'s evidence about WBA, along with evidence from Vogeley et al. (2001), points to a particular brain region as responsible for this function, it is natural to infer that inhibition of self-perspective is a vital aspect of mindreading.

Can TT accommodate this finding? The classical TT story about false-belief task errors is entirely different: It concerns a conceptual or representational deficit vis-à-vis false belief. This is nowhere in the right vicinity relative to the present findings. The other principal TT tool for explaining mindreading errors is poor intuitive theories. But WBA's problem, obviously, has nothing to do with a poor intuitive theory. It involves damage to a critical ability to inhibit self-perspective. The pivotal nature of this ability is central to ST, but not at all to TT. Because TT doesn't hold that accurate mindreading crucially adverts to one's own states (including one's own desires or emotions), inability to inhibit these states should make no difference under TT.[16]

Finally, proponents of TT might try to argue that beliefs about one's own current states are an important part of the process of inferring someone else's states. By their lights, what I have been calling the quarantining of *states* is really a matter of inhibiting *beliefs* about those states, that is, keeping such metabeliefs from playing a role in inferences about the target's states. WBA's problem is a loss in this inhibitory capacity. This maneuver, however, is at variance with characteristic or natural versions of TT. True, some theory-theorists appeal to "like-me" inferences as a basis for constructing theories about others (e.g., Meltzoff; see section 4.8). But it is rare for theory-theorists to argue that normal mentalizing inferences involve beliefs about currently active states of the self. Indeed, many theory-theorists are at pains to reject any such reliance on the self. Second, the maneuver now being considered requires the theory-theorist to say that mentalizers always have *accurate* metabeliefs about their current states. Why must they say this? In acts of projection, an *actual* state of the self is projected onto the target, whether the state is an evaluation state, a somatic state, or whatever. Theory-theorists now try to accommodate this by saying that the attributor metarepresents such states, and those metarepresentations influence his attribution. For this maneuver to work, however, the metabeliefs must be accurate; if they were inaccurate, attributions to the target would be biased toward other states, not toward the attributor's actual states. But that isn't the empirical finding. Now, how can the assumption of metarepresentational accuracy be rationalized under TT? TT has no account of first-person attribution that implies such systematic accuracy. Paradigm TT holds that first-person attribution is an affair involving complex inferences, and why should they be accurate? Finally, it is foreign to TT's spirit to assume that third-person attribution tasks require regular monitoring of all of one's own current states. Thus, TT cannot easily or naturally explain widespread egocentrism.

7.9 Input Inadequacy

In section 7.6, I argued that the existence of rampant egocentrism, such as the endowment effect, fits the ST story. But others have invoked similar materials to argue *against* ST. Prediction failure in the endowment effect, for instance, has been cited as a problem for ST. Nichols, Stich, and Leslie (1995) cite an early decision-prediction experiment concerning the endowment effect by Loewenstein and Adler (1995). A large group of (nonendowed) subjects examined a mug engraved with the school logo. Half of the subjects were asked to imagine that they possessed the mug on display and to predict whether they would exchange the mug for various amounts of money. All subjects were then presented with a mug and told that they could actually exchange the mug for cash. The results showed that predicting subjects had made substantial underpredictions. The mean predicted exchange price was $3.73, but the mean actual exchange price for the predictors was $5.40. The mean actual exchange price for subjects who didn't make a prediction was even higher: $6.46. Nichols et al. now pose a problem for ST:

> It is hard to see how an advocate of simulation theory can offer a principled explanation of the results. Obviously, the mistaken prediction cannot be the result of a difference between the psychological mechanisms of the predictor and the target since in this experiment the subjects are predicting their own decisions. Nor is it plausible for the simulation theorist to suppose that the Pretend Belief and Desire Generator would have a problem generating the pretend beliefs and desires that result from being told that one now actually owns the mug. For if the pretence mechanism that the simulation theorist posits can't handle simple cases

like pretending that one has been given a mug one has had ample opportunity to examine, then the pretence mechanisms must be very fallible indeed. And if that is the case, then it is a mystery why our predictions turn out to be correct as often as they do. For the theory theorist, by contrast, there is no puzzle about how the results are to be explained. Folk psychology [understood as a set of naïve theories] just doesn't include any information about the endowment effect. So when the effect plays a major role in determining behavior, predictions based on folk psychology get it wrong. (1995: 443–444)

Numerous other examples might be given in which a TT explanation looks more promising than an ST explanation, because it seems implausible that either differences in mechanism or inadequate inputs can account for the errors. Introductory psychology classes commonly describe Stanley Milgram's (1963) famous experiment, in which subjects were asked to administer increasingly severe electrical shocks to another person. Students are invited to predict what they themselves would do in that situation. They usually predict that they would not obey the "authorities." Judging by the results of the original experiment, however, these predictions must mostly be wrong. Can the problem here be a failure of inputs, the students' failure to imagine being in the situation? If not, the prediction must be the product of a bad theory, not a bad simulation. Rebecca Saxe (2005) cites this example, among others, as a presumptive case of theorizing rather than simulating.

I would not be surprised if many such predictions *are* based on theory rather than simulation. This is no embarrassment to the present hybrid position, which acknowledges that many instances of mindreading are executed wholly by theory rather than simulation. Unquestionably, we all have numerous theories—at least "mini-theories"—about our own psychological changes, as well as the changes of others. Every parent has fairly definite ideas of when their child gets hungry, fussy, or excited. (These are individualized generalizations, it might be said, rather than theories, but in any case, they're not simulations.) So I don't take issue with the claim that many alleged cases of theory-based mindreading in the literature are probably correct. At the same time, one shouldn't underestimate ST's ability to explain mindreading errors in terms of pretend input mistakes. This possibility holds for at least some of the cases cited by Nichols, Stich, and Leslie, as well as Saxe.

Pretend inputs can be inaccurate in two ways, through either an *excess* or a *deficiency* of inputs. The song tappers example illustrates the problem of excess. Deficiencies are harder to pinpoint, especially where an observer doesn't know exactly what mentally transpires in the target. What thoughts led Milgram's original subjects to obey the authorities in charge of the experiment? That is an open question. Whatever they were, students sitting in a classroom would not mentally reenact all the relevant features of those subjects' thoughts. It isn't easy to reenact the subtle psychological associations of an authority-laden situation when one's actual setting is entirely different. So it is quite plausible that students in the classroom do make self-predictions by E-imagination; it's just that their E-imaginative efforts are woefully deficient. The same might hold in endowment-effect cases. Recall that the only manipulation by Van Boven et al. (2000) that produced a reduction in egocentric empathy gaps was allowing buyers' agents to experience mug ownership. Why did mug ownership improve their predictions of sellers' behavior? Perhaps by making it easier to approximate the inputs sellers used in their decisions.

In reflecting on these matters, one mustn't conflate E-imagination with supposition. How hard can it be, Nichols, Stich, and Leslie exclaim, to pretend that one owns a mug? Pretend ownership is such an easy input, it seems, that if such pretense still leads to failure, simulation must be a very poor method. It then becomes a mystery why mindreading should so often succeed. One mistake lurking here is the possible confusion of E-imagination with supposition. Sure, it's easy to *suppose* one owns a mug. But supposition isn't E-imagination, or re-creation. Merely supposing one owns a mug doesn't re-create the psychological circumstances operative in a decision-making task. Analogously, I can easily suppose that I am now living in ancient Troy and observing Helen. What is not so easy is to create an accurate visualization of her. The requisite visual information isn't stored in my head. So although I can *try* to visualize Helen, I can't make the visualization faithful to a genuine seeing of her. This doesn't mean that my powers of visualization are *never*, or *rarely*, up to a simulative challenge. The powers are fine if they are accompanied by suitable knowledge or experience to guide the visualizing act. So Nichols et al. are not entitled to say that if simulation doesn't work in the mug ownership case, then it must be a terribly poor method in general.

This line of explanation critically appeals to information: Missing information often prevents an accurate (enough) simulation. But isn't information something characteristic of TT? Yes, but two points are relevant. First, although it is information, it isn't *lawlike* information of the kind distinctive of TT. Second, acknowledging that accuracy of inputs requires informational guidance doesn't undercut the simulational aspect of the cognitive performances in question; the inputs are inputs *for simulation*. The approach to ST adopted in this book does not try to keep information out of the processing picture.

7.10 Assigning Contents to Others

Discussions of high-level mindreading typically focus on "whole" propositional attitudes, that is, attitude-content pairs. This section is devoted to contents only. I explore the way(s) that mindreaders construct contents for others' intentional states. Do they theorize or simulate? I defend a hybrid treatment, but one that emphasizes simulation as the default procedure. Our fundamental, default procedure is to project our own basic concepts and combinatorial principles onto others.[17]

There could be cognizers whose interpersonal imputation of content proceeds purely by theorizing. For example, there might be a race of super-theorizers whose own conceptual repertoire they consider proprietary. They approach the conceptual repertoire of others "from a distance," prepared to impute radically different conceptual characteristics to others, even elementary concepts and principles of conceptual combination. A similar possibility is a field anthropologist who scrupulously keeps her own ontology out of the picture when approaching an alien culture's ontology. She doesn't assume that their ontology matches her own.

Is all this really possible? To make a coherent case for it, we may have to endow our supertheorizers with a philosophicoscientific theory of mental content. The theory would specify what content is in general and under what circumstances a creature has a mental state with identifiable content. Using this theory, the supertheorizers would specify satisfaction conditions for the possession of thought contents, even contents they themselves don't (even *can't*) possess. The theory might say that if a creature has cognitive faculties F and G and uses them in certain ways, it will have a thought content "θ," a content they themselves cannot instantiate because they lack faculties F or G.[18]

Although such supertheorizers are logically possible, *we* are not like them. We do not approach mindreading targets in so theorizing a spirit. Our default procedure is to mindread in a fundamentally biased, egocentric fashion. We project our own conceptual, combinatorial, and even ontological dispositions onto others, at least our *basic* conceptual, combinatorial, and ontological dispositions. This is not our universal practice, but it is our default practice.

I do not hold that humans make *no* use of theorizing in content ascription. On the contrary, they use a fair amount of theorizing (in a liberal sense of that term). Our fundamental or default practices, however, are of a projective, or simulative, character. Absent special circumstances, we presume our own mental contents to be suitable in kind to match those of our targets.[19] Of course, we don't succeed in matching a target's propositional representations unless we combine the right concepts in the right ways. The matching task is never trivial. But our default procedure is to *try*, at least, to capture a target's (propositional) content by attributing elements of our own thought contents. A radical theorizer wouldn't even attempt this.

These ideas can be amplified with the help of an example from Dan Sperber (1997). A person sometimes experiences the need for a concept unavailable in her own mental lexicon. For example, a thinker may encounter an expression in a public language, the intended meaning of which remains obscure. Young Lisa hears her science teacher say:

(7.1)   There are millions of suns in the universe.

Until that moment, Lisa understood *sun* as a proper name referring to a single object. She does not know what *sun* might mean as a common noun. She guesses that suns are things like *the* sun, but also that the teacher means something more specific than this, which she doesn't fully comprehend. Thus, we might ascribe to Lisa the following belief:

(7.2)   My teacher thinks that there are millions of "suns" in the universe, whatever the teacher means by "sun."

In thinking (7.2) Lisa metarepresents the teacher's belief. But because she doesn't possess the exact concept the teacher expresses with the word *sun*, and knows this, she cannot metarepresent his belief by *replicating* its content. She can still metarepresent the content by using a quotational device to supplement her mental lexicon. In Lisa's thought, *sun* metarepresents the yet-to-be developed concept with a mental placeholder. She needs this placeholder because she doesn't (yet) have the conceptual means of expressing the teacher's concept in her own repertoire. She can think *about* the teacher's concept, and hence about his entire thought content, without being able to think *with* that concept. Thus, metarepresentation can be accomplished in two different ways: either by replicating a target's thought content or by referring to it with a definite description ("the concept my teacher expresses with the word *sun*"). The latter is a theorizing way of metarepresenting the content.[20]

As this example illustrates, we sometimes, perhaps often, use a theorizing method to metarepresent a target's intentional contents. But we don't always use such a method, nor is it our default. Our default procedure is attempted replication or simulation. (Recall that our characterization of ST in chapter 2 does not require successful replication, even in "relevant respects," only attempted simulation.)

Sperber's example is of a piece with concepts generally known as "deferential concepts," a notion made prominent by discussions of Hilary Putnam (1975) and Tyler Burge (1979, 1982), in which people use terms that rely on the linguistic expertise of others. Users of these terms need not think of themselves as possessing the same concepts as the experts. They may understand the terms, at least in part, by way of definite descriptions of the kind just illustrated. If the concepts they associate with these terms are then used to metarepresent another person's thought content, this is a theorizing form of metarepresentation. The simulation-of-content thesis I am advancing here does not extend to deferential concepts. The simulation thesis I wish to advance only applies to nondeferential concepts, especially basic concepts and basic modes of conceptual combination.

To illustrate the role of simulation in content attribution, consider basic ontological concepts, for example, the concept of a material "object." Contemporary psychologists have propounded theories of object representation. According to the dominant theory, due primarily to Elizabeth Spelke, the concept of a whole object is the concept of a connected and bounded region of matter that maintains its connectedness and boundaries when in motion, and which is "maximal" in the sense that it is not a proper part of another self-connected object (Spelke, 1990, 1994; Soja, Carey, and Spelke, 1991; Casati, 2003). Whole objects so characterized are not the only things the human mind recognizes as "things" or "entities," but people have a strong representational bias or preference for whole objects. They "prefer" to represent the world in terms of such items, as evidenced in children's early word learning (Bloom, 2000, chapter 4). Very young children have a bias toward interpreting new words they hear as whole-object names, such as names for rabbits rather than rabbit ears. They also learn words that do not name solid, whole objects, for example, substance names (*water*), part names (*ear*), verbs (*run*), and adjectives (*yellow*). But there seems to be a whole-object bias, which isn't limited to word learning. In parsing the physical objects in a visual scene, a preference is shown for Spelke-objects. If asked to count the number of "objects" in a (fairly empty) room, people would not be stupefied, because counting by Spelke-object criteria makes it manageable. It wouldn't be manageable if one were equally disposed to count by any random criterion, including one that admits as objects arbitrary parts of Spelke-objects, or mereological sums of Spelke-objects. People are not so disposed, however. They have a natural bias toward whole objects.

Because all people have the same conceptual biases, they substantially share the same basic, intuitive ontology. In principle, creatures with the same basic ontology could use a theorizing method to ascribe contents to others, but, I submit, we are not like that. Our default tendency, when assigning contents to others, is to prefer whole-object concepts, just as whole-object concepts are preferred in our own thinking. In other words, our ontological preferences are projected onto others.[21] Moreover, they are initially projected not only onto people but also onto animals or anything else we mindread. So projection isn't the product of a special theory that other *people* resemble us in their basic ontological categories. Rather, our mentalizing propensity includes a default propensity to project our preferred categories onto any target.

Theory-theorists might respond by claiming that our basic ontology is subserved by a tacit theory that belongs to our cognitive system. The theory might consist in a set of principles, including the following:

P₁: Prefer a parsing of the world into whole objects rather than arbitrary parts of whole objects or arbitrary mereological sums of whole objects.

Mereological sums are entities composed of any random constituents, including spatiotemporally disconnected constituents like a chair and a bowl. Another principle of such a tacit ontological theory of ontology might be:

P_2: Prefer a parsing of the world into "good" parts rather than "bad" parts of whole objects.

"Good" parts of a body include an ear, a leg, or a head; a "bad" part would be a leg-plus-adjacent-third-of-the-torso. Precise criteria for part goodness would be included in a full articulation of the tacit theory.

Grant, for the sake of argument, that each person's cognitive system includes such tacit principles. This implies nothing about how to treat *other* people's ontological predispositions. What would be relevant to *folk psychology*, or *mentalizing*, would be a tacit theory about the ontological preferences of people in general, not merely principles for doing one's own ontologizing. Here is a sample law that might belong to such a theory:

L: In their material-object ontologizing, people in general prefer whole objects (Spelke-objects) both to arbitrary mereological sums and to arbitrary parts of whole objects.

Do people possess such a law? Well, how might they have come to possess it? Phylogeny and ontogeny are the obvious possibilities, which we consider in reverse order.

If such a law were learned in ontogeny, how would it be learned? How would one learn that others have a whole-object preference unless one were already disposed to believe this, or to project one's own ontological preferences? This is very close to Quine's (1960) famous "gavagai" problem. What behavioral evidence, he asked, would show an unbiased interpreter (a field linguist) that a speaker's word *gavagai* means *rabbit* rather than, say, *undetached rabbit part*? Would the speaker's behavior, verbal or nonverbal, resolve the issue? Quine despaired of the possibility that science could determine a speaker's meaning (or intention) and concluded that there is no fact of the matter to be determined. Others have resisted this conclusion, dismissing it as a consequence of Quine's excessive behaviorism. But it remains doubtful that we could learn the contents of a speaker's utterances, or infer the specific contents of their mental states, without bootstrapping from own content preferences (as ST proposes).[22]

Perhaps the folk-psychological law is hardwired rather than learned. Did evolution deposit such a folk-psychological law in our brains? The suggestion would be that evolution deposited *two* types of laws or principles in our brains, one to guide our own thinking in a whole-object-biased way and another to interpret other people's thinking as having the same whole-object bias. Is this a plausible "strategy" or "path" for evolution to have followed? Clearly, a more economical strategy was available. Once evolution had endowed our own thought patterns with a whole-object bias, why bother to program our brains with a second set of identical principles for mindreading the whole-object bias in others? Why not program our brains to project our own thought patterns onto others? This would yield the same result far more parsimoniously. That *this* is what evolution did is the simulationist hypothesis—a vastly more plausible hypothesis.

It is noteworthy that Quine himself was a simulationist about folk attribution of intentional states. He appealed to simulation—"empathy" was his term—to explain how we ascribe contents both in indirect quotation and in mentalistic idioms. Here is a passage from *Word and Object* (1960) that illustrates his approach:

> In indirect quotation we project ourselves into what, from his remarks and other indications, we imagine the speaker's state of mind to have been, and then we say what, in our language, is natural and relevant for us in the state thus feigned. . . . Correspondingly for the other propositional attitudes, for all of them can be thought of as involving something like quotation of one's own imagined verbal response to an imagined situation. . . . We project ourselves even into what from his behavior we imagine a mouse's state of mind to have been, and dramatize it as a belief, wish, or striving, verbalized as seems relevant and natural to us in the state thus feigned. (1960: 219)

Of course, Quine was also a persistent critic of content attribution, of the "intentional idiom" in general. His criticism, however, seems to have been predicated on ST (though not under that label). He contrasted the "essentially dramatic idiom" of propositional-attitude talk with the "scientific spirit" of behaviorist psychology (1960: 219), preferring the latter for both science and ontology. His simulationism led him to conclude that intentional ascription is a folk enterprise in a pejorative sense, not a proper exercise of scientific psychology. Quine's disciples and interpreters typically portray him as a charity-rationality theorist, highlighting his remarks about charity in radical translation. But the textual evidence indicates that his leanings were more simulationist.[23]

Quine exegesis aside, ample considerations support simulation as people's naïve approach to content metarepresentation, though this leaves room for a nonnegligible strand of theorizing as well, as explained previously.

7.11 Predicting Inference and Choice

Predicting people's beliefs and choices is a large part of mindreading. Many beliefs are formed by inference, so predicting these beliefs involves predicting inferences that lead to them. How is this task executed?

Start with a special case of inference prediction: predicting grammaticality judgments. If you were given a list of grammatical and ungrammatical sentences and asked to predict other English speakers' judgments of their grammaticality, how would you proceed? Paul Harris (1992) posed this question and answered in a way that seems right: You would use simulation. You would make the grammaticality judgments yourself and ascribe the same judgments to others.

How might a theory-theorist respond to this case? A theory-theorist might contend that, surely, all of one's own grammaticality judgments are made by means of a tacit theory, a theory of English grammar. Assume this is right. Still, a tacit theory of English grammar is not a *folk-psychological* theory. Its subject matter is syntax, not beliefs about syntax. Modularism in particular should acknowledge this. Grammaticality and beliefs about grammaticality are different domains, so they should have different modules devoted to them, and different theories.

A simulationist can live with the suggestion that grammaticality judgments are guided by a theory, or set of principles. In the previous section we argued that people assign basic ontological contents to other people's intentional states by deploying their own ontological preference principles. This is a simulational procedure. Similarly, as Harris speculated, people would probably predict other people's grammaticality judgments by running the examples through their own principles of grammar—again, a simulational method of judgment prediction.

The same treatment seems plausible for inference predictions. If I know what Johnny believes, how would I predict the further conclusions (or retractions) he would draw from these beliefs? As in the grammatical example, I may have a tacit set of principles that guide my own inferential steps. But these principles don't constitute a folk-psychological theory; they don't tell me how people in general make inferences. They only instruct me what conclusions to infer from various premises, not what other people will infer from those premises. In other words, they are the rules that drive, or govern, the operating procedures of my own *reasoning mechanism*. It is possible, of course, to apply these principles to the task of predicting other people's inferences. But such an application would simply consist in a simulation routine. It would be a familiar matter of pretending to have the specified beliefs of the target and feeding them into my reasoning mechanism to see what it outputs. Then I attribute that output to the target.

Interestingly, Nichols and Stich, who are erstwhile theory-theorists, now endorse essentially this simulationist story of inference prediction (Nichols and Stich, 2003: 123, 135). They first posit an inference mechanism to do the normal job of executing inferences. Next they posit a possible world box (PWB) that is initially used to run pretend scenarios but is also co-opted to mindread others by creating models of them in the PWB. Inference prediction is then explained by the inference mechanism operating on a model of the target's belief states built up in the mindreader's PWB. As they acknowledge, "This is, of course, a . . . process of a piece with those proposed by simulation theorists" (2003: 123).

Next let's turn to the prediction of choice. Just as people plausibly use their own ontological preferences to assign ontological content to others' intentional states, and use their own reasoning procedures to predict others' inferences, it is plausible that their default method in predicting others' choices is to rely on their own criteria of choice. Let's examine a well-documented pattern of choice to see how the simulation approach compares with theory-theory and rationality theory in the matter of prediction.

Kahneman and Tversky (1984) gave subjects the following problem:

> Imagine that you face the following pair of concurrent decisions. First examine both decisions, then indicate the options you prefer.
>   Decision (i). Choose between:
>
> A.   a sure gain of $240
> B.   25% chance to gain $1000 and 75% chance to gain nothing
>
> Decision (ii). Choose between:
>
> C.   a sure loss of $750
> D.   75% chance to lose $1000 and 25% chance to lose nothing

In decision (i), 84 % of the subjects chose A and 16 % chose B. In decision (ii), 87 % chose D and 13 % chose C. How would subjects respond if asked to predict the choices others would make? It's a good bet they would predict these same choices.[24] These are the choices they themselves would make (if they are typical), and they would project those choices onto others. This, of course, is what ST says. Assuming this is right, is it also what TT and RT would lead us to expect?

Begin with RT. RT holds that attributors interpret targets' beliefs in terms of logical constraints like consistency and deductive closure. What about attributions concerning decision and choice? A widely endorsed precept of formal rationality theory is the dominance requirement: An option should never be preferred to one that dominates it. Thus, if people predict choices by the constraints of rationality, they would never predict (or would be reluctant to predict) that people choose both A over B and D over C. This is because the conjunction of A and D is dominated by the conjunction B and C. Adding the sure gain of $240 (option A) to option D yields 25 % chance to win $240 and 75 % chance to lose $760. Similarly, adding the sure loss of $750 (option C) to option B yields 25 % chance to win $250 and 75 % chance to lose $750. Thus, choosing A and D over B and C is a violation of dominance in a set of concurrent decisions.[25] According to RT, this is not a prediction attributors would make about people's choices. But it's a good bet it *is* the prediction they would make.

Rationality theorists may respond that people don't predict choices in terms of genuine rationality but in terms of what they *think* is rational.[26] They're good at predicting others' choices because what the predictors think is rational corresponds to what their targets think is rational. This RT story, however, collapses into ST. The new RT story is that predictors project their own thinking about the target's choice situation onto the target, but this is just equivalent to the simulation story. Proponents of RT might respond: "No, we don't mean that predictors imagine making the choice themselves. We mean that they consult tacit *principles* of rationality; it's just that their principles aren't very sound from a normative standpoint." But what is meant in saying that these tacit principles are "consulted"? Doesn't it come down to their using a practical reasoning mechanism, or choice mechanism, that is governed by these principles? How does this differ from the ST story?

Turn now to TT. Do people have a folk-psychological theory of choice that could predict such decisions? Prospect theory is the theory of choice Kahneman and Tversky developed by considering such cases as the foregoing (see Kahneman and Tversky, 1979). It is widely regarded as a highly successful theory (good enough for a Nobel Prize). If it is indeed correct, then the choosing mind operates in accordance with prospect theory. But is it part of the folk-psychologizing mind to theorize that prospect theory describes naïve choice or preference? In other words, do naïve agents not only operate in accordance with prospect theory in making their own choices but also invoke this theory when considering how other humans operate? Prospect theory says that people are risk averse in choices involving sure gains and risk seeking in choices involving sure losses. Do people also *folk-theorize* that they and their kin are risk averse in choices involving sure gains and risk seeking in choices involving sure losses? Does either evolution or ontogeny conspire to make naïve mentalizers "rediscover" these features of prospect theory? Neither possibility has much plausibility. If people correctly predict such choices when given examples, their ability to do so must derive from applying their own operating principles and projecting its outputs onto their targets. In other words, their ability must derive from simulation.

7.12 Retrodictive Mindreading

As first noted in chapter 2, an attributor's main items of evidence for many target states are causal effects of those states, so the attributor's mind must proceed from known effects to sought-after causes. First-person verbal reports are one type of example. The attributor works backward from the target's verbal utterance to a prior mental state. Similarly, when an attribution is based on nonverbal behavior, the attributor makes a retrodictive or explanatory transition from the behavior to a preceding state. Can simulation figure in such retrodictions? Unless a mental process can run backward, simulation does not seem applicable. Simulation works in predictive cases because the attributor starts with simulated input states, lets a simulating process proceed forward from those initial states to an output state, and uses that output to predict. But how can simulation work when the mindreader must work backward from a known output to to-be-determined inputs? In chapter 6, special reasons were given why reverse mental processes are plausible for facial expression of emotion, but these reasons don't generalize. Mental processes are by-and-large unidirectional.

There are still prospects for simulation to play a role in retrodiction, via the generate-and-test strategy. The "generate" stage produces hypothesized states or state combinations that might be responsible for the observed (or inferred) evidence. Hypothesis generation is presumably executed by non-simulative methods. The "test" stage consists of *trying out* one or more of the hypothesized state combinations to see if it would yield the observed evidence. This stage might well employ simulation. One E-imagines being in the hypothesized combination of states, lets an appropriate mechanism operate on them, and sees whether the generated upshot matches the observed upshot.

One problem with the generate-and-test strategy is an excess of state combinations that might yield a given upshot. How can a cognitive system handle them all? Can it limit the search space? This is presumably accomplished by theorizing methods, perhaps with the help of prior simulations. So it seems likely that a hybrid method is essential to the generate-and-test strategy (as we remarked in connection with Model 1 in chapter 6).

I know of no theoretical analysis or experimental evidence that bears directly on simulation's role in retrodictive mental attribution. But there are other facets of cognition that may constitute instructive precedents for the generate-and-test strategy. I shall draw attention to psycholinguistics, where one pair of researchers find evidence for generate-and-test models of language comprehension. This is not a mindreading domain per se but close enough, perhaps, to be instructive.

Townsend and Bever (2001) propose an analysis-by-synthesis model of sentence comprehension, in the tradition of the Halle and Stevens (1964) model for speech recognition. The essential idea in Halle and Stevens's approach was that an initial preliminary analysis of the input is made, which then triggers the mechanism that generates grammatically possible forms in the language. The candidate output of the grammar is compared with the speech input. When there is a match, the system assigns the grammatical representation used to provide the match. Townsend and Bever articulate the gist of this approach with the help of a scrambled egg metaphor.

Producing speech is like taking an ordered lineup of different kinds of eggs, breaking them so that each overlaps with its neighbors, then scrambling them up a bit so there is a continuous egg belt, and then cooking them. Comprehension is analogous to the problem of figuring out how many eggs there were originally, exactly where each was located, and what kind it was.... [T]he analysis-by-synthesis model starts with a particular hypothetical egg sequence, scrambles and cooks them in a virtual kitchen, and then compares the resulting virtual omelet with the actual input. When the virtual omelet matches the actual omelet, the input and cooking sequence producing the virtual omelet is confirmed as the correct analysis. (2001: 160–161)

According to the Townsend-Bever version of analysis by synthesis, devices that exploit associative information of the sort emphasized in connectionist models are used to construct an initial quick-and-dirty parse. This first stage of the process can be considered "theorizing." After this "likely" meaning is assigned, the next stage is to map the meaning onto a syntactic structure. Finally, that structure is used to derive a surface structure, which is compared to the original (stored) sequential input. This final step is the "simulation" stage of the model.

Townsend and Bever offer a variety of empirical evidence to support their approach, most of which is too technical for present purposes. One non-technical example draws on Miller and Isard's (1963) finding that words forming a sentence sound clearer and are more resistant to interference than the same words in a mere list or an ungrammatical sentence. Townsend and Bever claim that the analysis-by-synthesis model explains this. When a sentence is understood, the synthesis (simulation) stage involves an *extra* representation of the surface form, used for comparison to the stored input. The presence of two representations, they say, explains the relative percep-tual clarity that Miller and Isard found: Words in sentences sound clearer because they have two mental resonances, not one.

7.13 A Rival Conception of the Simulation Routine

This final section of the chapter considers some contrasts between the version of simulation theory advocated here and the one proposed by Robert Gordon (1995b; 1996). One purpose of this discussion is to foreshadow and defend the upcoming treatments of other mentalizing topics in later chapters, specifically, first-person introspective attribution (chapter 9) and mental concepts (chap-ter 10).

Gordon (1995b) construes the *standard* version of ST (which he opposes) as involving three elements:

1. an analogical inference from oneself to others;
2. premised on introspectively based ascriptions of mental states to oneself;

3. requiring prior possession of the concepts of the mental states ascribed (1995b: 53).

Gordon thinks ST should distance itself from all these elements. The analogical inference element, he fears, threatens to make ST collapse into TT, and the doctrine of introspection burdens ST with a philosophically controversial position. His rationale for opposing the concept-possession element is elusive, but he clearly resists it.

Gordon proposes an alternative version of ST not hobbled by these commitments. On the usual version of ST, when I set out to predict your decision, I imagine myself in your situation. That leads to a pretend decision to do A. I introspect this pretend decision state and "transfer" it to you, assuming you are like me. This formulation, says Gordon, allows ST to drift into problematic waters.

When I simulate you, I do not imagine *myself* in your situation. Instead, what I imagine requires an "egocentric shift" or a "recentering" of the egocentric map. In imagination, the referent of the pronoun *I* becomes you. Such recentering is a "transformation" of myself into you, much as actors become the characters they play. "Once a personal *transformation* has been accomplished, there is no remaining task of mentally *transferring* a state from one person to another, no question of *comparing* [the target] to myself" (1995b: 56). According to Gordon, when I recenter my egocentric map on you, I do not consider what I, AIG, would think, want, or decide. I consider what *you* would do, which frees me from the task of making an analogical inference from me to you.

In evaluating Gordon's proposal, we must distinguish two questions: (a) Who is the *subject* of the imagining states and (b) what are the *contents* of the imagining states—including the labels or tags associated with them? The imagining states are, of course, actual states: The mentalizer actually engages in imagination or pretense. Moreover, the mentalizer is the subject of those states. She cannot literally transform herself, metaphysically, into the target of her attribution. She remains the same individual throughout the simulation exercise. On the other hand, she can label, or tag, her pretend states as belonging to somebody else. Indeed, a minimally competent simulator must do something like this (as noted originally in figure 2.3), especially if she attempts to track two or more targets concurrently. Pretend states must be tagged to keep track of their intended targets—and perhaps to keep them mentally distinguished from one's own nonimaginary states. If we speak of the "content" of an imagining state in a broad sense, which includes the tag or label, then that content can be said to refer to the simulated target. When Gordon speaks of simulation as a "transformation," one must be careful about its meaning. Gordon is right that within the *content* of an imagining state (the world of imagination), the pronoun *I* refers to the target. But the real-world identity of the subject of an imagining state does not undergo any change in virtue of the subject's imaginative act. The language of "transformation" is misleading on this point.

After presenting his "recentering" construal of the simulation routine, Gordon focuses on the alleged analogical *inference* from self to target, which he rejects. On this point we may agree. As discussed in section 2.3, it is questionable whether the movement from a pretend decision to do m to a belief that the target will decide to do m requires the use of an analogical premise, "The target is like me." On the other hand, we reviewed empirical evidence in section 7.6 that people's use of simulation *does* depend on judgments of similarity to the self. So it is unwise to insist on a version of ST that categorically denies this.

The second element of the "standard" ST view holds that attributors make an introspective identification of their own (final) pretend state and "transfer" it, or project it, onto the target. Gordon rejects this element as well. By contrast, I wish to retain the second element, including introspective identification. Notice an important difference between the (pretend) state of deciding to do m and the final (genuine) state of believing that the target will decide to do m. Unlike the pretend decision, the belief state is a *metarepresentation*. It represents another mental state, a future state of the target. Moreover, it characterizes that state in terms of content and attitude type. Where does this characterization come from? It isn't provided by any prior element in the causal chain. This is clearly true of the attitude type: being a decision. The immediately preceding state, of course, *is* a decision (in pretend mode). But a decision does not characterize itself *as* a decision; it doesn't metarepresent itself. So how does the system "know" from this decision that the target's future state will be a decision? To select "decision" as an item of metarepresentational content, some classification process is required, perhaps introspection or self-monitoring. Thus, as I interpret ST, it naturally invites an introspective approach to first-person attribution, which will be defended in chapter 9. As we saw in section 7.6, there is empirical evidence that third-person mindreading involves use of a brain region responsible for self-reference or self-reflection. And research reported in sections 7.7 and 7.8 shows that failure to inhibit one's own current states produces inaccurate, egocentric third-person mindreading. Normal inhibition of such states is presumably executed via the monitoring of those states.

Is the classification of one's decision a classification of it *as* one's own state, as a state of the self? This, of course, would lend support to the self-other "transference," which Gordon seeks to avoid. The state being classified is certainly a state *of* the self. It is less clear whether an attributor ascribes it *to* the self. While in simulation mode, we have said, each state is "tagged" as belonging to some target other than the current self: either another person entirely or the future self. From this point of view, it seems difficult to hold that the attributor "transfers" the state from self to other. Perhaps the best thing to say is that, while in simulation mode, pretend states are coded as belonging to something other than the current self, but when the simulation mode is exited, any (retrospective) representation of those states represents them as belonging to the (actual) self.

Finally, what about the third element in Gordon's list of no-no's: the prior possession of mental-state concepts? If mindreading includes mental-state attribution, if mental-state attribution is having a belief about a mental state, and if a belief about a mental state features mental-state concepts, then simulation-based mindreading (like all mindreading) requires mental-state concept possession. Because such concepts presumably aren't created on the fly, prior possession of them is necessary. Because all these assumptions are entirely plausible, Gordon's version of ST, which ducks the question of mental-state concept possession, is a tough row to hoe. On the approach favored here, ST ought to deliver a congenial account of mental-state concepts. I shall make a stab at such an account in chapter 10.

Notes

1. Actually, it is debatable whether even ordinary thinking about imagination requires it always to be under voluntary guidance. Budd (1989), White (1990), and Currie and Ravenscroft (2002) point out that a great deal of imagery—for example, dream imagery—isn't subject to voluntary control. Because all imagery is the product of imagination, not all imagination involves voluntary control. This is undoubtedly correct, but I am not certain that it is recognized in ordinary thought. Indeed, I am not even sure it's part of folk wisdom that dreaming is imagining.

2. The case of this patient might pose a challenge to the view that primary visual cortex is required for visual imagery, because the patient's infarctions involved an almost complete destruction of primary visual cortex. However, destruction of primary visual cortex was not complete. Islands of intact cortex were preserved.

3. In response to Chatterjee and Southwood (1995), Butter, Kosslyn, Mijovic-Prelec, and Riffle (1997) point out that their report of imagery in the face of cortical blindness did not use very sensitive measures of imagery, and the patients did have some intact medial occipital cortex.

4. Preserved imagery in the face of cortical blindness is not the only dissociation that poses prima facie difficulties for a vision–visual imagery correspondence thesis. Cerebral achromatopsia (failure to see colors) can be dissociated from the capacity to have colorful images, hemispatial neglect can be manifested independently in vision and imagery, and visual agnosia can occur with intact imagery ability (see Bartolomeo, 2002; Pylyshyn, 2003b: 405). But our discussion of the cortical blindness cases, including congenital cortical blindness, indicates that these various findings may not be insuperable.

5. Admittedly, Pylyshyn proceeds to speculate about the possibility that the reported finding doesn't even involve the visual system, let alone a cortical screen (2003b: 397). However, this is just speculation and not terribly plausible in my judgment.

6. Elsewhere he says that images differ from vision in at least the following three respects: (1) unlike percepts, images fade rapidly; (2) unlike percepts, images are very malleable; and (3) images are created from stored information (Kosslyn, 1994: 74).

7. It goes without saying that they do not share all of their relational properties, specifically, their ways of being causally generated. On my account, having different types of causes simply follows from being images versus percepts.

8. M. Wilson (2003) discusses some other interesting details concerning Schwoebel et al's patient CW, but these need not be pursued.

9. Currie and Ravenscroft (2002) argue that motor imagery is imagined perception of movement rather than imagined action. "The reason we spontaneously describe certain mental events as motor images is because those events seem, in various ways, like perceptions of movement, not because they seem like the movements themselves" (2002: 85). I would say that motor imagery is not the reproduction of perception of a movement but the reproduction of an inner, central event that *plans*, *orders*, or *launches* a movement. This explains the case of patient CW. The central event, when produced by imagination, is normally followed by inhibition, so motor production doesn't occur. But intrinsically it is still very similar to a counterpart event that actually launches movement. In other words, an imagination-produced central event is a good surrogate of a normal, action-producing central event. One simulates the other.

10. Barsalou and Gallese, among others, cite these kinds of experiments as supportive of an "embodied" view of the mind (Barsalou et al., 2003; Gallese, 2003). I am cautious of the embodiment theme, at least as the central construct for the explanation of mindreading. More precisely, embodiment seems to play a role in some but not all kinds of mindreading. In this context, it bears repetition that my use of the term *enactment* does not carry the connotation of motoric activity (as it does in the embodiment literature). As far as terminology goes, one may E-imagine desiring that p, for example, without engaging motoric systems.

11. The researchers were interested in perceived similarity judgments because, drawing on Heal (1986), they assumed that people use the simulation heuristic, or self-reflection, only when they judge their target to be similar to self.

12. Mitchell et al. (2005) do not claim that this wholly arbitrates between ST and TT, because some versions of TT, they say, leave open the possibility that knowledge about the self could be a useful basis for theorizing about others. But they don't specify which version of TT they have in mind or discuss its viability. I raise questions about such self-oriented versions of TT in section 7.8.

13. However, there is independent evidence supporting this suggestion. For example, Ames (2004) found that people more readily project their own goals and predilections onto similar targets (e.g., people sharing the same hobbies) than dissimilar ones.

14. One might wonder whether the Mitchell et al. (2005) study really tapped a *high-level* mindreading process. In the mentalizing task of their study, subjects viewed facial photographs and assessed how *pleased* the targets looked. Isn't this a FaBER task, which we have treated as a paradigm of low-level mindreading? Assuming that "being pleased" qualifies as an emotion, it is true that this was a FaBER task. However, we shouldn't assume that the execution of *all* FaBER tasks has the earmarks of low-level mindreading. There may be no mirroring system associated with this task. Indeed, the brain-scanning evidence points to the recruitment of the regions typically

involved in high-level mindreading (e.g., dorsal MPFC). This is the rationale for treating the study under the heading of high-level mindreading.

15. Thus, I am proposing that first-person *future* mindreading is just as open to simulation as third-person mindreading. That invites the question: What about first-person *past* mindreading? Could ST be extended to that domain? Karen Shanton (unpublished) argues that it can. She argues, first, that a large slice of first-person past mindreading uses autonoetic memory. Second, autonoetic memory is a matter of mental simulation, in the sense we have given it. Third, Shanton adduces striking evidence that projection effects of the kind reported in the remainder of this section also occur in autonoetic memory.

16. Notice, moreover, that whereas Saxe, Carey, and Kanwisher (2004) suggest that the processing of different mental states (e.g., knowledge, beliefs, desires) relies on distinct functional and neural mechanisms, Samson et al.'s (2005) data indicate that there may be common processes for the different mental states. That fits better with ST than TT, where the latter would tend to invoke different naïve theories for different mental states.

17. This thesis has much in common with Jane Heal's thesis that simulation involves "co-cognition" (Heal, 1998). However, Heal appears to *equate* co-cognition with simulation, which I think is a mistake. Although content-simulation is a fundamental part of mindreading, it doesn't exhaust mindreading. Ascribing attitudes and other mental-state types is also a core part of mindreading. In responding to Heal's co-cognition thesis, Nichols and Stich (1998) complain that no actual theory-theorist denies the co-cognition thesis, or imputes to attributors massive content theoretization. This is correct, but only because theory-theorists haven't pursued the logic of TT to its natural conclusion. Just as full-tilt TT includes the thesis that human mentalizers represent attitude types in theorizing terms, so it should feature the thesis that human mentalizers represent attitude contents in wholly theorizing terms. That is a relevant thesis to dispute, as it is disputed here.

18. An example of theorizing about concepts in this fashion is Peacocke (1992).

19. Content holists will firmly deny that one person's mental contents bear any close resemblance to another person's mental contents, simply because each content in a person's head is fixed by the entire web of other contents in her head. Because webs of content differ substantially across individuals, their respective contents will not be very similar (despite agreements in verbal utterances, for example). Two responses to the content holist are in order. First, it is a very questionable doctrine about the "real" nature of mental content (Fodor and Lepore, 1992). Second, even if holism is correct about the real nature of mental content, naïve cognizers, unaware of this philosophicoscientific truth, might proceed with a content-resemblance *aim* that guides simulation.

20. In a rather loose or weak sense of "theorizing," in that no laws or generalizations are invoked by a definite description of the kind in question.

21. As used in this section, "projection" is not intended to connote inappropriateness. It is used in the more generic sense introduced in chapter 2.

22. In a paper published after this book was in press, Vann McGee (2005) presents a philosophy of language–based line of argument for the simulation, or empathy, approach (though his concerns are somewhat orthogonal to the present ones). McGee proposes a reconfiguration and solution to Quine's problem of inscrutability of reference that prominently includes the assumption that third-person interpretation

proceeds by empathetic identification or imaginative projection. Oddly, McGee fails to mention that Quine himself was an empathy theorist.

23. Here is how Quine developed the theme in *Pursuit of Truth* (1990):

> Empathy dominates the learning of language, both by child and by field linguist. In the child's case it is the parent's empathy. The parent assesses the appropriateness of the child's observation sentence by noting the child's orientation and how the scene would look from there.... We all have an uncanny knack for empathizing another's perceptual situation, however ignorant of the physiological or optical mechanism of his perception. (1990: 42)

> Martha empathizes with Tom's perception that it is raining just as the field linguist empathizes the native's perception that a rabbit has appeared. (1990: 62)

> We even hear "Tom perceives that the train is late." Consider how one would get on to using that sentence.... The evidence is not assembled deliberately. One empathizes, projecting oneself into Tom's situation and Tom's behavior pattern, and finds thereby that the sentence "The train is late" is what comes naturally. Such is the somewhat haphazard basis for saying that Tom perceives that the train is late. (1990: 63)

24. Why am I confident that these predictions would be correct? After all, in endowment-effect studies by Loewenstein and colleagues, subjects consistently made errors in predicting other people's valuations, precisely because (it was argued) they were projecting their own attitudes. In the present case, however, there is no reason to expect underlying valuation gaps between predictor and target. In the original Kahneman-Tversky study, there was very high uniformity across subjects in each of the two choices. So here there appears to be no comparable interpersonal valuation gaps of the kind that produce prediction errors in endowment-effect cases.

25. Another principle of normative rationality that is routinely violated is invariance (Kahneman and Tversky, 1984).

26. Kelby Mason has emphasized this possible line of response.

8

Ontogeny, Autism, Empathy, and Evolution

8.1 Overview

Chapters 6 and 7 made a case for third-person simulational attribution, especially in adults. But adult attribution doesn't exhaust the subject of third-person mindreading. Does simulationism also comport with developmental findings? Evidence about mentalizing is often drawn from other quarters as well, including pathologies like autism. Does ST fit with what is currently known about autism? More theoretical questions about simulation are also part of the current debate. Some writers link simulation to the currently popular architecture of control theory (featuring so-called internal models). What are the merits of this idea? Others speculate about the evolutionary roots of simulation. Can ST compete with TT in offering a plausible evolutionary story of mindreading? This chapter tackles the foregoing topics, plus many more.

Some prefatory comments are in order about the comparatively tentative nature of some of the evidence marshaled in parts of this chapter. Extenuating circumstances should be borne in mind. In the area of early childhood development, experimental manipulations with unambiguous interpretations are hard to come by. Moreover, because TT ideas have dominated the landscape in developmental psychology for years, comparatively little has been done to explicitly pit ST against TT on developmental topics. In the area of autism, the phenomenon is so complex and multifaceted that it's extremely difficult to find a single theory that explains everything. So the reader should not expect totally conclusive evidence. Rather, evidence adduced here should be weighed in conjunction with evidence from previous chapters. In making an overall judgment of ST's epistemic status, one should heed the advice of philosophers of science and consider the "consilience" (concurrence) of the evidence, the way that varied strands of evidence hang together. From this perspective, this chapter's evidence is helpful and instructive, even when it isn't, by itself, wholly dispositive.

8.2 Gaze Following and Intention Tracking

Given the profusion of developmental research and our limited space, the discussion must be confined to a handful of topics in development. This section looks at two mentalizing phenomena in the first 2 years of life: the tracking of attention and intention. Both are approached in the context of Meltzoff's work on imitation and mentalizing. Section 8.3 explores a connection between role play and mentalizing, and 8.4 examines false-belief task performance from an ST perspective.

Gaze following, or joint visual attention, is widely regarded as an important milestone in mentalizing. This phenomenon appears around 9 to 10 months of age. The child follows the mother's gaze, and presumably her attention, toward one and the same object. Arguably, this is a sign that the child understands the mother as having a mental state—attention—vis-à-vis the object in view. Around the same age, normal children also begin to point things out with an outstretched finger ("proto-declarative" pointing), directing other people's attention to an object they have in mind. This might also reveal an implicit awareness that the person they are communicating with can acquire a shared mental state by looking at the same object. These phenomena led Baron-Cohen (1995) to postulate a special module, the shared attention mechanism (SAM), with a distinctive role in mindreading. Importantly, autistic children are deficient in the development of both joint visual attention (Sigman, Mundy, Sherman, and Ungerer, 1986; Loveland and Landry, 1986) and proto-declarative pointing (Baron-Cohen, 1989; Mundy, Sigman, Ungerer, and Sherman, 1986). Baron-Cohen appealed to these deficits in autism to support his nativist-modularist approach to the subject. SAM was posited as one of the modules impaired in autism.

There is dispute about the timing and significance of joint visual attention. Some researchers (Corkum and Moore, 1995, 1998) take a conservative stance toward the earliest manifestation of joint visual attention and deny that it betokens mindreading at that stage. But almost everyone agrees that it evidences mindreading by the second year of life. There is also considerable research about what visual cues, exactly, elicit gaze following (Woodward, 1998; Woodward et al., 2001; Johnson, 2003). But these topics will not occupy us here. Of interest here is what can be learned about the possible role of simulation from this stage of mindreading.

In section 4.9, we encountered Meltzoff in the guise of an unorthodox theory-theorist endorsing privileged access to first-person mental states. We also noted in Meltzoff some simulationist leanings, with his suggestion that infants learn about the minds of others via "like-me" inferences that center on imitation. In a recent paper, Meltzoff (2005) takes additional steps in a simulationist direction with his treatment of gaze following and intention tracking.

Famously, Meltzoff and Moore (1977, 1983) discovered that infants as young as 42 minutes can imitate certain facial gestures such as tongue protrusion. But how do infants manage to correlate a seen tongue with their own tongue they have never seen? Their imitative ability indicates that, at some level of processing, they can map actions they see performed by others onto actions of their own body represented "from the inside" (proprioceptively). The newborn thinks, "That seen event is like this felt event." Meltzoff proceeds to argue that the infant's ability to interpret the bodily acts of others in terms of their own acts—and similarly for experiences—provides leverage on the problem of other minds.

Meltzoff (2005) applies this idea to gaze following. Infants in the first year of life imitate head movements and eye blinking (Meltzoff, 1988; Meltzoff and Moore, 1989). So infants can register the similarity between their own head movements and those of others and between their own eyelid closures and those of others. Infants' subjective experiences gained from turning in order to see could thus be used to make sense of like actions in others. In addition, an infant's experience is that eye closure cuts off the infant's own perceptual access. If an infant can map the eye closures of others onto his own eye closures (an ability demonstrated by imitating blinking), these mappings may provide data for understanding perception in others. Brooks and Meltzoff (2002) showed that 12- to 18-month-old infants have a better understanding of the effect of a person's eyes being closed than they do of a person being blindfolded. When they see someone whose eyes are closed, they correctly do not follow their head turning, but they mistakenly follow the head turning of a blindfolded model. Presumably, this is because they have first-person experience associated with eye closure but no experience of blindfolds blocking their view.

This interpretation was tested in a gaze-following experiment with blindfolds (Meltzoff and Brooks, 2003). One group of 12-month-old infants was given first-person experience with blindfolds. The world went black when they were blindfolded and became visible again when the blindfold was removed. Then these infants were tested on gaze following when a blindfold was put over the eyes of a model. The infants did not turn and follow the head movements of the blindfolded model. A control group of infants were allowed to familiarize themselves with the same blindfold but without experiencing view blockage. This manipulation had no effect. The control group mistakenly followed the blindfolded person's "gaze" when she turned her head.

Simulation could now enter the picture in roughly the following way. When a "trained" infant observes an open-eyed, nonblindfolded person turn and gaze in a certain direction, the infant can simulate that person as having some visual experience of an object in the direction of gaze and attending to the object. So the infant turns its own head to obtain a visual experience of the object. When the infant observes a closed-eyed person or a blindfolded person turn her head, the infant can simulate the model as having no visual experience (or black visual experience). So the infant does not follow the model's head turning.

Another well-known discovery of Meltzoff (1995) is that 18-month-old toddlers imitate the unsuccessful acts of adults they observe. A demonstration was arranged in which an adult "accidentally" overshot his target in a task or had his hand slip several times on an object so that the goal was not achieved. At least this is how another adult would interpret the behavior: in terms of an unfulfilled intention. The question was whether a toddler would also attribute such an intention, whether it would "read through" the observed body movements to an underlying goal that wasn't observed. The measure of the toddlers' interpretation was what they reenacted, and what they in fact reenacted were unobserved movements that attained the goal, not the observed movements. Thus, they apparently inferred goals that were at variance with what they saw. (The manipulated objects and modes of manipulation were unfamiliar, so they didn't just infer goals from prior exposure to successful specimens of behavior of that type.)

Meltzoff (2005) explains this phenomenon in terms of the child's projection of his own experience onto the model. As background, he comments that infants in their second half-year of life are obsessed with the success and failure of their plans. They mark self-failures with special labels. Psycholinguistic research shows that among the child's earliest words are "uh-oh" and (in England) "oh bugger." Very early on, they use these terms to comment on a mismatch between their own intentions and real-world outcomes (Gopnik and Meltzoff, 1986). They also experiment with unsuccessful efforts by trying and trying again until the solution comes under voluntary control. Thus, infants could construe a model's failed attempts in terms of their own experience with their own intentions. Putting this in simulationist terms (which Meltzoff does not do, though he comes close), a child in Meltzoff's (1995) experiment could imaginatively identify with the observed model and simulate his trying and failing. Because the simulation would comport both with the child's own prior experience and what is observed in the model's behavior, it would be readily accepted as the interpretation of the model's mental state. The child would then act out of this same, initially simulated, intention when reenacting the observed behavior.

8.3 Role Play and Mindreading

Imitation has become an important topic in its own right within social cognitive science (Hurley and Chater, 2005; Meltzoff and Prinz, 2002; Nadel and

Butterworth, 1999). In this section, I explore one way that imitation—in an extended sense—appears to be linked to the development of mindreading. First I shall report on the ways that creative role play constitutes a kind of simulation (Goldman, 2005). Empirical evidence will then be adduced supporting the notion that such "practice" at simulation makes a positive contribution to children's mindreading.

Normal children engage in role play from the age of 2, acting out the role of a person or creature. Role play, as defined by Paul Harris (2000), is a species of pretend play in which a child impersonates a character, such as a mother, a bus driver, or a soldier. One can also project a role onto an object like a doll or toy, which serves as a prop for the role. I shall interpret role play as *extended* imitation. Ordinary imitation is behavioral duplication of an observed action, whether of its goal, its means, or both. Actions are typically imitated shortly after they are observed, though deferred imitation, involving substantial delays, is also encountered. By "extended" imitation, I mean three things. First, there may be no existing individual whose behavior is imitated; the imitated performance may be that of an imaginary character. Second, even if a model exists, imitation may not copy any specific token behavior of the model. The actor may know that a certain general kind of behavior is prototypical of a given role, but she may instantiate that behavior very creatively. Third, role play is "extended" imitation insofar as it involves more than mere *behavioral* copying. It involves *imitation* as well, that is, attempts to enact in one's own mind a target's mental states or processes. Evidently, children's role play involves such mental simulation, as manifested by verbal and nonverbal behavior.

Harris (2000: 30) illustrates such cases with the use of dolls or toys as props. Children often speak as if they are experiencing a role from the viewpoint of the invented person or character. They use deictic terms appropriate to the character and give expression to emotions, sensations, and needs of the character. For example, John at 21 months is playing with his jack-in-the-box and often impersonates Jack. If Jack's hand is poking out when the lid of the box is closed, John says, "Ouch, ouch. Boo-hoo" (his word for "hurt") (Wolf, 1982: 319). From 2 to 3 years of age, children often conjure up imaginary characters who accompany them over many months. Insofar as they mentally track the character, this is an instance of (high-level) mental simulation. Thus, one may hypothesize that mental simulation is an extension of the more primitive phenomenon of bodily imitation.

Role play appears to make a positive contribution toward the development of mindreading. Children who engage in more joint play than others, including role play, subsequently perform better on mindreading tasks, but no such connection is found for solitary pretense, which involves just objects and props rather than role play (Astington and Jenkins, 1995; Schwebel, Rosen, and Singer, 1999). Taylor and Carlson (1997) checked whether 3- and

4-year-old subjects had previously invented an imaginary character. Those 4-year-olds who had invented such a character performed better on belief tasks, even when age and verbal ability were controlled for. No effect was found for 3-year-olds, but few of them had engaged in this type of role play.

Is role play a cause of enhanced mindreading ability? Perhaps it is only an effect rather than a cause, or perhaps both are effects of a common cause (e.g., IQ). Youngblade and Dunn (1995) addressed the first worry with the following study: Toddlers were assessed for pretend play first at 33 months and then 7 months later. Pretend play at 33 months was linked to better performance in belief tasks at 40 months. Because 33 months is prior to the third birthday, when children usually fail verbal false-belief tasks, it is unlikely that variation among the children was an effect of a preexisting false-belief competence.[1]

It appears, then, that vivid deployment of simulational exercises directed at imaginary characters facilitates mindreading competence. This is to be expected if mindreading involves important simulational elements, but not predictable if it lacks such elements. Convergent evidence comes from the fact that autistic children, who are often impaired in advanced mindreading, show early deficiencies in role play.

8.4 False-Belief Tasks, Simulation, and Inhibitory Control

The most studied milestone in mindreading development is false-belief task performance, and explaining the change between 3 and 5 years (on the standard tests) is a crucible for any theory. ST would try to explain it pretty straightforwardly. Given a false-belief scenario, a simulator must simulate the target with a pretend belief that contravenes what he knows to be true. He must use this feigned belief rather than his genuine one to predict (or retrodict) the target's belief. In a switched location task, for example, he must use a pretend belief that the object is in location L, when he knows that it's really in location L*. In a deceptive container task, when asked what he previously thought was in the container, he must use a pretend belief that it was an object of type T, though he now knows that it was really an object of type T*. In both tasks, he must quarantine or inhibit his genuine belief to keep it from infecting his simulation. Perhaps the transition from 3 to 5 (or 4) years is marked by an enhanced capacity to do this job.

I shall now present more evidence in support of the executive function approach to this transition, which was previously scouted in chapters 4 and 5. We are concerned, in particular, with the inhibitory control variant of the executive function approach. Much was said in chapter 7 about quarantine failure and mindreading errors, including neuropsychological evidence linking an impairment in self-perspective inhibition with mindreading errors (section 7.8). So we already have a great deal of evidence for the plausibility of this approach. But chapter 7 wasn't explicitly addressed to developmental questions. It is that developmental trajectory we revisit here.

"Executive functioning" refers to processes that monitor and control thought and action, including self-regulation, planning, behavior organization, cognitive flexibility, and response inhibition. Inhibitory control is an executive ability that enables someone to override "prepotent" (i.e., dominant, habitual) tendencies. In the case of mindreading, an attributor must focus on what the target believes rather than on what the attributor himself knows, or believes, to be the case. False-belief mindreading tasks require an attributor to override the natural tendency to reference reality (as one believes it to be). On this approach, children's failures on standard measures of false belief, appearance-reality, deception, and other aspects of theory of mind stem from the difficulty of overriding the tendency to reference reality. A crucial enabling factor for childhood advances in mentalizing may be advances in inhibitory control.

Stephenie Carlson and Louis Moses (2001) did a wide-ranging study of the relationship between false-belief task performance and inhibitory control in children. As background to their data, they adduced the following evidence: Important developmental changes occur in inhibitory control during the period that the indicated changes in mentalizing take place, between ages 3 and 6 (Diamond and Taylor, 1996; Frye et al., 1995). Moreover, they cited evidence from (older) brain-imaging studies that implicated the frontal lobes as the seat of mentalizing abilities (Fletcher et al., 1995; Gallagher et al., 2000; Frith and Frith, 2003); the frontal lobes are similarly believed to be heavily involved in executive functioning. Finally, autistic individuals show impairments on classic executive functioning tasks, such as the Wisconsin Card Sort and Tower of Hanoi tasks (Hughes and Russell, 1993; Ozonoff, Pennington, and Rogers, 1991), as well as on the relevant mentalizing tasks. Thus, Carlson and Moses suggested that inhibitory control and mindreading attainments share a common developmental timetable and a common brain region, and their joint absence appears to yield a common psychopathology, namely, autism.

In Carlson and Moses's own study, children were tested on a battery of four mentalizing tasks, including two false-belief tasks, plus a battery of 10 inhibitory control tasks. Mentalizing tasks included the "location false belief" task, the "contents false belief" task (deceptive container task), a deceptive pointing task, and an appearance-reality task. The 10 inhibitory control tasks all required children to respond counter to a prepotent tendency. In the day-night task, for example, the prepotent response was to say "day" for a picture of the sun and "night" for a picture of the moon. Subjects were instead required to say the opposite of what the picture shows. In the grass-snow task, children were required to point to the color that is opposite to its associate, namely, green for "snow" and white for "grass." Carlson and Moses found significant correlations in performance in almost all of the correlations between the 10 inhibitory control measures and the 4 theory-of-mind measures. In 35 of 40 cases, the "partial" correlations, controlling for age, gender, and verbal ability, were positive. Every inhibitory control measure was significantly related to the theory of mind battery (i.e., overall) scores; conversely, every theory of mind measure was significantly correlated to the inhibitory control battery. The correlation between the two batteries themselves was especially high (.66). These results are broadly consistent with those of Frye et al. (1995), who did similar tests. Thus, the research strongly suggests that executive functioning is centrally implicated in mindreading development in this class of tasks. Although the correlational nature of the Carlson and Moses study does not directly resolve the direction of causality issue, Hughes (1998) found that executive functioning at age 3 predicts mindreading performance 1 year later better than mindreading predicts executive functioning across that age span.

Although Carlson and Moses do not mention ST, it is highly consistent with their findings, as previously indicated. Chapter 7 adds substantial new evidence that bolsters their approach. Section 7.7 demonstrated that even adults have trouble preventing their own knowledge (or other mental states) from inappropriately seeping into their mindreading processes and biasing them. Section 7.8, concerning patient WBA, demonstrated that impairment in self-perspective inhibition produces massive, egocentrically biased mindreading errors (at least on high-inhibition false-belief tasks). Finally, the study by Birch and Bloom (2003) lends specific support to the relevance of inhibitory control to the childhood improvement on false-belief tasks between 3 and 5 years. They found that the magnitude of the inhibitory difficulty, which they characterize as a curse-of-knowledge effect, decreased with age in subjects ranging from 3 to 5 years.

On the other hand, Saxe, Carey, and Kanwisher (2004) have taken issue with the inhibitory control story of false-belief task errors by appeal to neuroimaging results. They claim that belief attribution and inhibitory control rely on distinct neural systems. "At least for adults, then, false belief attribution may not depend on inhibitory control during task performance" (2004: 101). However, the evidence from patient WBA, discussed in section 7.8, runs counter to Saxe et al.'s claim. WBA suffered a right hemisphere stroke and showed a lesion to the right inferior and middle frontal gyri extending into the right superior temporal gyrus. His neuropsychological assessment included problems in executive control, especially in inhibition, shifting, and rule detection. This inhibition problem seemed to be specifically responsible for his egocentrically biased errors in false-belief tasks and a variety of other mindreading tasks. Recall also that Samson et al. (2005) pointed to the close correspondence between WBA's areas of lesion and those analyzed by Vogeley et al. (2001) that link self-perspective to theory of mind. So there is ample reason to doubt the interpretation of Saxe et al. (2004). Thus, to the extent that ST is not only consistent with, but also positively favored by, the inhibitory control story of mindreading (see section 7.8), ST provides the best fit with accumulated findings on a prominent class of mindreading errors identified in developmental psychology, social psychology, and neuropsychology.

8.5 Autism and Simulation

A link between autism and mentalizing deficits was established in the mid-1980s, in articles by Baron-Cohen, Leslie, and Frith (1985, 1986). A theoretical account of autism is now seen as another crucible for theories of mentalizing. Because autism has become a more widespread clinical problem, it attracts increasing attention for multiple reasons. A recent theory of autism constitutes a good fit with simulationism, though at first blush it may seem outlandish.

Autism is a complex neurodevelopmental disorder, though its neurological specifics are not well understood. It was first identified by Leo Kanner and Hans Asperger in Vienna in the early 1940s, and one hypothesis about its nature that Asperger (1944) originally advanced will occupy our attention. There are many facets to the autism syndrome. Clinically, it is a disturbance in the ability to establish normal relationships with peers, typically accompanied by delay in the acquisition of language, especially the communicative or pragmatic aspects of language. Autism is usually characterized by "aloneness." The social disability of autism is often accompanied by obsession with "objects" rather than persons, starting at an early age. Autistic individuals commonly engage in repetitive, monotonous activities with, for example, numbers or mechanical systems. This might include fluent and persistent mathematical calculations, such as calendrical calculations about the days of the week on which various dates have fallen. Childhood signs of autism include a paucity of imaginative play and an absence of normal expressive behaviors such as eye contact. It was originally thought that about 75 percent of autistic individuals have below-average IQ, but the percentage of "high-functioning" autistics, with normal or even above-average intelligence, is now estimated to be about half. Some high-functioning autistics start speaking on time but suffer from social and communicative disabilities. These are now diagnosed as having Asperger's syndrome, a variant of autism. Many researchers have concluded that the core of autism is a brain dysfunction that impairs mentalizing. In Baron-Cohen's (1995) terminology, it is a condition of "mindblindness." This feature of autism, of course, is what chiefly interests us here.

I shall discuss three theories of autism, but I'll highlight one that best fits ST. This theory was originated by Asperger:

> The autistic personality is an extreme variant of male intelligence. Even within the normal variation, we find typical sex differences in intelligence.... In the autistic individual, the male pattern is exaggerated to the extreme. (Asperger, 1944)

This extreme-male-brain theory of autism has been adopted and elaborated by Simon Baron-Cohen (2003, 1999; Baron-Cohen and Hammer, 1997). Though initially quite curious, perhaps even repugnant, Baron-Cohen's evidence is quite impressive (at least by my lights). The emphasis on male versus female personality types, however, does not capture the analytical core of Baron-Cohen's hypothesis. The analytical core is that there are two kinds of cognitive activity that normal humans display, which Baron-Cohen calls *empathizing* and *systemizing*. People who suffer from autism are extremely deficient in empathizing but often extreme systemizers. Statistically speaking, females are likely to be relatively strong on empathizing and less strong on systemizing, whereas males, conversely, are often strong on the systemizing dimension and weak on the empathizing dimension. Autism is an extreme case of the latter combination. Not coincidentally, in people diagnosed with high-functioning autism, or Asperger's syndrome, the sex ratio is at least 10 males to every female.

Baron-Cohen formulates his thesis quite succinctly, and his formulations make clear its relationship to simulationism:

> Autism is an empathy disorder: those with autism have major difficulties in "mindreading" or putting themselves into someone else's shoes, imagining the world through someone else's eyes and responding appropriately to someone else's feelings. (2003: 137)

> Empathy involves a leap of imagination into someone else's head. While you can try to figure out another person's thoughts and feelings by reading their face, their voice and their posture, ultimately their internal world is not transparent, and in order to climb inside someone's head one must imagine what it is like to be them. (2003: 24)

Clearly, Baron-Cohen has become an empathy theorist of mindreading, a simulation theorist. Mindreading is equated with putting oneself in someone else's shoes, or head.[2] Oddly, he never mentions the label "simulation theory," despite its prominence in the mindreading literature. Nonetheless, this is apparently his position, though few details are supplied. Moreover, the second cognitive activity he stresses, systemizing, looks very much like "theorizing" as people in the mentalizing community have characterized it. Autistic individuals, especially those with Asperger's syndrome, are said to be very good at systemizing, or theorizing, but that, according to Baron-Cohen, doesn't much help them mindread, except in quite superficial ways.

Baron-Cohen provides a vivid example of someone with Asperger's syndrome, a Cambridge University mathematician named Richard Borcherds, who was a winner of the Fields Medal, the equivalent in mathematics of the Nobel Prize. Despite his facility with anything mathematical, Borcherds was puzzled by his sense of alienation from people. He found people to be complex, mysterious beings who were hard to comprehend. He knew that they have emotions and thoughts—he wasn't completely mindblind—but he found it difficult to know *which* emotions and thoughts they were having at a given time.

> The straightforward cases presented no difficulty for him. He could work out that someone might be sad if they got hurt or if they did not get what they wanted, and that they would be happy if they did get what they wanted. He could even appreciate that someone might be sad if they *thought* they were getting something that they did not want. Yet this is no great shakes, since even the average six-year-old child can work that out.
>
> The social world is far more sophisticated than this and moves at a tremendous speed. When people came round to his home, conversation and interaction would become confusing to him, even though it was just the ordinary stuff of everyday chat between a group of friends. Faced with this sea of words and hidden meanings, of exchanges of glances and smiles, of innuendo and double-entendre, of bluff and deception, embarrassment and camouflaged flirtation, it was just all too much. It went over his head. (Baron-Cohen, 2003: 155–156)

Thus, as Baron-Cohen describes him, Borcherds used a nonstandard "systemizing" procedure to "work out" simple mental-state ascriptions, but he was not adept at using the empathic (simulational) techniques that normal people use, and this kept him from mindreading at the pace and level required for fluent social interaction. Asked if he used e-mail to chat with people, or if he had friends he liked to spend time with, Borcherds said that his use of e-mail was restricted to work-related information exchange. He didn't really have friends as such, though colleagues would sometimes visit his apartment. He would often leave them to chat with his wife and withdraw into a book. He could be with another person, one to one, but in a group he would get confused and withdraw. It had always been this way.

In supporting his thesis that females are, *on average*, prone more toward empathizing and males more toward systemizing, Baron-Cohen draws on anecdotes plus a variety of statistical and experimental studies. By systemizing, Baron-Cohen means the drive to analyze, explore, and construct systems. A systemizer likes to figure out how things work or to extract the underlying rules that govern the behavior of a system. This is done to understand and predict the system or to invent a new one. It is significant that autism is known to have a genetic basis, and a preponderance of fathers of people with autism work in engineering, computing, and scientific professions. However, systemizing is associated not only with science. Systems can be as varied as a vehicle, a plant, a library catalog, a musical composition, or even an army unit. They all operate on inputs and deliver outputs, using "if-then" correlational rules (2003: 3). Baron-Cohen adduces evidence in support of the claim that, on average, boys are more naturally inclined to systemize and girls to empathize. For example, girls' speech has been described as more cooperative, more reciprocal, and more collaborative. Girls more readily make space for the other's point of view, enabling the other to save face because they feel that their point has been accepted (Leaper, 1991; Maccoby, 1998). To support the notion that gender differences are not merely culturally acquired, Baron-Cohen reports a study in his lab by Jennifer Connellan and Anna Batkti. They videotaped 100 1-day-old babies who were shown both a smiling face and a mobile made from a ball the same size and color as the face but with rearranged features. To make the mobile look more mechanical, they hung material from it that moved every time the larger mobile moved. The girl babies looked longer at the face, and the boy babies looked longer at the mobile (Connellan, Baron-Cohen, Wheelright, Batkti, and Ahluwalia, 2001). This was on the first day of life.

One might object to Baron-Cohen's theory on the grounds that it doesn't comport well with low-functioning autistic children, especially those who engage in wild, uncontrolled activity, like screaming and throwing excreta. There isn't much that smacks of "systemizing" in these children. But autism is an extremely complex and varied syndrome, and no going theory covers all of its dimensions. To the extent that Baron-Cohen's theory accounts for mindreading deficits and other cognitive aspects of autism, it has substantial explanatory value and should be evaluated favorably.

Analytically speaking, however, Baron-Cohen's discussion of empathizing leaves something to be desired. There seem to be three distinct senses, dimensions, or types of empathy, as Baron-Cohen understands the term, but he doesn't distinguish them carefully: (1) "Empathy" can refer to the use of E-imagination or simulation when reading others' mental states. This seems to be lacking in autistics. (2) "Empathy" can refer to high motivation or interest in knowing other people's mental states. This ingredient is also lacking in autistics. They seem uninterested in other people's mental lives as compared with the properties of (selected) "systems." (3) Individuals who are "empathic" not only are interested in knowing what others feel but also have caring reactions to those feelings. Autistics, by contrast, are relatively indifferent toward other people's feelings, though not as cold as psychopaths.[3] When Baron-Cohen discusses the empathic propensities of females, as a group, he talks about all three of these dimensions jointly, without carefully distinguishing them. The problem is that his evidence in support of greater empathy among females than males tends to be strong for dimensions (2) and (3) but rather unspecific for dimension (1), the principal dimension of interest here. However, the general portrait drawn of autistics and their lack of empathizing is a compelling one. This much, certainly, can be said: *If* Baron-Cohen were right about autism—in particular, right about deficits in the first (cognitive) dimension of empathy—this would provide strong evidence for ST, because it would show that a major clinical population known to be deficient in mindreading is also deficient in the use of simulation for mindreading.

I turn now to a second prominent theory of autism, the executive dysfunction theory. In the preceding section, we encountered the idea of executive function and dysfunction, although the focus there was one type of executive dysfunction: inhibitory control. Executive function more broadly is needed to keep several tasks going at the same time and switching between them. They are vital for high-level decisions to resolve conflicting responses, override automatic behavior, and inhibit inappropriate impulsive actions. Neuropsychologists associate these abilities with a high-level supervisory system lodged primarily in the frontal lobes. The second theory of autism is that autism is fundamentally an impairment of this system, a theory that has been pursued by several investigators (Ozonoff et al., 1991; Pennington et al., 1997; Hughes and Russell, 1993; Russell, 1997). Executive dysfunction might account for a number of traits frequently observed in autism. One is repetitive activity. Repetitiveness can be seen as a natural consequence of the lack of higher-level executive control, which produces excessive perseveration. Another feature strongly associated with autism is difficulty in switching tasks or mind-set from doing one thing to doing another. Switching ability is tested by the Wisconsin card-sorting test, on which autistics perform poorly.

To the extent that proper executive functioning involves adequate inhibitory control, and an inhibitory control deficit could impede simulation-based mindreading (section 8.3), the executive dysfunction theory of autism might be consistent with ST. However, as Baron-Cohen points out, not all people with autism or Asperger's syndrome, who show clear deficits in mindreading, have executive dysfunction problems. Richard Borcherds has considerable difficulties in empathizing and mindreading but not a trace of executive dysfunction (Baron-Cohen, 2003: 177).

A third theory of autism is the "weak central coherence" theory of Uta Frith, presented in the first edition of her book *Autism: Explaining the Enigma* (1989). Central coherence is a tendency to focus on the large picture of things rather than the bits and pieces that make it up. Once a jigsaw puzzle has been assembled, one sees the picture as a whole and even has a hard time seeing the pieces as individual pieces. Someone with weak central coherence, however, would continue to attend to the separate fragments. Frith suggested that autistics are characterized by weak central coherence and therefore have trouble appreciating the relations between parts and wholes. The idea was tested by comparing normal and autistic children on a hidden figures task (Shah and Frith, 1983). For normal children, embedded shapes are swallowed up by the bigger figure and therefore hard to find. Autistic children, however, scored above average for their mental age. Frith's hypothesis was that understanding subtle social interactions requires massive integration of multimodal information. Individuals who are weak at such integration would find it hard to acquire a theory of mind. However, in the second edition of her book, Frith (2003) concedes that mentalizing may not require massive amounts of information integration. Also, contrary to what she previously assumed, some people with autism may actually have a preference for strong rather than weak central coherence (2003: 167). Baron-Cohen questions the weak central coherence theory on the ground that autism often involves an intact or even superior systemizing ability, and this ability involves keeping track of multiple elements in a larger system (2003: 177). However, if it turned out that the weak central coherence theory of autism were correct, this might well be consistent with ST. Effective simulation might require informational integration.

The final chapter is yet to be written on the enigma of autism.[4] But some of the currently prominent theories, including the most intriguing and promising one, by my lights, are fully compatible with ST. Indeed, it is precisely a deficit in interpersonal mental simulation, also called empathizing, that seems to characterize autistic individuals. In the next section, I consider another theory of autism, not a competitor of the empathy theory but a possible originating cause of autism. This theory proposes a mirror-neuron dysfunction as the underlying cause.

8.6 Autism and Mirror-Neuron Dysfunction

The first to propose a detailed model linking autism to mirror-neuron dysfunction were Williams, Whiten, Suddendorf, and Perrett (2001). They speculated that impaired development of the mirror-neuron system could lead to impaired imitation. This, in turn, could lead to impaired social and communication abilities, including joint attention, theory of mind, empathy, and even the pragmatic dimensions of language, all of which are characteristics of autism spectrum disorders (ASD).

Williams et al. pointed to research by Rogers and Pennington (1991) that identifies a possible link between autism and imitation deficits. In a recent update, Rogers, Hepburn, Stackhouse, and Wehner (2003) found that children with autism were significantly more impaired in oral-facial imitation, imitation of actions on objects, and overall imitation abilities than controls, including both normal children and children with other developmental disorders. Williams et al. suggested an intimate connection between imitation disorders and mindreading impairments, especially on a simulation approach to mindreading. Like the attribution of mental states (under ST), imitation involves translating another person's perspective in terms of one's own. The same holds for empathy, which also involves a self-other translation. Thus, an early imitation deficit could lead to a cascade of other deficits commonly associated with ASD. Finally, if imitation deficits were a product of a mirror-system dysfunction, that would establish a developmental pathway from mirror-neuron dysfunction to autism. There are now many analyses proposing that the mirror system plays an essential role in imitation. Giacomo Rizzolatti (2005) argues that a necessary prerequisite for imitation is matching an observed action with its motor representation, and such matching is normally performed by the motor mirror system. Marco Iacoboni (2005) advances a similar thesis. Thus, a damaged mirror-neuron system could easily be responsible for an imitation deficit.

Is there specific evidence of a mirror-neuron dysfunction in people with ASD? V. S. Ramachadran and colleagues have studied this in the laboratory by looking at brainwaves believed to be associated with mirror neurons, specifically, electroencephalography (EEG) mu frequency band oscillations. At rest, sensorimotor neurons, including mirror neurons, spontaneously fire in synchrony, leading to large-amplitude EEG oscillations in the 8 to 13 Hz (mu) frequency band. When subjects perform an action, these neurons fire asynchronously, thereby decreasing the power of the mu-band EEG oscillations. During observed hand actions, the mirror-neuron system is the only network that has been identified to be active in this area of cortex. This suggests that mu wave *suppression* in response to observed actions can be used as a selective measure of mirror-neuron system functioning.

Oberman et al. (2005) therefore set out to test whether individuals with ASD would show dysfunction in mirror-neuron activity as reflected by mu suppression. That is, would ASD subjects *fail* to show mu suppression in situations where normals would show it? They had subjects perform several tasks, including moving their own hands and watching a video of a moving hand. The control group showed significant suppression from baseline in mu oscillations at each electrode during both the self-initiated hand movement condition and the observed hand movement condition. The ASD group also showed significant mu suppression during the self-initiated hand movement condition but, crucially, not during the observed hand movement condition. Thus, there does indeed appear to be an association between ASD and impairment in the mirror-neuron system. This finding does not undercut Baron-Cohen's theory that ASD is related to empathy deficits; it may even support the empathy theory because of the linkage between mirroring and some kinds of low-level empathy. However, the Oberman et al. study demonstrates impairment only in the *motor* mirror system, not in mirror systems for pain or the emotions, which are more intimately associated with empathy. So more work must be done before we can say with confidence that Baron-Cohen's empathy theory is supported by the mirror-neuron dysfunction story.

8.7 A Dual-Process Theory of Empathy

We slipped into the topic of empathy through the back door, through Baron-Cohen's approach to autism. But empathy deserves sustained treatment as a central topic in social cognition, and also because of its close relation to simulation (some writers use the two terms interchangeably). Empathy is a complex topic because there are almost as many approaches to it as researchers in the field (Preston and de Waal, 2002). I make no attempt to provide a comprehensive overview of approaches to empathy. Instead, I focus on a specific treatment of empathy that parallels the duplex theory of simulational mindreading presented in chapters 6 and 7. It resembles our theory in advocating a dual-process account of empathy. Dual-process theories of the mind are ubiquitous in psychology. There is considerable agreement about a principled difference in the mind between automatic and controlled processes (Chaiken and Trope, 1999; Wegner and Bargh, 1998; Egeth and Yantis, 1997; Stanovich, 2004). Although my high-level versus low-level distinction does not precisely match the automatic-controlled contrast, there is substantial overlap.[5] Thus, the approach to empathy summarized next adds theoretical weight to the idea of a high-low distinction in mindreading.

The duplex theory of empathy to which I refer is that of Sara Hodges and Daniel Wegner, who distinguish systematically between automatic and controlled empathy (Hodges and Wegner, 1997). Let us begin with automatic empathy. Without restricting empathy to the realm of emotion, Hodges and Wegner view emotional contagion as a paradigm of automatic empathy. They discuss contagion patterns like some of those encountered in chapter 6, though without the neurological underpinning. Hodges and Wegner's article predates the work on mirror systems and the cognitive neuroscience of emotion reading that we highlighted in chapter 6, so their story differs in detail from the one told in that chapter. Specifically, they endorse what I called "reverse simulation" (Model 2), whereas I opted for "unmediated resonance" (Model 4). Nonetheless, the contagion phenomena they subsume under the heading of automatic empathy overlap considerably with the resonance phenomena treated in chapter 6.

The phenomena discussed by Hodges and Wegner consist in emotional and cognitive contagion and priming, often via facial, vocal, and postural feedback. When we see a happy face, our smiling muscles react (Bush, Barr, McHugo, and Lanzetta, 1989; Dimberg, 1988), and when we see a pained expression, our facial muscles react in the way they would if we were pained (Vaughan and Lanzetta, 1981). These events of mimicry occur to some degree even when people are asked to inhibit their facial expressions, a strong indicator that automatic activation is occurring. As an apparent result of this mimicry, people come to feel the same emotion they have observed, apparently through feedback from the enervated facial muscles (Adelmann and Zajonc, 1989). The causal mediation of facial feedback, described in section 6.3 as "reverse simulation," is partially mooted by recent discoveries that even people with paralyzed facial muscles (due to Mobius syndrome, e.g.) seem to undergo the same emotions. This finding, along with the discovery of mirroring systems, is what led us to prefer an unmediated resonance model to the facial feedback model. But whatever the exact path or route, its automaticity is undisputed.

Many striking findings of automatic feedback were reported in the 1980s and 1990s, extensively reviewed in Hatfield, Cacioppo, and Rapson (1994). For example, Kellerman, Lewis, and Laird (1989) investigated the link between feedback from behavioral expressions of love, such as long, unbroken, close-up gazes, and feelings of love. They asked men and women to gaze into one another's eyes continuously for 2 minutes, then asked them how romantically they felt about one another. Three control conditions were devised. In one, a subject gazed into the other's eyes, but the other looked away. In another, both subjects gazed at one another's hands. In a third, subjects gazed into one another's eyes—but only to count how often the other blinked. As predicted, the mutual gaze subjects reported greater feelings of romantic love, attraction, interest, warmth, and respect for one another than subjects in the control conditions. In an example of vocal feedback, Siegman, Anderson, and Berger (1990) asked people to talk in a variety of vocal styles about topics that made them furious. Some subjects were asked to speak softly and slowly, others to speak normally, and still others to speak loudly and fast. Both men and women felt less angry and had slower heart rates and lower blood pressure when they carefully modulated their voices. When subjects spoke harshly, they got angrier and more physiologically aroused. These two examples do not address the interpersonal transmission of emotion but only the automaticity with which one's own behavior and posture elicit emotion.

Hodges and Wegner allow for cognitive as well as emotional empathy and stress that cognitive empathy can also be quite automatic. Baldwin and his colleagues suggested that just a reminder of another person can evoke automatic cognitive empathy. Baldwin and Holmes (1987) found that when participants were reminded of their relationship either with their parents or with their friends, they judged a sexually permissive story more in line with the standards of the group of which they were reminded. Adoption of others' perspectives can also affect a person's view of the self. If you take the perspective of someone highly critical of you, it can make you feel like so much "chopped liver" (Hodges and Wegner, 1997: 317). When participants in another study were primed with subliminal pictures of authority figures, such as the pope, they made more critical self-judgments (Baldwin, Carrell, and Lopez, 1990).

Hodges and Wegner characterize automatic empathy as having the inertia of running or tumbling downhill, whereas controlled empathy is as effortful as climbing a mountain. In attempts to reach the mountain peak, we search for grips, holds, and trails to help us on our way. Similarly, in trying to achieve empathy, we seek out aids to help us. We identify items of information in our experience or memory that will trigger automatic empathy. Sometimes we also seek to control empathy by controlling our actual exposure or imagination-evoked exposure to empathy-inducing stimuli. Exactly how we seek to control empathy is a function of our motivations, which can be various.

We may be motivated to control empathy for moral reasons, to figure out how other people should be treated (see chapter 11). Empathy may also be controlled for less noble goals, for example, to figure out how others feel in order to manipulate their behavior. Our motivation vis-à-vis empathy is not always for greater empathy. Sometimes we want to avoid getting into someone else's shoes because of the associated costs. Film viewers may control their level of emotional empathy with the victim of an atrocity by looking away from the screen during the ugly part. In a study by Shaw, Batson, and Todd (1994), subjects who knew they would have an opportunity to provide high-cost (time-consuming) help to a homeless person were less likely to choose to hear a highly empathy-inducing appeal from the homeless man than a nonempathy-inducing plea from him.

Hodges and Wegner argue that the suppression of perspectives is sometimes more difficult than their production. The fact that perspectives often occur automatically means that they are thrust into the mind and are therefore difficult to control. Wegner (1994) offered a theory of "ironic processes" of mental control, which Hodges and Wegner (1997) apply to the case of empathy. The ironic process theory proposes that every act of mental control invokes two cognitive search processes: a conscious operating process that searches for thoughts that will produce the intended mental state and an ironic *monitoring* process that searches for thoughts that indicate a failure to produce the intended state. In the case of perspective production, then, part of the mind is attempting to exert the control, and part is testing the effectiveness of that control. A curious result is that an attempt to control our empathy in the absence of enough conscious mental capacity unleashes a failure-inducing monitoring process that wreaks havoc with our intended mental state. The effect of the monitor is precisely to oppose the intended state rather than to promote it.

The value of Hodges and Wegner's work for the present project is twofold. First, it demonstrates the psychological robustness and complexity of perspective-taking processes. Second, it shows that both automatic and controlled perspective taking are essential to a comprehensive understanding of the phenomena. The merits of this duplex approach redound to the merit of our somewhat similar duplex treatment of simulation processes. For readers initially skeptical of a duplex approach to simulation, the present material supplies additional rationale.

8.8 Mirroring and the Unity of Social Cognition

Against this background, it is relevant to comment on the role of mirror mechanisms in the theory of simulation and social cognition more generally. Gallese, Keysers, and Rizzolatti (2004) offer a highly "unificationist" approach to simulation and social cognition. They write:

> In this study we provide a unifying neural hypothesis on how individuals understand the actions and emotions of others. Our main claim is that the fundamental mechanism at the basis of the experiential understanding of others' actions is the activation of the mirror neuron system. A similar mechanism, but involving the activation of viscero-motor centers, underlies the experiential understanding of the emotions of others. (2004: 396)

Although this passage highlights actions and emotions, the title of the article, "A Unifying View of the Basis of Social Cognition," suggests a more ambitious thesis, embracing all aspects of social cognition. At a minimum, Gallese, Keysers, and Rizzolatti propose that all *simulational* phenomena should be understood in mirroring, or resonance, terms.

As Sperber (2005) points out, however, there are many varied forms of social cognition, not all of which involve understanding mental states. Some social cognition consists in classifying people by their sex, age, profession, ethnicity, and the like, to derive predictions about their character and behavior. Obviously, this cannot be identified with mentalizing. Even if we narrow the focus from social cognition to mentalizing, it is hard to make a case for mirroring as the foundation of it *all*. Mirroring is a highly automatic process, as the Parma group insists. If perspective taking (or E-imagination) is a core part of interpersonal simulation for mindreading, and if controlled processes comprise an important factor in perspective taking, then the prospects for understanding mentalizing wholly in terms of mirroring, or resonance, are not encouraging. This is supported by considerations of the previous section.

We should not overlook the possibility that controlled processes are ultimately reducible to, or ontogenetically explicable in terms of, mirroring systems. This is possible in principle, but I am unaware of any supporting evidence for such a thesis. The dominant view in current psychology is that controlled processes are of a different type or order than automatic processes like mirror systems. Perhaps the scenario sketched by Williams et al. (2001), discussed in section 8.6, is intended to be a scenario in which normal mirror systems ultimately lead to *high-level* mindreading. But this theme is not well articulated or empirically supported in their treatment.

Although I am skeptical of the ambitious version of the Gallese-Keysers-Rizzolatti thesis, I am also unpersuaded by Jacob and Jeannerod's (2005) critique of their work. Jacob and Jeannerod address the prospects of what they call "the motor theory of social cognition," whose goal, they write, "is to derive human social cognition from human motor cognition" (2005: 21). Among several references they cite as endorsements of this idea is Gallese and Goldman (1998). But the latter article does not embrace the idea that all of social cognition is derivable from motor cognition. Indeed, I don't even think that all *simulation* involves motor cognition. Nor does Gallese endorse this, to judge from a recent online paper in which he writes: "According to the use I make of this notion, embodied simulation *is not conceived of as being exclusively confined to the domain of motor control*, but rather as a more general and basic endowment of our brain" (Gallese, 2004; emphasis in the original).[6] Perhaps Jacob and Jeannerod's interpretation of our view in Gallese and Goldman (1998) results from the assumption that all mirroring phenomena are motor phenomena. This assumption is unwarranted. True, the earliest mirroring systems, which inspired the "mirror" terminology, were motoric systems, but in recent years the range of detected mirroring systems has substantially expanded.

8.9 Shared Representations

The literature on simulation theory contains a good bit of talk about "shared representations." What does this mean? The phrase has two different possible referents: either equivalent mental events *across* individuals or equivalent mental events *within* an individual. Consider the cross-individual sense first. In motor mirroring, the same type of neural event occurs in an organism executing an action and in an observer. In affective resonance, the same emotion occurs in one person and also (substantially attenuated) in an observer. Thus, one type of event is "shared" across individuals. In more elaborate cases, someone might use his motor system to track the kinematics of another person's action, which is driven by that person's motor system. Observers can anticipate targets' handwriting by running their own motor systems to replicate those of their targets (Orliaguet, Kandel, and Boe, 1997; Kandel, Orliaguet, and Viviani, 2000; Chaminade, Meary, Orliaguet, and Decety, 2001).

The within-individual sense of "shared representations" is what interests me at this juncture. The idea is that a simulation-style mindreader creates (or tries to create) replicas of his target's states. Pretend states are created that are approximate equivalents of genuine states occurring in the first-order business of cognition. The chief difference between them lies in their respective origins, which could be forgotten as cognition proceeds. So how does the cognitive system manage to segregate these more-or-less equivalent states? Isn't there a danger of confusion? This issue was encountered in various forms in chapter 7. Visual imagery might be confused with genuine seeing; motor imagination might be confused with genuine motor planning or execution. In mindreading, genuine states might slip into a simulation where they don't belong. Indeed, this was found to be a pervasive problem in mindreading, giving rise to egocentric errors. In chapter 2, our diagrams suggested that an attributor "tags" pretend states with a label for the intended target. But does the cognitive system really have a tagging procedure?

To the extent that these problems exist, their existence supports the simulation approach, which is the main point of the present section. But it would be good to have additional evidence that this is a real problem for the brain and that it devotes processing resources to its solution. Some attention has been given to this issue in the literature, which we shall briefly examine.

Jean Decety and collaborators have investigated this issue and argue that a certain region of the brain, the right inferior parietal lobule, is the principal locus of responsibility for executing this task (Ruby and Decety, 2001, 2003, 2004; Decety and Chaminade, 2003). Ruby and Decety often identify the task as distinguishing between first- and third-person perspectives. The first question is whether there is a real commonality between representations across these perspectives that might give rise to a problem, and the second question is what the brain does to solve the problem. A meta-analysis by Grèzes and Decety (2001) established that common brain regions are involved during action generation, action simulation, and action observation. But there must also exist a neural-level distinction between first- and third-person perspective representation. So Ruby and Decety (2001) asked subjects to imagine either their performing a given action (first-person perspective) or the experimenter performing the same action (third-person perspective). According to ST, there should be an overlap between regions involved in first- and third-person perspective, and their results show that this is partly true. Several areas are common to both perspectives, including the SMA, precentral gyrus, precuneus, and MT/V5. But the overlap is not complete. There were increases in the parietal, cingulate, and frontal cortices for third-person simulation when compared with first-person. In particular, Ruby and Decety highlight the activation of right inferior parietal cortex as critical, supporting this interpretation by evidence from clinical neuropsychology and brain-imaging studies of schizophrenic patients. A patient with an abscess in the right parietal cortex believed his body to be controlled by external forces. He made statements such as "My head is empty," "I have no thoughts," and "I feel hypnotized" (Mesulam, 1981). Schizophrenic patients show hyperactivation of the right inferior parietal cortex and misattribute self-generated acts to external entities (Spence et al., 1997).

A second study by Ruby and Decety (2003) investigated the neural correlates of the self-other distinction at the conceptual (rather than the motor)
level. Medical students were presented with written sentences related to health
sciences and instructed to make a judgment about them according to their own
perspective or according to what they thought a layperson would believe.
Again, the right inferior parietal lobe was significantly activated in the third-
person versus first-person contrast. A third study by Ruby and Decety (2004)
asked subjects to adopt either their own or their mother's perspective in response to verbally described situations involving social emotions. The main
effect of third-person perspective as compared to first-person was, again,
significant activation in the right inferior parietal cortex (also in the ventromedial prefrontal cortex). Finally, Decety and Chaminade (2003) explored the
neural correlates of sympathy, or empathy. They remark that although empathizing necessitates a sharing of affect (across individuals), it also requires a
minimal distinction between self and other (within the subject). They therefore
view it as noteworthy that their tasks recruited the right inferior parietal
lobule.

It may be complained that although these studies shed light on *where* the
activity of drawing self-other distinctions takes place, little light is shed on
how these distinctions are drawn. Fair enough—we certainly want more information on the "how" of the activity. But the studies do provide additional
evidence that there is a recurring problem with a recurring solution, which
cuts across domains from the motor to the conceptual to the emotional. In this
case, the existence of a problem is mostly attested to by the pathological
cases. But without neuroimagining studies of normals, we would have a hard
time interpreting the pathologies. The existence of the self-other problem and
the fact that it seems to have a common solution across multiple domains fits
very well with the entire ST framework.[7]

8.10 Simulation and Control Theory

A popular approach to many topics in contemporary neuroscience is control
theory. Several theorists see control theory as a framework in which ST might
be embedded. It therefore behooves us to examine control theory and evaluate
the prospects for a synthesis of it with ST.

Control theory is a product of engineering or cybernetics. Its application to
motor cognition and other domains of cognition is substantially the handi-
work of Daniel Wolpert and coworkers (Wolpert, Ghahramani, and Jordan,
1995; Wolpert, 1997; Wolpert and Kawato, 1998; Wolpert and Ghahramani,
2000; Wolpert, Doya, and Kawato, 2004). Control theory can be illustrated
by a simple adaptive control system, or servomechanism, like a thermostat.[8]
The elements of such a system are (1) a target or reference signal (e.g., the

desired room temperature); (2) an input signal (actual room temperature), which is a joint result of (3) exogenous events in the environment (nightfall) and the output of the control system (level of heat output); (4) a comparator, which determines whether the target and input signals match (has the room reached the desired temperature?); (5) output, which is determined by comparison between target and input signals (heat output is turned up); and (6) a feedback loop, by which output has effects on the succeeding input signal (actual room temperature rises).

The motor system can be viewed as a feedback loop in which the outputs are motor commands and the inputs are sensory consequences of action (Wolpert and Ghahramani, 2000). Motor commands generate contractions in the muscles, causing the musculoskeletal system to change its configuration. This leads to a variety of different changes in body configuration, depending on the nature of the physical objects we interact with. The body's current state is not directly accessible to the central nervous system (CNS). The CNS has access only to sensory feedback from which it estimates the state of the body. The task of producing accurate and fast movements is complicated by time delays in the transduction and transport of sensory signals to the CNS. Thus, sensory information cannot be used to guide the initial part of a movement, and skilled performance requires feed-forward control.

By general consensus, there is an internal device that helps address these problems. When motor commands are issued to the musculature, duplicate signals called "efference copy" are also produced. It is hypothesized that the central nervous system also contains "forward models," that is, internal computational mechanisms that use efference copy to predict sensory consequences of motor acts. The predictions are based on past associations between similar motor acts and their experienced sensory consequences. Using forward models to predict sensory consequences is faster than waiting for the executed movements to produce those consequences. One piece of evidence for forward models is the cancellation, or attenuation, of predicted sensations. Externally caused tactile stimulation, such as a tickle, is experienced as more intense than the same stimulation when self-produced (Blakemore, Wolpert, and Frith, 1998). This is explained by the operation of a forward model. A forward model makes a sensory prediction, which is compared with the actual sensory consequences of the act. If the act has been self-produced, the actual consequences will match the predicted ones, and the sensations will be perceptually attenuated. So, if you tickle yourself, you won't feel it very much. By contrast, externally caused sensations—for instance, tickles by other people—are not attenuated in perception. The proffered explanation is that the forward model doesn't predict externally caused sensations. Absent a matching prediction, the system interprets the sensation as externally caused and allows you to feel it saliently.

How is this framework related to simulation theory? Gallese (2001, 2003, 2005) argues that resonance phenomena, of the sort discussed in chapter 6, constitute an empathic link between individuals. We share, he says, a multiplicity of states with others. To capture the richness of the experiences we share with others, he introduces a conceptual tool called "the shared manifold of intersubjectivity" (2001: 44–45). Although the shared manifold is operationalized at three different levels (phenomenological, functional, and subpersonal), Gallese finally embeds the shared-manifold approach within the control-theoretic framework of forward models. Indeed, the control-theoretic framework is introduced when defining *simulation*:

> I will use the term *simulation* in a way that is close to the third definition given above [omitted here]: *an implicit mechanism meant to model the objects and events that the mechanism itself is supposed to control while interacting with them.* The term interaction is considered here in its broadest sense. Simulation is a *control functional mechanism*, its function being the modeling of the objects to be controlled. Indeed, a current authoritative view on motor control envisages simulation as the mechanism employed by forward models to predict the sensory consequences of impending actions (see Wolpert, Doya, Kawato, 2004). According to this view, *the predicted consequences are the simulated ones*. (Gallese, 2003: 521, emphasis in the final sentence is added)

Does Gallese mean to define *interpersonal* simulation, of the sort illustrated by resonance or mirroring phenomena, in terms of these control-theoretic ideas? That is not clear to me. On the one hand, resonance phenomena are precisely what the "shared manifold of intersubjectivity" seems intended to capture. On the other hand, it is unclear how the control functional approach would actually apply to this case, examined in detail. Consider resonance phenomena involving disgust or pain. How do they satisfy or instantiate the stated definition? Suppose you inhale a foul odor, which provokes disgust in you. When I observe your facial expression, my disgust system produces a corresponding disgust feeling in me. Thus, a simulation relation holds between your disgust feeling and mine. But how is this relation captured by Gallese's definition and related remarks? The definition says that simulation is a "mechanism." Which mechanism instantiates the definition in this case, and which event does it succeed in simulating? The mechanism is presumably my disgust-producing system—the anterior insula, to keep things simple. Which event does it simulate? According to the definition, it should be an event that the mechanism is meant to *model* and *control* while interacting with it. Does my anterior insula interact with your disgust feeling, and does it control that feeling of yours? No. So the definition does not authorize the desired conclusion that your disgust feeling is simulated.

The final sentence of the passage from Gallese says that the simulated events are the predicted events. In control theory, the predicted events are typically sensory consequences, that is, sensory events experienced in the simulator. But what might these sensory consequences be where I am the simulator? Whatever they are, they cannot include *your* disgust experience.

In short, it seems impossible to combine Gallese's control-theoretic definition of simulation with the interpersonal, replicationist sense of simulation.

Another simulation-oriented application of control theory (inspired by Gallese's proposals and Prinz's work on common coding of perception and action) is under development by Susan Hurley (2005a, 2005b, forthcoming). Hurley advances five different "layers" of adaptive feedback control, which she calls the "shared-circuits model." She uses the model to show how a shared information space for action and perception can be the basis of a shared information space for self and other. There isn't room here for a detailed examination of her complex and multifaceted construction. Instead, I want to look at a presupposition of her approach, the alleged simulationist character of control theory.

In the computational study of motor control, forward and inverse systems are said to "model" certain transformations (e.g., from motor commands to sensory consequences or from desired consequences to actions). In what sense of "model" do CNS systems model these transformations? It might be the computationalist sense, where modeling is creating and using a complex set of representations or descriptions of a target subject. In this sense, a model of a transformation is a theory of it. In support of this interpretation, notice that in Wolpert and Kawato's (1998) MOSAIC model of control, forward models are said to provide probabilities for use in certain calculations. Such probabilities, namely, probabilistic representations, are the stuff of theories. Models are also spoken of as containing "information." Wolpert and Gharhamani write: "Internal models, both forward and inverse, capture information about the properties of the sensorimotor system" (2000: 1216). Similarly, there is much talk of models being "learned" and "updated," where the learning and updating of models is naturally interpretable as the learning of theories. On the basis of these considerations, it is natural to understand the internal-model framework as proceeding within the general framework of computationalism, to which the theory-theory approach is closely allied.

But some of the terminology used by these writers suggests a different interpretation. Wolpert and collaborators frequently use such terms as *mimic* and *simulate* to describe the activity of internal models. Wolpert, Ghahramani, and Jordan say that forward models "*mimic* the causal flow of a process" (1995: 1880). Wolpert writes: "The ... feedforward process ... uses the efferent outflow along with the current state estimate to predict the next state by *simulating* the movement dynamics with a forward model" (1997: 213; emphasis added). Wolpert, Doya, and Kawato write: "On the basis of computational studies it has been proposed that the CNS internally *simulates* aspects of the sensorimotor loop in planning, control and learning" (2004: 310, emphasis added).

In section 2.4, we contrasted two senses of "simulation": the computational-modeling sense and the replication sense of simulation. I argued that the appropriate sense of simulation for a theory of mindreading is the replication sense, which fits most work in the ST tradition. But I suspect it's the computational-modeling sense of simulation that is suitable for control theory. Indeed, the replication interpretation seems highly implausible in certain contexts. Wolpert, Doya, and Kawato write that a forward model "acts as a neural simulator of the musculoskeletal system *and environment*" (2004: 310, emphasis added). Could a forward model in the CNS replicate the *environment* (in some interesting way)? That is quite a stretch. What ought to be meant is that a forward model *represents* or *describes* (some aspects or dimensions of) the environment. This is entirely tangential to the replication sense of simulation.

Admittedly, Wolpert and colleagues (along with others like Grush, 2004) may intend the replication sense of "simulation." That is how Patricia Churchland (2002), for example, interprets them. The more important question is not whether this is their intention but whether this construal is appropriate. Granted that CNS systems engage in "modeling" in *some* sense, should this modeling be understood in a replicational sense? Physiological studies that motivated the efference copy construct underlie the basic framework, and the phrase "efference copy" evokes the idea of a neurocognitive item that duplicates, replicates, or resembles another neurocognitive item. But efference copy is only a small part of the overall theory. The internal models posited by control theory, all built up by associative learning, do not lend themselves very well to the simulationist conception.[9] If control theory can indeed be firmly grounded in a suitably replicational sense of simulation, I would welcome it. But the issue awaits full resolution.

8.11 Evolution of Mindreading

Mindreading is a pivotal activity of the human social brain, arguably one that sets us apart as a species. Unsurprisingly, there is abundant curiosity about its evolution. Perhaps light can be shed on the subject by reflecting on the possible account of mentalizing that best fits an otherwise well-supported phylogenetic account.

Most efforts in this direction focus on the mindreading of propositional attitudes. Two hypotheses about the selectional advantages of mindreading are commonly proffered. First, reading another person's mind can help one anticipate that person's future behavior. Second, knowing how to induce false belief in the other can advance one's self-interest. Humphrey formulated the first of these as follows:

> In evolutionary terms it must have been a breakthrough.... Imagine the biological benefits to the first of our ancestors who developed the ability to make

realistic guesses about the inner life of his rivals; to be able to picture what another was thinking about and planning to do next. (Humphrey, 1984)

The second hypothesis, that mindreading subserves "Machiavellian intelligence," or tactical deception, is founded on the thought that deception is something our primate forebears could do (Byrne and Whiten, 1988, 1991). Baron-Cohen (1995) advanced evolutionary hypotheses about four mind-reading modules, three of which "feed into" the central module, ToMM, that executes propositional-attitude reading.

Most of these speculations presuppose the TT story of mindreading, and their proponents rarely discuss whether the proposed evolutionary story fits better with TT or with ST.[10] However, the evidence for most of the evolutionary stories is quite debatable. It would be preferable to examine mind-reading terrain where the phylogenetic materials are more solid. This holds for some of the face-based emotion recognition examples discussed in chapter 6. So this section is devoted to reflections on these emotional systems, the adaptive value of contagion, and how contagion could be transmuted into certain kinds of mindreading routines, namely, *simulational* routines.[11]

I begin with disgust, relying heavily on Lawrence and Calder (2004). Garcia (1989, 1990) has argued for two mammalian defense systems, "external" and "internal." The internal, or "gut," defense system evolved under the pressure of plants and animals that employ toxins to fend off foragers and predators. This gut defense system is associated with distaste reactions. When odor is compounded with taste in acquisition, odor alone acts like taste, an internal cue. It is known that damage to the gustatory neocortex of the rat, located in the agranular insular cortex, impairs the distaste reaction. Rats lesioned in the agranular insular cortex do not appear to experience the hedonic shift in taste that normally occurs when an ingested item is accompanied by illness. In humans, lesions to the presumably homologous area of the gustatory insula impair reactions to bitter tastes (Pritchard, Macaluso, and Eslinger, 1999). Rozin and Fallon (1987) proposed that the human emotion of disgust evolved from the mammalian distaste response. A "core" disgust system is constructed from the distaste food rejection system via a process akin to evolutionary preadaptation in which the disgust response is attached successively to a variety of things that are offensive within any particular culture. Tomkins (1963) argued that primary disgust is frequently induced by the display of disgust in others, that is, that disgust faces are a pan-cultural disgust stimulus. The data from patient NK (Calder, Keane, Manes, Antoun, and Young, 2000) support this disgust contagion proposal, as do the imaging data from the Wicker at al. study (2003) (see section 6.1).

Regarding anger, Lawrence and Calder (2004) report the well-supported view that there are two broad categories of aggression: "self-defensive" aggression and aggression concerned with competition for, and defense of, valued resources, including territory, a mate, or a place in a rank order. The second type of aggression, appetitive/competitive/offensive aggression, relies on a distinct motivational system. Action patterns associated with this form of aggression have much in common across various mammalian species, and the human emotion of anger is related to activation of this system (Blanchard and Blanchard, 1984). The dopamine system has been implicated in the production of offensive responses in the processing of conspecific aggression signals in a wide variety of species. In vivo microdialysis experiments in rats have shown that dopamine levels are elevated during social-agonistic encounters, and ex vivo dissection experiments in mice show altered dopamine levels following aggressive behavior (Hadfield, 1983). The latter study also found increases of dopamine in mice who merely witnessed fighting but were prevented from participating. In humans, dopamine D2 levels are increased when they play a competitive-aggressive video game (Koepp et al., 1998). As we know from the Lawrence-Calder experiment reported in section 6.1, acute dopamine block-ade produces a selective disruption in the recognition of anger displayed in faces but leaves intact the recognition of other facial expressions. Apparently, the disruption works by interfering with the mechanism of anger contagion that normally occurs and normally underpins the recognition of anger in facial expressions.

Two evolutionary steps are needed to explain face-based recognition for any emotion: the evolution of contagion mechanisms and the evolution of emotion recognition from contagion. The discussion that follows closely follows the proposals of Sripada and Goldman (2005). Contagion mecha-nisms for emotions presumably evolved because it was adaptive for the self to experience a given emotion E when others, especially conspecifics, ex-perienced E and displayed that experience facially. For example, disgust is experienced in response to a harmful food item. If an individual observes a conspecific making an avoidance-associated response to an ingested food item, it would be adaptive for that individual to make the same response vis-à-vis that food item, to induce avoidance. A similar logic applies to other sources of disgust, such as disease or putrefaction, the avoidance of which would also be adaptive. In the case of competitive anger, the same logic again applies. It may be adaptive to become aggressive and angry when you ob-serve a conspecific become aggressive and angry (toward you). Hence, mech-anisms for anger contagion may evolve over time.

Once emotion contagion mechanisms are in place, how might this lead to mindreading? It is common for natural selection to build new capacities from existing ones. Traits that originally evolved for other uses and are subse-quently co-opted for a new purpose are called *exaptations* (Gould and Vrba, 1982). If a contagion mechanism for a given emotion state is already in place, this mechanism might be co-opted for a new purpose, that of mindreading. If a contagion mechanism for emotion E exists, this implies that occurrences of

E in a sender S tend to be copied, or triggered, in a receiver R. Once such an emotion-copying process is established, it can readily be exapted into simulational (resonance-based) mindreading. If the occurrence of E in sender S reliably triggers a corresponding state E in observer R, then R is in a position to capitalize on her own experience of E and impute it to S. R simply has to acquire a propensity to classify her own state appropriately and assign the so-classified state to S. Thus, there is an available evolutionary pathway to a simulation routine for FaBER, and it isn't obvious that there is any comparably available evolutionary pathway to a theory-based routine for FaBER.

Assuming that the foregoing account is roughly correct for FaBER, and perhaps for other low-level mindreading processes as well, what are the implications for the evolution of high-level simulational mindreading? It is unlikely that the story could be quite so simple. According to chapter 7, high-level mindreading depends crucially on the process of E-imagination, specifically, interpersonal applications of E-imagination. It is not difficult to conceive of evolutionary accounts of *intra*personal E-imagination, including visual imagination and motor imagination (see Currie, 1995a; Dennett, 1978c). But the step to *inter*personal uses of E-imagination is a large one, and the step to interpersonal uses *for mindreading* is another large step.

Now, the interpersonal use of E-imagination for mindreading is essentially a matter of learning to take another person's perspective, and the capacity for perspective taking may have evolved from mirror-neuron activity in primates, where an observer undergoes the same goal-related event in his premotor cortex as the creature he observes. This might be related to the link between mirror-matching and simulational mindreading first proposed by Gallese and Goldman (1998). This hypothesis is intriguing, but it faces challenges, including the following one. As emphasized in section 8.6, perspective taking, or enactive imagination, is a fairly controlled process, whereas mirroring-matching activity is a highly automatic one. These may be entirely different types of processes, though they share certain (simulational) characteristics, just as spontaneous smiling and voluntary smiling are distinct processes, using entirely different sets of muscles. Other complications are associated with high-level mindreading, including its possible relation to language (see chapter 4). So I offer no further speculations about the evolution of high-level simulational mindreading. I rest content in the hope that a little progress has been made in sketching the evolution of low-level mindreading in simulation-friendly terms.

Notes

1. It can be objected that the evidence is still purely correlational and does not directly speak to a causal relationship. Indeed, it would be preferable to have an intervention study to strengthen the claim. (Thanks here to Andrea Heberlein.)

2. It may be countered that Baron-Cohen's position is not so clearly simulationist. He frequently describes mindreading in the language of "inferring" and employs the label "theory of mind." This is not very dispositive, however, because "inferring" can be used neutrally, to characterize the steps of mindreading according to any approach, and the label "theory of mind" can also be used quite neutrally. I think his use of the term "empathy," together with the quoted passages, makes my interpretation compelling. Admittedly, he probably didn't contemplate alternative theoretical frameworks in writing *The Essential Difference*.

3. Some researchers would disagree about autistics being indifferent to others' feelings. Uta Frith (2003: 111–112) suggests that although autistics have difficulty with high-level ("intentional") empathy, they are unimpaired with respect to low-level ("instinctive") empathy. (Thanks here to Philip Robbins.) However, there are findings that support autistic impairments in low-level (emotional) empathy, as well as high-level (cognitive) empathy. In a study by Charman et al. (1997), an experimenter acted as if he had hit his thumb with a hammer and made facial and vocal expressions of distress (cries of pain). None of the 10 autistic children studied, age 20 months, showed any facial sign of concern, whereas most normally developing children did. Similarly, Oliver Sacks (1995: 269) tells the story of a 12-year-old autistic girl who reported to a teacher: "Joanie [another student] is making a funny noise." Joanie was weeping.

4. A fourth theory of autism is the amygdala theory; the amygdala is known to be abnormal in autism. However, I won't explore this additional theory. In any case, it may not be incompatible with the empathy theory.

5. In particular, the examples of nonconscious E-imagination discussed in section 7.4, especially those analyzed in terms of priming, are standardly classified as automatic rather than controlled. But I entertained the possibility that those examples belong in our high-level category rather than the low-level one.

6. Similar passages can be found in other writings by Gallese, for example, "The discovery of mirror neurons in the monkey premotor cortex has unveiled a neural matching mechanism that, in the light of more recent findings, appears to be present also in a variety of *nonmotor-related* human brain structures" (2001: 46; emphasis added).

7. For further exploration of self-other problems and simulation, see Jeannerod and Pacherie (2004). They cite additional clinical evidence that is relevant. I don't pursue their analysis in detail because it ventures into the vexed issue of the "self," which considerations of space preclude here. For a book-length treatment of the self from a neuroscience perspective, see Metzinger (2003).

8. This illustration is borrowed from Hurley (in press).

9. In recent writings, Wolpert and colleagues endorse further replicationist-sounding themes for certain *special* topics in control theory. Wolpert, Doya, and Kawato (2004) suggest that during action observation, one's own motor system can be used to understand the actions of others, that is, for detecting and identifying biological motion: "There the observer uses his own multiple modules to try to simulate the observed percept" (2004: 314). This idea has been suggested by a number of other writers, including Knoblich and Prinz (2001), Knoblich and Flach (2001), and Decety and Grèzes (1999). Gallese may have this material in mind in citing the Wolpert et al. work. But it doesn't follow from this special application that the *general* control-theoretic framework of internal models should be understood in replicational terms.

Indeed, it isn't entirely clear that Wolpert et al. intend their approach to instantiate simulation in the sense we have specified here (R-simulation). Let me quote some relevant passages at length:

> Skilled motor behavior relies on accurate predictive models of both our own body and external objects and environments. As the dynamics of our body changes during development, and as we experience tools that have their own intrinsic dynamics, we constantly need to acquire new models and update existing models. Thus, forward models are not fixed entities but must be learned and updated through experience. Learning a predictive model is relatively straightforward. By comparing the predicted and actual outcome of a motor command a prediction error can be generated. Well-established computational learning rules can be used to translate these errors in prediction into changes in synaptic weights that will improve any future predictions of a forward model. We can consider a similar forward or predictive model for social interaction. In this case another person's response to my motor commands or communicative behavior is modeled. Again, discrepancies between anticipated and actual behavior can be used to refine such a model. Therefore, by monitoring one's own action and the response of others, it is possible to learn a predictive model of the likely behavior of someone in response to our actions.
>
> We propose that the reason we are able to solve the problem of learning internal models of other people is because of the similarity of brains across people. We propose that the uniqueness of human communication relies on our brains being similar. This allows the brain to use this fact to train a good internal model of another person's brain. We will review how having a similar motor system (brain and musculoskeletal system) between two people enables us to use the mappings between our actions and our own mental states as *a priori* information to bootstrap any learning of another person's internal models. (2004: 310, 311–312)

Although there is undoubtedly a "flavor" of R-simulation in the Wolpert et al. text, a careful reading suggests a CM-interpretation instead. Consider the very final sentence of the foregoing material. "Mappings" between our actions and mental states sound like rules or generalizations between the two types of variable. They are things that forward models represent, theory-like things. Similarly, the claim that these mappings are a priori *information* suggests that the internal models use the mappings in a theorizing fashion. In other words, a theory of one's own motor system is used to acquire a theory of someone else's system. To my ears, this sounds more like theorizing than R-simulation.

10. An exception here is Humphrey, who sketches a form of ST.

11. In chapter 6, we promoted the idea that emotion contagion is a resonance or mirroring system, and section 6.7 considered the proposal that mirroring systems are not hardwired but instead arise from Hebbian learning. This section obviously sets aside the Hebbian learning possibility and explores the more common assumption that mirror systems have an innate basis.

9

Self-Attribution

9.1 The Special Method View

The last three chapters focused almost exclusively on mental attribution to others. But our agenda has a slot for self-attribution as well: How do people detect and classify their own (current) mental states? Any comprehensive theory of mentalizing must answer this question. ST does not directly offer an answer; no simulation theorist claims that simulation itself is used in first-person attribution, at least attribution of *current* states. On the other hand, the version of ST presented here presupposes a special role for the classification of one's own states. Third-person mindreading by simulation borrows classifications of one's own states to classify states of another. In decision prediction, for example, one makes a simulated decision, metarepresents it as a decision with a specific content, and attributes it to the target. So under ST, classification of one's own state plays a role even in third-person ascription.[1]

Setting aside this distinctive feature of ST, self-attribution is a prominent topic in philosophy, commonly discussed under the heading of "self-knowledge." The label "self-knowledge," however, introduces certain issues peripheral to our agenda. Knowledge is a thick epistemological concept, connoting more than just attribution or belief. Philosophers understand knowledge as something like justified true belief, or reliably formed true belief. In keeping with my resolve to avoid in-depth treatment of epistemology (section 1.2), this chapter trips lightly over these issues, concentrating on the simpler question of how classifications of one's own states are arrived at, whether accurately, reliably, justifiably, or otherwise. An account of first-person mindreading isn't obliged to establish that first-person mindreading is more reliable than third-person mindreading or to explain why first-person mental beliefs are better warranted than third-person mental beliefs. We won't ignore these questions entirely, but the focus is on epistemologically *neutral* facts about self-attribution, facts on which the epistemological status of self-knowledge—or self-delusion—might supervene.[2]

So, the main question in this chapter is how attributors select specific mental-state descriptors for self-attribution. How do they classify episodes of their mental life as tokenings of certain sensations, emotions, or propositional attitudes rather than others? It is one thing to have, or experience, a mental state and something else to attribute such a state, to have a belief about it. How do attributors classify or "type" current states as belonging to certain mental categories rather than others?

A general epistemological doctrine in this domain is the doctrine of *privileged access*. This doctrine holds that people are in an authoritative position vis-à-vis their own mental states, that their sincere claims about them have a favored position. There is some sort of *asymmetry* between first-person and third-person situations, such that first-person reports have a higher credibility or trustworthiness than third-person reports. If this asymmetry is legitimate, what accounts for it? What special relationship does a person bear to her own mental states as compared with those of others? Of course, the standard doctrine of asymmetry presupposes that third-person attribution is based on theory-like inference from the target's observed behavior and environment; special first-person access is said to contrast with that scenario. This contrast may need adjustment when we contemplate a simulationist account of third-person attribution in which first-person classification participates. But for the moment, to get up and running, let's assume the standard view of third-person attribution.

How should a presumed asymmetry between first- and third-person attribution be accounted for? One answer is what I'll call the *special method* view. This comes in a weak form and a strong form. According to the weak form, people have a special *process* or *method* of accessing or detecting their own current mental states, a method that cannot be applied to the states of others. The strong form embraces both this and the additional thesis that the special method is epistemologically superior, where superiority consists in greater reliability than third-person methods, or the ability to confer greater justification or warrant for one's resulting beliefs. Because I am downplaying epistemological questions, I shall pay only limited attention to the reliability or justification-conferring power of different methods. I shall principally concern myself with the weak form of the special method view: Is there a distinctive method for first-person mindreading, and what is its nature?

One conception of the special method, a conception I'll defend, features the thesis that the special method is that of "introspection," "inner sense," or self-monitoring. What "introspection" means is controversial, and the version of it I'll defend will not be very orthodox. But the idea is often associated with a quasi-perceptual model of mental-state apprehension. The process of identifying one's pains, emotions, or beliefs is modeled on perceptual processes of seeing or hearing objects or sounds. Just *how* similar introspection is to perception, or inner sense to outer sense, is a matter of dispute. Often accompanying an introspective or monitoring version of the special method view is the claim that it classifies a mental state token by recognizing in it some *features* or *criteria* associated with the selected mental type. For example, one classifies a target state as "thirst" or "anger" by recognizing in it features criterial to one's concept (or conception) of thirst or of anger. Such recognition does not require inference from premises about one's own behavior or other peripheral events. This type of approach is sometimes called "Cartesian,"[3] but various types and degrees of Cartesianism are available for adoption or rejection, as we shall explore later.

There are many reasons why the special method view, and especially its quasi-perceptual variant, has been greeted with skepticism. Philosophers and psychologists alike find it unpersuasive, even repugnant. As this chapter unfolds, we shall examine and rebut various grounds for skepticism found in the philosophical and psychological literatures. Next I critically discuss several recent variants of the special method view and finally turn to my own favored version of that view.

9.2 Philosophers' Doubts about the Cartesian Model

Philosophical resistance to anything that smacks of a Cartesian model is often associated with Wittgenstein's attack on the possibility of a private language (see especially Wittgenstein, 1953: section 258). Here is a standard version of Wittgenstein's argument: According to Cartesianism, self-knowledge involves the use of a vocabulary for labeling mental events that is essentially private. This means that there are no procedures—at least no public procedures—by which to verify whether a term from such a vocabulary is applied in the same way as when initially introduced. This implies that there is no standard of correctness or incorrectness, no difference between getting the term's use right versus getting it wrong, which undercuts the claim that a genuine *language* is in use. Two crucial replies are available to the private language proponent (Fodor, 1975: 69–70). First, there is no reason why mental terms need be epistemically private in Wittgenstein's sense. If mental events are neural events, then all the mental events involved in application of a mental code are in principle publicly accessible. Second, the argument makes the mistake of assuming that because the user of a private language (or his community) cannot *verify* the correctness or incorrectness of its applications, there isn't *in fact* a difference between correct and incorrect applications. This is an objectionable form of verificationism. To be sure, there are alternative inter-pretations of Wittgenstein's private language argument (e.g., Wright, 1991, 1998; McDowell, 1991, 1998), but none is really convincing. Each has one or more questionable premises or presuppositions.

A second source of doubt about the Cartesian model arises from a competing positive approach to privileged access, also due to Wittgenstein. In everyday epistemic practice, a person's sincere claim of being in a simple mental state is accepted by others as very strong evidence for his really being in that state. It is part of our "language game" to confer authoritativeness on such claims. Wittgenstein's thesis is that this feature of our language game is not founded on any other story congenial to Cartesianism. The facts of our language game are just "brute" or "bedrock," even "primitively constitutive" of what it is to be in these mental states. Elizabeth Fricker (1998) calls this the "artefact of gram-mar" theory, and Crispin Wright (1998) calls it the "default view." As Fricker rightly points out, however, the fact that our everyday epistemic practice confers prima facie warrant on first-person mental reports is compatible with underlying Cartesian ideas. Maybe our social-epistemic practice confers warrant on first-person reports *because* such reports are based on introspection, a reliable method of detection. To show that epistemic practices are "bedrock" rather than explicable in terms of introspective reliability needs considerable argument. Even if Wittgenstein were right that social-epistemic practices are not indebted to introspection, appeal to social-epistemic practices doesn't explain which methods *are* used in classifying (or avowing) one's own mental states. How this is done—whether at the "personal" or "subpersonal" level—is precisely the question we wish to answer, and no story at the level of social-epistemic practices can provide an explanation. There are scientific stories to tell about how cognitive tasks like perceptual judgment, language learning, and reasoning about numbers are executed. Why shouldn't there be a scientific story to tell about mental self-attribution?

A third objection to the special method view is that first-person privileged access arises not from a contingently reliable process or a special method of recognition but from a logical or metaphysical immunity to error. This "logical" solution looks especially plausible with respect to the *subject* of first-person mental ascription. Isn't the self-ascriber of a pain immune to "error through misidentification" when she says, or believes, "I have such and such a pain (or belief)"? How could she be wrong about who has, or "owns," the mental state?[4] Logical or metaphysical infallibility, however, does not carry over to the mental-state type. Error is at least possible—perhaps even common—with respect to mental types. So how can distinctive first-person access be explained through error immunity of a logical or metaphysical sort?

One version of the noncontingency approach is due to Tyler Burge (1985, 1988, 1996). Burge identifies a special class of first-person mental judgments—called "cogito" judgments—that are necessarily true. These are judgments of the form "I am thinking that I am thinking that p." These judgments are contextually and automatically self-verifying, because a subject's thinking such a thought *makes* the thought content true. No distinctive method for arriving at such judgments need be posited. Nothing like this holds in the case of third-person mental attribution. So the first-person/third-person asymmetry is explained without positing a special *method* for detecting one's own thoughts.

Granting Burge's point about the class of judgments he calls "cogito" judgments, the point obviously does not generalize to all first-person judgments. "I am thinking that I have a headache" is not self-verifying, because the thought that I have a headache does not make it true that I have a headache. In general, the cogito type of analysis does not apply to sensations, an important subclass of mental states. The analysis equally fails to generalize to attitude types other than thinking (Boghossian, 1989). Consider "I am thinking that I hope the drought will end soon." Although having such a reflective thought makes it true that one entertains the content "that the drought will end soon," it does not make it true that one *hopes* this content will be realized. Thinking that one Φs that p does not entail Φing that p unless thinking (logically) entails Φing, but thinking doesn't entail hoping.

Burge might say that even if self-verification does not explain privileged access for all cases, at least it explains it for some. I would reply that there is a strong prima facie case for a (substantially) *unified*, or *homogeneous*, account of first-person privileged access. There appears to be a strong unity or similarity among different kinds of mental states with respect to special access, so any disunified explanation has a nonnegligible count against it. This is one reason why a "logical" or "metaphysical" approach looks unpromising.[5]

I turn next to Sydney Shoemaker's (1996) views on self-knowledge. Shoemaker contends that the inner sense view of self-knowledge presupposes the occurrence of mental states or events that are *independent* of the method used to determine their occurrence. He calls this "the independence condition" and disputes its fulfillment. He claims, instead, "that there is a conceptual, constitutive connection between the existence of certain sorts of mental entities and their introspective accessibility" (1996: 225). On one conception of what mental states are, says Shoemaker, it would be conceptually possible for a person to be in mental states without knowing or believing that he is—even if he had the concepts needed for forming such beliefs or knowledge. In other words, it would be conceptually possible to be systematically ignorant of these states. He characterizes this scenario as one of systematic *self-blindness*. However, argues Shoemaker, self-blindness is conceptually impossible, a thesis he defends in intricate detail. Hence, our knowledge or belief about our own mental states is not a contingent matter but something conceptually guaranteed. Because this violates the independence condition, which the special method view presupposes, the special method view (and its inner sense variant) is untenable.

Shoemaker embeds the independence condition into what he calls the "broad perceptual model" of introspection, which he rejects. A discussion of this phase of his argument is deferred to section 9.5. Here I restrict myself to another perception-like model of introspection that Shoemaker discusses (and also rejects): the "object-perception" model. There isn't room to discuss all features of this model, but I'll comment on one of them. Ordinary sense perception, says Shoemaker, involves distinctive sense experiences. When I see a lilac bush in bloom, I experience a visual presentation of this flowery bush, a presentation distinct both from the bush itself and from any belief I might form about the bush. Nobody thinks that in being introspectively aware of a sensation or thought, one has yet another sensation or experience that is "of" the first sensation or thought and constitutes its "appearing" a particular way (Shoemaker, 1996: 207; see Lyons, 1986: chapter 5). In other words, introspective awareness of mental states has no distinctive phenomenology associated with it. There is no introspective character analogous to the "lookishness" of vision or the "soundishness" of audition. In this respect, introspection is unlike ordinary sense perception. But Shoemaker properly grants that this disanalogy is insufficient to declare a moratorium on the analogizing of introspection to sense perception. Inner sense might resemble outer sense in *some* respects, though not *all*. I agree with this general stance. Disanalogies like the absence of phenomenology should not exclude (quasi-) perceptual models of introspection.

In recent years, a new kind of worry has arisen for the privileged access thesis, one arising from content externalism. Content externalism is the thesis that the contents of propositional attitudes are individuated at least in part by environmental factors; content does not supervene on a thinker's intrinsic properties. The thesis is due to Putnam (1975) and Burge (1979), influenced especially by Putnam's Twin Earth thought experiment. Content externalism appears to make trouble for privileged access. How can a subject know the contents of his thoughts by introspective awareness, given that the external world is presumably inaccessible to introspection? This problem is pressed by Paul Boghossian (1989), Michael McKinsey (1991), and Jessica Brown (1995), for example. Others defend the compatibility of externalism and privileged access. Brian McLaughlin and Michael Tye (1998) point out that there are multiple ways of interpreting each of the crucial concepts: content, externalism, and privileged access. Under some interpretive combinations, externalism and privileged access are compatible.

Because a full treatment of these topics gets very technical—in ways tangential to this book's focus—I shall not tackle the content-externalism problem in any detail. Another reason to keep it at arm's length is that the problem is officially about self-*knowledge*, one of those "thick" epistemo-logical questions we have set aside. Nonetheless, toward the end of the chapter, we'll see that the theory of content self-attribution offered here promises the bonus of coping smoothly with content externalism.

9.3 Cognitive Science-Based Doubts about Privileged Access

Many psychologists and cognitive scientists are very leery about privileged access in general (first-person/third-person asymmetry) and the Cartesian model in particular. Grounds for doubt are grouped here into three categories: (i) methodological doubts about introspection, (ii) evidence for confabulation rather than introspection, and (iii) evidence of a common inferential method in first- and third-person mentalizing.

9.3.1 Introspection as a Scientific Methodology?

Historically, psychology challenged the legitimacy of introspection as a method of psychological science. This challenge was so potent during the behaviorist era that the very word *introspection* became—and largely remains—taboo, though nowadays many cognitive scientists are comfortable with the term *(self-)monitoring*. The historical rap against introspection was twofold. First was the complaint that introspective reports are not reliable ("valid," in psychological terminology), because introspective reports of men-tal phenomena from different laboratories gave conflicting stories, so some of those reports had to be wrong. The headline case was the dispute between German introspectionists (mostly in Würzberg) and American introspec-tionists (led by E. B. Titchener at Cornell) about the existence of imageless thought. According to the story, subjects gave different reports, depending on their respective laboratories. Hence, introspection cannot be a "superior" method of detecting states or properties of the mind. Second was a complaint about the "privacy" of introspection. Objective science requires objective methods, that is, public or intersubjective methods rather than private ones, but introspection is the paradigm of a private method.

The first complaint is questionable in historical terms. After reviewing the Würzburg and Cornell results, Monson and Hurlburt (1993) argued that subjects in the two laboratories actually reported identical observations, but these were given different interpretations by the theorists. Nonetheless, it is certainly right that restrictions must be imposed on the kinds of mental properties that introspection can be counted on to reveal. Introspection may be reliable vis-à-vis some questions and less reliable or wholly unreliable vis-à-vis others. Early psychologists tried to use introspection to uncover the microstructure of cognition, and that is clearly beyond its powers (Goldman, 2004). But this concession leaves open the possibility that gross features of conscious life can be accurately identified by introspective means. However, all these points are incidental for the present inquiry, which asks whether there is a distinctive first-person method, reliable or unreliable. Psychologists should not trust subjects' introspective reports if introspection isn't a reliable method of ascertaining what is reported, but psychologists can nonetheless conclude that naïve people do *use* introspection in forming beliefs about their mental states. So the question of whether cognitive science should rely on introspective reports is separable from the question—our question—of whether ordinary people use introspection as their default method of self-attribution.

A similar point applies to the privacy issue. There are interesting questions of what is so good about publicity (intersubjectivity) or so bad about privacy, and what exactly these properties are (Goldman, 1997). But these questions are tangential to the ones before us. Introspection may indeed be a private process (in one relevant sense), and that *may* disqualify it for purposes of science (though I have argued to the contrary, in Goldman, 1997, 2000b, 2004). But this does not matter for present purposes. If people do use a private method for self-ascribing mental states, so be it. Our present enterprise is to get straight what they actually do, not to pass epistemological or methodological judgment on their practice.

That people use something like introspection can be made compelling by considering the implausibility of alternatives. I believe that I currently intend to walk into my study and remove a particular book from the shelf. What leads me to think I have this intention? Might it be inferred by theoretical reasoning? From what evidence would it be inferred—current behavior? past behavior? So far I have taken no step toward the study, so current behavior provides no clue. Nor do I have any past track record of taking that particular book off the shelf, so past behavior is no help either. The obvious explanation is that my intention belief is obtained directly rather than inferentially.

Nowadays it is not uncommon for cognitive scientists to posit introspection, or at least self-monitoring, to account for experimental findings. Here is an example from Willem Levelt (1990: 13), writing on the production of speech. A speaker can detect trouble in his own internal speech before he has fully articulated the troublesome element. This is presumably what happened in the following recorded self-correction: "To the left side of the purple disk is a v-, a horizontal line." There is reason to assume that the speaker began to articulate the word *vertical*; he briefly had a *plan* or *intention* to articulate "vertical," which he abandoned near the start of its articulation. What happened, according to Levelt, is that the plan for saying "vertical" was available or accessible to the self-monitoring system, and it was found to have a nonintended meaning. Thus, a self-correction in mid-word was effected. The crucial point for our purposes is that the only good explanation in the offing assumes that the agent has a system, or process, for detecting his own current plan, a species of mental state. This is one simple example of how a self-monitoring process is a crucial posit in some area of cognitive science.

9.3.2 Self-Ascription by Confabulation

Other cognitive science researchers, however, cite evidence for methods of self-ascription quite different from introspection. For example, some research indicates that people self-ascribe by a process of confabulation—the fabrication of ill-supported explanatory stories. This process is of a piece with theorizing, so the method of self-ascription, on this view, would be the same as the assumed method of other-ascription.

In a widely cited article, Richard Nisbett and Timothy Wilson (1977) reported evidence of subjects confabulating stories about the causes of their mental states. At a shopping mall, they mounted a display table with four pairs of identical panty hose and asked passersby which pair they preferred and what their reasons were. In a previous version of the study, they had ascertained that there was a strong position effect. The panty hose were labeled A, B, C, and D, from left to right. Pair A was preferred by only 12 percent of the participants, pair B by 17 percent, pair C by 31 percent, and pair D by 40 percent for a statistically significant effect. In the main study, when people were asked the reason for their choice, people pointed to some attribute of the preferred pair, such as its superior knit, sheerness, or elasticity. Nobody spontaneously mentioned position effect as the cause of her preference. When specifically asked whether their choice had been influenced by position, almost all said of course not (the lone exception being a participant who was taking three psychology courses). Thus, participants seemed totally unaware of what was in fact causing (or influencing) their preference, and their claim about what influenced it was merely a confabulation. They simply made conjectures about what might have produced their preference.[6] Nisbett and Wilson's published article drew the eye-catching conclusion: People have "little or no introspective access to higher order cognitive processes."

A second study providing evidence for confabulation was done by Michael Gazzaniga (1992; Baynes and Gazzaniga, 2000). This involved split-brain patients, who had undergone surgical separation of their two hemispheres. In such commissurotomy patients, the left hemisphere, which usually controls the production of speech, is no longer in communication with the right hemisphere. Stimuli can be given separately to each hemisphere, which does not communicate this information to its mate, as normally occurs when the corpus callosum is intact. When a visual stimulus is flashed to the right brain only, it can produce manual responses, but it cannot verbally respond to this experience. The talking left hemisphere, on the other hand, is blind to the stimulus. So what is the patient's verbal response when asked about a stimulus flashed to the right brain, or asked about a manual action produced by the right brain in response to such a stimulus?

In one test, a patient's left brain saw a chicken claw and the right brain saw a snow scene, and the patient was asked to choose an associated item from an array of pictures placed in full view of both hemispheres. The patient responded by choosing the shovel with the hand connected to the right brain (the left hand) and by choosing a chicken with the hand connected to the left brain (the right hand). The left brain matched the chicken claw and the right brain matched the snow scene. When the patient was asked why he chose these items, the talking left hemisphere replied, "Oh, that's simple. The chicken claw goes with the chicken, and you need a shovel to clean out the chicken shed" (Gazzaniga 1992: 124; based on Gazzaniga and LeDoux, 1978). Evidently, the left hemisphere was simply confabulating. It had no idea, really, why the shovel had been selected, because it had no information about the snow scene. It just made up a story to connect the shovel to a chicken. This story was not a readout from a mental process of choosing the shovel; choosing the shovel occurred in the right hemisphere, and the left hemisphere was wholly ignorant of that process. When challenged to explain the choice of the shovel, the left hemisphere fabricated a story.

Gazzaniga relied on this kind of finding to hypothesize a left-brain-based module called the interpreter. The interpreter's job is to give explanations of the agent's behavior by creating plausible theories. Such interpretations may provide very inaccurate accounts of what really transpires, and their creation is a far cry from a special "channel" to mental states that figures in a Cartesian model.

Confabulation is a pretty compelling account of the split-brain example. One might quibble (is it really a quibble?) that this isn't a genuine case of *first-person* attribution, because the disconnected hemispheres underlie two separate streams of consciousness. When the left hemisphere explains the right hemisphere's action by appeal to a certain thought or intention, it isn't attributing that mental-state to *itself*. I will not press this response, however. I grant that first-person mental-state attribution sometimes consists in confabulation. It does not follow, however, that confabulation is the only method, or the principal method, of first-person attribution. Indeed, cases of confabulation may be relatively rare. Standard cases of first-person attribution may involve introspection or self-monitoring. This is the theory I wish to embrace, and the resulting overall theory might be called a *dual-method* theory.[7] To sustain the privileged access theory, it suffices that a substantial range of mental attributions are executed by a special, distinctive method that works (fully) only in the first person. That there is a second, backup method, which can be used equally for first- and third-person attribution, doesn't detract from privileged access.

Nisbett and Wilson seemed to deny privileged access more broadly. Their denial has recently been recanted by the second author, Wilson. What he and Nisbett meant to deny, says Wilson (2002), is privileged access to the *causes* of one's behavior, and to the mental *processing* that produces feelings, judgments, and behaviors. People do have privileged access to a great deal of information about themselves, such as the content of their current thoughts and memories and the object of their attention.

> The fact that people make errors about the causes of their responses does not mean that their inner worlds are a black box. I can bring to mind a great deal of information that is inaccessible to anyone but me. Unless you can read my mind, there is no way you could know that a specific memory just came to mind, namely an incident in high school in which I dropped my bag lunch out a third-floor window, narrowly missing a gym teacher who happened to walk around a corner at just the wrong time. Isn't this a case of my having privileged, "introspective access to higher order cognitive processes"? ... Although we often have access to the results of these processes—such as my memory of the lunch-dropping incident—we do not have access to the mental processes that produced them. I don't really know, for example, why that particular memory came to mind, just as the participants in the panty-hose study did not know exactly why they preferred pair D over A. (Wilson, 2002: 105)

And in a further passage:

> To the extent that people's responses are caused by the adaptive unconscious, they do not have privileged access to the causes and must infer them, just as Nisbett and I argued. But to the extent that people's responses are caused by the conscious self, they have privileged access to the actual causes of these responses; in short, the Nisbett and Wilson argument was wrong about such cases. (Wilson, 2002: 106)

These passages concede to privileged-access theorists everything they really want, or deserve. No careful privileged-access theorist should claim that people have introspective access to the causes of their behavior, especially *qua* causes, or to the cognitive processes that run their mental lives. But Wilson now concedes that people do have privileged access to much of their conscious lives, even to the conscious causes of their responses.[8]

Although Wilson has recanted a hefty chunk of his earlier confabulation story, intriguing new research adds fresh potential support to the confabulation story. Johansson, Hall, Sikstrom, and Olsson (2005) did an interesting study on self-reports of choice behavior. Participants were shown pairs of photographs of female faces and asked to choose which face they found most attractive. Immediately after their choice, they were asked to verbally describe the reasons for their choice. Unknown to them, on certain trials, the experimenter executed a covert exchange of the two faces immediately after they made their choice and as they were asked to explain their reasons. Thus, as they were describing their reasons, what they were looking at (as the face they had ostensibly chosen) was the nonchosen face. Each subject completed 15 face pairs, three of which were thus manipulated. Surprisingly, there was a very low level of detection that an exchange had occurred. Only 13 percent were detected concurrently. Although it might be expected that reports given for nonmanipulated and manipulated trials would differ in many ways, the analysis revealed no group differences (on three analytic categories) between the reports in the two types of trials. Moreover, in some manipulated trials, the "reasons" cited for the choice specified features that could not possibly be about the original choice. Where the actual choice was a blond, for example, and the experimenter was now displaying the nonselected brunette, the participant said, "I chose her because she had dark hair." Thus, the authors conclude, participants sometimes (perhaps regularly?) confabulated their reasons.

There is a different possible explanation for these findings, however. It seems likely that a participant is commonly attending to the photograph currently being perceived and forming new reasons on the fly, even though the conversation is *supposed* to concern his reasons for the choice made a moment earlier. This is rendered plausible by several psychological considerations. First, the representation of an earlier display can decay quickly or be overridden by a new stimulus. A detailed representation of a previous stimulus might last only 0.5 seconds (Simons and Rensink, 2005), less than the time between the choice made and the request for reasons. Second, the participant is engaged in a repetitive task, to identify attractive features in a currently displayed stimulus. When looking exclusively at a single photo during a reasons-giving segment, this photo will be the prepotent stimulus and tend to dominate his thoughts about features, even if the perceived face isn't the one just chosen. Prepotency of the currently perceived photo might be compared to the well-known Stroop task. Just as a person can't help *reading* a printed word, even when asked to identify its color, so the participant might be unable to avoid identifying attractive features of the currently viewed face, though he is supposed to be reporting the attractive features pinpointed a few seconds earlier. If this is right, the subject isn't literally confabulating; he is reporting respects of attractiveness genuinely operative in his current thinking. He may be introspecting these respects. I find this explanation more compelling than the wholesale-confabulation story toward which Johansson et al. seem to lean.

9.3.3 Developmental Evidence for Self-Other Symmetry

Another family of arguments against a distinctive method of first-person attribution comes from developmental research and allied research in psychopathology. Theory-theorists of the child-scientist stripe contend that developmental evidence strongly supports *parallelism*, or *symmetry*, between self- and other-attribution. Here are Gopnik and Meltzoff (1994) on the alleged self-other similarity in young children's mindreading:

> The evidence suggests that there is an extensive parallelism between children's understanding of their own mental states and their understanding of the mental states of others.... In each of our studies, children's reports of their own immediately past psychological states are consistent with their accounts of the psychological states of others. When they can report and understand the psychological states of others, in the cases of pretense, perception, and imagination, they report having had those psychological states themselves. When they cannot report and understand the psychological states of others, in the case of false beliefs and source, they do not report that they had those states themselves. (1994: 179–180)

Of particular importance are deceptive container tasks that we reviewed in chapter 4 (Gopnik and Astington, 1988; Gopnik and Slaughter, 1991; Perner et al., 1987). There it was found that 3-year-olds make mistakes about their "immediately preceding" beliefs about what was in the container. Initially, children believe that Smarties are in the tube, but later they say that they had thought that pencils were in the tube. This mistake parallels one they make when asked about others' beliefs. Gopnik (1993) concludes that in both cases the child's mindreading is guided by a theory that does not countenance false beliefs. Although there is a strong impression that self-awareness is immediate and direct, this is an illusion, says Gopnik. She draws a parallel with the judgments of experts. "Experts experience their knowledge as immediate and perceptually based; in reality, however, it depends on a long theoretical history. Similarly, we, as experts in commonsense psychology, may experience our theoretical knowledge of the intentionality of our psychological states as if it were the result of direct perception" (1993: 2). The Cartesian model of self-knowledge, and its implied asymmetry between self and other, is simply an illusion.[9]

Theory-theorists claim that children and adults make self-attributions by theoretical reasoning, so it would be extremely helpful if they told us exactly which lines of reasoning are used. Presumably the premises of mindreading inferences are supposed to be propositions about the target's current behavior and environment, perhaps supplemented by previously known propositions about past behavior and mental states. Can these resources account for problematic cases? Consider Wilson's example of recalling out of the blue a certain high school incident. How would an agent come to believe by theoretical reasoning that he is experiencing such a memory? Which current behavior of his, which features of the environment, and which knowledge of his own past jointly enable him to infer that he is currently experiencing such a memory? Surely, he has no evidence that would inferentially lead to this self-ascription. Nevertheless, he makes that self-ascription, evidently by a different means.

Such cases are easily multiplied, so a heavy burden of argument lies on theory-theorists. Do their empirical findings bear that burden? Return to the deceptive container task. The mistaken self-attributions in that class of cases are all attributions about the past, not about currently held beliefs. No introspectivist, or defender of privileged access, holds that past mental states are available for introspective access, only current mental states. Gopnik would reply that a bad-memory account of the data is rendered implausible by the fact that the same subjects had no trouble remembering other past states of theirs. There is ample empirical evidence, however, that memory or some other information-processing problem posed a difficulty for 3-year-olds in this task, as discussed in chapter 4. When given various memory aids, their performance significantly improved.

A great deal of additional empirical evidence bears on the claim of first-person/third-person parallelism. Nichols and Stich (2003: 168–192) provide a comprehensive analysis of this literature, with the clear conclusion that the putative parallelism doesn't hold up and fails precisely in ways that favor a dual-method approach that includes self-monitoring or introspection. Let me review several highlights of their analysis.

Nichols and Stich adduce three sets of findings from the developmental literature that support asymmetric methods for self-oriented versus other-oriented tasks. First, Wimmer et al. (1988) let children in two conditions either look in a box or not look in a box. They were then asked, "Do you know what is in the box or do you not know that?" Three-year-olds performed very well on this first-person task. For the third-person version of the task, they observed somebody else either look or not look in a box and were asked whether that person knows or doesn't know what is in the box. The children did significantly worse on this third-person version of the question.

Second, in studies of children's ability to characterize pretense, Rosen, Schwebel, and Singer (1997) found that young children have difficulty characterizing the pretenses of others. Children watched characters sitting on a bench but pretending to be on an airplane. When the children were asked whether the characters were thinking about being on an airplane or thinking about sitting on a bench outside their school, 90 percent of the children answered incorrectly. By contrast, in Gopnik and Slaughter's (1991) experiments, children of the same age did perfectly well on questions about what they themselves were pretending or imagining. Gopnik and Slaughter also report that 3-year-olds didn't do well on "level-2" perspective-taking tasks in the other-person version. But when a similar task was given in a first-person version, 3-year-olds did very well indeed—surprisingly well, the authors comment.

Third, Nichols and Stich present evidence from psychopathology that supports an asymmetric approach. Some investigators of autism claim that evidence supports a symmetrical, purely theorizing approach to self-attribution. Both Baron-Cohen (1989) and Carruthers (1996) claim that autistic children's performance on appearance-reality tasks provides evidence that they lack self-awareness, and because it is otherwise well known that autistics are deficient in mindreading others, this supports symmetry. As Nichols and Stich point out, however, the failure of the autistic subjects in the pertinent studies ran the wrong way for purposes of this argument. According to the TT approach, autistics suffer from an impaired general mechanism for mindreading. This mechanism is allegedly used for first- as well as third-person ascriptions, so a symmetry hypothesis would predict trouble for autistics in forming beliefs about how objects *look* to them, in other words, appearance beliefs. They should not have had trouble forming beliefs about reality. In the target study, though, autistic subjects had exactly the reverse problem.

Other appeals to autism in an attempt to bolster the symmetric approach involved introspective reports from adults with Asperger's syndrome. Uta Frith and Francesca Happé (1999) contended that a study of theirs with Hurlburt (Hurburt, Happé, and Frith, 1994) strengthens the hypothesis that adults with Asperger's syndrome suffer from impaired self-awareness. Nichols and Stich reject this interpretation based on a reexamination of the data. For instance, one of the adult subjects, Robert, reported that when he was probed for his current experience he was:

> "trying to figure out" why a key that he had recently had made did not work. This figuring-out involved picturing an image of the key in the door lock, with his left hand holding and turning the key. (Hurlburt et al. 1994: 388)

This report reveals Robert to be someone capable of reporting his current thinking, in this case, quite imagistic thinking. Although Hurlburt and colleagues had expected their subjects to have difficulty with the experience sampling method (see section 9.6), this was true for only one subject, Peter, and even he could talk about his current experience. Thus, subjects who show impaired third-person mindreading have intact first-person mindreading. This comports with the view that reading one's own mind operates via a different process than reading the minds of others.

Robbins (2004) takes exception to the Nichols-Stich evaluation of the autism evidence. However, he also adds evidence of dissociation in the other direction (intact third-person mindreading, defective first-person mindreading). Passivity-symptomatic schizophrenics, who are impaired at first-person mindreading, exhibit normal performance on third-person mindreading tasks (Corcoran, 2000). Thus, even if Nichols and Stich are wrong about their autism conclusion, there is ample evidence from the totality of sources cited to scuttle the theory-theorists' broad claim of parallelism between first- and third-person mindreading methods.

Of course, the version of ST developed here assigns a significant common element to first- and third-person mindreading. Both use something like introspection as *part* of a simulation-plus-projection routine. On the other hand, this is only one part of such a routine. Simulation generally involves additional parts, that is, trying to take a target's perspective and running it through some cognitive operation(s). Thus, asymmetries or nonparallelisms between first- and third-person mindreading are perfectly consistent with ST.[10]

9.4 Monitoring Mechanisms, Ascent Routines, and Perceptual Displacement

I turn now to Nichols and Stich's (2003) positive theory of self-attribution, which wisely endorses a special-method approach, but one that suffers from salient problems. By identifying these problems and similar problems confronting two other related approaches, I can pinpoint some features that a better special-method theory should possess. Nichols and Stich present their theory quite compactly, as follows:

> To have beliefs about one's own beliefs, all that is required is that there be a Monitoring Mechanism (MM) that, when activated, takes the representation p in the Belief Box as input and produces the representation *I believe that p* as output. This mechanism would be trivial to implement. To produce representations of one's own beliefs, the Monitoring Mechanism merely has to copy representations from the Belief Box, embed the copies in a representation schema of the form: *I believe that ____*, and then place the new representations back in the Belief Box. The proposed mechanism (or perhaps a distinct but entirely parallel mechanism) would work in much the same way to produce representations of one's own desires, intentions, and imaginings. (2003: 160–161)

Is this an adequate account of self-monitoring?

One lacuna in the Nichols-Stich account is their silence about an entire class of mental states: sensations, or somatic states, including pains, itches, thirst, and the like. Their approach makes it very difficult to accommodate these states. According to philosophical orthodoxy, sensations lack representational content, but representational content is precisely what the Nichols-Stich theory utilizes in its account. Without an associated propositional content for sensations, it is wholly unclear how they can be handled by the theory. The theory is a syntactic theory, which says that a monitoring mechanism operates on the syntax of the mental representations monitored. But, at least on the traditional account, neither pain nor thirst has syntax. Now Nichols and Stich may opt for a representationalist account of sensations, thereby transforming them into propositional attitudes. But they show no sign of this. Moreover, is it plausible that each pain has a unique proposition-sized representation associated with it? It is usually assumed that each pain has numerous properties, and people can introspect and report on quite a few of these: location, character (e.g., sharpness or dullness), intensity, and so forth. An adequate theory of self-monitoring should accommodate these prima facie facts about introspectibility, whereas the Nichols-Stich theory lacks the resources for doing so.

If Nichols and Stich go representationalist about pain, one presumes they would posit a separate monitoring mechanism for pain, just as they do for perception. Indeed, the quoted passage from their book contemplates a distinct monitoring mechanism for each attitude type! If this strategy is pursued for sensations, there will be a separate monitoring mechanism for each sensation type as well. What a profusion of mechanisms! Nor is it clear exactly how many such mechanisms there must be. Is there a separate mechanism for each sensation descriptor and attitude descriptor in natural language?[11] What ever happened to the parsimony Nature is credited with in their previous chapter, where it was argued that evolution would rather reuse a preexisting mechanism than evolve a separate new mindreading mechanism?

Suppose Nichols and Stich acknowledge the superiority of a single monitoring mechanism. Would that pose a difficulty for their theory? Focusing on attitudes, it leaves completely unanswered the question of how the monitoring mechanism decides which attitude *type* a targeted mental state belongs to. Is it a belief, a desire, a hope, an intention, or what? The theory implies that MM takes a representation out of a box, forms a new representation with the prefix "I Φ that ...," and then adds the new representation to the belief box. But how does it know which attitude type to substitute for 'Φ'? This might be easy if boxes in the Nichols-Stich diagrams symbolized genuine brain boxes. A monitoring mechanism might simply keep track of which box the initial sentence was taken from. But on the standard philosophical use of box symbolism, boxes are merely convenient shorthand for functional roles. Nichols and Stich say quite explicitly that this is how their boxology is intended (2003: 11). The question therefore arises how the monitoring mechanism determines that a given piece of syntax occurring in the mind has this or that functional role. We are told nothing about this. The problem can be avoided by positing a separate monitoring mechanism for each attitude type. If each mechanism is specialized for its proprietary attitude type, it knows what prefix to assign before putting an attributed syntax into the belief box. As we have seen, however, a separate monitoring mechanism for each attitude type is an incredibly unparsimonious model.

Another question concerns the strength or intensity of a propositional attitude. I can make judgments about the strength or intensity of a belief, desire, or hope of mine (how accurately is another question). How does the monitoring mechanism judge this dimension of an attitude token? The Nichols-Stich theory offers no clue and seems devoid of resources to address the question. Theirs is a "syntactic redeployment" theory, which characterizes self-monitoring as the manipulation and repositioning of a piece of mental syntax. Because strength or intensity is quite independent of mental syntax, the theory is a nonstarter vis-à-vis this dimension of mental self-attribution.

I do not mean to suggest that redeployment accounts have nothing going for them. In fact, my own positive theory will incorporate redeployment as one component. But *pure* redeployment theories, of which the MM theory is an example, are fundamentally inadequate, principally because of their failure to account for type selection. Another example of a pure redeployment theory is the ascent-routine theory, which suffers from the same debility.

This approach was first proposed by Gareth Evans (1982) and in recent years has been promoted by Robert Gordon (1995b, 1996). Evans describes the ascent procedure as follows: "I get myself in a position to answer the question whether I believe that p by putting into operation whatever procedure I have for answering the question whether p" (1982: 225). Gordon also presents the ascent routine using the belief illustration "the way in which adults ordinarily determine whether or not they believe that p is simply to ask themselves the question whether or not p" (1996: 16). The procedure is presumably to be completed as follows. If one answers the whether-p question in the affirmative, then one "ascends" a level and also gives an affirmative answer to the question "Do I think/believe that p?" Except for the boxological metaphor, this is only minimally different from the MM account. One might translate Evans and Gordon into boxologese by saying that you start with "p" in your belief box, prefix "I believe that" to "p," and add the resulting representation to the belief box.[12]

The chief problem for the ascent-routine approach is the same one confronting the MM approach: The basic procedure is described only for the mental classification of belief and lacks a clear account of classifying other attitudes or sensations. To illustrate just for the attitudes, how does the approach deal with the self-ascription of hope? Suppose the question is whether you *hope* team T won its game yesterday. Can you use the ascent routine to answer this question? Obviously, answering the first-level question "Did team T win its game yesterday?" will not help you determine whether you hope that team T won. What question, then, should you ask? Gordon provides no reason to think there is a distinctive question for each attitude type. Finding a representation at the first level that can be redeployed at the attitudinal level is a plausible maneuver for content ascription. But it's a nonstarter for the second component of propositional attitude ascription, selecting the attitude *type*.

There is another serious problem with the ascent-routine approach even when applied to belief. When its proponents say that a mindreader "answers" the whether-p question in the affirmative, what exactly does this mean? Does "answering" mean *vocalizing* an affirmative answer to the whether-p question? This won't cover cases of self-ascription where no answer is vocalized. So what transpires when the whether-question is answered subvocally? Does one simply say the words silently to oneself? The words could be "said" with or without endorsement. What is necessary, then, is that one *judges* the answer to be "p," that is, occurrently believes the answer to be "p." All right, but what is the next step in the ascent routine? Having judged that p, how does the mindreader arrive at an (affirmative) answer to the question "Do I think/believe that p?" Obviously, the next step must be a determination *that* one has judged that p. Here we effectively reencounter our original problem! Without a story of how this "determination" is executed, the account is fatally incomplete. No such story is given.

Another example of a pure redeployment theory is Fred Dretske's (1995) displaced-perception theory of introspection. Although Dretske calls his approach a theory of introspection, he denies that introspection involves "looking inward." Dretske defends a representational theory of mind that is externalist, in the sense that it portrays mental events as being constituted not by the intrinsic character of the events occurring inside but by the relations these events bear to external affairs. He further claims that one doesn't *know* about mental states by looking at them but by looking outward at the external states of affairs that give them (by virtue of their "indicator function") their representational content. He draws analogies to other cases in which one comes to know facts about certain objects by seeing *different* objects. He calls this "displaced perception." I see how much I weigh not by looking at myself but by looking at the bathroom scale on which I stand. I see how much gas remains in the gas tank not by looking at the gas tank but by looking at a gauge on the dashboard. Like many representational theories of mind, the attractions of Dretske's theory are mainly on the content dimension. It goes some distance toward explaining how contentful mental states have their propositional contents, so one can understand (if not agree with) the proposal that learning a current state's content might involve looking outward rather than inward. However, representational theories of mind are much weaker on the question of what makes a mental-state token a state of a particular kind (e.g., a desire, a belief).

For related reasons, it is hard to see how such a theory can make sense of the idea that one classifies the attitude type of a current state by looking outward. Dretske acknowledges that externalist theories have this sort of problem: "The problem centers not on the content, but on the attitude (the relation) one has to that content" (1995: 54). Having noted the problem, however, he dismisses it all too quickly. We are "absolute authorities," he says, about our thought contents, but "not very good (in fact, I think, very bad) about the attitudinal aspect of these mental states" (1995: 55). His strategy is to deny introspective knowledge of the attitudinal aspect and thereby relieve himself of any responsibility to explain attitudinal knowledge (or belief).

This is unconvincing. Introspection commonly gives us knowledge of the attitude types of our current mental episodes, as much as of their contents. I can know as easily that I am *wondering* whether it will rain today as *whether it will rain today* is what I am wondering. Moreover, given our agenda, the central issue is not the knowledge question. An introspectionist theory of first-person mindreading owes us an explanation of how introspective beliefs or self-attributions are arrived at, whether or not they qualify as knowledge (or attain any other distinctive epistemic status). Dretske's theory offers no help on this crucial matter.

9.5 Introspection and Attention

In this section, I examine the role of attention and make two points. First, if attention is an important facet of introspection, this bolsters the case for an interesting parallel between introspection and external perception. Second, appreciating the role of attention in introspection puts us in a position to deflate Sydney Shoemaker's argument from self-intimation against the quasi-perceptual model of introspection.

A psychological technique for studying introspection has been devised by Russell Hurlburt (1990, 1993, 1997; Hurlburt and Heavey, 2001), called descriptive experience sampling (DES). Hurlburt and Heavey (2001) describe the technique as follows:

> DES uses a beeper to cue subjects, at random times, to pay immediate attention to their ongoing experience at the moment they heard the beep. They then jot down in a notebook the characteristics of that particular moment, and subsequently (within 24 hours) describe the characteristics of that sampled moment in an in-depth interview. Those interviews ask only one question (although it is phrased in a wide variety of ways): *"What was occurring in your inner experience at the moment of the beep?"* (2001: 400)

According to Hurlburt and Heavey, using DES reveals thoughts that the subject does not initially know about, even though they are conscious. For example, used with a subject called Donald, the technique revealed that Donald had frequent angry thoughts about his children. Before sampling, Donald had no knowledge about this kind of thinking. These "angry-toward-children" thoughts were not unconscious but were in fact freely available at the moment of each sampling beep. "Donald simply characteristically neglected to remember the existence of these thoughts" (Hurlburt and Heavey, 2001: 403). It could be argued that although Donald didn't remember an extended pattern of such thoughts, he must have been aware of each such thought at the time of its occurrence, not only "aware" in the sense of experiencing the thought but in the sense of self-ascribing it at the time. But why assume this? Why assume that people constantly self-ascribe every mental state they occupy at any given time? This would betray either a mistaken identification of first-order consciousness with higher-order consciousness or would invoke the controversial assumption that first-order consciousness is always accompanied by reflective awareness. The latter assumption is entailed by higher-order thought analyses of consciousness, which hold that what it *is* for a state to be conscious is to be accompanied by a higher-order state that reflects on it. But such analyses are quite problematic (Goldman, 1993b). Among other things, they are forced to postulate the "reduplication" of all conscious mental states, requiring a dubious allocation of enormous cognitive resources.[13]

If we grant Hurlburt and Heavey's contention that most of Donald's angry-toward-children thoughts were not self-ascribed until he became a subject for the DES technique, then it seems natural to conclude that the beeps called Donald's *attention* to these thoughts, and only under its aegis did he judge that he had them. So introspective self-attribution does not occur continuously without the guidance of attention. It requires or is at least facilitated by attention, although this attention can occur automatically rather than voluntarily or through external intervention (like a beep). Hurlburt and Heavey report a similar case of "a woman suffering from borderline personality disorder, who discovered through DES that she nearly always experienced multiple visual images, usually with extremely negative content. Before sampling, [she] had no knowledge of the multiplicity of her visual awareness or its consistent negativity, despite the ubiquity of both characteristics" (2001: 403). Again, the subject did not spontaneously self-ascribe these characteristics of her experience, although they were conscious. Attention was required to elicit these self-ascriptions.

Jonathan Schooler and colleagues (2004) have made somewhat similar findings. They developed a paradigm to study lapses of metaconsciousness during reading. Participants read passages of text and were supposed to indicate every time they caught their minds wandering ("zoning out"). In addition, participants were probed intermittently and asked to indicate if they had been zoning out at that moment. The results indicated that they were often caught zoning out by the probes when they had been unaware that they were zoning out just prior to the probes. It required attention—often probe-spurred attention—to trigger reflective awareness via introspection.

Does this important role for attention in introspection find a parallel in external perception? Yes. A powerful role for attention has recently been established through the phenomena of change-blindness and inattentional blindness. In studies of change blindness, O'Regan and colleagues (O'Regan, 1992; O'Regan, Rensink, and Clark, 1999) showed observers natural scenes and asked them to detect cyclically repeated changes, for example, a large object shifting, changing color, or appearing and disappearing. By making the change co-occur with an eye saccade, an eye blink, or a cut in a film sequence, their attention is not called to this change. And when they don't attend to the change, despite the fact that it is large and in full view, they are typically unaware of it. Even when eye measurements show they are looking directly at the change, they don't become aware of it (as a change).

How are these points relevant to the viability of a quasi-perceptual model of introspection? The first point is that introspection and perception resemble one another in the importance of attention. Second, attention seems to act like an orienting organ in introspection, analogous to the shift of eye gaze or the sniffing of the nose. Shoemaker (1996) argues that introspection is disanalogous to sense perception because it lacks an orienting organ that can get the subject into an appropriate relation to the cognitive target (1996: 204–205). I disagree. The "organ" of introspection is attention, the orientation of which puts a subject in an appropriate relation to a targeted state.

Shoemaker considers this proposal but dismisses it (1996: 219). He claims we do not attend to sensory experiences—the mental events themselves—but rather to the intentional objects of those experiences. He says the same for intentional states. We do not attend to those states per se, merely to their possibly nonexistent intentional objects. This seems inconclusive to me. Why not say that we—or, rather, our cognitive systems—pay attention to both the states *and* their intentional objects?

As mentioned in section 9.2, Shoemaker's resistance to the quasi-perceptual model appeals heavily to a certain alleged feature of sense perception that he calls the "independence condition." Objects known by sense perception are independent of their being so known; their existence is conceptually independent of there being mechanisms that make such knowledge possible (1996: 224–225). In the case of mental states, by contrast, Shoemaker says that their existence is not independent of their being known. There could not be creatures that have mental states but are introspectively "blind" to them. Another way of saying this is that the states are *self-intimating* (in a weak sense): Being in one of these states tends—under certain conditions—to produce the (correct) belief that one is in that mental state (1996: 222).

Defense of a self-intimation thesis depends on building the right "conditions" into the account, or definition, of each mental state. One such condition is that a creature occupying the state must have the necessary *concept* of the state to form suitable beliefs about its instances. Also, if what we said about attention is correct, *being* in state M does not guarantee believing that one is; one first has to attend to state M. Now if, in this fashion, all the causally necessary conditions for generating the belief are specified in the "under-certain-conditions" clause, it won't be surprising to get Shoemaker's weak self-intimation thesis. But why, then, would weak self-intimation undercut independence? One could equally say that it is a "conceptual" or a priori matter that if a stone exists, then *under certain conditions* there will be a belief that the stone exists. We merely have to build into "certain conditions" the existence of a perceiver with organs oriented toward the stone, and so forth. The fact that there might be a conceptual or a priori truth of this sort doesn't impugn the ontological independence of the stone. The same holds,

I submit, for the ontological independence of mental states from second-order, introspective beliefs about them. Finally, because first-order mental states and second-order beliefs about them are ontologically independent of one another, the second-order beliefs can be the result of causal processes that track the mental states.[14]

9.6 Introspection and Consciousness

I now want to raise questions about the connection between introspection and consciousness. Nichols and Stich write as if all our beliefs, desires, and the like can be monitored by a monitoring mechanism. This is a bit surprising. What about unconscious, or covert, desires and beliefs of the sort posited by rafts of cognitive scientists, as well as Freudian theorists? Are these available to introspection? That is doubtful. The same problem arises for what philosophers call "standing" or "dispositional" desires and beliefs, as opposed to "occurrent" or "activated" ones.[15] One of my current standing beliefs is that such-and-such is my social security number, but this isn't a belief I can currently monitor or introspect, because it isn't in working memory. True, if I am asked what my social security number is, I can rapidly retrieve the information from long-term memory. But this involves activating the standing or dispositional state, yielding a new working-memory state. This state, and the information contained in it, can be monitored or introspected, but the merely dispositional state cannot be monitored. If these points are correct, an adequate theory of self-monitoring should incorporate these wrinkles.

I am substantially attracted to the view that introspection can be directed only at conscious, activated states. But this view is not beyond challenge. Is it clear, for example, that the thoughts Hurlburt and Heavey uncovered with their DES technique were already conscious prior to their subjects directing attention at them? Perhaps they were only rendered conscious by the beacon of attention. Is it clear that the zoning-out activities caught by Schooler's probes were already conscious prior to being revealed by his probes? Again the answer is unclear. Another problematic set of cases is especially important for us, because they bear on our earlier argument for ST. In our discussion of FaBER in chapter 6, we concluded that FaBER tasks are executed by simulation. In each of the four FaBER models considered in chapter 6, there is a stage at which the system classifies an (attenuated) emotion as belonging to one emotion category or another. Presumably, this is "direct" classification, or introspection. But throughout our discussion of FaBER, we allowed that the operative processes, whatever they are, transpire below the level of consciousness. So these acts of introspection are targeted at unconscious states, contrary to the thesis now under discussion. Moreover, this kind of case is not unprecedented, or even uncommon, in different parts of cognitive science. So it would be unwise to push the thesis that the scope of introspection is restricted to conscious states. Perhaps philosophers confine the term *introspection* to conscious events, but this terminological point is not of great interest. We can simply replace "introspection" as our favored label for the classification process that interests us, opting instead for such labels as "monitoring," "inner sense," or perhaps "apperception."

9.7 What Properties Does Introspection Use for Mental Classification?

It is time to turn to the central questions for a theory of direct introspection or monitoring, the theory that there is an introspection system, or process, that identifies current mental states by inner recognition (rather than inference). Before proceeding, however, we need to clarify our basic understanding of introspection and say something about the assumption that it is a unitary operation. There is certainly some ambiguity in the use of the term *introspection*. For example, it can refer either to a process of *inquiry*, directed at mental states, or to a process of *answering* such an inquiry.[16] In the former sense, introspection is inwardly directed attention, which chooses selected states for analysis. In the latter sense, it is the process of analyzing or classifying selected states. In the remainder of this discussion, we focus on the latter process: analysis or classification. Jesse Prinz (2004) holds that introspection "fractionates" into additional senses or types. For example, in addition to introspecting information currently being perceived, he says that people introspect their memories, as when they are asked what they had for breakfast this morning and respond, "Orange juice and a scone." In other words, according to Prinz, episodic retrieval is a type of introspection. This strikes me as excessive proliferation of varieties of introspection. I prefer to regard memory retrieval as a nonintrospective cognitive act, one that creates a new working-memory state that can then be introspected.

Let me turn now to the central issues. I propose to treat introspection (the "answering" half of introspection) as a perception-like process. More precisely, *part* of introspection will be treated as perception-like. Now if part of introspection is perception-like, that part should include a transduction process.[17] A transduction process features inputs—events or properties to which the process is causally sensitive—and outputs—representations generated in response to these inputs. Two central questions therefore arise: What are the input properties for introspection, and what are the outputs? The outputs of introspection are representations of token mental states that classify them along one or more of the following dimensions: (1) the general category of the token state (e.g., belief, desire, pain, anger, heat sensation, visual representation), (2) the content of the state, and (3) the strength or intensity of the state. A token visual state, for example, might be classified as being of the type *seeing* and as having the content "There are three bowls on the table." Of course, the visual state itself would *have* the content it has whether or not it is introspected. Introspection, however, might "re-represent" its content (not in the visual format). On the account I wish to offer, the content aspect of introspection is not perception-like but proceeds rather by redeployment (or a cousin thereof). This matter is deferred until section 9.8. Introspection is perception-like, however, in the way it recognizes or classifies the target state in terms of its general category and in terms of such characteristics as strength or intensity. How this might be accomplished is what we are about to examine (the examination continues in chapter 10). Actually, the aim here is quite modest and preliminary, because no details are available in the current state of knowledge. The first step is to rebut the claim that introspection couldn't be a perception-like process (even in part) because it couldn't work by transduction. There are no properties that would serve as appropriate inputs. This section considers the options, to see whether there are any viable candidates.

Is there a family of properties to which introspective classification might be sensitive, properties that enable such a system to make reliable, accurate introspective classifications a respectable percentage of the time?[18] What features of token mental states could an introspective mechanism "pick up," detect, or utilize in making its classifications? Here are four possible answers:

1. Functional properties.
2. Phenomenal properties.
3. Representational properties.
4. Neural properties.

For many of these answers, large problems loom in the metaphysics of mind. For example, phenomenal properties are often said to supervene on physical properties, and it's problematic whether such supervenient properties can serve as causes. This worry is stressed by Jaegwon Kim (1993, 1998). Such metaphysical issues are too complex to adjudicate here, so my discussion merely alludes to the metaphysical debates without exploring them in depth. We can make progress toward a tentative view without resolving all of these delicate issues.

9.7.1 Functional Properties

For many philosophers of mind, functional properties are a favored answer to the question of how the folk represent mental-state types. Each mental-state concept is allegedly associated with a functional role, a pattern of causal-subjunctive relationships among stimulus inputs, other mental states, and behavioral outputs. The functional role associated with belief, for example, might consist in having a tendency to interact with other beliefs to generate deductive and inductive inferences and having a tendency to interact with desires to produce decisions or actions. Functional properties, however, are poor candidates for being the properties to which an introspective system is sensitive. This is not because mental-state tokens *lack* functional properties; they certainly have such properties. But from the fact that they have functional properties, it doesn't follow that these properties are the causally relevant factors in introspection. Here is an analogy from vision. A dollar bill has the high-level property of being a unit of monetary currency. When a person sees a dollar bill, however, this monetary property is not causally relevant to the visual system. The properties causally operative in vision are the dollar's shape, color, texture, and so forth. Putting the matter in terms of the transduction process, the dollar-related properties that are inputs to the visual system are physical features of the *optical image* at the back of the eye, which itself is produced by the ambient optical array that is influenced by the shape, color, texture, and other factors of the dollar. We want to know the analogue in the introspective domain of the causally operative features of the optical image.

For present purposes, functional properties have two crucial features: They are subjunctive, or dispositional, and they are relational. Both pose difficulties for the idea that they might be directly detected by introspection (Goldman, 1993a). Can a perception-like system directly detect a dispositional property? Can vision, for example, detect the water solubility of a lump of sugar? Not if it isn't currently dissolving. It can detect a lump's color and perhaps texture. From these (categorical) features, it might be *inferred* that the lump is made of sugar, from which it might be inferred (given background information), that it is soluble in water.[19] But vision cannot directly detect that a given (unimmersed) lump is water soluble. Similarly, if a target mental state possesses a dispositional or subjunctive property, it's hard to see how that property of the token state could be directly causally registered in the introspection process. Now turn to the relational character of functional properties. The functional role associated with pain would include a tendency to cause the system to have an aversion to the state, to want to get rid of it. The trouble is that an introspective system couldn't tell by direct introspection of a target (alone) that it has this relational character. It would have to check whether the state goes on to produce (or be accompanied by) an appropriate aversion. This is not how introspection is supposed to work.

When the dispositional and relational characteristics of functional roles are combined, the problems only get worse. The functional role associated with a desire for goal G includes a disposition to choose action A *if* A is believed to be the best means to G. Now suppose a subject seeks to determine, introspectively, whether an indexed mental token m is a desire for G but doesn't actually think that A is the best means to G. How could the introspective system determine whether this part of the functional role is satisfied? It must figure out whether the following subjunctive is true: "m would lead to a choice of A if A were believed to be the best means to G." How would the introspective system do this when the specified belief isn't in the cognitive system? The larger cognitive system might simulate a belief that A is the best means to G and see what simulated choice emerges. But this would hardly qualify as introspection. Moreover, it would provide no help unless the system could classify the simulated belief *as* a belief that A is the best means to G and could classify the resulting choice *as* a choice of A. But how could the system make these classifications if it can appeal only to functional, namely, dispositional-relational, characteristics?[20] In light of all these problems, functional properties are poor candidates for playing a critical role in introspection.

9.7.2 Phenomenal Properties

Are the input properties for introspection phenomenal properties? Remember that we want to identify the introspectively discriminated properties associated with *all* mental-state types. Could phenomenal properties serve this role? Here are three possible objections to this approach.

(i) As mentioned previously, it is widely held that phenomenal properties are causally impotent, because they supervene on physical properties. Only the physical supervenience base, it is thought, has causal powers. So how could phenomenal properties be the input side to the transduction process of introspection?

(ii) According to orthodoxy, attitudes do not have phenomenal properties, but we certainly introspectively discriminate occurrent tokens of the different attitude types. We recognize introspectively whether an indexed occurrent state is a desire or a fear, a belief or a doubt. The problem here is not simply that occurrent attitude tokens are (allegedly) lacking in phenomenology. Even if all occurrent attitude tokens had some phenomenology, this would not guarantee the possibility of typing them *by* their phenomenology. For this, it would be necessary that each type have a *distinctive* phenomenal property (or set of properties) that could serve as the causal trigger of the corresponding introspective classification. It is this latter, more demanding, condition that seems so improbable.

(iii) If it is granted that nonconscious mental states can be introspected (or monitored), that is a problem for the phenomenal-properties answer, because nonconscious states presumably lack phenomenal properties.

There are possible replies to each of these objections, though theorists with different commitments will judge their plausibility differently. In reply to problem (i), many philosophers of mind dispute the claim that supervenient properties are precluded from causal efficacy because there is causation at a lower level (Fodor, 1989; McLaughlin, 1989; LePore and Loewer, 1989; Yablo, 1992). Turning to objection (iii), at least a few philosophers believe that qualia are not restricted to conscious states (Rosenthal). If this is correct, even nonconscious states might have phenomenal properties available for detection. Finally, in reply to objection (ii), a growing number of philosophers are sympathetic to the nontraditional view that occurrent tokens of the attitudes have phenomenal features (Flanagan, 1992; Goldman, 1993a; Levine, 1993; Strawson, 1994; Chalmers, 1996; Siewert, 1998; Peacocke, 1998; Horgan and Tienson, 2002; Pitt, 2004). What has not been convincingly argued, however, is that each attitude type has distinctive phenomenal features. This is the major sticking point, I believe, for the phenomenal properties approach.

9.7.3 Representational Properties

The representationalist approach would say that the properties of mental tokens that serve as inputs to the introspection process are representational properties. Because the question before us is how introspection identifies or recognizes the *type* of a mental-state token, we are not here talking about the propositional contents (if any) of such tokens. In addition to any such content, the theory would have to hold that each type *qua type* has distinctive representational or intentional properties, and these are what play a causal role in introspection.

How might this work for phenomenal, or qualitative, mental-state types, like pain or sight? Representationalists like Dretske (1995), Harman (1990), Lycan (1996), and Tye (1995, 1997, 2002) purport to reduce phenomenal properties, at least sensory and perceptual phenomenal properties, to representational facts.[21] For example, to undergo a pain is to have a sensory representation of a certain sort of bodily disturbance. The disturbances vary with the pains, but whether it's a throbbing pain, a stabbing pain, or an ache, to be in pain is to represent some region of the body as undergoing some kind of damage or disturbance. Applied to the present problem, the idea would have to be that the introspection system takes the information "bodily damage occurring" as input and outputs the classification, "the system is in pain." An advantage of this approach is that intentional or informational properties are more respectable, in both philosophical and cognitive scientific circles, than "raw" phenomenal properties. Furthermore, there would be no difficulty in extending introspection to nonconscious states. It is uncontroversial that nonconscious states have intentional properties, so if introspection can detect intentional properties, it can operate on nonconscious mental tokens as well as conscious ones.

The suggestion on the table, then, is that occurrent state tokens of each type are type-recognizable by virtue of representational features distinctive to the type. Every belief token has some representational features specific to belief. Every desire token has other representational features specific to desire. These features are inputs to the introspective process by which tokens of belief and desire are recognized as beliefs and desires, respectively. But is this at all plausible? Can beliefs be distinguished from desires, can decisions be distinguished from vacillations, by means of type-specific representational contents? It's very unclear what the distinguishing representational contents might be. One and the same propositional content can be either believed or desired. I can either want a certain piece of legislation to be defeated or believe that it will be defeated. What distinguishes a state of believing from a state of desiring with the same content isn't a matter of some further intentional content.

If this point isn't conclusive, consider a related problem. Within the same attitudinal category, token states differ in strength or intensity. Beliefs can be weak or firm; desires can be mild or fervent. The intensity properties of token states can be discriminated and classified. But do intensity differences reside in something intentional or representational? One might try to express strength of conviction in terms of probabilistic content. Perhaps strong belief in p consists in believing "p is highly probable," and weak belief in p consists in believing "p is more probable than not." But this cannot be the right story. First, young children who don't yet grasp probabilistic contents (or anything equivalent) can still have beliefs of varying strengths, from firm to tentative. Second, any probabilistically qualified proposition ("p, with probability n") can itself be believed more or less strongly. At the bottom level, degrees of belief must be a psychological matter of the state, not a matter of its propositional content. Thus, I don't see how representational content can be the basis for introspectively identifying either the type of a mental token or its intensity.

9.7.4 Neural Properties

Neural properties seem like natural candidates for the causal inputs to the introspection process, and they would be advantageous for several reasons.[22] No challenge can be raised to their causal efficacy, and their detectability would be the same whether they were the substrate of conscious or of nonconscious mental states. Obviously, a bewildering array of types of neural properties might be relevant, and I won't say a great deal about the choice to be made. Nonetheless, for concreteness, let me illustrate the approach by discussing an example where the neurophysiology is tolerably well understood, an example that deals with the introspective discrimination of sensory types (not their detailed contents).

A. D. Craig (2002) proposes a new account of what he calls *interoception* (not to be confused with introspection), which is the sense of the physiological condition of the entire body. This account rests on an improved understanding of the functional anatomy of a certain neurophysiological system, the lamina I spinothalamocortical system. This system conveys signals from small-diameter primary afferents that represent the physiological status of all tissues of the body. In primates, lamina I spinothalamic neurons project to a dedicated thalamocortical relay nucleus, the posterior part of the ventromedial nucleus, or VMpo. The VMpo is small in the macaque monkey thalamus but proportionately very large in the human thalamus. Embedded in VMpo, which Craig calls "interoceptive cortex," are the cortical representations of several highly resolved, distinct sensations, including pain, temperature, itch, muscular and visceral sensations, sensual touch, and other feelings from the body. There are two classes of neurons that signal sharp pain and burning pain, which selectively receive inputs from Aδ-nociceptors and polymodal C-nociceptors, respectively. In addition, there are two types of thermoreceptive lamina I cells that respond selectively to cooling or to warming, distinct types of chemoreceptive cells that respond selectively to histamine or to noxious chemicals, and other classes that respond selectively to muscle or joint afferents or to mechanical "slow brush" (tickle). Drawing on this description, the neural properties approach might say that when people introspectively classify these different types of sensations, the classification rests on a discrimination of the different classes of neural cells that are currently activated in the VMpo system. A high level of activation in one class of cells generates the introspective classification "pain" (or "sharp pain"), a high level of activation in a different class of cells generates the introspective classification "tickle," and so forth.[23]

The distinction between interoception (in Craig's sense) and introspection should be emphasized. Interoception is the perception of the physiological status of bodily tissues. It culminates in sensations, often described by neuroscientists in representational terms as sensory representations of tissue status in different bodily regions. I construe these sensory representations (à la Tye, 1997) as the sensory content of the sensations. Introspection, as I propose to understand it, is a *further* response to these sensations: It is the (meta-) representation and classification of those perceptions in mental-state terms. This classification is executed, under the neural-properties proposal, on the basis of which groups of cells are activated.

The neural-properties approach seems particularly promising for sensation types because there are dedicated neural circuits for different types of sensation. But such circuits are unlikely to be available for the propositional attitudes. Does this fact scotch the neural-properties approach? No. The existence of distinctive neural properties that are usable by an introspection device does not require dedicated circuits. A dedicated circuit involves the "front end" of a mental-event type, and introspection isn't concerned with the front end. So the neural-properties approach remains very promising.

On balance, then, neural properties seem to be the best answer to the question (posed in section 9.7) of what the inputs are to the introspection process. Again, it is assumed that if introspection is a perception-like process, it must involve transduction, and transduction must involve some input properties. So the case for perception-like introspection depends on the existence of a suitable family of input properties. Neural properties seem to be the right family of properties (unsurprisingly). More specifics would undoubtedly be helpful, but they are not essential for present purposes. We are concerned here with the (fairly abstract) thesis that introspection is a perception-like process, and this requires that there be *some* family of input properties, whatever its precise membership. What we have tried to establish—or, more accurately, make plausible—is that there is such a family.

The next question that naturally flows from the foregoing is what the output properties are for the introspection process. As indicated in section 9.7, these must be representations, or representation-events, of certain types. What these might be is explored in chapter 10.

9.8 Redeployment and Translation

Visual perception is a complex process involving multiple components. It involves processing by shape, color, texture, orientation, depth, and so forth. Visual experience is a seamless whole, because the products of different processes have been "bound" together in a final representation. Nonetheless, the components of visual processing are distinct. Similarly, I conjecture that introspection involves two or more distinct components, at least one for mental types and a different one (or two) for mental contents. The representation of mental types is accomplished by a perception-like recognition process, in which a given occurrent token is mapped into a mental category selected from a relatively smallish number of types. The representation of mental contents cannot be accomplished in the same way, because there is no smallish number of content types to which a token's content can be mapped.

Suppose I entertain a fond hope that our new puppy will not pee on our Oriental rug, and, in an introspective act, I so classify my state's content. Is this content classification achieved by recognition? Is the state's content mapped into a preestablished content category "Our new puppy won't pee on the Oriental rug"? This is unlikely. Imagine that I have never before entertained precisely this content; it has just been newly generated from my conceptual repertoire by productive processes of thought. The most plausible story, then, of how I "introspect" the content is that I simply *redeploy* it. The hope's content is replicated in the metarepresenting state. However, redeployment cannot be the story of the type classification, the classification of the target state as a hope. The metarepresentation does not redeploy or replicate hope because it is not itself a hope; it is a belief or judgment.

The redeployment approach to content self-attribution is endorsed by Christopher Peacocke (1999), who, as far as I know, coined the term *redeployment*. There are other advantages to the redeployment account, as Peacocke makes clear, advantages related to knowledge and content externalism. Redeployment contributes to an explanation of how second-order self-ascriptions can be sensitive to the externally individuated contents of first-order attitudes without the thinker having to rely on evidence about his environment (1999: 251). But this topic goes beyond our current purview.

Redeployment per se, however, has trouble with cases where the first-order state represents the content in a different format than introspection uses. Suppose that the first-order representation is a visual representation rather than a belief representation. Suppose I accurately self-ascribe a visual perception as follows: "I see a toy truck under the sofa." My perceptual state presumably uses a visual code to represent the toy truck and its relation to the sofa. When I mindread this state, however, the metarepresentation presumably doesn't use the visual code. As Nichols and Stich (2003) suggest, not every mental code is admissible into the belief box, and the visual code is one of the inadmissible ones. So an introspection system or monitoring mechanism cannot simply borrow the visual representation, prefix it with "I believe that," and place the resulting representation into the belief box. In other words, it cannot simply *redeploy* the target state's content when that content is represented in a visual format. There must be an intramental *translation*, from one mental code to another. This differs from mere redeployment, so translation must be added to the family of introspection processes to complete the story.

Note, however, that the translation process is often quite partial, especially when the introspection system is operating on sensory or perceptual states, construed representationally. As Tye emphasizes, the phenomenal content of sensory representations is very rich, much richer than the conceptual content available to introspective re-representation (Tye, 1995). So although introspective classification may involve some sort of translation of the sensory representations, the translation is limited and approximate. This leads Tye to speak of the sensory representations as having "nonconceptual" content, an acceptable proposal under some interpretations of nonconceptual content, but perhaps not all.

Let me briefly summarize the proposed model of introspective self-attribution. It characterizes introspective self-attribution as being subserved by three distinct processes: recognition, redeployment, and translation. Recognition is used in typing the target state, whether it's a contentful or noncontentful state. Recognition is also used for classifying the target state in terms of supplementary features like strength or intensity. For contentful target states, introspection uses either redeployment or translation to produce the content assignment contained in the metarepresentation.

If this model is right, a problem familiar from other areas of cognitive science arises. How does the introspective system "bind" the results of the several processes, so that appropriate outputs of recognition are paired with appropriate outputs of redeployment or translation? I hazard no guess as to how this binding problem is solved. But it is no knock against a theory that it generates interesting questions for research, especially questions with well-studied analogues in other domains. It is well recognized in cognitive science, for example, in the study of visual attention, that there must be methods by which different properties or features are "bound" or integrated into a single object (Treisman, 1996; Treisman and Gelade, 1980). Something similar seems to be necessary in introspective self-attribution.

Notes

1. As discussed briefly in section 7.13, there are possible versions of ST in which one doesn't attribute the pretend state *to* the self; it is not labeled as one of *my* states. Nonetheless, it is a state *of* the self that is classified. So the theory must come to terms with how one classifies one's own states.

2. Epistemological questions in this territory are addressed in Goldman (2004).

3. Some writers restrict the term *Cartesian* to theories that focus on phenomenological features essentially "private" to the agent (Fricker, 1998). I shall not be endorsing an account of first-person attribution that is Cartesian in that sense.

4. There is considerable discussion in the cognitive science literature, much of it centered on schizophrenia, about how even errors of misidentification can occur. But this topic will not be explored here.

5. This point applies to a different sort of explanation Burge offers for privileged access, namely, the special role reflective thoughts play in critical thinking (see Burge, 1996). This explanation will be restricted to intentional states, and will not carry over to sensations. Other problems with this approach are noted by Peacocke (1996) and Macdonald (1998).

6. Actually, a more cautious conclusion would be this. The participants were ignorant of *one* of the contributing causes of their preference, namely, the position of the preferred item in the array. There may well have been additional contributing mental causes, however, and these might have included judgments about the very factors they mentioned. The fact that all pairs of panty hose were identical doesn't show that a participant passerby didn't *judge*, say, the sheerness of one pair to exceed that of the others. So when someone mentioned sheerness as a cause of her preference, perhaps she was accurate, and not confabulating. A (comparative) sheerness judgment may indeed have been *one* of the causes of the preference, and she may have introspectively detected that cause. (Whether she could have introspectively detected *that* it

was a cause is more problematic. In my view, however, the introspectability of causal relations has never been part of a Cartesian theory.)

7. Nichols and Stich (2003) also endorse a dual-method theory.

8. In the rest of his book, Wilson argues that the causal role of conscious thought has been overrated, citing among other things Wegner's (2002) work on the illusion of conscious will. But as I stress in the text, introspectionism is adequately supported if people have introspective access to their conscious states, even if they don't have introspective access to the *causal efficacy* of these states vis-à-vis other states or events. (The causal efficacy of consciousness is all that people like Wegner raise doubts about.)

9. There are a couple of passages in Gopnik (1993) that clash starkly with this interpretation.

> One possible source of evidence for the child's theory may be first-person psychological experiences that may themselves be the consequence of genuine psychological perceptions. For example, we may well be equipped to detect certain kinds of internal cognitive activity in a vague and unspecified way, what we might call "the Cartesian buzz.". . . [O]ur genuinely *special and direct access* to certain kinds of first-person evidence might account for the fact that we can draw some conclusions about our own psychological states when we are perfectly still and silent." (1993: 11, emphasis added)

These passages seem to be an endorsement of a limited Cartesian model, restricted perhaps to the phenomenology of experience rather than to intentional states like belief and desire. Limited as it is, it would seem to be a major concession to the privileged access position and hence at odds with everything else Gopnik writes both in this paper and elsewhere. So I am inclined simply to discount it as something of an aberration.

10. It might seem that the combination of impaired first-person mindreading and intact third-person mindreading should be inconsistent with ST, although this combination is reported by Corcoran (2000) for some schizophrenics. However, Corcoran specifically cites a study by Langdon et al. (1997), where the reported first-person impairments were problems on *recall* of past intentions. Recall problems may have nothing to do with problems concerning introspection.

11. J. Prinz (2004) advocates the notion of a multiplicity, or "spectrum," of introspection mechanisms. But he doesn't adequately address the problems I am raising.

12. Thanks to Eric Schwitzgebel for noting the similarity between the ascent-routine approach and redeployment accounts. Nichols and Stich also fail to notice the similarity (as I initially did); they take issue with Gordon's approach.

13. It might appear that not only first-order states must be "duplicated" but higher-order states as well, yielding a series of infinite regresses. However, one can stop such regresses by saying that a lower-level state is rendered conscious by being the object of even a *nonconscious* higher-order state. That is Rosenthal's (1993) strategy.

14. There is a moderately close parallel between Shoemaker's line of argument and that of Crispin Wright (1989), in which Wright argues against an "inward perception" model of intention detection. Wright argues that intention is an "extension-determining concept," which means, roughly, that there is an a priori connection between our judgments and the extension of the concept. Wright proceeds to argue that because intention is an extension-determining concept, it is inappropriate to think of us as

detecting our intentions. Holton (1993) critiques Wright along lines somewhat similar to my critique of Shoemaker. To take one of Holton's examples, suppose we define a *correctly functioning thermometer* as one that accurately registers the temperature within a certain range. The definition offers us an a priori guarantee that correctly functioning thermometers will not get things wrong. Nevertheless, there is no temptation to deny that such thermometers *detect* the temperature: They do so in a straightforward causal way.

15. Notice that my term *belief* is applied to both standing and occurrent (activated) states. Some philosophers prefer the term *judgment* for the occurrent variety of belief. Until now, when I have discussed the introspection of beliefs and desires, I have had the occurrent variety in mind.

16. Some of the inquiring processes seem to be effortful and some automatic. The answering processes, by contrast, seem to be wholly automatic, not at all subject to control.

17. Talk of a transduction process is metaphorical in the case of introspection, because it is not literally being proposed that introspection involves a change in the form of *energy* by which information is transmitted.

18. Here I introduce a weak reliability constraint. This is why my earlier expression of "disinterest" in epistemological issues like reliability was slightly qualified.

19. Many philosophers argue that color properties must be analyzed dispositionally. But if so, we must conclude that the presence of colors, *so understood*, isn't what vision (directly) detects.

20. Thanks to Kelby Mason for help in articulating these problems.

21. In recent writing, Tye (2002) distinguishes two senses of *qualia*. In one sense, qualia are introspectively accessible properties of experience. In this sense, he says, qualia exist and are properly understood in representational terms. In a second sense, qualia are intrinsic, introspectively accessible, and *nonrepresentational* qualities of experience. In this sense, he dismisses qualia as a philosophical myth (2002: 447).

22. Of course, mental-state dualism, which holds that mental tokens are not physical states, would not allow that such token states have neural properties. But it might allow a subtler doctrine, under which, say, a subject's brain instantiates certain neural properties whenever a certain type of mental state is instantiated.

23. Craig indicates that a "re-representation" of the interoceptive cortical image in VMpo occurs in the anterior insular cortex of the nondominant (right) hemisphere, possibly unique in humans. This area, he says, may constitute a basis for the subjective evaluation of one's condition, that is, "how you feel." There are two ways, I comment, in which this proposal might be interpreted. The anterior insular cortex area may be the real substrate of feelings (or the subjective/affective dimension of feelings), or it may be the substrate of what I am calling the introspective classification of feelings.

10

Concepts of Mental States

10.1 Mentalizing and Concepts of the Mental

One of the principal problems on our agenda is how the folk understand or conceptualize mental states. When people attribute a desire, a belief, a pain, or an emotion, whether to self or to other, what is their representation of the state attributed? In the case of propositional attitudes, representing an entire mental state involves representing both its type and its content. The focus in this chapter, however, is exclusively types—emotion and sensation types as well as attitude types. The problem of representing, or conceptualizing, contents was addressed in sections 7.10 and 9.8. Of course, a mentalizer who attributes a particular belief must possess, and deploy, a concept of belief, and this concept must differ from her concepts of desire, intention, pain, anger, and the like. Concepts of all such mental-state types I'll call mental concepts. What can be said about the nature of mental concepts?

A prior question is: What are concepts (for a review, see Laurence and Margolis, 1999)? In the philosophical literature, "concept" is ambiguous in at least two ways. There is a *psychological* sense of "concept" in which a concept is a mental representation of a category, something literally in the head. If there is a language of thought, a concept might be a (semantically interpreted) word in the language of thought. If there are multiple languages of thought, a concept might be a word, or group of words, in one or more of these languages. Thus, the concept *horse*(often written in capitals: HORSE) might be a mentalese word that applies to all and only horses. To possess a concept is to have some such mental representation as part of one's cognitive repertoire. A second sense of "concept" is the *Fregean* sense. In contrast with the psychological sense, Frege (1892) conceived of concepts ("senses") as abstract entities, graspable by different individuals but not literally in anybody's head. In the present chapter, mental concepts will be discussed exclusively in the psychological sense of the term.

Two different aspects of mental concepts are of interest: their *vehicles* and their *contents*. A concept's vehicles are the specific mental representations, or types of mental representation, that comprise the concept, including the "structure" of such vehicles.[1] A concept's content is its satisfaction conditions, the conditions an object or state must satisfy to qualify as an instance of the concept or to belong to its extension. In the general theory of concepts, both topics are extremely fraught issues, which we cannot treat in full generality. The hope is to shed some light on a particular class of concepts, the mental ones.

Our treatment of mental concepts will be influenced by our treatment of introspection in chapter 9. There it was argued that introspection is a common, indeed standard, way by which people recognize, discriminate, or detect the mental types of one's current mental tokens. Is there, in general, a connection between methods for discriminating objects in a domain and the concepts of those object types? Some approaches to concepts endorse such links. If this is right, and if introspection is the standard first-person method for mental-state recognition, then introspective representations of mental states could play a pivotal role in the account of mental concepts. This is the route I shall pursue.[2]

My treatment of mental concepts (partly) in terms of introspective representations diverges notably from typical treatments of mental concepts under the TT approach. As we saw in chapter 9, most proponents of TT give little or no credence to the idea of a special method for detecting one's own mental states. Theory-theorists typically insist that mental states are "abstract" and "unobservable," so there is presumably no way for introspection, a putative form of inner observation, to get a fix on them.[3] Thus, no such process as introspection could be of help in understanding mental concepts.

Even among simulationists, a role for introspection is controversial. As noted in section 7.13, Gordon expunges introspection from his version of ST. Indeed, he dispenses with any use of mental concepts in mindreading by rejecting a final step of simulation in which a (simulated) mental state is classified under a mental concept. By my lights, omitting classification from mindreading changes the subject. So this chapter continues to assume that mindreading involves mental classification, that is, application of mental concepts. The question therefore arises, what is the nature of mental concepts? As indicated, I divide this question into two parts, the first concerning vehicles and the second concerning contents. Vehicles are treated in sections 10.2 through 10.4, and content in sections 10.5 and 10.6.

10.2 An Introspective Code for Mental-
Concept Representation

My central thesis is that mental concepts (partly) employ *introspection-derived*, or *introspection-associated*, mental representations. The hypothesis is that there is a proprietary code, the *introspective code* (I-code), used to represent types of mental categories and to classify mental-state tokens in terms of those categories. This idea is not dissimilar to one advanced by William Lycan (1996: 59–61), who speaks of introspective concepts as semantically primitive lexemes of our language of thought, used in second-order representations of the subject's own first-order psychological states. However, I want to embed this general approach in a framework that acknowledges the multiplicity of mental codes or representational formats. I assume that one and the same distinctive code could be used both to represent various mental categories (e.g., belief and intention) and to classify currently observed token states in terms of these categories (*"that* state now occurring is an intention"). Let me illustrate my approach in examining an analogous case: the case of vision and visual representation.

A number of vision scientists, including David Marr (1982) and Irving Biederman (1987, 1990), conjecture that visual object recognition partly proceeds in terms of shape-based representations of objects and their parts. Biederman postulates that we code physical object types like *cup*, *lamp*, or *tree* in terms of characteristic parts of such objects, each part being a specifiable shape. The shapes in question are volumetric units like cylinders, which Biederman calls *geons* (for "geometrical ions"). In addition to the geonic representations, Biederman's theory employs a small set of relations by which a pair of geons can be related, such as top-of, side-connected-to, and larger-than. Biederman says that different combinations of geons and relations among them can be used to represent object categories like *cup*, *lamp*, and *tree*. For example, a roughly cylindrical geon would be the main part of a cup, and it would be side-connected to a handle-shaped geon. The same two geons could be used to represent a pail, where the handle geon bears the top-of relation to the cylindrical geon. Biederman does not claim that the geonic code is the only code for representing object names or categories. The same object names can also be coded in another format, a modality-neutral format. In such a format, *cup* might be represented as "container for drinking, with a handle."

When we see a cup or a tree, says Biederman, high-level vision forms an active, geon-based representation of the target object. The system then tries to match the geonic and relational elements in the perceptual representation of the target to a corresponding combination of elements and relations in a stored representation of an object type. When a close enough match is found, the target object is categorized as a member of the matched type. Of course, cups and trees can be actively represented even when we don't see them. Jones might inform me by telephone that there is currently a cup on his desk. In representing Jones's unseen cup, I might visualize it in a geonic representational format or, alternatively, in a modality-neutral, partly functional, representation: a container for drinking, with a handle. Analogously, my proposal for mental concepts is that they include at least two representational types, that is, representations in two representational codes or formats: the postulated I-code and a more generic conceptual code.

The I-code being hypothesized would have a proprietary vocabulary, proprietary in the same sense that Biederman's geonic vocabulary is proprietary to visual cognition. The vocabulary of the I-code would be used to characterize one's own internal states, not in causal-functional terms but in terms of properties accessible to introspection. The introspective vocabulary would in no way be "reducible" to causal-functional vocabulary. It is difficult to say what introspective properties or dimensions there may be,[4] but let us speculate about some possibilities. Three possible dimensions, or parameters, are (1) the doxastic, or credal, dimension; (2) the preference or valence dimension; and (3) the bodily feeling dimension. "Sureness" or certainty would be one value of the doxastic parameter, doubt another value, and disbelief a third. Desire would be one value of the valence parameter, indifference a second, and aversion a third. Concerning bodily sensations, there would be a multitude of finely delineated categories.

Our coding of mental-state concepts might utilize combinations of the foregoing parameter values, just as our coding of physical object types may utilize different combinations of geons and geonic relations. For example, HOPE may represent a mental-state category that combines desire on the valence dimension and doubt, or uncertainty, on the doxastic dimension. FEAR, in a nonaffective sense of the term, may represent aversion on the valence dimension and uncertainty on the doxastic dimension. ("Sammy fears that his score won't be high enough to win the competition.") PAIN may represent a certain raw feeling together with a negative valence toward it. Each of these concepts may also have associated features coded in a *nonintrospective* vocabulary or format, as will be discussed in the next section. Here the discussion is restricted to the introspective vocabulary, or I-code.

Notice that although the I-code is used to represent many mental states with phenomenal, or phenomenological, character (which is not to say that all mental states have phenomenal character), it does not follow that the introspective format has an *additional* phenomenal character of its own. Indeed, I assume that the I-code itself has no independent phenomenology.

10.3 Mental-Concept Representation
and Multiple Formats

An instructive precedent for reflecting on how multiple codes or formats might be used in mentally representing a single word or category can be found in the work of Ray Jackendoff (1996). Jackendoff presents this idea, which he calls "representational modularity," in the following passage:

> The general idea is that the mind/brain encodes information in many distinct formats or "languages of the mind." There is a module of mind/brain responsible for each of these formats. For example, phonological structure and syntactic structure are distinct levels of encoding, with distinct and only partly commensurate primitives and principles of combination. Representational Modularity therefore posits that the architecture of the mind/brain devotes separate modules to these two encodings. (1996: 1)

It is not essential to my application of the multiple-format idea that the formats or levels of representation be *modules*, so I ignore this aspect of Jackendoff's proposal. Jackendoff is ultimately interested in the problem of how we talk about what we see. How does the mind/brain encode spatial information in visual terms, how does it encode spatial information in linguistic terms, and how does it communicate between the two formats or levels of representation? In the case of language and spatial cognition, he postulates two modules that he calls *conceptual structure* (CS) and *spatial representation* (SR). Roughly speaking, CS encodes propositional representations, whereas SR is the locus of "image schema" representations. CS is an encoding of linguistic meaning that is independent of the particular language whose meaning it encodes. It is an "algebraic" representation in the sense that conceptual structures are built up out of discrete primitive features and functions. SR contrasts with CS in being geometric (or quasi-topological) in character rather than algebraic, something like Biederman's geonic system.

We come now to the most pertinent element in Jackendoff's theory for present purposes. Lexical items like "dog," says Jackendoff, can be paired with a number of representations in different formats, which collectively specify its "meaning" (for the subject in question). "Dog," for example, might be paired with representations in three formats, CS, SR, and an auditory format, yielding something like the following:

CS: Individual, Type of Animal, Type of Carnivore
          Function: (often) Type of Pet
SR: [3-D model with motion affordances]
Auditory: [sound of barking]

Jackendoff goes on to say that these materials might be considered "the nonlinguistic knowledge one has of dogs—the 'concept' of a dog, much of which could be shared by a nonlinguistic organism" (1996: 12).

I shall treat Jackendoff's representation schema for (the concept) DOG as a prototype for representations of mental concepts such as BELIEF, DESIRE, and FEAR. As indicated, however, I postulate an additional representational code, the I-code. Notice that some of the same dimensions represented in the I-code (e.g., the doxastic and valence dimensions) might also be represented in a nonintrospective code, perhaps Jackendoff's CS. Jackendoff himself postulates that different representational modules sometimes have similar representational contents, although they are expressed in different encodings (for example, via different primitives and different principles of combination). Without such similarities, it would be impossible for different modules to communicate with one another within the brain. Thus, Jackendoff says that the notions of physical objects and physical motion are presumably shared by the SR system and the CS system. On the other hand, details of object shapes, such as the shape of a violin or a butter knife or a German shepherd's ears, would be naturally encoded in SR but not readily expressible in CS. Analogously, the I-code I am postulating would lend itself to representing certain features of mental states not readily represented in CS.

To further clarify what I have been saying, the suggestion is that I-coded representations are *among* the representations that figure in mental-state concepts like BELIEF, DESIRE, FEAR, and LOVE. However, they probably do not exhaust the representations that figure in these mental concepts. Just as Jackendoff's sample account of DOG includes material in the vocabulary of CS, so each mental concept may also contain CS constituents[5] and may even describe causal-functional materials. The present approach doesn't exclude such representational elements; it just declines to assign them an exclusive or even primary role in mental-state representation.

The vast majority of self-attributions of current mental states, I suspect, use introspection only. An introspective representation of a current mental-state token is matched to some constituent of a mental concept, for instance, DESIRE, and this generates a classification of the state token as an instance of DESIRE. More specifically, the introspective representation serves as default evidence for the token state being a desire and, absent defeating evidence, yields that classification. Similarly, introspective representations can be used in the course of simulation processes to generate third-person attributions.

In special circumstances, self-attribution might proceed by theoretical inference or confabulation, and an inferential (nonsimulative) route may be a fairly common method of third-person attribution. Theoretical inference in third-person attribution is fully compatible with our hybrid account and was even admitted as a nonstandard strategy for first-person attribution under our dual-method approach (section 9.3.2). In all such cases, behavioral or functional constituents of the mental concept would come into play, just as CS (rather than geonic) representations presumably come into play when forming a testimony-based belief that a cup is on Jones's desk.

Information of the functional variety might even override information of an introspective variety. For example, introspective information might initially favor classifying a state as "love," but behavioral/functional information may trump that initial classification. This raises the question of how the two kinds of information are weighted in the process of categorization. I offer no specific theory of the categorization process.

If there is a proprietary introspective code, are we consciously aware of it? We are certainly aware of the visual and auditory forms of representation, even if we don't naïvely think of them *as* representational formats. Are we analogously aware of an introspective form of representation? That is doubtful. We are aware of *what* is coded by introspection but not of the coding per se. If there is a coding system, it is a silent partner. But the same is true of Jackendoff's representational format CS. We are aware of *what* it codes but not of the coding system itself.

Still, is it really plausible to postulate a wholly new system of representation or discrimination, previously unheralded in cognitive science? New research and/or theorizing sometimes impels cognitive scientists to postulate previously undetected or untheorized coding systems. An excellent example is the coding system associated with the dorsal visual stream. Research on both monkeys and humans indicates that there are two different streams of visual information that extend outward from primary visual cortex: the ventral stream and the dorsal stream. These two streams have a sharp division of labor (Milner and Goodale, 1995). The ventral stream mediates what we ordinarily think of as visual object perception; the dorsal stream mediates the visual control of skilled action, without giving rise to visual awareness. A well-studied patient, D.F., who has damage to her ventral stream pathway, is unable to indicate the size, shape, and orientation of an object, either verbally or manually, when simply looking at it. Nonetheless, when she reaches out to grasp it, she shows normal preshaping and rotation of her hand (Goodale, Milner, Jakobson, and Carey, 1991). This successful motor guidance is due to her intact dorsal system. Evidently, the dorsal system employs a distinct, visuomotor coding system, using moment-to-moment information about the disposition of objects in an egocentric frame of reference to mediate the control of goal-directed acts (see Milner and Goodale, 1995). Obviously, I do not claim to have comparable neurophysiological evidence in support of an I-coding system. But theoretical considerations of the sort offered here are also evidentially relevant.

What is the relationship between the I-coding system and the mental-state lexemes of natural language? No simple isomorphism between the two should be expected. The I-coding system is presumably much richer than the resources of natural language (especially what is *lexically* encoded in natural language), just as the geonic coding system offers far greater taxonomic resources than our linguistic system of physical-object labels. Nonetheless, there must be some partial mapping, or interface, between the I-system and the linguistic taxonomic system for mental states. The details of such a mapping go beyond our present purview.

10.4 Introspection-Based Concepts and Self-Directed Recognitional Concepts

Another approach to mental concepts that rummages in the same philosophical neighborhood as the one sketched here is Brian Loar's (1990, 2003) theory of self-directed recognitional concepts. Loar's account is concerned with the narrower class of phenomenal concepts, rather than mental concepts more broadly, but its philosophical motivations are sufficiently similar to those of the present account to merit an exercise in "compare and contrast."[6]

Loar introduces a class of concepts called recognitional concepts. They are type-demonstrative concepts that have the form "x is one of *that* kind." These type demonstratives are grounded in dispositions to classify, by way of perceptual discriminations, certain objects, events, and situations. Suppose you go into the California desert and spot a succulent never seen before. You become adept at recognizing instances and gain a recognitional command of their kind, without a name for it. You are disposed to identify positive and negative instances and thereby pick out a kind. In forming recognitional concepts, one always presupposes a general type to which the kind belongs: four-legged animal, plant, physical thing, perceptible event. So a recognitional concept will have the form "physical thing of that (perceived) kind" or "internal state of that kind," and so forth. Recognitional abilities, says Loar, depend on no consciously accessible analysis into component features; they can be irreducibly gestalt.

Phenomenal concepts, according to Loar, are a special class of recognitional concepts, a species of *self-directed* recognitional concepts. They are type demonstratives that derive their reference from a first-person, or introspective, perspective: "that type of sensation," "that feature of visual experience." The properties picked out, Loar argues, are physical-functional properties of the brain. Although the properties picked out, or referred to, by phenomenal concepts are physical-functional properties of the brain, the phenomenal concepts themselves are conceptually independent of physical-functional descriptions. They are not theoretical, or causal-functional, concepts of brain states; instead, they pick out physical-functional properties of the brain "directly."

One point of difference between my scheme of introspective concepts and Loar's is that his phenomenal concepts are presented as *abilities* or *dispositions*. A phenomenal concept is a disposition to pick out positive and negative instances of the kind in question (a phenomenal kind). By contrast, my hypothesized introspective representations are supposed to be the *categorical bases* of such dispositions. They are the distinctive representations of introspection by which one sorts current experienced states as pains or itches, or as feelings of warmth or cold.

A second point of difference is that Loar implies that recognitional concepts lack any analysis into component features.[7] By contrast, I am hypothesizing that there is a cognitive system, namely, the introspective system, that possesses and deploys descriptive or predicative resources for distinguishing mental-state types. The I-system is not reduced to making an internal gesture, or demonstration, toward mental tokens of the kind in question. It represents the various internal states by means of descriptive features, predicates in a proprietary vocabulary not readily expressible in natural language. This is akin to the relationship between Jackendoff's SR (spatial representation) and CS (conceptual structure). The shapes of a violin, a butter knife, or a German shepherd's ears are naturally encoded in SR but not in CS. It is not clear whether Loar definitely intends his phrase "recognitional concept" to preclude any set of component descriptive features. If he does, then my theory further diverges from his recognitional-concept theory.

A third major difference between my theory and Loar's is one of scope: Mine includes, but is not exhausted by, phenomenal concepts. My theory also hopes to accommodate the self-ascription of beliefs and other states for which phenomenal character is dubious. This might seem to constitute a major gulf between Loar's approach and mine. But Loar himself makes room for *non*phenomenal self-directed concepts as well, so my approach may be on the same track as this added feature of his account.

In discussing nonphenomenal self-directed recognitional concepts, Loar asks us to consider blindsight. Some cortically damaged people are phenomenally blind in restricted retinal regions but, when prompted, can guess with a fair degree of accuracy whether (say) a vertical or horizontal line is presented. He then asks us to extend the example by imagining a blindsight that is exercised spontaneously and accurately ("superblindsight"). Finally, he shifts the discussion to internal properties and asks us to conceive of a self-directed recognitional ability, which is like the previous ability in being phenomenally blank and spontaneous but which discriminates an internal property of one's own. If this recognitional ability were suitably governed by the concept "that state," the resulting concept would be a self-directed recognitional concept that is phenomenally blank. This acknowledged possibility of nonphenomenal self-directed recognitional concepts makes Loar's account even closer to mine. Of course, I am proposing that the foregoing description is (roughly) true not merely of some possible mental concepts but of many of our actual mental concepts.

Finally, Loar makes remarks about the "projective" use of self-directed recognitional concepts in third-person ascription that fit nicely with our simulationist approach. Loar holds that recognitional concepts in general are "perspectival," in the sense that their reference is determined from a certain constitutive perspective. In the case of phenomenal concepts, we acquire them from a first-person perspective "by discriminating a property in the having of it" (Loar, 2003: 302). When we then use the concepts to ascribe states to others, we are "projecting" them from our own case. The third-person ascriptions have the form "x has a state of this sort," where the demonstrative gets its reference from an actual or possible state of one's own. It should be obvious how congenial this is to our simulationist approach.

To reiterate, I do not say that introspection-based concepts exhaust the character of mental concepts as conveyed by a natural-language mental predicate. I propose only that they comprise a large part of their character and occupy a special role in first-person classification.[8]

10.5 The Contents of Mental Concepts: The Causal-Covariation Approach

The preceding discussion dealt with the representational vehicles by which introspection classifies first-order mental states. These vehicles are (syntactic) elements of the I-code. I now turn to the *contents* of such vehicles, specifically, the contents of introspective concepts. The theory of content is much-contested terrain, offering many complex alternatives. Because of the unsettled questions in this terrain, concerning both content in general and mental concepts in particular, I won't try to offer an unequivocal answer to our question about content. However, one conclusion important to this book will be defended throughout the discussion (mostly implicitly). This conclusion is that all of the most promising approaches to mental-concept contents fit comfortably within the ambit of an introspection-based approach and contrast with views favored by pure theory-theorists or rationality theorists. Thus, although there is no single theory of mental-concept content that I find wholly satisfactory, the best answers on the table mesh with the theoretical stance defended in previous chapters.

The literature on mental-concept contents is delicate and controversial, partly because it bears quite directly on the metaphysical issue of physicalism versus nonphysicalism. Readers might like a clear pronouncement on mental-concept contents precisely because of this linkage. But it should be recalled (section 1.2) that I deliberately kept this topic off the present agenda; it is simply too large and complex. However, the discussion that follows reflects some of the angles on mental-concept contents that tilt different philosophers toward different metaphysical conclusions (or accommodate their antecedent metaphysical views).

I focus on two approaches to concept contents: the causal-covariation approach and the two-dimensional approach. The first is examined in this section and the second in the sequel. A cousin of the causal-covariation approach is the information-theoretic approach pioneered by Dretske (1981, 1988). According to this approach, the content or meaning of a sign or mental symbol is a function of what it indicates or signifies. Tracks in the woods mean, or indicate, that there are deer in the woods because the tracks wouldn't be there unless deer were there. Similarly, certain perceptual representations in the head might mean, or have the content, "dog," because such representations wouldn't be tokened unless a dog were present. Applied to cases of interest here, the theory would say that certain I-representations might mean, or have the content, "belief" or "pain," because such representations wouldn't be tokened unless a belief or a pain, respectively, were currently in the subject's mind (and monitored by the introspection system). In Fodor's hands, the informational approach was transmuted into a causal-covariation theory that says (very roughly) that a representation R expresses the property P in virtue of its being a law that things that are P cause tokenings of R in some specified ("normal") circumstances (Fodor, 1990, 1998).[9] The reference to "normal" circumstances calls attention to a major problem for this theory: the problem of error, or misrepresentation. I'll ignore this problem, because it's tangential to our concerns.

Let us return to the framework in which we were discussing I-coded concepts. When the concept BELIEF is tokened in the introspection system, as the result of monitoring a current belief, what property of the (first-order) belief plays the causal role? The answer is crucial, because under the causal-covariation theory the causally efficacious property should comprise the content of BELIEF (at least the introspection-based constituent of BELIEF). Recall now that section 9.7 tilted toward the view that neural properties are the causal inputs to the introspection-transduction process. Shall we conclude, then, that some *neural* property possessed by beliefs is the content of the introspective constituent of BELIEF? And similarly, should we conclude that some neural property distinctive of pains constitutes the content of the introspective constituent of PAIN, because such a property would be the causal input to introspection that triggers PAIN? These answers will invite complaints. In the case of PAIN, at least, shouldn't the content be a phenomenal property rather than a neural property?[10]

One problem facing the phenomenal-property proposal, as reviewed in section 9.7, is the causal status of phenomenal properties. Phenomenal properties presumably supervene on physical properties and would therefore (at least according to Kim, 1998) be merely epiphenomenal and noncausal. One direct response to this problem is to dispute the contention that supervenient properties are causally inefficacious (Fodor, 1989; McLaughlin, 1989). A second possible response is to amend the informational or covariation approach by omitting the causation requirement. The amended theory could require merely nomological covariation, not causation.

Another possible way to proceed is to abandon a *pure* informational or covariation theory and introduce elements from inferential role semantics (usually considered a rival approach). The distinctive content of the introspective concept PAIN would then be determined not simply by the cause of its tokenings but by the patterns of inferential interaction between such tokenings and other pieces of information in the user's mind. It is not clear, however, how this will help. Which candidate for content would it favor, and why? Another approach is to appeal to "modes of presentation" to identify the property that constitutes this concept's content. Fodor (1998: 13ff.) indicates a preference for the mode-of-presentation approach as a way of dealing with Frege's puzzle of how the concept of Hesperus (the evening star) differs from the concept of Phosphorus (the morning star) when the two concepts are coreferential (both refer to Venus). Unfortunately, it is radically unclear what might be the requisite modes of presentation for introspective concepts of mental states.

A chief attraction of Loar's type-demonstrative approach is its (apparent) applicability to the Frege-type puzzle as concerns the mental and the physical. The type-demonstrative approach allows us to say that a phenomenal concept of pain is different from a physical-functional concept of pain, although the two are coreferential (they both pick out a physical-functional *property*). But does Loar mean to say that the two concepts share the same *content*? That's what an informational or covariation approach would dictate, but it seems unsatisfactory. A phenomenal concept does not seem to represent a type of state *as* a physical state (especially not as a *neural* state).

We encounter here a very difficult problem in the theory of content, not entirely unique to concepts of the mental. Introspection-based mental concepts have two characteristics that create difficulties for a theory of content. First, the root of all talk and theorizing about content is the desire to explain what a representation means. Such explanations are always couched in terms of some representational code, normally a natural language. However, the formats of some mental representations do not lend themselves to characterization or explication in natural language; they are not readily expressible (or translatable) into the code of the content-specifying theory. This creates one difficulty for a theory of content, which I'll call the *inexpressibility problem*. Introspection-based mental concepts obviously have the inexpressibility problem. A second problem is related to the distinctiveness of the I-code but not its untranslatability into natural language. The problem is that when two representations are in different formats, then even when they represent one and the same object or property, it is tempting to think of them as differing in content. For example, we can represent the roughness of a surface's texture either tactilely or visually. Two such representations are obviously quite different, though the represented property, roughness, is the same. One is tempted to say that the two representations differ in content, but it's unclear how a theory of content should accommodate this. Modes of presentation have been introduced to provide assistance when referring thoughts seem underindividuated, but when the contents of perceptual representations are in question, it isn't clear what *further* modes of presentation might be invoked. I'll call this the *format distinctiveness* problem. Theories of content can run into trouble from either of these problems. When both are present, as in the case of introspection-based mental concepts, a theory of content is seriously challenged.

10.6 The Contents of Mental Concepts: The Two-Dimensional Approach

Perhaps we have been barking up the wrong tree. Perhaps it's just misguided to think that a concept's content can be identified with the property (or *a* property) that causes the concept's tokenings. This section examines another approach. The approach starts with the assumption that a concept's content should be identified with an associated intension, a function that maps each possible world to an extension, a class of things that satisfy the concept in that world. Within this general framework, David Chalmers (1996, 2003a, 2003b) distinguishes two types of intensions and highlights one of them as the key to capturing the content of phenomenal concepts. Because phenomenal concepts are the most discussed troublemakers for a theory of introspection-based concepts, let's examine Chalmers's framework.[11]

Chalmers (2003b) distinguishes four different types of phenomenal concepts, all of which he illustrates for phenomenal redness. The first three phenomenal concepts are relational concepts. One is the community relational concept, glossed as "the phenomenal quality typically caused in normal subjects in my community by paradigmatic red things." Second is the individual relational concept, glossed as "the phenomenal quality typically caused in me by paradigmatic red things." Third is a demonstrative or indexical concept of phenomenal redness of the sort Loar proposes. A demonstrative like "this quality" or "this sort of experience" has a character (in the sense of Kaplan, 1989) that fixes reference in a context by picking out whatever quality is ostended in that context. In the actual world, each of these three concepts refers to the same (nonrelational) property, namely, phenomenal redness.

Chalmers argues that there is also a fourth type of phenomenal concept in the vicinity, one that picks out phenomenal redness *directly* rather than relationally. This concept is needed to identify what Frank Jackson's (1982, 1986) color-deprived Mary gains when she learns for the first time what it is like to see red. Mary learns that seeing red has such-and-such quality, and the new concept she acquires is "such-and-such." Chalmers calls this a *pure phenomenal concept.* This concept is needed, he says, to make sense of the "cognitive significance" of Mary's new knowledge. Mary can now think the new thought "this quality is R," where "this quality" expresses a demonstrative (and hence relational) concept, whereas "R" expresses the pure phenomenal concept. Such a thought, says Chalmers, is cognitively significant rather than trivial. It expresses an identity that is knowable only a posteriori, not a priori, because no a priori reasoning can rule out the hypothesis that she is now ostending some other quality entirely. Chalmers concludes that pure phenomenal concepts are distinct from the other three types of phenomenal concepts. The pure phenomenal concepts are crucial for expressing certain truths, such as the truth about Mary.

Chalmers analyzes the relations among these concepts by using a two-dimensional framework for representing the content of concepts (Chalmers, 2003a). The two-dimensional framework distinguishes two dimensions, or components, of content: the primary (or epistemic) component and the secondary (or subjunctive) component.[12] Very roughly, the primary component captures a "narrow" sense of content, and the secondary component expresses a "wide" sense of content. When an identity $A = B$ is a posteriori (e.g., "The person before me is my uncle"), the concepts A and B have different primary intensions. When A and B are rigid concepts and the identity is true, A and B have the same secondary intension. So the four phenomenal-redness concepts have different primary intensions from one another but the same secondary intension.[13]

Now, if we seek to interpret introspection-based concepts of the sort I have been discussing along the lines of any of Chalmers's phenomenal concepts, which one might it be? It couldn't be any of the three relational concepts, because the introspective concepts I have been discussing are not supposed to be relational (not relational in *those* ways, anyway). The best candidate is Chalmers's pure phenomenal concept. However, I hesitate here. Chalmers goes on to explain that the referent of a pure phenomenal concept is "somehow present inside the concept's sense, in a way much stronger than in the usual cases of 'direct reference'" (2003b: 233). I confess to being quite unclear how the referent of a concept—in this case a phenomenal quality—could manage to get "inside" the sense of the concept. So while I acknowledge the attractions of a pure phenomenal concept, especially the way that its primary intension permits a satisfactory treatment of Mary's newly acquired knowledge, I am not eager to endorse this solution to our problem of content.[14]

There is an additional, important, reason why such a solution doesn't adequately serve our purposes. Chalmers's proposal concerns phenomenal concepts, but there is no reason to feel confident that all introspection-based mental concepts are phenomenal concepts.[15] It is questionable, for example, whether any phenomenal property is associated with BELIEF or INTENTION. Thus, it is not clear how Chalmers's proposal could generalize to our problem of identifying contents for all mental concepts.

To conclude, I don't have a satisfactory theory of the content of intro-spection-based mental concepts. This is not an embarrassment, however, be-cause the lacuna is largely traceable to the gnarled and messy state of the general theory of content. The theory encounters special difficulties when confronted by representations with the two troublemaking features identified earlier: *inexpressibility* and *format distinctiveness*. Concepts in the I-code are prime examples of such troublesomeness. An acceptable comprehensive theory would presumably help resolve such problems of content, but no such theory is currently available. Note that our chief competitors, the theory-theory and the rationality theory, are in a worse position to identify the contents of mental concepts. They ignore introspection-based concepts en-tirely, and they certainly lack the resources to connect mental-concept con-tents with introspective self-ascription.[16] By contrast, our account of the introspection-based "character" of mental concepts is a promising element in a story of introspective self-ascription. Although we come up short on the topic of content, this is not a sign that our general approach is on the wrong track.

10.7 Concepts and the Epistemic

In this section, I consider a possible objection to my account of mental con-cepts suggested by Jerry Fodor's (2001, 2004) critique of a certain broad philosophical approach to concepts. Fodor purports to demolish this entire tradition of concept theorizing, a tradition he calls *concept pragmatism*, though a better label, I think, is *concept epistemicism*.[17] He associates this view with the last hundred years of Anglophone philosophy of mind and language. On this view, concepts are construed epistemically. More specifi-cally, "Concept pragmatism either is or contains the thesis that concept pos-session is constituted by certain epistemic capacities" (2004: 32). One such epistemic capacity is a capacity to sort objects into kinds, based on perception, for example. Concept epistemicism holds that to have a concept C is, inter alia, to be able to sort objects in C's extension. To have the concept DOG, for example, is to be able to sort dogs from nondogs. Similarly, concept episte-micism might say that possessing the concept BELIEF is, inter alia, having the ability to sort beliefs from other mental states. Fodor's contention, by contrast, is that "*no* concepts are constituted by epistemic possession conditions" (2001: 8).

Now my approach to mental concepts, especially its introspection-based component, is a pretty clear exemplification of concept epistemicism. In-trospection is a method by which cognizers sort their first-order mental-state tokens according to types represented by the concepts. To have an I-concept associated with BELIEF is to have the capacity to sort tokens of belief from tokens of other mental-state types. Although I haven't emphasized the reliability of introspection, this is implied by introspection's sensitivity to the properties distinctive of the various mental-state types in question. Indeed, I have strongly implied that I-concepts are recognitional concepts, not in Loar's sense of being sorting dispositions (full stop), but in the sense of being categorical bases of sorting dispositions. So if Fodor has cogent objections to concept epistemicism, they presumably extend to the variant of concept epistemicism embodied in my approach to I-concepts.

What are Fodor's objections to concept epistemicism? Fodor's main objection (the only one I'll consider here) concerns the requirement of compositionality. The principle of compositionality requires that constituent concepts transmit all their semantic properties to their hosts. Thus, the possession conditions for RED SQUARE must include the possession conditions for RED and the possession conditions for SQUARE. The trouble arises if one imposes recognitional conditions for the constituent concepts, because recognitional conditions don't transmit to complex concepts. Having the concept RED may be sufficient for being able to recognize red things in favorable circumstances, and having the concept SQUARE may be sufficient for being able to recognize square things in favorable circumstances. But it doesn't follow that having the concept RED SQUARE is sufficient for being able to recognize red squares in favorable circumstances. This is because the favorable conditions for recognizing red things might be ipso facto *un*favorable for recognizing square things (2001: 8). Fodor concludes that at least *some* concepts, namely, the complex ones, which have compositional structure, are not constituted by recognitional capacities (2001: 8).

I respond as follows.[18] Fodor is systematically ambiguous, perhaps even confused, about what a plausible version of concept epistemicism would maintain and what is required by a plausible principle of concept composition. Concept epistemicism should not require that a recognitional requirement be *part* of any concept, that is, that such a requirement be included in the concept as if it were a constituent. Rather, a reasonable form of concept epistemicism would maintain that, for *some* concepts (e.g., primitive concepts), possession of these concepts requires *satisfaction* of a recognitional requirement. If RED is primitive, then possessing RED requires satisfying a suitable recognitional requirement vis-à-vis instances of RED. This recognitional requirement, however, need not be transmitted to complex concepts of which the primitive concept is a constituent. Complex concepts needn't be subjected to the same recognitional requirement, at least not in virtue of compositionality. What a plausible compositionality principle requires is only that the *semantic content* of a primitive concept be transmitted to any complex ("host") concept of which it is a constituent. The recognitional requirement, however, is not part of the semantic content of a primitive concept such as RED. The recognitional requirement is only a *constraint* on (primitive) concept *possession*; it is not part of the concept's semantic content. The semantic content of RED, for example, might be the property of being red (e.g., being disposed to reflect certain wavelengths). That property must indeed be transmitted to the semantic content of RED SQUARE. But there is no necessity that the recognitional requirement for *possession* of RED be transmitted to the concept RED SQUARE. Although one could formulate concept epistemicism so that it also imposes this possession condition on complex concepts, this would be a poorly chosen formulation. One cannot demolish an entire approach by pointing to failings of some ill-chosen version of it. Once Fodor's critique of concept epistemicism is defused in this fashion, my own account of I-concepts is freed from any taint of being an instance of a generally unsustainable approach.

10.8 A Comprehensive Theory

We have now completed our defense of a comprehensive simulation-based theory, addressing the four central questions laid out in chapter 1. Evidence was presented for extensive simulation in third-person mindreading (chapters 6–7). Significant simulationist ingredients were found in matters of development, psychopathology, and evolution (chapter 8). Self-attribution was seen to be a predominantly introspective affair, which accommodates the role of self-attribution in simulational routines (chapter 9). Finally, our story is completed by this chapter's account of mental concepts, which assigns a distinctive role to an introspective code.

Notes

1. It is unclear at what level of description vehicles or mental representations are most fruitfully characterized, presumably at some functional or functional-architectural level.

2. Fodor denies that there is any intimate connection between concepts and recognition procedures. His argument is examined in section 10.7.

3. Gopnik and Wellman write: "All these characteristics of theories ought also to apply to children's understanding of mind, if such understandings are theories of mind. That is, such theories should involve appeal to abstract unobservable entities, with coherent relations among them" (1992: 148). Similarly, Scholl and Leslie write: "Children become competent reasoners about mental states even though they cannot see, hear or feel them" (1999: 133).

4. The nature of these properties is not inferable from the properties discussed in section 9.7, the input properties to introspective "transduction." An apt analogy is the optical image at the back of the eye, which doesn't by itself determine how the human color system structures color representations. Color representation also depends on the opponent-processing system that helps constitute our color-processing apparatus (Hurvich and Jameson, 1957).

5. I use the term *constituent* loosely, not in Fodor's restrictive sense of "constituent."

6. Actually, Loar's principal motivation is to defend physicalism from challenges like that of Jackson's (1982, 1986) "knowledge argument." That metaphysical issue is quite peripheral to our present concerns.

7. More precisely, he says they "depend on no *consciously accessible* analysis into component features" (2003: 298).

8. Of course, a simulationist approach implies that they also play an important role in third-person classification.

9. A related approach with considerable popularity is the teleosemantic theory of content, advocated by Millikan (1989), Papineau (1987), and others.

10. Of course, many physicalists claim that phenomenal properties *are* physical properties, but that's a highly contentious issue.

11. It should be noted that Chalmers's theory is not a full-fledged theory of content on a par with, say, the causal-covariational approach. In particular, it does not purport to be a "naturalization" of content that provides sufficient conditions in physical terms for an item's having a certain content.

12. The preferred terminology in Chalmers (2003a) is "epistemic" and "subjunctive." I use the "primary" versus "secondary" terminology to avoid confusion in the ensuing section, where there is discussion of "concept epistemicism."

13. The primary intension of the pure phenomenal concept R is distinct from the others because it picks out phenomenal redness in all worlds, which is not true of the primary intensions of the others.

14. Chalmers (personal communication) says that the quoted sentence was only meant as a metaphorical illustrative remark and doesn't play an essential role in his account. If it doesn't help, it can just be ignored. However, we do need to understand what it means for a concept to pick out a property "directly." Does it, perhaps, consist in a causal relationship with the property rather than a constitutive relationship? Chalmers evinces no attraction to causal theories of content, so this seems unlikely. But what, then, is the "directness" relationship?

15. In earlier work (Goldman, 1993a), I gave provisional support to the idea that even the propositional attitude types have distinctive phenomenal characteristics. However, I now wish to retract that support (or at least put it on hold). The I-coding system hypothesized in this chapter is intended to provide the sketch of an account of mental concepts that would accommodate introspective classification of attitudes without having to postulate distinctive phenomenal characteristics for the various attitude types.

16. Of course, space has been left for *some* TT-like elements in our overall account of mental concepts, specifically in the nonintrospective components of mental concepts. But these components cannot exhaust the content of mental concepts. Although color-deprived Mary may have some of the same understanding of red as ordinary people do, she does not have a full understanding of it (until she is exposed to what it looks like). Similarly, a full understanding of mental concepts is not exhausted by nonintrospective components.

17. The thesis of concept epistemicism is unrelated to Chalmers's epistemic component of content.

18. After completing my response, it was called to my attention that Recanati (2002) and Schiffer (unpublished) make somewhat similar responses.

11

The Fabric of Social Life

Mimicry, Fantasy, Fiction, and Morality

11.1 Behavioral Mimicry and Social Bonds

This final chapter explores the warp and woof of social life. It shows how many of our distinctively human social traits are interwoven with simulational propensities. The discussion isn't restricted to mentalizing; it strolls through other topics related to simulation, including the psychological underpinnings of social bonds, our fascination with fiction, and the relevance of simulation and empathy to moral theory.

Our picture of today's world is dominated by the specter of terrorism; it's hard not to think of the human race as embroiled in feuds, warfare, and violence. From another perspective, however, it can seem surprising how extensive and strong are the bonds that hold people together, strangers as well as kin, supporting all sorts of social structures and patterns of interaction. What forges and maintains these bonds? Are there hidden sides of human psychology that promote the creation and maintenance of interpersonal bonds? This section looks at one social psychological approach to the question, focused on behavioral mimicry. Behavioral mimicry is germane to simulation because it's a species of interpersonal simulation, though not (on its face, at any rate) a species of mental simulation.

The topic of unconscious mimicry has a considerable history, going back at least to Adam Smith (1759/1976). Chapter 6 reviewed evidence of automatic facial mimicry, but automatic mimicry is not restricted to the face. Postural mimicry has been observed in many studies (Scheflen, 1964; La France, 1979, 1982; La France and Broadbent, 1976), and so has rhythmic synchrony in speech and bodily movement (Bernieri, 1988; Condon and Ogston, 1966; see

Hatfield et al., 1994, for a review). Zajonc, Adelmann, Murphy, and Nie-denthal (1987) found that couples grow to resemble each other the longer they are together, a pattern that could be the product of years of unconscious mimicking of a partner's facial expressions. Until recently, there has been no baseline or control group with which to measure amounts of mimicry, and one statistical test suggested that it didn't occur more often than chance (Bernieri, 1988). Against this background, Tanya Chartrand and John Bargh (1999) studied the phenomenon with more experimental controls.

They approached the subject from the perspective of experiments reported in section 7.4. In contrast with previous studies, Chartrand and Bargh hypothesized that mimicry occurs not only between people who have prior "rapport" with one another but also among strangers. They theorized that mimicry is an automatic product of what Wilhelm Prinz (1990) calls a "common-coding" principle: a shared representational system for perceiving and performing behaviors. (Prinz's shared representational system is a cousin of the mirror-system theory.) Thus, Chartrand and Bargh view behavioral mimicry as proceeding without conscious choice or guidance, prompting their label "the chameleon effect." They conjecture that automatic behavior matching serves as social "glue" that produces empathic understanding and liking between people, without their deliberately intending to bring this about.

Chartrand and Bargh's first experiment tested unintentional mimicry between strangers. Each participant was paired with a partner—really a confederate—and they were placed in a room together, seated about a meter apart. The participant could see the partner's mannerisms during the interaction. Under a cover story, the participant and the partner took turns describing various photographs. The confederate adopted a preselected mannerism and facial expression throughout the interaction, either rubbing his face or shaking his foot and either smiling or maintaining a neutral face. After all photographs had been described, a second partner (also a confederate) was brought in for another session with photographs, and this one displayed the "other" mannerism and facial expression (rubbing her face versus shaking her foot, and smiling versus not smiling). From each confederate's expression, there was a significant effect on the participant. Participants smiled more times per minute when they were with the smiling confederate than with the neutral-faced confederate. They rubbed their faces more times when in the presence of the face-rubbing confederate than with the foot-shaking confederate, and shook their feet more times with the foot-shaking confederate than with the face-rubbing confederate. Thus, individuals took on mannerisms and facial expressions of those around them without any intention or reason to do so.

The automaticity of the chameleon effect was evidenced by participants' failure to mention the partners' mannerisms during debriefing questions.

Their debriefing comments suggested total lack of awareness that they had mimicked the confederate. Moreover, the chameleon effect did not seem to be goal dependent—for example, not dependent on an affiliation goal. This was evidenced by the fact that the participants did not mimic the foot-shaking and face-rubbing behaviors of the smiling confederate to the exclusion of the nonsmiling confederate. Finally, because the confederates' behavior was predetermined and standardized, it was clear who was mimicking whom, hence the causal direction of the effect. It also excluded any third factor as the cause of the behavioral similarity.

What adaptive function might be served by the chameleon effect? Chartrand and Bargh's second experiment asked whether behavior matching is related to greater liking and rapport between the interactants. Their hypothesis was that it serves the basic human need to belong and to form and maintain stable relationships. Automatically behaving in a similar manner to other group members keeps an individual from standing out as different and helps prevent social distance from other group members. La France (1982) had previously found that students frequently displayed the same postural configuration as that of the teacher, and the extent of postural similarity was positively correlated with the students' ratings of rapport, involvement, and togetherness. Additional studies have also found that behavioral mimicry leads to emotional convergence between interacting partners (Charney, 1966; Trout and Rosenfeld, 1980).

In Chartrand and Bargh's second experiment, confederates either mirrored the behavioral mannerisms of the participant throughout the interaction or engaged in neutral mannerisms (control condition). Afterward, participants completed a questionnaire that asked them to report how much they liked the partner and how smoothly the interaction had gone. Participants liked the partner more when the latter had mirrored the participant than in the control condition. They also reported smoother interaction when there had been mirroring. However, participants weren't aware they had been mimicked. During the debriefing, they were asked whether they noticed anything in particular about the confederate's behavior or mannerisms. Only 1 of 37 participants in the mimicking condition noticed that the confederate had used a similar mannerism, and that sole participant didn't interpret it as mimicry.

Not everyone engages in mimicry to the same extent. Chartrand and Bargh speculated that one individual difference related to mimicry is empathy. They distinguish between two senses of "empathy," cognitive and affective, where cognitive empathy is equated with perspective taking. To measure perspective taking, they used the perspective-taking subscale of Davis's (1980) Interpersonal Reactivity Index, which assesses the tendency to spontaneously adopt the psychological point of view of others. They divided their participants into high and low perspective takers and found that high perspective takers engaged in significantly more mimicking than did low perspective takers. By contrast, there was no main effect of empathic concern (affective empathy) on the frequency of mimicking.

Chartrand and Bargh conclude that cohesion and liking within a group are promoted by unconscious mimicking of one another's facial expressions, postures, and mannerisms. This chameleon effect also contributes, they suspect, to effective behavior coordination among group members. This is not unlike schools of fish or flocks of birds, which achieve synchrony and immediacy in behavior coordination as an automatic and direct effect of perception on behavior (Reynolds, 1987, 1993).

11.2 Coordination, Fantasy, and Erotic Stimulation

As just noted, the chameleon effect appears to be a perception-driven affair. This characterizes *one* level of human sociality but hardly exhausts the human capacity for coordination or affiliation. Compared with other species, human coordination is relatively free of requirements of mutual perception. Social coordination and cooperation can be mediated by indirect, long-distance communication, utilizing a variety of communication technologies (the Internet being only the most recent, vivid example). Common to all such communication is high-level mindreading. If the arguments of earlier chapters are correct, a large chunk of such mindreading involves E-imagination. Cooperation also occurs in the absence of communication, and E-imagination can be helpful here as well.

An intriguing example is found in the functional neuroimaging literature. A group of neuroeconomists, McCabe, Houser, Ryan, Smith, and Trouard (2001), studied the brain activity of individuals who played standard two-person "trust and reciprocity" games while ensconced in a scanner. In any given game, a subject's opponent was either another human or a computer (and subjects were told which was the opponent for each game). In a trust game, one can make moves that are either cooperative or noncooperative. Half of the subjects consistently attempted cooperation when playing with human counterparts. Within this group, regions of prefrontal cortex (especially medial prefrontal cortex) were more active when playing a human than when playing a computer (which used a fixed and known probabilistic strategy). Within the group of noncooperators, no significant differences were found in prefrontal activation between computer and human conditions. One possible explanation (not offered by McCabe et al.) is that cooperators, when playing against other humans, engaged in E-imagination-driven thinking, whereas noncooperators and cooperators, when playing against computers, used purely theoretical, strategic-driven thinking.

E-imagination seems particularly crucial in other idiosyncratic corners of human life. Consider the quirky obsession with the "lives of the rich and famous." This absorption includes high levels of devotion to the private lives of selected individuals, expressed in the consumption of gossip, books and magazine stories, films and television shows, or desires to display their names, signs, styles, or emblems. Targeted individuals include the living and the dead, heroes and villains. What is the source of such preoccupations? Perhaps sheer curiosity. The rich and famous are statistically unusual in various respects, which might spark the intellect to dwell on their atypical features. As a complete explanation, this seems weak. Curiosity hardly explains the unique niche that the rich and famous occupy in some people's fantasies and daydreams. A more compelling explanation is that these are acts of E-imagination in which they adopt the celebrity's persona and feel "what it is like" to be him or her, what it feels like to hit the game-winning home run and receive the crowd's accolades.

Even if this is right, why is mental impersonation of precisely *this* group so attractive? There may be no single answer. Perhaps it's not just the pleasure of vicariously enjoying the luxuries and attention lavished on the stars, but it's also satisfying, for different reasons, to vicariously undergo their pains and anguish, their failed romances, their bouts with addiction and depression. The latter can generate the feeling that one isn't so bad off oneself (see section 11.8.2). Whatever the reason, vicarious immersion in the lives of the rich and famous is rampant.

Fascination by erotic materials is another popular pursuit that enlists interpersonal mental simulation. To introduce this theme, consider a distinctly nonerotic example. In a passage quoted in section 1.5, Adam Smith describes a reader's pleasure being enlivened by sympathy with another's:

> When we have read a book or poem so often that we can no longer find any amusement in reading it by ourselves, we can still take pleasure in reading it to a companion. To him it has all the graces of novelty; we enter into the surprise and admiration which it naturally excites in him, but which it is no longer capable of exciting in us; we consider all the ideas which it presents rather in the light in which they appear to him, than in that in which they appear to ourselves, and we are amused by sympathy with his amusement which thus enlivens our own. (1759/1976: 14)

A parallel phenomenon seems to be part of the erotic power of sexually arousing depictions. Of course, visual or verbal depictions of a sexual target's body or behavior can be erotically arousing in themselves. But, equally clearly, an observer's erotic arousal can be enhanced and enlivened by the depiction of a partner who is erotically aroused by the target. Like Smith's reader, the observer's arousal can be heightened by mental projection into the partner's shoes (or whatever), that is, by simulating the partner's arousal. People who engage in ménages à trois presumably exploit such sympathetic or empathetic mechanisms to heighten their sexual pleasure.

11.3 Fiction and E-Imagination

Fiction, or narrative in general, has a powerful hold on the human mind and is a staple of every human culture. Everyone agrees that understanding fiction requires imagination. But is *simulative* imagination at work here, that is, E-imagination? One philosopher who apparently denies this is Shaun Nichols (2004a).

Nichols adopts a cognitive architecture developed together with Stephen Stich (Nichols and Stich, 2003) and applies it to the role of imagination in fiction. Their architecture appears to countenance what I call supposition but no other variety of E-imagination. The architecture is presented in boxological terms, where each box depicts a cognitive system or kind of state. For present purposes, we can focus on three boxes: the belief box, the desire box, and the possible world box, later called by Nichols the pretend box. Each box is understood to specify a distinct functional role. The boxes can contain representation tokens. In the case of the pretend box, the job of the tokens is not to represent the world as it is but to represent what the world would be like given some set of "assumptions" (Nichols and Stich, 2003: 28). Nichols and Stich speak of the pretend box as containing pretense "premises" (2003: 29). The language of "assumptions" and "premises" clearly intimates supposition rather than E-imagination more generally. Moreover, they elsewhere express skepticism about the existence of pretend desire (Nichols and Stich, 2000), which again suggests a restriction of pretense to pretend belief, that is, supposition. Although I have allowed the possibility that supposition might be a species of E-imagination, I don't think that Nichols and Stich share my conception of E-imagination. So Nichols's approach to imagination and fiction seems quite different from the one I contemplate (and will elaborate on later).

The first question, then, is whether Nichols's comparatively "thin" conception of imagination, namely, supposition, adequately accounts for imagination's role in the experience of fiction. Returning to his boxological approach, what is the difference between belief representations (i.e., representations in the belief box) and pretense representations (i.e., representations in the pretense box)? Not the *content* of the representations, says Nichols, because pretense representations and beliefs can have exactly the same content. The natural cognitivist proposal, he says, is that pretend representations differ from belief representations by their *function* (Nichols, 2004a: 130). Just as desires are distinguished from beliefs by their characteristic functional roles, so pretenses are distinguished from beliefs by their functional roles. One thing they have in common, though, is that both kinds of representations use the "same code." This is a crucial theme in his article, entitled "Imagining and Believing: The Promise of a Single Code." Here is why sameness of code is important, says Nichols:

If pretense representations and beliefs are in the same code, then mechanisms that take input from the pretense box and from the belief box will treat parallel representations much the same way. For instance, if a mechanism takes pretense representations as input, the single-code hypothesis maintains that if that mechanism is *activated* by the occurrent belief that *p*, it will also be activated by the occurrent pretense representation that *p*. More generally, for any mechanism that takes input from both the pretense box and the belief box, the pretense representation *p* will be processed much the same way as the belief representation *p*. I will count any theory that makes this claim as a "single-code" theory. (2004a: 131)

Nichols seeks to use the single-code theory for his explanatory project in the theory of fiction. He wants to explain why pretense representations used by consumers of fiction have affective consequences comparable to those of belief representations. His answer is to appeal to the single-code hypothesis:

According to the single-code hypothesis, . . . the emotional systems will respond to pretense representations much as they do to parallel beliefs. That is, if the pretense representation that *p* gets processed by an affective mechanism, the affective outputs should parallel those of the belief that *p*. (2004a: 131)

So, Nichols's idea is to explain the fact that pretense representations are processed by affective systems in "much the same way" as beliefs by appeal to the fact that the two types of representations use the same code. This purported explanation is unconvincing. I assume it's in the nature of an explanation that the explaining facts (the "explanans") should imply, or at least make probable, the fact to be explained (the "explanandum"). How does this apply here? It would have to be the case that if two tokens of the same representation, in one and the same code, are "housed" or "contained" in two different states (or boxes), then it's either guaranteed or quite probable that these representations will be processed equivalently by the same cognitive mechanism. Is this plausible?

I think not. As we've seen, talk of cognitive "boxes" is talk of functional roles. Different boxes have different functional roles associated with them, and this applies to the pretense and belief boxes. Now, functional roles are specified largely by dispositions to interact with other states and mechanisms in the larger cognitive system. Given that pretense differs from belief in functional role, why should it be true that "for any mechanism that takes input from both the pretense box and the belief box, the pretense representation *p* will be processed much the same way as the belief representation *p*"? It could happen, of course, that some selected mechanism would process a pretense representation p and a belief representation p equivalently. But why is this implied, predicted, or made probable, for a random mechanism? Having a representation in a given code is only one component of the complex state of affairs (the propositional attitude token). Another component is the box that contains the representation, that is, the attitude type. Why is sameness of code *sufficient* to guarantee, or even make probable, the equivalence of treatment by processing mechanisms? On the contrary, one would think that the distinctive functional role associated with each box or attitude type would also be relevant. And it would tilt in the general direction of difference in treatment. So why does sameness of code imply, or make probable, sameness of treatment?

Let's reflect more on Nichols's proposal. Consider the case of desire and belief. Desire representations and belief representations should also share the same code. Otherwise, how could desires and beliefs "talk" with one another, which they have to do when a person executes practical reasoning?[1] Despite a shared code, desires and beliefs with the same content (believing that p and desiring that p) are certainly not processed in an equivalent way. By parity of thinking, why should pretenses and beliefs be processed in an equivalent way? Or take a second example. Agnosticism is a distinct attitude type from belief. In the Nichols-Stich approach to cognitive architecture, there should therefore be a belief box and an agnosticism box, and their respective representations would surely use the same code. But this hardly makes it reasonable to expect content-equivalent inputs from these two boxes to generate equivalent outputs.

Of course, I am not disputing the explanandum fact that Nichols seeks to explain, namely, that pretense representations, as used by consumers of fiction, produce similar effects as beliefs. Nichols cites experimental evidence in support of this similarity thesis. Vrana, Cuthburt, and Lang (1989) and Lang, Levin, Miller, and Kozak (1983), for example, did work concerning imagination and fear. In one experiment, virtually all subjects presented with an imaginary scenario involving a snake encounter showed physiological signs (elevations in heart rate and skin conductance) associated with genuine (belief-prompted) fear. Moreover, fearful reactions to a passage about snakes produced more powerful reactions in people with a phobic fear of snakes. Like Nichols, I would like to explain facts such as these.

If we think of imagination in terms of E-imagination, we will be better positioned to explain people's emotional responses to fiction. It's of the essence of E-imagination that it aims to produce a state that replicates, in relevant respects, some "genuine" mental state: believing that p, hoping that p, seeing f, and so forth. To the extent that E-imagining succeeds, the states it produces will indeed have similar functional properties to the genuine states they mimic. At least this will be so to the extent that imagination-produced states aren't kept "off-line." Some examples of this are reported later. But such similarities don't arise simply because pretense representations use the same representational code as the mimicked states. Gregory Currie has advocated the E-imagination approach as the proper approach to fictional engagement (Currie, 1995a, 1995b, 1997; Currie and Ravenscroft, 2002). Currie rightly stresses that the relevant type of E-imagination is not restricted to E-imagining *belief*; it includes, for example, E-imagining desire.[2]

According to the E-imagination hypothesis, affective responses to fiction occur because fiction serves as a series of textual or theatrical props that fuel a viewer's or reader's E-imagination into producing all sorts of surrogate states. The states are surrogates of believing, seeing, desiring, and so forth, and many bear a close resemblance to their natural, nonsurrogate counterparts. Thus, just as the natural counterparts are apt to generate certain emotions, the surrogates are apt to generate roughly similar emotions.

Tamar Gendler (2003) cites several instructive empirical studies in which imagining being in various states has yielded effects rather similar to being in the corresponding genuine states. In one experiment, children were shown and permitted to inspect two opaque empty boxes. They were then asked to imagine either that one of the boxes is occupied by a nice, friendly rabbit or by a mean and horrible monster. The experiment continued with the researcher asking the child whether she might leave the room to get the child a little gift. In four cases—all where the child had been asked to imagine a monster—the child was unwilling to let the researcher depart (Harris, 2000: 173–180). In another study, Rozin and Nemeroff (1991) presented adults with two bottles and invited them to pour sugar into each one. Subjects were then asked to affix a "sugar" label to one bottle and a "sodium cyanide" label to the other. Although subjects were happy to report that both bottles contained sugar, many nonetheless showed a marked reluctance to eat from the bottle labeled "cyanide." Labeling, it appears, activated imagining, and imagining verged on belief.

Obviously, these cases do not show that imagination-produced states and their natural counterparts have perfectly equivalent consequences. But no such strong showing is needed to account for an intriguing range of similarities in engagements with fiction. Moreover, affective consequences of imagination seem to be more similar than nonaffective consequences, and these are the ones that occupy center stage in discussions of mental reactions to fiction.

11.4 Simulation and Fiction: Clarifying the Debate

A number of other issues have been raised about imaginative, or simulational, involvement in fiction. Many, though not all, of these issues concern the involvement of emotion. Kendall Walton (1990, 1997), for example, raises questions and doubts about the correctness of saying that observers have emotional or other psychological attitudes vis-à-vis things in fictional worlds. To say we have psychological attitudes toward fictional entities, Walton argues, "is to tolerate mystery and court confusion" (1990: 196). Writing about Charles, who watched a film about green slime, Walton writes: "[Charles] may . . . have been genuinely frightened. . . . But he was not afraid of the slime" (1990: 197). It is tempting to read this merely as a comment about the intentional object of

Charles's experience, that is, that Walton is merely denying that a "fear of" relationship holds between Charles and the slime. This comports with the following passage: "My negative claim is *only* that our genuine emotional responses to works of fiction do not involve, literally, fearing, grieving for, admiring fictional characters" (1997: 38). But other passages suggest a different interpretation, namely, that the emotion may not be real but merely fictional or imaginary. In his book *Mimesis*, Walton says that Charles's fear is merely fictional, in his special sense of "fictional" that refers to games of make-believe. Again in his 1997 article, he continues to express doubt about the reality of the emotion: "Surely spectators of *Romeo and Juliet* not only realize, in imagination, the tragedy that befalls the young lovers, but also grieve for them *in imagination*—whether or not we suppose that their experiences amount to grieving for them in reality" (1997: 47, italics added).

In my view, it's a mistake to deny real emotional states to Charles. Two questions must be separated: (1) What is the relatum of Charles's mental state? (2) What attitude or emotion *type* does Charles's mental state instantiate (fear, outrage, sorrow, etc.)? Obviously, no mental state has any *de re* relationship to a nonexistent entity. This is a general problem I won't try to tackle. For present purposes, it is question (2) that is crucial, and here I see no reason to deny that Charles experiences fear. Walton, however, offers another reason for declining to ascribe genuine fear to Charles:

> I will argue that being afraid is in certain respects similar to having . . . a belief [that the feared object poses a threat] . . . and that Charles's state is not relevantly similar to that of believing that the slime endangers him; hence he does not fear it. (1990: 197)

That fear necessarily involves a belief or judgment of the indicated sort is a thesis endorsed by so-called cognitive or judgmentalist theories of emotion. Here is a more detailed rendering of a cognitive theory that Walton finds "not implausible":

> To be (really) afraid of a tornado . . . is to have certain phenomenological experiences (quasi fear) as a result of knowing or believing that one is endangered by the tornado. What makes the state one of *fear* rather than anger or excitement is the belief that one is in danger, and what makes the tornado its object is the fact that it is the tornado that one takes to be dangerous. (1990: 244–245)

The claim in this passage that I wish to deny is not that the belief plays a role when we ascribe an object to an emotion but the claim (in the second sentence) that what makes a state one of fear rather than anger or excitement is the belief that one is in danger. The suggestion is that each type of emotion has an associated belief that must cause the token emotion if it is to qualify as a token of the target type. To qualify as fear, for example, an emotion must have an endangerment belief in its etiology.

I dispute this thesis on psychological grounds. Recall the material in chapter 6 on emotion transmission or contagion. Seeing a fearful person's face induces a subthreshold state of fear in the observer. Seeing a disgusted person's face induces a subthreshold state of disgust in the observer. The observer may not be conscious of the emotion, but it is still experienced (at least "undergone"). If we want to *classify* or *type* the emotion, it surely should be classified as fear in the first case and disgust in the second. However, contrary to the judgmentalist theory, there need be no belief of the canonical sort in the state's etiology. The initially fearful person may believe he is in danger, but the observer—who perhaps doesn't see what frightens the target—need not also believe himself to be in danger. So Walton's reason for denying that Charles's fear is genuine fear is unpersuasive.

Assuming that consumers of fiction have genuinely emotional engagements with fiction, is this the result of simulation, that is, imaginative identification with persons related to the fictional work, for example, with some characters described in the work? Currie holds that simulation is central both to working out what is fictionally the case, primarily with respect to a character's experience, and with regard to how and why we care about and affectively respond to fictional characters (Currie, 1995b: 153–154). Similarly, Susan Feagin (1996) argues that although there are important differences between empathizing with real people and empathizing with fictional characters, simulation underlies both types of empathy.

Noel Carroll, by contrast, rejects the view that our engagement with fiction typically involves taking up characters' points of view or simulating characters' psychological states (Carroll, 1990, 1998, 2001). He writes:

> We do not typically emote with respect to fictions by simulating a character's mental state; rather . . . we respond emotionally to fiction from the outside. Our point of view is that of an observer of a situation and not . . . that of the participant in the situation. When a character is about to be ambushed, we feel fear for her; we do not imagine ourselves to be her and then experience "her" fear. (2001: 311–312)

Carroll offers several arguments in support of this position (instructively summarized in Coplan, 2004). First, readers' emotions have different objects from those of the characters. We feel *for* the character, which isn't the same as simulating her fear. Second, readers often have different (usually, more) information than the characters do, which commonly generates different emotions. In the opening sequence of *Jaws*, viewers who know that a killer shark is nearby have different emotions than the character swimming in the water, who is happy and carefree in her ignorance. Third, readers often experience desires and preferences with regard to narrative outcomes that differ from the desires and preferences of the characters. Even when we care about the characters, we do not necessarily want them to get what they want.

These are good reasons to challenge the notion that the reader or observer of a fictional narrative usually adopts the perspective or position of a character or protagonist. But characters aren't the only candidates for the "targets" of simulation by consumers of fiction. Currie (1997) has advanced a different (and to my mind more plausible) account, namely, that one usually adopts the position of a hypothetical "reader of fact" (or observer of fact). This is a hypothetical person who observes or learns of the events portrayed in the narrative as if these events were facts (unlike a real reader or filmgoer who encounters the events as segments of a work of fiction). A fictional work, such as a novel or a film, is presented at the entry level as an account of a series of events as if they were happening or did happen. This is not to suggest that an optimal aesthetic appreciation of the work accrues from adopting this simple perspective on the narrative to the exclusion of any other. Still, it is hard to follow a narrative at all, to imbibe what it is intended to convey, without using this perspective as a *baseline* for all further responses to the work. A typical narrative text or film is a *prop* that induces one to adopt the factual-reader or factual-observer perspective. Films make it highly compelling—at least in a prereflective, precritical stance—that one is seeing an unfolding scenario from the camera's perspective. It takes no creativity to E-imagine being such a hypothetical observer; the filmic medium makes it difficult to avoid doing so, which helps account for its power. In Walton's (1990) terminology, it is difficult to avoid "making believe" as a simulative response. Again, I do not suggest that taking the perspective of a hypothetical reader or observer of fact exhausts the stance of an actual reader or viewer, especially a sensitive one, but it's an important part of an actual consumer's stance.

The hypothetical-observer-of-fact theory readily accommodates Carroll's points. A hypothetical observer commonly has different information about the goings-on than characters do, and this breeds different emotions or emotional objects. A hypothetical observer of the *Jaws* scenario knows a shark is around and therefore feels fear *for* the swimmer; he doesn't feel *her* fear, because she doesn't have any. At the same time, the actual observer (who is simulating the hypothetical observer) feels fear, at least simulated fear, because E-imagined or make-believe knowledge that a shark is around produces (when fed into suitable emotion-generating equipment) fear or fearlike output. As ST maintains from the start, cognitive mechanisms that operate on E-imagined input states produce roughly the same sorts of outputs as their genuine, nonimagined counterpart inputs produce.

None of this precludes the idea that there is *also* perspective taking of characters. Either the reader or observer "directly" simulates a character or she simulates a hypothetical-observer-of-fact simulating a character. The latter, indirect possibility is a bit more baroque, though by no means impossible, so I shall focus on the former possibility. There is empirical research, summarized by Harris (2000) and by Coplan (2004), that people track the perspective of one or more protagonists when they read narratives. This research supports the idea that character simulation is a common form of mental engagement with fiction.

Rinck and Bower (1995) had subjects memorize the diagram of a building and objects located within it. Then they had their subjects read narratives describing characters' movements and activities within the building. While reading, they were probed with sentences referring to memorized objects in the building's rooms. The consistent finding was that readers more quickly processed sentences describing objects close to the current location of the protagonist. The interpretation was that readers were experiencing the narrative from the spatiotemporal standpoint of the protagonist and were moving through the building "with" the protagonist. Other studies by Black, Turner, and Bower (1979), Rall and Harris (2000), and Bryant, Tversky, and Franklin (1992) lend further support to this idea. Finally, Gernsbacher, Goldsmith, and Robertson (1992) did a series of experiments indicating that readers often process the emotional implications of narrative events from the standpoint of one of the protagonists. Subjects read narratives in which a central character was likely to feel a particular emotion. They were then probed with target sentences, which included emotion terms that either matched the emotional state of the character or did not match it. They hypothesized that if readers appraise narrative events from the character's perspective, then target sentences matching the character's emotions should be processed more quickly than sentences not matching it. This is exactly what they found. By itself, this doesn't firmly support a simulational account as contrasted with a theorizing account. However, a study by Harris and Martin (unpublished) provides additional support for the simulation, or empathizing, account (see Harris, 2000: 70).

Matthew Kieran has offered a number of objections to the simulation theory of fictional engagement as *he* construes it (a construal responsive to earlier claims by simulationists like Currie and Feagin). Kieran construes the following two-part claim:

(1)   When I want to really understand the nature of a character's experience and their attitude toward their own experience (what their character is really like), then I need to simulate. A deep understanding of fictional characters requires simulation, though a shallow understanding of them need not.

(2)   In order to capture the full nature of our affective responses to a narrative, we must understand the simulation process that we go through as readers— because that simulation process is central to our acquiring an understanding of characters. (Kieran, 2003: 69–70)

Kieran denies that an understanding of characters requires me, as reader, to imagine myself in their shoes. It doesn't even require me to simulate the narrator or other hypothetical observer of the scene. To support these claims,

Kieran presents the opening of Dickens's *Hard Times*, which portrays Gradgrind delivering some emphatic statements about his teaching philosophy. Gradgrind's appearance and speaking mannerisms are described in vivid detail. Kieran claims that our understanding of and affective response to Gradgrind do not require simulation.

A wise simulationist should first respond by objecting to Kieran's formulations of the "simulation thesis" as unnecessarily strong in certain respects. They are phrased in terms of simulation being "needed" or "required" for understanding. A simulationist might respond that simulation is something readers naturally *do*, even if it isn't something they are required to do to achieve understanding. She might add that when Kieran concludes that we acquire a deep and sophisticated understanding of Gradgrind just by making inferences (not Kieran's exact wording) from Dickens's description of him, how does Kieran purport to know this? The question of simulation versus inference is the nub of the ST-TT dispute, a matter not readily settled in the armchair. So Kieran is not entitled to conclude that simulation by the reader isn't needed, or isn't used. Finally, turning to the second part of Kieran's simulation thesis, concerning affective responses, the *Hard Times* passage is a weak example for Kieran's purposes. Dickens's description of Gradgrind portrays his appearance as square-legged, square-shouldered, and hard set, his carriage as obstinate, and his voice as inflexible, dry, and dictatorial. Introspectively, my affective reaction to these descriptions seems to arise from the visual and auditory imagery I create in my mind of Gradgrind's appearance and speech. In other words, I imagine myself being present in the schoolroom and witnessing the scene described by Dickens. Whether or not I *need* to imagine this to elicit these affective reactions, it seems to me that I actually do it, contrary to what Kieran implies.

A second point of Kieran's is that readers often appreciate things about the dispositions and character of a fictional protagonist that the protagonist herself does not recognize because of unconscious motivations or self-deceptions. Such understanding could not be achieved by simulation, because if only simulation were used, the reader's understanding would be limited by the same factors limiting the protagonist's self-understanding. This is a good point, but what simulationist claim does it refute? No reasonable proponent of simulation in narrative understanding would claim that all understanding of fictional protagonists proceeds by simulation of *them*. In particular, the point ignores the hypothetical-reader-of-fact version of the simulation theory of fictional engagement. If at least one "side" of the (actual) reader simulates the hypothetical-reader-of-fact, then both could certainly recognize and understand things about the target protagonist that she herself doesn't recognize or understand.

To summarize, I have argued that simulation in the form of E-imagination does indeed play a significant role in the consumption of fiction. A fully adequate account of engagement with fiction requires a richer kind of imagination than mere supposition, namely, E-imagination. The exact role of E-imagination is multifaceted and complex, sometimes involving characters and sometimes involving "hypothetical observers (or readers) of fact."

11.5 Simulation and Moral Theory

The remainder of this chapter turns to moral psychology and moral philosophy. If mental simulation is acknowledged as a core feature of the human mind, what impact should this have, if any, on moral theory? Connections between simulation and moral theory might be charted via the closely linked notions of empathy and/or perspective taking. A number of moral psychologists and moral philosophers propose close ties between moral judgment or moral motivation, on the one hand, and either empathy or role taking. Among psychologists, these are leading themes of Jean Piaget (1932/1948), Lawrence Kohlberg (1984), C. Daniel Batson (1991), and Martin Hoffman (2000); among moral philosophers, they had a central place in Schopenhauer's (1841/ 1965) account of morality and a lesser but significant place in the writings of R. M. Hare (1963, 1981). More recently, it has been stressed by Martha Nussbaum (2001) and in previous work of my own (Goldman, 1992b, 1993c) and Robert Gordon (1995a).

There are several different passageways through which simulation or empathy might enter the theater of moral philosophy. My discussion is organized around three such passageways. The first passageway is through metaethics, which investigates the foundations and metaphysical status of moral judgment. Two competing traditions in metaethics are moral rationalism and moral sentimentalism. According to rationalism, a tradition most saliently associated with Kant, morality is grounded in reason or rationality. Sentimentalism is the view that morality is grounded in feelings, emotions, or sentiments; Hume is its most influential representative. Empathy, perspective taking, or simulation might be invoked by moral sentimentalism in its account of core moral judgment, because moral judgments might be said to rest, in paradigmatic cases, on homologous or resonant feelings that arise in observers of harms inflicted on others. Moral sentimentalism might also invoke empathy or perspective taking as the most promising account of moral motivation, assumed to be something like care or concern for others. The question arises whether core moral motivation is really driven by perspective taking, an issue that can be addressed by examining the early development of moral motivation in children and impairments of moral motivation in psychopathology, for example, psychopathy. These matters will occupy us in section 11.6.

Second, empathy, perspective taking, or simulation might also enter moral theory at a less foundational level. Any normative ethics that admits effects on happiness, or hedonic states, as *one* of the criteria for judging moral actions or social policies has to worry about how moral agents can determine the relevant hedonic consequences of a prospective action. What *epistemic tools* do moral judges have for determining other people's hedonic states? Simulation or role taking might be highly relevant here, as a fundamental method for arriving at such determinations. This wouldn't imply that simulation is infallible, however, or undeserving of critical assessment. On the contrary, it becomes essential to undertake such assessments, which we do in section 11.7.

Third, empathy or simulation might be introduced into moral theory not merely as an epistemic tool but as a major factor in the production of pleasurable experience and people's self-assessment of their state of happiness or well-being. These topics are explored in section 11.8.

11.6 Development, Psychopathology, and Altruistic Motivation

Both philosophy and psychology are witnessing resurgent interest in sentimentalist approaches to moral judgment (e.g., Gibbard, 1990; Blackburn, 1998; Haidt, 2001; Greene, Sommerville, Nystrom, Darley, and Cohen, 2001). I shall give extended attention to a recent treatment of sentimentalism by Shaun Nichols (2004b), partly because Nichols's book merits attention and partly because it takes the empathy or perspective-taking approach seriously and offers significant challenges to it. The most important strand of current sentimentalism is a collection of views about how moral judgments are actually made, that is, what types of cognitive factors are responsible for core moral judgment. A second important topic is what gives rise to moral motivation, especially altruistic motivation. That is where our story begins. Guided by Nichols's discussion, we examine signs of altruistic motivation in young children.

As we have remarked before, different things can be meant by "empathy." If we follow Eisenberg and Strayer's (1987) definition as "vicarious sharing of affect," empathy can be achieved in at least two ways: by "catching" another's affect via emotional contagion or by adopting the other's perspective (using E-imagination). There is pretty clear evidence that newborn infants undergo emotional contagion. Simner (1971) presented newborn infants with tapes of various auditory stimuli: spontaneous crying by a newborn infant, spontaneous crying by a 5-month-old infant, a computer-generated crying sound, and white noise of equivalent sound intensity. The newborns cried significantly more in reaction to the tape of the newborn crying than to the other stimuli.[3] However, catching another's affect is a long way from having an attitude toward the other that bears some semblance to a moral attitude. In particular, catching someone else's distress doesn't yet constitute a form of altruistic motivation, such as concern or a desire to help.[4] A "directed" motivation to help would require mindreading of the other, attributing to the other a state of distress or discomfort. This is not entailed by emotional contagion per se. When do young children demonstrate these capacities?

In a corpus of cases described by Bartsch and Wellman (1995), there are verbal transcripts for four children before the age of 2, and in each case the child is attributing pain to another person well before the second birthday. So pain attribution emerges quite early. The same is true of children's demonstration of comforting behavior appropriately directed to the target's distress. In experimental studies of 1-year-old children by Zahn-Waxler and Radke-Yarrow (1982), crying elicited comforting behaviors, as did coughing and gagging. Moreover, the children often comforted the target in appropriate ways. Zahn-Waxler and Radke-Yarrow describe one instance in which the mother of a 19-month-old child hurt her foot. The child exhibited concern, ran over, said "hurt foot," and rubbed the mother's hurt foot (1982: 124). Thus, the children seem to engage in the kind of mindreading necessary for intentional, directed, comforting behavior.

Nichols now poses the question of whether this is compatible with empathy as rendered by the perspective-taking (simulation) account. He objects that children under the age of 2 have limited mindreading abilities, in particular, severe deficiencies in the capacity to take the perspective of others (2004b: 49). Until the age of 4, they fail the standard false-belief task and similar tasks. Thus, because toddlers provide core cases of altruistic motivation but lack the requisite perspective-taking capacities, this is a serious prima facie argument against perspective-taking accounts.

There are three replies to this objection. First, Nichols's story about the mindreading limits of 2-year-olds is now dated. In light of Onishi and Baillargeon's (2005) study indicating that 15-month-old children attribute false belief, it can no longer be asserted that this is beyond the capacity of 2-year-olds (section 4.4). Second, troubles on standard false-belief tasks do not demonstrate weakness in taking another's perspective. Problems with standard false-belief tasks are problems with *inhibiting* the first-person perspective (section 8.4), which should be distinguished from (problems with) adopting a third-person perspective. Third, we have provided evidence for both low- and high-level simulationist mindreading. What Nichols calls perspective taking corresponds to high-level simulation; contagion corresponds to low-level simulation. As he himself recognizes, low-level simulation (e.g., mirroring, or resonance) might enable 2-year-olds to make third-person attributions of pain and distress. Nichols doesn't dispute that 2-year-olds engage in this kind of mindreading; he only denies that they do it by perspective taking. But because perspective taking is high-level simulation, it isn't the only option available in our duplex version of ST.

Nichols next raises problems associated with autism. Mindreading researchers generally agree that perspective taking is seriously compromised in autism. Nonetheless, says Nichols, autistic children *are* responsive to distress in others (Bacon, Fein, Morris, Waterhouse, and Allen, 1998; Blair, 1999a; Yirmiya, Sigman, Kasari, and Mundy, 1992). For example, in a study by Blair (1999a), autistic children were shown pictures of threatening faces and distressed faces, and they showed the normal pattern of heightened physiological response to both sets of stimuli. Thus, although autistic children have a deficit in perspective taking, they do respond to distress in others. Moreover, autistic individuals engage in comforting behavior, as shown by Sigman, Kasari, Kwon, and Yirmiya (1992). These findings, says Nichols, collectively pose a problem for the perspective-taking account of altruistic motivation, which predicts that perspective-taking deficits in autistics should be accompanied by deficits in altruistic motivation (Nichols, 2004b: 58).

One possible response is to challenge the claim that autistic children have no deficiency in distress responsiveness. Some researchers report impairments in autistics' responsiveness to distress (chapter 8, note 4). Charman et al. (1997) had an experimenter act as if he had hit his thumb with a hammer and make facial and vocal expressions of distress. None of the 10 autistic subjects (age 20 months) showed facial signs of concern, whereas most normally developing children did. However, if we go along with studies cited by Nichols, in which autistic children display heightened physiological response to distressed faces, then low-level simulation, or contagion, is implicated, possibly the presence of a mirror system. Once again, our duplex form of ST offers a rich enough palette of options to deal with the data.

Nichols next argues that psychopathy poses the inverse problem from autism. Psychopaths lack remorse and empathy and are deceitful and manipulative (R. D. Hare, 1991). Moreover, they show abnormally low physiological response to suffering in others (Blair et al., 1997; Blair, 1999b). Nonetheless, psychopaths are capable of perspective taking; they perform as well as normal adults on standard perspective-taking tasks (Blair et al., 1996). So how can perspective taking be pivotal for altruistic motivation? Being good at perspective taking doesn't translate into concern or altruism.

Nichols proceeds to hypothesize a cognitive mechanism called a concern mechanism. This mechanism "takes as input representations that attribute distress, for example, 'John is experiencing painful shock,' and produces as output affect that, inter alia, motivates altruistic behavior" (2004b: 56–57). The concern mechanism, he conjectures, is what is impaired in psychopathy.[5] Continuing his argument against the perspective-taking account, he contends there is a double dissociation between perspective taking and the concern mechanism. Autistic children have impaired perspective-taking abilities but an intact concern mechanism. Psychopaths, by contrast, have a normal capacity for perspective taking but a deficit in the concern mechanism.

These considerations might be a problem for a theory that aims to account for altruistic motivation *entirely* in terms of perspective taking. But no such theory is being proposed here. Specifically, no central role in altruistic motivation is being assigned to *high-level* simulation. On the other hand, *low-level* simulation does seem to be a key ingredient in core altruistic motivation. As reported previously, psychopaths have an abnormally low physiological response to suffering in others. Also recall the finding reported in section 6.1 that psychopaths have a paired deficit in face-based recognition of fear. This seems to signal impairment in low-level simulation of fear, which may be coupled with impaired low-level simulation (or contagion) of distress. These impairments, however, have nothing to do with impairments in E-imagination, or perspective taking. Intact perspective taking, however, is not *sufficient* for concern or altruistic motivation. We can agree with Nichols that there is something like a concern mechanism. This might be triggered, in normals, by low-level simulation or resonance. But it also might be triggered, later on, by perspective taking, though not in psychopaths. In other words, psychopaths may possess and deploy perspective taking for high-level mindreading, but this doesn't imply activation of the concern mechanism, which, as Nichols conjectures, might be one important thing damaged in psychopaths.

This is all I shall say about simulation's role within sentimentalist metaethics. Let me close this section with a few words about simulation's possible role within rationalism. A common theme in rationalism is that moral principles should be *universalizable*, a central tenet of Kant's (1785/1959) moral philosophy. There are many ways to develop the universalizability theme, and some invoke the idea of considering matters from other people's point of view or from one's own point of view in a hypothetical situation. This is where perspective taking, or high-level simulation, might enter the picture. One variant of this idea is the impartial spectator theory, advanced by Frances Hutcheson and Adam Smith, among others. On this approach, morality would be determined by projecting ourselves into the shoes of an impartial judge and seeing how such a person would view the matter. John Rawls (1971) does not write explicitly about perspective taking. Nonetheless, his key idea is to identify principles of justice by asking what basic principles of social organization would be chosen by people in a certain hypothetical situation, namely, the "original position," where choices are made under a "veil of ignorance." This is, in effect, a kind of ideal perspective-taking approach. Next, consider the golden rule, a principle found in at least eight world religions: Christianity, Confucianism, Buddhism, Hinduism, Islam, Judaism, Taoism, and Zoroastrianism.[6] The golden rule is readily understood as an invitation to test a proposed action by imagining yourself on the "receiving" end of it and seeing whether you would find it acceptable. Finally, consider the moral theory of R. M. Hare (1963, 1981). Though not a rationalist in metaethics, Hare endorses a universalizability test in normative ethics, which we shall explore in the following section. The point of the present paragraph is simply to take note of the fact that role taking, or imagination-based simulation, plays a nonnegligible role in a variety of moral theories, not just in sentimentalism.

11.7 Empathy as an Epistemic Tool

I turn now to the second possible application of mental simulation to moral theory. As noted before, Hare regarded imaginative identification with others as a crucial step in moral reasoning, as indicated in this passage:

> He [i.e., B] must be prepared to give weight to A's inclinations as if they were his own. This is what turns selfish prudential reasoning into moral reasoning. It is much easier, psychologically, for B to do this if he is actually placed in a situation like A's *vis-à-vis* somebody else; but this is not necessary provided that he has sufficient imagination to envisage what it is like to be A. (1963: 94)

He makes the point more fully and explicitly in a later book:

> I have to know what it will be *like* for [the other person]. . . . We shall have to keep carefully in mind the distinction between knowing that something is happening to someone, and knowing *what it is like for him*. It is the latter kind of knowledge which, I am proposing, we should treat as relevant, and as required for the full information which rationality in making moral judgments demands. (1981: 91–92)

Hare evidently views imaginative identification, or simulation, as an essential epistemic tool for moral judgment.

Peter Singer defends Hare's theory, saying that something like it provides the only way of resolving ethical disputes (1981: 101ff.). He later summarizes his own position as follows: "I have been arguing that . . . universalizability does require that we put ourselves in the place of others and that this must then involve giving weight to their ideals in proportion to the strength with which they hold them" (1988: 152).

Richard Holton and Rae Langton (1999) consider the value of imaginative identification as an epistemic tool in some detail. They specifically formulate the issue in terms of simulation theory, citing the version I provided in Goldman (1992b). First, they point out that putting oneself in others' shoes can yield two kinds of information. It can play a role (A) in discovering the preferences of others and (B) in discovering who has preferences. Under (A), simulation might enable us to know what people want and how much they want it. It might even give us a basis for interpersonal utility comparisons (as discussed in Goldman, 1995). (B) might be even more fundamental. "The thought experiment of putting oneself in the shoes of others might be used to find out not simply how to compare preferences, but whether there are any preferences there to compare" (Holton and Langton, 1999: 213). Thus, simulation might be used to determine the domain of moral salience.

In the end, however, Holton and Langton are skeptical about the value of empathetic or simulational thought experiments. Such exercises can provide the desired information about others' mental states, they point out, only if we are similar enough to those to whom we should show moral consideration. But are we similar enough? Our fellows are physiologically similar, they concede, but that might not be enough. We can have little conception of what it is like to be mentally ill in certain ways, for example, to be a psychopath. Does that mean that such a person is outside the domain of moral salience? Surely they ought not to be, argue Holton and Langton. What about non-human animals? Holton and Langton put the problem this way: "If the method of simulation barely gets us beyond the average guy, there seems little hope of its getting us as far as we need to get with the non-human animals" (1999: 223). Hare, they remark, is remarkably sanguine. In one passage, he recommends thinking ourselves into the position of bears and in another suggests that he can even think his way into the position of a trout. Holton and Langton are less sanguine. The problem is especially pressing for someone like Singer (the principal target of their article), who has devoted so much work to the inclusion of nonhuman animals in the moral domain.

Holton and Langton also worry about relying on imaginative identification as a source of moral motivation.

> Perhaps it works. But if it does, it will skew our concern to those for whom we find imaginative identification easy. It will invite precisely the kind of parochialism that an impartialist moral theory rejects. We are familiar with the problem that long-lashed large-eyed animals get a disproportionate share of our concern—that the killing of baby seals provokes more outrage than the killing of coypu. A motivation that is based on an ability to empathize is equally parochial. (1999: 226)

So they take a distinctly negative stance toward empathy's role in ethics: "We object to the idea that empathy provides the basis for ethics" (1999: 228–229).

Holton and Langton's worries about empathy as an epistemic tool are not misplaced, but their reservations are partly a response to an excess of exuberance by certain proponents of empathy, especially Hare. We need not say that empathy is *the* (unique) basis for ethics, especially when addressing its role as epistemological tool. A more cautious stance would say that empathy, or simulation, is psychologically the most primitive and pervasive method for identifying mental states in others. This doesn't mean it should be relied on, in its raw form and to the exclusion of other methods, for determining other people's mental states.

At this juncture, we cross the self-imposed boundary of the book's main agenda, namely, the study of naïve methods of mental attribution independent of their reliability or accuracy. Here reliability is precisely what interests us. We have already inspected factors that add fuel to Holton and Langton's worries about simulation. We have seen how quarantine failure, for example, can distort third-person attribution. Holton and Langton's own concerns are also on target and germane to ethics.

But should it be surprising that our most primitive faculty for a given epistemic job is inadequate for certain applications? And should we suppose that nature restricts us to this single faculty? Naked eyesight is a very imperfect tool for many epistemic tasks, such as determining the distances of celestial objects or the properties of minute objects. For these epistemic tasks, vision must be augmented with instruments like telescopes and microscopes, or it must be supplemented with an entirely different faculty, scientific reasoning. That vision is incapable of detecting all physical magnitudes doesn't demonstrate its epistemic worthlessness or show that it shouldn't be relied on even in a limited range of application. Analogous points hold for interpersonal mental simulation. Our natural simulational endowment—or pair of endowments (resonance and E-imagination)—is a great epistemic boon. Our species's capacity for detecting others' mental states would have been greatly compromised if Mother Nature hadn't bestowed these gifts on us. Our ability to engage in rapid and nuanced social interaction might be impossible without them, as would be the complex cooperative projects that mark the highpoints of human civilization. This lesson is learned from autism. Autistics commonly report that rapid and subtle social interaction—heavily involving mindreading—is just an uninterpretable blur. Deficiencies in simulative capacities wreak havoc with their social aptitudes.

Nonetheless, neither kind of mental simulation is an ideal mental-state detector for all applications of interest. Their limits are especially salient for interspecies applications. Most other species lack the sorts of facial expressions that could trigger responses in human resonance systems. We can't recognize emotions and feelings in the faces of fish the way we recognize them in human faces. Still, with the help of neuroscience, we can make plausible inferences to the existence of pain in fish. Scores of polymodal nociceptor sites just like ours are found in the head and neck of rainbow trout.

When it comes to empathy with other humans, the most frequently discussed limit is its parochialism. Empathic responses occur more readily vis-à-vis individuals who are salient, currently perceived, spatially closer to us, or bear greater resemblance to us. Many ethicists, however, argue that our moral obligations to distant and personally unknown individuals are as strong as obligations to nearer and personally known individuals. Thus, stirrings of empathy might not be equal to the task. The moral circle, as Singer (1981) calls it, is in danger of being drawn too narrowly.

Granting this point, the proper lesson is that simulation must be augmented with helpful devices, just as vision is augmented by telescopes and microscopes. In chapter 7, I argued that E-imagining is guided by information, including perceptually derived and stored information. To accurately E-imagine the situation of an anonymous and distant individual, it helps to receive detailed information about that person's life experience and an image of her and her immediate environment. Thus, news coverage of ongoing wars, famines, and other catastrophes are more effective when they supply biographical details of selected individuals, as well as photographs or visual footage. For most people, purely statistical information is ineffective at generating compassion. The question arises whether perceptual, individualized information is comparatively effective because it produces more accurate and detailed E-imagination (a purely epistemic result) or because it better activates the motivational aspect of empathy (care, concern, compassion). The answer is probably both. The point is that even if unassisted empathy is only a qualified guide to morality, its use as an epistemic tool can be enhanced and extended so that its utility for practical ethics is much more satisfactory.[7]

11.8 Empathy and the Quality of Life

Historically, the agenda of ethics included the question of how to attain the happy life. A core topic of ancient moral theory, it figures less centrally in contemporary ethics, retaining some popularity in the utilitarian but not the deontological tradition. Nonetheless, it deserves attention, perhaps under the heading "moral psychology." It's certainly of interest to contemporary psychology, one branch of which studies the determinants of happiness, subjective well-being, and the like. The processes of empathy, or simulation, can make contributions to this inquiry, the last of the three I am reviewing.

Moral theorists consider events within an individual that make for a happy or unhappy life. These might include (1) pleasures and pains; (2) satisfaction or frustration of desires, goals, and preferences; and (3) things that are objectively good or bad independent of our desires, such as knowledge, liberty, and development of natural abilities. These three categories figure in Derek Parfit's (1984: 3–4) classification of what he calls "self-interest" theories. I shall also pursue this general approach, focusing on the first two categories that feature subjective experiences.[8] However, I'll pursue the topic at a lower level than philosophers usually do: the level of the "mechanics" of subjective hedonic experience. At this level, we examine causal processes of the mind responsible for hedonic experiences and their subjective evaluation. In this brief foray, I highlight one narrow dimension of the subject that simulation theory can illuminate: how social mental interactions influence the quality of life.

11.8.1 Recursive Reciprocal Contagion

Many of life's most intense and memorable pleasures have a distinctly social character. They involve interactions with others, often masses of others. Here is a sampling of popular social events that seem to generate high levels of pleasure or keenly felt satisfaction.

Cocktail parties
Religious revival meetings
Sporting events
Rock concerts
Victory celebrations
Parades

In each case, there may be asocial aspects of a participant's experience that contribute to the resulting pleasure or satisfaction. Each partygoer imbibes some potables, munches on some delicacies. Each concertgoer has a moving musical experience. Each partisan at a victory celebration gets satisfaction from a valued mission accomplished. But these relatively asocial aspects of the experience don't account for all of the hedonic quality. These elements of the experience could occur in an alternative, isolated setting. One could enjoy the same drinks and munchables alone at home; one could listen to the same music or watch the victory celebration on TV. The hedonic qualities of these privatized versions of the experiences would pale by comparison with their crowd-immersion counterparts. What accounts for these preferences?

Reciprocal contagion, I submit. Recall (section 11.2) Adam Smith's description of a companion's amusement enlivening one's own. This is hedonic contagion. It also occurs at parties, comedy events, sporting events, and so forth. Amusement is transmitted, of course, by laughter, so radio and television used to employ canned laughter to increase the audience's amusement. The basic process here is emotion contagion, which we have treated under the heading of low-level mental simulation. All of the social events on my list readily breed emotion and mood contagion on a large scale. Unlike Smith's example, moreover, they commonly involve quantities of *reciprocal* contagion. It's not just a matter of X's positive affect enhancing Y's, but also of Y's affect in turn enhancing X's, and Z's, and so on. This enhancement process, moreover, is recursive; one cycle builds on its predecessor without limit. When many people are involved, the outcome can be a remarkable hedonic "high" for each individual.

Gustave Le Bon (1896) wrote about the mysterious forces that operate in crowds. He thought that crowd membership contributes to an enlargement of the ego, the release of impulses, and heightened suggestibility. But he also recognized the element of mood and affect contagion in crowds. Hatfield, Cacioppo, and Rapson (1994) highlight this contagion potential of crowds, which coincides at the two-person level with the phenomena we described under the headings of affective resonance (chapter 6) and behavioral mimicry (section 11.1). Our twenty-first-century understanding of the psychology and neuroscience of these simulation phenomena should elevate them above the level of mere curiosities. They are fundamental properties of the mind that must be inserted into any balanced portrait of human nature, as well as any treatment of the mechanics of hedonic experience. This social dimension of cognition and affect is fundamental to human well-being. It's no wonder that loneliness is typically associated with a comparatively low level of life satisfaction.

Two important caveats should be made. First, I don't mean to imply that all hedonic contagion effects involve mood or affect or that they all involve low-level resonance. Perceptual channels mediate low-level resonance, but simulation effects can also occur via E-imagination. A political campaign worker who cannot attend a victory rally can still "engage" with her coworkers in imagination. The pleasure she derives from goal satisfaction can be enlivened by that of her coworkers in something like the way that Smith's reader has his pleasure enlivened by that of a companion. Unlike Smith's reader, the campaign worker doesn't observe the celebration of her coworkers, but a similar effect of pleasure enhancement is achieved by imagination.

Second, happiness does not require living in crowds. Recursive reciprocal contagion occurs in dyads as well as crowds. Prime examples of recursive reciprocal contagion in dyads include sexual passion (the arousal of each member of the dyad heightens the arousal of the partner), conversations with intimate friends, and parent-infant interactions. It is no coincidence that these experiences hit the top of the charts in common lore, fiction, and/or philosophy. (Actually, only friendship makes it to the top of the philosophy charts, while parent-offspring relationships are routinely ignored in the curiously adult-only philosophical tradition.)

11.8.2 Simulation-Based Framing

Contagion-enhanced pleasure isn't the only way simulation influences well-being or self-assessed well-being. The second path of influence I'll describe concerns the way people evaluate their well-being. Such evaluations are influenced by comparisons with others, comparisons often determined by simulation.

A preliminary comment is in order about the ostensible distinction just drawn between well-being and self-assessment of well-being. Shouldn't we be interested only in the former, not the latter? The trouble is that there may be no firm distinction here. Psychologists find that one cannot simply add up the countless experiences people undergo through life and expect that "sum" to equal the feeling of well-being they report when reflecting on their lives. The subjective sense of well-being proves to be weak, labile, and sometimes counterintuitive. Poor people are sometimes happier than rich ones, patients 3 years after a cancer operation are found to be happier than a healthy control group, and paralyzed accident victims are more content with their lives than one might expect (Campbell, 1981). Moreover, measures of well-being have a low test-retest reliability (consistency), usually hovering around .40. So is there a determinate state of personal well-being that exists independently of a person's assessment of it? That is questionable. Perhaps, then, what should be counted as a person's present happiness is how he or she is disposed to respond to a question like "Taking all things together, how would you say things are these days?" If so, there is no principled distinction between well-being and self-assessed well-being (Kahneman and Tversky, 2000: parts 8 and 9).

Looking at personal assessments of well-being, we find them to be very context dependent. For example, Strack, Schwarz, and Gschneidinger (1985) instructed subjects in one group to recall and write down a very negative event in their lives, while subjects in another group were instructed to recall and write down a very positive event in their lives. Within each group, half of the subjects were asked to recall a recent event, and half were asked to recall a past event. Subjects were then asked to rate their well-being on a 10-point scale. An unsurprising result was that recalling a positive recent event made people feel good, and thinking about a negative recent event made people feel less happy. The results for past events were more surprising. Ratings of well-being were higher for those who recalled a past negative event than for those who recalled a past positive event. There seem to be a substantial effect of comparison of one's present with one's past.

Schwarz and Strack (1991) found another striking comparison effect. Subjects evaluated their own lives more favorably when they met a handicapped experimental confederate or listened to such a confederate describe the life difficulties created by his severe medical condition. The impact of the confederate's description was even more pronounced when the seating arrangements rendered the confederate visible while the subject was filling out the happiness report.

I now wish to speculate that comparison effects can be expected to flow from simulation processes. The simulation literature suggests that people routinely track the mental states of others in their immediate environment. This would make it easy to use others as standards of comparison in assessing one's own well-being. A study by Sebanz, Knoblich, and Prinz (2003) showed that people track the motoric mental states of another person working alongside them, even though the two actors are responsible for entirely independent tasks. This tracking is apparently done by representing the other's actions in a functionally equivalent way as one's own actions, just as simulation theory predicts. The study did not examine hedonic states or states of well-being. But if people habitually track the hedonic mental states of others in the way that they track their motoric mental states, the results of such mindreading could establish baselines for self-judgments of well-being.

There is independent evidence in social psychology that people make creative, sometimes self-deceptive, comparisons with imagined others to help them cope with their own problems. Shelley Taylor (1989) illustrates this point with statements of creative comparisons made by cancer patients:

> From a woman whose breast cancer was treated with a lumpectomy (removal of the lump) rather than a mastectomy (which involves removal of the entire breast): "I had a comparatively small amount of surgery. How awful it must be for women who have had a mastectomy. I just can't imagine. It would seem to be so difficult."
>
> The remarks of a woman who had a mastectomy: "It was not tragic. It worked out okay. Now, if the thing had spread all over, I would have had a whole different story for you."
>
> An older woman with breast cancer stated: "The people I really feel sorry for are these young gals. To lose a breast when you're so young must be awful. I'm 73. What do I need a breast for?"
>
> A younger woman stated: "If I hadn't been married, I think this thing would have really gotten to me. I can't imagine dating or whatever knowing you have this thing and not knowing how to tell the man about it." (1989: 171)

Taylor's point is that one can see oneself as better off than others if one picks the right dimension and then proceeds creatively. This is what victims often seek to do.

In addition to such controlled and creative invention of comparison cases, I suggest that people routinely use their literal, noncontrolled mindreading of others as a basis for self-comparison. These "others" include both individuals in the perceptual environment and individuals in the extended environment, such as characters known through the media or through literature who have made an impression on the mind. Assuming that mindreading is executed substantially by simulation, this is highly relevant to self-assessments of well-being. Such self-assessments may be our best guide to, if not the very essence of, life satisfaction.

11.9 Conclusion

This final chapter has provided a small sample of the enormous range of human experience that can be adequately understood only with attention to the mind's habits of interpersonal simulation. The sample included the automatic establishment of social bonds through mimicry, the enhancement of pleasures through identification with others, the role of imagination in engaging with fiction, the roots of altruistic motivation, the epistemic limits of simulation, and the subtle ways that interpersonal comparisons influence life satisfaction. If even a fragment of what we have sketched is correct, simulation is a key concept not only for philosophy of mind and the science of social cognition but also for any systematic attempt to grasp the elements of human sociality. Earlier chapters showed how evidence from cognitive science lends powerful empirical support to the existence and robustness of simulational phenomena.

This chapter has shown how simulational phenomena can illuminate many other topics of pivotal concern to philosophy and the humanities.

Notes

1. After reading a previous draft of this material, Nichols (personal communication) commented that he doesn't think that desires and beliefs use the same code. That's because he takes code talk as a metaphor for the "computational features" of a representation. This raises many delicate issues, and I confess that I lose my grip on Nichols's code talk at this juncture. The view needs to be spelled out in more detail, including a spelling out of the entire boxology architecture.

2. Nichols (2004a) counts off-line simulation theory (as represented by Currie, for example) as a version of the single-code account. But this is a bit misleading, because simulationists don't think it's merely the representational code that does the explanatory work in treating the puzzle of fiction and the emotions.

3. Humans are not the only species that shows empathic responses. Rats were first trained to press a lever for food. Then the setup was changed so that the lever sometimes provided food but also shocked another rat, which was visible in another chamber. Rats would choose to eat less so as to avoid hurting other members of their species. Later experiments with monkeys yielded similar findings (Hauser, 2000; cited in Bloom, 2004). Whether these animal studies implicate mindreading is an open question.

4. As Peter Goldie puts the point, empathy is consistent with indifference: "You can imagine the other's suffering, yet simply disregard it, or you might empathize with a person who has committed a terrible crime, yet feel no sympathy for you think he thoroughly deserves his punishment" (1999: 420).

5. Nichols's concern mechanism seems to be inspired by, and modeled on, Blair's violence inhibition mechanism (VIM). For problems he finds with VIM, see Nichols (2004b: 11–16).

6. The Buddhist text *Udana-Varga* (5, 1) formulates the rule as follows: "Hurt not others in ways that you yourself would find hurtful." Thanks to Derek Parfit for references on the golden rule.

7. For more on this theme, see Hoffman (2000) and Bloom (2004: 140–151).

8. It is not wholly clear that the desire-satisfaction approach is a subjective-experience approach. If it focuses on desire *fulfillment* (realization) irrespective of whether the agent is informed of this fulfillment, then it isn't a subjective-experience approach. But I'll assume that the approach focuses on a related experience, either knowledge of fulfillment or a feeling of satisfaction arising from such knowledge.

References

Aarts, H., and Dijksterhuis, A. (2002). Comparability is in the eye of the beholder: Contrast and assimilation effects of primed animal exemplars on person judgments. *British Journal of Social Psychology* 41: 123–138.

Adelmann, P., and Zajonc, R. (1989). Facial efference and the experience of emotion. *Annual Review of Psychology* 40: 249–280.

Adolphs, R. (1995). Fear and the human amygdala. *Journal of Neuroscience* 15: 5879–5891.

―――. (2002). Recognizing emotion from facial expressions: Psychological and neurological mechanisms. *Behavioral and Cognitive Neuroscience Reviews* 1(1): 21–62.

Adolphs, R., Damasio, H., Tranel, D., Cooper, G., and Damasio, A. R. (2000). A role for the somatosensory cortices in the visual recognition of emotion as revealed by three-dimensional lesion mapping. *Journal of Neuroscience* 20(7), 2683–2690.

Adolphs, R., Gosselin, F., Buchanan, T. W., Tranel, D., Schyns, P., and Damasio, A. R. (2005). A mechanism for impaired fear recognition after amygdala damage. *Nature* 433: 68–72.

Adolphs, R., and Tranel, D. (2000). Emotion recognition and the human amygdala. In J. P. Aggleton, ed., *The Amygdala: A Functional Analysis*, 2nd ed. (587–630). Oxford: Oxford University Press.

Adolphs, R., Tranel, D., Damasio, H., and Damasio, A. (1994). Impaired recognition of emotion in facial expressions following bilateral damage to the amygdala. *Nature* 372: 669–672.

Adolphs, R., Tranel, D., Hamann, S., Young, A. W., Calder, A. J., Phelps, E. A., Anderson, A., Lee, G. P., and Damasio, A. R. (1999). Recognition of facial emotion in nine individuals with bilateral amygdala damage. *Neuropsychologia* 37: 1111–1117.

Ames, D. R. (2004). Inside the mind reader's tool kit: Projection and stereotyping in mental state inference. *Journal of Personality and Social Psychology* 87: 340–353.

Anderson, A. K., and Phelps, E. A. (2001). Lesions of the human amygdala impair enhanced perception of emotionally salient events. *Nature* 411: 305–309.

Aniskiewicz, A. S. (1979). Autonomic components of vicarious conditioning and psychopathy. *Journal of Clinical Psychology* 35: 60–67.

Armstrong, D. M. (1968). *A Materialist Theory of the Mind*. New York: Humanities Press.

———. (1980). *The Nature of Mind, and Other Essays*. Ithaca, NY: Cornell University Press.

Asch, S. E. (1946). Forming impressions of personality. *Journal of Abnormal and Social Psychology* 41: 258–290.

Asperger, H. (1944). Die "Autistischen Psychopathen" im Kindesalter. *Archiv fur Psychiatrie und Nervenkrankheiten* 117: 76–136.

Astington, J., and Gopnik, A. (1988). Knowing you've changed your mind: Children's understanding of representational change. In J. Astington, P. Harris, and D. Olson, eds., *Developing Theories of Mind*. Cambridge: Cambridge University Press.

Astington, J., and Jenkins, J. M. (1995). Theory of mind development and social understanding. *Cognition and Emotion* 9: 151–165.

Bacon, A., Fein, D., Morris, R., Waterhouse, L., and Allen, D. (1998). The responses of autistic children to the distress of others. *Journal of Autism and Developmental Disorders* 28: 129–142.

Baldwin, M. W., Carrell, S. E., and Lopez, D. E. (1990). Priming relationship schemas: My advisor and the pope are watching me from the back of my mind. *Journal of Experimental Social Psychology* 26: 435–454.

Baldwin, M. W., and Holmes, J. G. (1987). Salient private audiences and awareness of the self. *Journal of Personality and Social Psychology* 52: 1087–1098.

Bargh, J. A., and Chartrand, T. (1999). The unbearable automaticity of being. *American Psychologist* 54(7): 462–479.

Bargh, J. A., Chen, M., and Burrows, L. (1996). Automaticity of social behavior: Direct effects of trait construct and stereotype activation on action. *Journal of Personality and Social Psychology* 71: 230–244.

Baron-Cohen, S. (1989). Perceptual role-taking and protodeclarative pointing in autism. *British Journal of Developmental Psychology* 7: 113–127.

———. (1995). *Mindblindness: An Essay on Autism and Theory of Mind*. Cambridge, MA: MIT Press.

———. (1999). The extreme male brain theory of autism. In H. Tager-Flusberg, ed., *Neurodevelopmental Disorders*. Cambridge, MA: MIT Press.

———. (2003). *The Essential Difference: The Truth about the Male and Female Brain*. New York: Basic Books.

Baron-Cohen, S., and Hammer, J. (1997). Is autism an extreme form of the male brain? *Advances in Infancy Research* 11: 193–217.

Baron-Cohen, S., Leslie, A., and Frith, U. (1985). Does the autistic child have a "theory of mind"? *Cognition* 21: 37–46.

———. (1986). Mechanical, behavioral, and intentional understanding of picture stories in autistic children. *British Journal of Developmental Psychology* 4: 113–125.

Barsalou, L. W., Niedenthal, P. M., Barbey, A. K., and Ruppert, J. A. (2003). Social embodiment. In B. H. Ross, ed., *The Psychology of Learning and Motivation* (Vol. 43). San Diego, CA: Academic Press.

Bartels, A., and Zeki, S. (2000). The architecture of the colour centre in the human visual brain: New results and a review. *European Journal of Neuroscience* 12: 172–193.

Bartolomeo, P. (2002). The relationship between visual perception and visual mental imagery: A reappraisal of the neuropsychological evidence. *Cortex* 38(3): 357–378.

Bartsch, K., and Wellman, H. (1995). *Children Talk about the Mind.* New York: Oxford University Press.

Batson, C. D. (1991). *The Altruism Question: Toward a Social-Psychological Answer.* Hillsdale, NJ: Lawrence Erlbaum.

Baynes, K., and Gazzaniga, M. S. (2000). Consciousness, introspection, and the split-brain: The two minds/one body problem. In M. S. Gazzaniga, ed., *The New Cognitive Neurosciences*, 2nd ed. (1355–1368). Cambridge, MA: MIT Press.

Bechara, A., Tranel, D., Damasio, H., Adolphs, R., Rockland, C., and Damasio, A. R. (1995). Double dissociation of conditioning and declarative knowledge relative to the amygdala and hippocampus in humans. *Science* 269: 1115–1118.

Behrmann, M., Moscovitch, M., and Winocur, G. (1994). Intact visual imagery and impaired visual perception in a patient with agnosia. *Journal of Experimental Psychology: Human Perception and Performance* 20: 1068–87.

Bennett, J. (1978). Some remarks about concepts. *Behavioral and Brain Sciences* 1: 557–560.

Benton, A. L., Hamsher, K., Varney, N. R., and Spreen, O. (1983). *Contributions to Neuropsychological Assessment.* New York: Oxford University Press.

Bernieri, F. J. (1988). Coordinated movement and rapport in teacher-student interactions. *Journal of Nonverbal Behavior* 12: 120–138.

Bertolo, H., Paiva, T., Pessoa, L., Mestre, T., Marques, R., and Santos, R. (2003). Visual dream content, graphical representation and EEG alpha activity in congenitally blind subjects. *Cognitive Brain Research* 15: 277–284.

Beschin, N., Basso, A., and Sala, S. D. (2000). Perceiving left and imagining right: Dissociation in neglect. *Cortex* 36: 401–414.

Biederman, I. (1987). Recognition-by-components: A theory of human image understanding. *Psychological Review* 94: 115–147.

———. (1990). Higher-level vision. In D. N. Osherson, S. M. Kosslyn, and J. M. Hollerbach, eds., *Visual cognition and action: An invitation to cognitive science*, Vol. 2, (41–72). Cambridge, MA: MIT Press.

Birch, S. A. J., and Bloom, P. (2003). Children are cursed: An asymmetric bias in mental-state attribution. *Psychological Science* 14: 283–286.

———. (2004). Understanding children's and adults' limitations in mental state reasoning. *Trends in Cognitive Sciences* 8: 255–260.

Bird, C. M., Castelli, F., Malik, O., Frith, U., and Husain, M. (2004). The impact of extensive medial frontal lobe damage on "Theory of Mind" and cognition. *Brain* 127(Pt 4): 914–928.

Bisiach, E., and Luzzatti, C. (1978). Unilateral neglect of representational space. *Cortex* 14: 129–133.

Black, J. B., Turner, T. J., and Bower, G. H. (1979). Point of view in narrative comprehension, memory, and production. *Journal of Verbal Learning and Behavior* 18: 187–198.

Blackburn, S. (1998). *Ruling Passions: A Theory of Practical Reason*. Oxford: Oxford University Press.

Blair, R. J. R. (1999a). Psychophysiological responsiveness to the distress of others in children with autism. *Personality and Individual Differences* 26: 477–485.

———. (1999b). Responsiveness to distress cues in the child with psychopathic tendencies. *Personality and Individual Differences* 27: 135–145.

———. (2002). A neuro-cognitive model of the psychopathic individual. In M. Ron, ed., *Disorders of Brain and Mind II*. Cambridge: Cambridge University Press.

Blair, R. J. R., Jones, L., Clark, F., and Smith, M. (1997). The psychopathic individual: A lack of responsiveness to distress cues? *Psychophysiology* 34: 192–198.

Blair, R. J. R., Mitchell, D. G. V., Peschardt, K. S., Colledge, E., Leonard, R. A., Shine, J. H., Murray, L. K., and Perrett, D. I. (2004). Reduced sensitivity to others' fearful expressions in psychopathic individuals. *Personality and Individual Differences* 37: 1111–1122.

Blair, R. J. R., Mitchell, D. G. V., Richell, R. A., Kelly, S., Leonard, A., Newman, C., and Scott, S. K. (2002). Turning a deaf ear to fear: Impaired recognition of vocal affect in psychopathic individuals. *Journal of Abnormal Psychology* 111: 682–686.

Blair, R. J. R., Sellars, C., Strickland, I., Clark, F., Williams, A. O., Smith, M., and Jones, L. (1995). Emotion attributions in the psychopath. *Personality and Individual Differences* 19: 431–437.

———. (1996). Theory of mind in the psychopath. *Journal of Forensic Psychiatry* 7: 15–25.

Blakemore, S.-J., and Decety, J. (2001). From the perception of action to the understanding of intention. *Nature Reviews Neuroscience* 2: 561–567.

Blakemore, S.-J., Wolpert, D. M., and Frith, C. D. (1998). Central cancellation of self-produced tickle sensation. *Nature Neuroscience* 1(7): 635–640.

Blanchard, D. C., and Blanchard, R. J. (1984). Affect and aggression: An animal model applied to human behavior. In R. J. Blanchard and D. C. Blanchard, eds., *Advances in the Study of Aggression*, Vol. 1 (1–62). Orlando, FL: Academic Press.

Block, N. (1978). Troubles with functionalism. In C. W. Savage, ed., *Perception and Cognition, Minnesota Studies in the Philosophy of Science*, Vol. 9 (261–325). Minneapolis: University of Minnesota Press.

Bloom, P. (2000). *How Children Learn the Meaning of Words*. Cambridge, MA: MIT Press.

———. (2004). *Descartes' Baby: How the Science of Child Development Explains What Makes Us Human*. New York: Basic Books.

Bloom, P., and German, T. (2000). Two reasons to abandon the false belief task as a test of theory of mind. *Cognition* 77: B25–B31.

Boghossian, P. (1989). Content and self-knowledge. *Philosophical Topics* 17: 5–26.

Botterill, G., and Carruthers, P. (1999). *The Philosophy of Psychology*. Cambridge: Cambridge University Press.

Brandt, S. A., and Stark, L. W. (1997). Spontaneous eye movements during visual imagery reflect the content of the visual scene. *Journal of Cognitive Neuroscience* 9(1): 27–38.

Brooks, R., and Meltzoff, A. N. (2002). The importance of eyes: How infants interpret adult looking behavior. *Developmental Psychology* 38: 958–966.

Brown, J. (1995). The incompatibility of anti-individualism and privileged access. *Analysis* 53(3): 149–156.

Brugger, P., Kollias, S. S., Müri, R. M., Crelier, G., Hepp-Raymond, M.-C., and Regard, M. (2000). Beyond re-membering: Phantom sensations of congenitally absent limbs *Proceedings of the National Academy of Sciences USA* 97(11): 6167–6172.

Bryant, D. J., Tversky, B., and Franklin, N. (1992). Internal and external spatial frameworks for representing described scenes. *Journal of Memory and Language* 31: 74–98.

Buccino, G., Binkofski, F., Fink, G. R., Fadiga, L., Fogassi, L., Gallese, V., Seitz, R. J., Zilles, K., Rizzolatti, G., and Freund, H.-J. (2001). Action observation activates premotor and parietal areas in a somatotopic manner: An fMRI study. *European Journal of Neuroscience* 13(2): 400–404.

Buccino, G., Lui, F., Canessa, N., Patteri, I., Lagravinese, G., Benuzzi, F., Porro, C. A., and Rizzolatti, G. (2004). Neural circuits involved in the recognition of actions performed by nonconspecifics: An fMRI study. *Journal of Cognitive Neuroscience* 16: 114–126.

Buchel, C., Price, C., Frackowiak, R. S., and Friston, K. (1998). Different activation patterns in the visual cortex of late and congenitally blind subjects. *Brain* 121: 409–419.

Budd, M. (1989). *Wittgenstein's Philosophy of Psychology*. London: Routledge.

Burge, T. (1979). Individualism and the mental. *Midwest Studies in Philosophy* 4: 73–121.

———. (1982). Other bodies. In A. Woodfield, ed., *Thought and Object*. New York: Oxford University Press.

———. (1985). Cartesian error and the objectivity of perception. In R. Grimm and D. Merrill, eds., *Contents of Thought* (62–76). Tucson: University of Arizona Press.

———. (1988). Individualism and self-knowledge. *Journal of Philosophy* 85: 649–663.

———. (1996). Our entitlement to self-knowledge. *Proceedings of the Aristotelian Society* 96: 91–116.

Bush, L. K., Barr, C. L., McHugo, G. J., and Lanzetta, J. T. (1989). The effects of facial control and facial mimicry on subjective reactions to comedy routines. *Motivation and Emotion* 13: 31–52.

Butter, C., Kosslyn, S., Mijovic-Prelec, D., and Riffle, A. (1997). Field-specific deficits in visual imagery following hemianopia due to unilateral occipital infarcts. *Brain* 120: 217–228.

Butterworth, G. (1991). The ontogeny and phylogeny of joint visual attention. In A. Whiten, ed., *Natural Theories of Mind*, (223–232). Oxford: Blackwell.

Byrne, R., and Whiten, A. (1988). *Machiavellian Intelligence: Social Expertise and the Evolution of Intellect in Monkeys, Apes and Humans*. Oxford: Oxford University Press.

Byrne, R., and Whiten, A. (1991). Computation and mindreading in primate tactical deception. In A. Whiten, ed., *Natural Theories of Mind* (127–141). Oxford: Blackwell.

Cacioppo, J. T., Klein, D. J., Berntson, G. G., and Hatfield, E. (1993). The psychophysiology of emotion. In M. Lewis and J. M. Haviland, eds., *Handbook of Emotions*. New York: Guilford.

Calder, A. J., Keane, J., Cole, J., Campbell, R., and Young, A. W. (2000). Facial expression recognition by people with Mobius syndrome. *Cognitive Neuropsychology* 17(1–3), 73–87.

Calder, A. J., Keane, J., Manes, F., Antoun, N., and Young, A. W. (2000). Impaired recognition and experience of disgust following brain injury. *Nature Neuroscience* 3: 1077–1078.

Campbell, A. (1981). *The Sense of Well-Being in America*. New York: McGraw-Hill.

Camerer, C., Loewenstein, G., and Weber, M. (1989). The curse of knowledge in economic settings: An experimental analysis. *Journal of Political Economy* 97: 1232–1254.

Carey, S. and Johnson, S. C. (2000). Metarepresentation and conceptual change: Evidence from Williams syndrome. In D. Sperber, ed., *Metarepresentations* (225–264). New York: Oxford University Press.

Carlson, S. M., and Moses, L. J. (2001). Individual differences in inhibitory control and children's theory of mind. *Child Development* 72: 1032–1053.

Carlson, S. M., Moses, L. J., and Hix, H. R. (1998). The role of inhibitory processes in young children's difficulties with deception and false belief. *Child Development* 69: 672–691.

Carnap, R. (1956). The methodological character of theoretical concepts. In H. Feigl and M. Scriven, eds., *Minnesota Studies in Philosophy of Science*, Vol. 1 (38–76). Minneapolis: University of Minnesota Press.

Carr, L., Iacoboni, M., Dubeau, M.-C., Mazziotta, J. C., and Lenzi, G. L. (2003). Neural mechanisms of empathy in humans: A relay from neural systems for imitation to limbic areas. *Proceedings of the National Academy of Sciences, USA* 100: 5497–5502.

Carroll, N. (1990). *The Philosophy of Horror, or Paradoxes of the Heart*. London: Routledge.

Carroll, N. (1998). *A Philosophy of Mass Art*. New York: Oxford University Press.

Carroll, N. (2001). *Beyond Aesthetics: Philosophical Essays*. Cambridge: Cambridge University Press.

Carruthers, P. (1996). Autism as mind-blindness: An elaboration and partial defence. In P. Carruthers and P. K. Smith, eds., *Theories of Theories of Mind*, (257–273). Cambridge: Cambridge University Press

Casati, R. (2003). Representational advantages. *Proceedings of the Aristotelian Society* 2003: 281–298.

Chaiken, S., and Trope, Y. (1999). *Dual-Process Theories in Social Psychology*. New York: Guilford.

Chalmers, D. (1996). *The Conscious Mind: In Search of a Fundamental Theory*. New York: Oxford University Press.

Chalmers, D. (2003a). The components of content (revised version). In D. Chalmers, ed., *Philosophy of Mind* (608–633). New York: Oxford University Press.

———. (2003b). The content and epistemology of phenomenal belief. In Q. Smith and A. Jokic, eds., *Consciousness* (220–272). Oxford: Oxford University Press.

Chaminade, T., Meary, D., Orliaguet, J.-P., and Decety, J. (2001). Is perceptual anticipation a motor simulation? A PET study. *NeuroReport* 12: 3669–3674.

Charman, T., Swettenham, J., Baron-Cohen, S., Cox, A., Baird, G., and Drew, A. (1997). Infants with autism: An investigation of empathy, pretend play, joint attention, and imitation. *Developmental Psychology* 33: 781–789.

Charney, E. J. (1966). Psychosomatic manifestations of rapport in psychotherapy. *Psychosomatic Medicine* 28: 305–315.

Chartrand, T. L., and Bargh, J. A. (1999). The chameleon effect: The perception-behavior link and social interaction. *Journal of Personality and Social Psychology* 76: 893–910.

Chatterjee, A., and Southwood, M. (1995) Cortical blindness and visual imagery. *Neurology* 45: 2189–2195.

Cherniak, C. (1986). *Minimal Rationality*. Cambridge, MA: MIT Press.

Chomsky, N. (1975). *Reflections on Language*. New York: Pantheon.

Churchland, P. S. (2002). Self-representation in nervous systems. *Science* 296: 308–310.

Churchland, P. M. (1981). Eliminative materialism and the propositional attitudes. *Journal of Philosophy* 78: 67–90.

———. (1988). *Matter and Consciousness*, rev. ed. Cambridge, MA: MIT Press.

Clements, W. A., and Perner, J. (1994). Implicit understanding of belief. *Cognitive Development* 9: 377–394.

Collingwood, R. G. (1946). *The Idea of History*. Oxford: Clarendon Press.

Condon, W. S., and Ogston, W. D. (1966). Sound film analysis of normal and pathological behavior patterns. *Journal of Nervous and Medical Disease* 143: 338–347.

Connellan, J., Baron-Cohen, S., Wheelwright, S., Batkti, A., and Ahluwalia, J. (2001). Sex differences in human neonatal social perception. *Infant Behavior and Development* 23: 113–118.

Coplan, A. (2004). Empathic engagement with narrative fictions. *Journal of Aesthetics and Art Criticism* 62: 141–152.

Corcoran, R. (2000). Theory of mind in other clinical conditions: Is a selective "theory of mind" deficit exclusive to autism? In S. Baron-Cohen, H. Tager-Flusberg, and D. J. Cohen, eds., *Understanding Other Minds: Perspectives from Developmental Cognitive Neuroscience* (391–421). Oxford: Oxford University Press.

Corkum, V., and Moore, C. (1995). Development of joint visual attention in infants. In C. Moore and P. J. Dunham, eds., *Joint Attention: Its Origins and Role in Development* (61–83). Hillsdale, NJ: Erlbaum.

———. (1998). The origins of joint visual attention in infants. *Developmental Psychology* 34(1): 28–38.

Cosmides, L., Tooby, J., and Barkow, J. H. (1992). Introduction: Evolutionary psychology and conceptual integration. In J. H. Barkow, L. Cosmides, and J. Tooby, eds., *The Adapted Mind: Evolutionary Psychology and the Generation of Culture* (3–15). New York: Oxford University Press.

Craig, A. D. (2002). How do you feel? Interoception: The sense of the physiological condition of the body. *Nature Reviews Neuroscience* 3: 655–666.

Craik, K. (1943). *The Nature of Explanation*. Cambridge: Cambridge University Press.

Craver-Lemley, C., and Reeves, A. (1987). Visual imagery selectively reduces vernier acuity. *Perception* 16: 599–614.

Csibra, G., Biro, S., Koos, O., and Gergely, G. (2003). One-year-old infants use teleological representations of actions productively. *Cognitive Science* 27: 111–133.

Csibra, G., Gergely, G., Biro, S., Koos, O., and Brockbank, M. (1999). Goal attribution without agency cues: The perception of "pure reason" in infancy. *Cognition* 72: 237–267.

Currie, G. (1995a). Imagination and simulation: Aesthetics meets cognitive science. In M. Davies and T. Stone, eds., *Mental Simulation* (151–169). Oxford: Blackwell.

———. (1995b). *Image and Mind: Film, Philosophy and Cognitive Science*. Cambridge: Cambridge University Press.

———. (1997). The paradox of caring: Fiction and the philosophy of mind. In M. Hjort and S. Laver, eds., *Emotion and the Arts* (63–77). Oxford: Oxford University Press.

Currie, G., and Ravenscroft, I. (2002). *Recreative Minds*. Oxford: Oxford University Press.

Currie, G., and Sterelny, K. (2000). How to think about the modularity of mind-reading. *The Philosophical Quarterly* 50: 145–160.

Damasio, A. (1994). *Descartes' Error*. New York: Grosset/Putnam Press.

———. (1999). *The Feeling of What Happens*. New York: Harcourt Brace.

Damasio, A. R., Tranel, D., and Damasio, H. (1990). Face agnosia and the neural substrates of memory. *Annual Review of Neuroscience* 13: 89–109.

Darley, J. M., and Latane, B. (1968). Bystander intervention in emergencies: Diffusion of responsibility. *Journal of Personality and Social Psychology* 8: 377–383.

Darwin, C. (1872/1965). *The Expression of the Emotions in Man and Animals*. Chicago: University of Chicago Press.

Dasser, V., Ulbaek, K., and Premack, D. (1989). The perception of intention. *Science* 243: 365–367.

Davidson, D. (1970). Mental events. In L. Foster and J. Swanson, eds., *Experience and Theory*. Amherst: University of Massachusetts Press. Reprinted 1980 in *Essays on Actions and Events* (207–225). Oxford: Oxford University Press.

———. (1984a). *Inquiries into Truth and Interpretation*. Oxford: Oxford University Press.

———. (1984b). Thought and talk. In *Inquiries into Truth and Interpretation* (155–170). Oxford: Oxford University Press.

———. (2001). Knowing one's own mind. In *Subjective, Intersubjective, Objective* (15–38). Oxford: Oxford University Press.

Davies, M. (1987). Tacit knowledge and semantic theory: Can a five per cent difference matter? *Mind* 96: 441–462.

Davies, M., and Stone, T. (2001). Mental simulation, tacit theory, and the threat of collapse. *Philosophical Topics* 29: 127–173.

Davis, M. H. (1980). A multidimensional approach to individual differences in empathy. *Catalog of Selected Documents in Psychology* 10: 85.

Decety, J., and Chaminade, T. (2003). Neural correlates of feeling sympathy. *Neuropsychologia* 41: 127–138.

Decety, J., and Grèzes, J. (1999). Neural mechanisms subserving the perception of human actions. *Trends in Cognitive Sciences* 3: 172–178.

Decety, J., Jeannerod, M., and Preblanc, C. (1989). The timing of mentally represented actions. *Behavioral and Brain Research* 34: 35–42

Dennett, D. (1978a). Beliefs about beliefs. *Behavioral and Brain Sciences* 1: 568–570.

———. (1978b). Intentional systems. In D. Dennett, *Brainstorms* (3–22). Montgomery, VT: Bradford.

———. (1978c). Why the law of effect won't go away. In D. Dennett, *Brainstorms* (71–89). Montgomery, VT: Bradford.

———. (1987). *The Intentional Stance.* Cambridge, MA: MIT Press.

de Villiers, J. (2000). Language and theory of mind: What are the developmental relationships? In S. Baron-Cohen, H. Tager-Flusberg, and D. Cohen, eds., *Understanding Other Minds: Perspectives from Developmental Cognitive Neuroscience,* 2nd ed. (83–123). Oxford: Oxford University Press.

de Villiers, J., and de Villiers, P. A. (2000). Linguistic determinism and false belief. In P. Mitchell and K. Riggs, eds., *Children's Reasoning and the Mind* (191–228). Hove, England: Psychology Press.

Diamond, A., and Taylor, C. (1996). Development of an aspect of executive control: Development of the abilities to remember what I said and to "Do as I say, not as I do." *Developmental Psychology* 29: 315–334.

Dijksterhuis, A., and van Knippenberg, A. (1998). The relation between perception and behavior, or how to win a game of trivial pursuit. *Journal of Personality and Social Psychology* 74(4): 865–877.

———. (2000). Behavioral indecision: Effects of self focus on automatic behavior. *Social Cognition* 18: 55–74.

Dilthey, W. (1977). *Descriptive Psychology and Historical Understanding.* The Hague: Martinus Nijhoff.

Dimberg, U. (1988). Facial electromyography and the experience of emotion. *Journal of Psychophysiology* 2: 277–282.

Dimberg, U., and Thunberg, M. (1998). Rapid facial reactions to emotional facial expressions. *Scandinavian Journal of Psychology* 39, 39–45.

Dimberg, U., Thunberg, M., and Elmehed, K. (2000). Unconscious facial reactions to emotional facial expressions. *Psychological Science* 11(1): 86–88.

Dominey, P., Decety, J., Brouselle, E., Chazot, G., and Jeannerod, M. (1995). Motor imagery of a lateralized sequential task is asymmetrically slowed in hemi-Parkinson's patients, *Neuropsychologia* 33: 727–741.

Dretske, F. (1981). *Knowledge and the Flow of Information.* Cambridge, MA: MIT Press.

———. (1988). *Explaining Behavior: Reasons in a World of Causes.* Cambridge, MA: MIT Press.

Dretske, F. (1995). *Naturalizing the Mind.* Cambridge, MA: MIT Press.

Egeth, H. E., and Yantis, S. (1997). Visual attention: Control, representation, and time course. *Annual Review of Psychology* 48: 269–297.

Eisenberg, N., and Strayer, J. (1987). Critical issues in the study of empathy. In N. Eisenberg and J. Strayer, *Empathy and Its Development* (3–13). New York: Cambridge University Press.

Ekman, P. (1992). Are there basic emotions? *Psychological Review* 99(3), 550–553.

Ekman, P., and Friesen, W. V. (1976). *Pictures of Facial Affect*. Palo Alto, CA: Consulting Psychologists Press.

Ekman, P., Levenson, R. W., and Friesen, W. V. (1983). Autonomic nervous system activity distinguishes among emotions. *Science* 221: 1208–1210.

Emery, N. J., and Clayton, N. S. (2001). Effects of experience and social context on prospective caching strategies by scrub jays. *Nature* 414: 443–446.

Epley, N., Keysar, B., Van Boven, L., and Gilovich, T. (2004). Perspective taking as egocentric anchoring and adjustment. *Journal of Personality and Social Psychology* 87:329–339.

Epley, N., Morewedge, C. K., and Keysar, B. (2004). Perspective taking in children and adults: Equivalent egocentrism but differential correction. *Journal of Experimental Social Psychology* 40: 760–768.

Evans, G. (1981). Semantic theory and tacit knowledge. In S. Holtzman and C. Leich, eds., *Wittgenstein: To Follow a Rule*. London: Routledge and Kegan Paul.

———. (1982). *The Varieties of Reference*, J. McDowell, ed. Oxford: Oxford University Press.

Fabricius, W., and Imbens-Bailey, A. (2000). False beliefs about false beliefs. In P. Mitchell and K. Riggs, eds., *Children's Reasoning and the Mind* (267–280). Hove, England: Psychology Press.

Fadiga, L., Fogassi, L., Pavesi, G., and Rizzolatti, G. (1995). Motor facilitation during action observation: A magnetic stimulation study. *Journal of Neurophysiology* 73: 2608–2611.

Farah, M. J. (1984). The neurological basis of mental imagery: A componential analysis. *Cognition* 18: 245–272.

Farah, M. J., Soso, M. J., and Dasheiff, R. M. (1992). Visual angle of the mind's eye before and after unilateral occipital lobectomy. *Journal of Experimental Psychology: Human Perception and Performance* 18:241–246.

Feagin, S. (1996). *Reading with Feeling: The Aesthetics of Appreciation*. Ithaca, NY: Cornell University Press.

Festinger, L. (1957). *A Theory of Cognitive Dissonance*. Evanston, IL: Row, Peterson.

Flanagan, O. (1992). *Consciousness Reconsidered*. Cambridge, MA: MIT Press.

Flavell, J. H., Flavell, E. R., and Green, F. L. (1983). Development of the appearance-reality distinction. *Cognitive Psychology* 15: 95–120.

Fletcher, P., Happé, F., Frith, U., Baker, S., Dolan, R., Frackowiak, R., and Frith, C. (1995). Other minds in the brain: A functional imaging study of "theory of mind" in story comprehension. *Cognition* 57: 109–128.

Flombaum, J. I., and Santos, L. R. (2005). Rhesus monkeys attribute perceptions to others. *Current Biology* 15: 447–452.

Fodor, J. A. (1975). *The Language of Thought*. Scranton, PA: Crowell.

———. (1983). *The Modularity of Mind*. Cambridge, MA: MIT Press.

———. (1987). *Psychosemantics*. Cambridge, MA: MIT Press.

———. (1989). Making mind matter more. *Philosophical Topics* 17: 59–79.

———. (1990). *A Theory of Content and Other Essays*. Cambridge, MA: MIT Press.

———. (1998). *Concepts, Where Cognitive Science Went Wrong*. Oxford: Oxford University Press.

———. (2000). *The Mind Doesn't Work That Way : The Scope and Limits of Computational Psychology*. Cambridge, MA: MIT Press.

————. (2001). Language, thought and compositionality. *Mind and Language* 16: 1–15.

————. (2004). Having concepts: A brief refutation of the twentieth century. *Mind and Language* 19: 29–47.

Fodor, J. A., and Lepore, E. (1992). *Holism, A Shopper's Guide*. Cambridge, MA: Blackwell.

Fogassi, L., Ferrari, P. F., Gesierich, B., Rozzi, S., Chersi, F., and Rizzolatti, G. (2005). Parietal lobe: from action organization to intention understanding. *Science* 308:662–667.

Forguson, L., and Gopnik, A. (1988). The ontogeny of common sense. In J. Astington, P. Harris, and D. Olson, eds., *Developing Theories of Mind*. Cambridge: Cambridge University Press.

Frege, G. (1892). Ueber Sinn und Bedeutung. Translated in P. Geach and M. Black, eds., *Translations from the Philosophical Writings of Gottlob Frege* (1952), 56–78. Oxford: Blackwell.

Freud, S. (1915/1953). Instincts and their vicissitudes. *Collected Papers*, 4. London: Hogarth.

Fricker, E. (1998). Self-knowledge: Special access versus artefact of grammar—A dichotomy rejected. In C. Wright, B. C. Smith, and C. Macdonald, eds., *Knowing Our Own Minds*, (155–206). Oxford: Oxford University Press.

Frith, U. (1989). *Autism: Explaining the Enigma*. Oxford: Blackwell.

————. (2003). *Autism: Explaining the Enigma*, 2nd ed. Malden, MA: Blackwell.

Frith, U., and Frith, C. D. (2003). Development and neurophysiology of mentalizing. *Philosophical Transactions of the Royal Society*, series B. 358: 459–473.

Frith, U., and Happé, F. (1999). Theory of mind and self consciousness: What is it like to be autistic? *Mind and Language* 14: 1–22.

Frye, D., Zelazo, P., and Palfai, T. (1995). Theory of mind and rule-based reasoning. *Cognitive Development* 10: 483–527.

Fuller, G. (1995). Simulation and psychological concepts. In M. Davies and T. Stone, eds., *Mental Simulation* (19–32). Boston: Blackwell.

Funk, M., Brugger, P., and Shiffrar, M. (2005). Hand movement observation by individuals born without hands: Phantom limb experience constrains visual limb perception. *Experimental Brain Research* 164: 341–346.

Gale, E., de Villiers, P., de Villiers, J., and Pyers, J. (1996). Language and theory of mind in oral deaf children. In A. Stringfellow, D. Cahana-Amitay, E. Hughes, and A. Zukowski, eds., *Proceedings of the 20th Annual Boston University Conference on Language Development*, Vol. 1. Somerville, MA: Cascadilla.

Gallagher, H. L., Happe, F., Brunswick, N., Fletcher, P. C., Frith, U., and Frith, C. D. (2000). Reading the mind in cartoons and stories: An fMRI study of "theory of mind" in verbal and nonverbal tasks. *Neuropsychologia* 38: 11–21.

Gallese, V. (2001). The "shared manifold" hypothesis: From mirror neurons to empathy. *Journal of Consciousness Studies* 8 (5–7): 33–50.

————. (2003). The manifold nature of interpersonal relations: The quest for a common mechanism. *Philosophical Transactions of the Royal Society of London B, Biological Science* 358: 517–528.

————. (2004). Intentional attunement. The mirror neuron system and its role in interpersonal relations. http://www.interdisciplines.org/mirror/papers/1/10/1.

———. (2005). "Being like me": Self-other identity, mirror neurons and empathy. In S. Hurley and N. Chater, eds., *Perspectives on Imitation: From Neuroscience to Social Science*, Vol. 1 (101–118). Cambridge, MA: MIT Press.

Gallese,V., Fadiga, L., Fogassi, L., and Rizzolatti, G. (1996). Action recognition in the premotor cortex. *Brain* 119: 593–609.

Gallese, V., and Goldman, A. (1998). Mirror neurons and the simulation theory of mindreading. *Trends in Cognitive Sciences* 2: 493–501.

Gallese, V., Keysers, C., and Rizzolatti, G. (2004). A unifying view of the basis of social cognition. *Trends in Cognitive Sciences* 8: 396–403.

Gallistel, C. R. (1990). *The Organization of Learning*. New York: Crowell.

———. (2000). The replacement of general-purpose learning models with adaptively specialized learning modules. In M. Gazzaniga, ed., *The New Cognitive Neurosciences*, 2nd ed. (1179–1191). Cambridge, MA: MIT Press.

Garcia, J. (1989). Food for Tolman: Cognition and cathexis in concert. In T. Archer and L.-G. Nilson, eds., *Aversion, Avoidance and Anxiety* (45–85). Hillsdale, NJ: Erlbaum.

———. (1990). Learning without memory. *Journal of Cognitive Neuroscience* 2: 287–305.

Garcia, S. M., Weaver, K., Moskowitz, G. B., and Darley, J. M. (2002). Crowded minds: The implicit bystander effect. *Journal of Personality and Social Psychology* 83: 843–853.

Gazzaniga, M. S. (1992). *Nature's Mind: The Biological Roots of Thinking, Emotions, Sexuality, Language, and Intelligence*. New York: Basic Books.

Gazzaniga, M. S., and LeDoux, J. E. (1978). *The Integrated Mind*. New York: Plenum.

Gelman, R., and Williams, E. (1998). Enabling constraints on cognitive development. In D. Kahn and R. Siegler, eds., *Cognition, Perception and Language*, Vol. 2, *Handbook of Child Psychology*, 5th ed. New York: Wiley.

Gendler, T. (2003). On the relation between pretense and belief. In M. Kieran and D. M. Lopes, eds., *Imagination, Philosophy, and the Arts* (125–141). London: Routledge.

Gergely, G., and Csibra, G. (2003). Teleological reasoning in infancy: The naïve theory of rational action. *Trends in Cognitive Sciences* 7(7): 287–292.

Gergely, G., Nadasdy, Z., Csibra, G., and Biro, S. (1995). Taking the intentional stance at 12 months of age. *Cognition* 56: 165–193.

German, T., and Leslie, A. (2000). Attending to and learning about mental states. In P. Mitchell and K. Riggs, eds., *Children's Reasoning and the Mind* (229–252). Hove, England: Psychology Press.

Gernsbacher, M. A., Goldsmith, H. H., and Robertson, R. R. W. (1992). Do readers mentally represent characters' emotional states? *Cognition and Emotion* 6: 89–111.

Gibbard, A. (1990). *Wise Choices, Apt Feelings*. Cambridge, MA: Harvard University Press.

Gilbert, D. T., Gill, M. J., and Wilson, T. D. (2002). The future is now: Temporal correction in affective forecasting. *Organizational Behavior and Human Decision Processes* 88(1): 430–444.

Gilovich, T., Griffin, D., and Kahneman, D., eds. (2002). *Heuristics and Biases: The Psychology of Intuitive Judgment*. Cambridge: Cambridge University Press.

Gilovich, T., Savitsky, K., and Medvec, Y. H., (1998). The illusion of transparency: Biased assessments of others' ability to read one's emotional states. *Journal of Personality and Social Psychology* 75: 332–346.

Goel, V., Grafman, J., Sadato, N., and Hallett, M. (1995). Modeling other minds. *Neuroreport* 6: 1741–1746.

Goldenberg, G., Muellbacher, W., and Nowak, A. (1995). Imagery without perception: A case study of anosognosia for cortical blindness. *Neuropsychologia* 33: 1373–1382.

Goldie, P. (1999). How we think of others' emotions. *Mind and Language* 14: 394–423.

Goldman, A. (1986). *Epistemology and Cognition.* Cambridge, MA: Harvard University Press.

———. (1989). Interpretation psychologized. *Mind and Language* 4: 161–185. Reprinted in M. Davies and T. Stone, eds., *Folk Psychology* (74–99). Oxford: Blackwell (1995).

———. (1992a). In defense of the simulation theory. *Mind and Language* 7(1–2): 104–119.

———. (1992b). Empathy, mind and morals. *Proceedings and Addresses of the American Philosophical Association* 66, 3: 17–41. Reprinted in M. Davies and T. Stone, eds., *Mental Simulation* (185–208). Oxford: Blackwell (1995).

———. (1993a). The psychology of folk psychology. *Behavioral and Brain Sciences* 16: 15–28.

———. (1993b). Consciousness, folk psychology, and cognitive science. *Consciousness and Cognition* 2: 364–382.

———. (1993c). Ethics and cognitive science. *Ethics* 103: 337–360.

———. (1995). Simulation and interpersonal utility. *Ethics* 105: 709–726.

———. (1997). Science, publicity and consciousness. *Philosophy of Science* 64(4): 525–545. Reprinted in Goldman (2002b).

———. (2000a). Can science know when you're conscious? Epistemological foundations of consciousness research. *Journal of Consciousness Studies* 7(5): 3–22. Reprinted in Goldman (2002b).

———. (2002a). Simulation theory and mental concepts. In J. Dokic and J. Proust, eds., *Simulation and Knowledge of Action* (1–20). Amsterdam: John Benjamins.

———. (2002b). *Pathways to Knowledge, Private and Public.* New York: Oxford University Press.

———. (2003). Conceptual clarification and empirical defense of the simulation theory of mindreading. In C. Kanzian, J. Quitterer, and E. Runggaldier, eds., *Persons: An Interdisciplinary Approach.* Vienna: Obvahaupt.

———. (2004). Epistemology and the evidential status of introspective reports. *Journal of Consciousness Studies* 11(7–8): 1–16.

———. (2005). Imitation, mind reading, and simulation. In S. Hurley and N. Chater, eds., *Perspectives on Imitation: From Neuroscience to Social Science*, Vol. 2 (79–93). Cambridge, MA: MIT Press.

———. (2006) (in press). Imagination and simulation in audience responses to fiction. In S. Nichols, ed., *The Architecture of the Imagination.* Oxford: Oxford University Press.

Goldman, A., and Sripada, C. (2005). Simulationist models of face-based emotion recognition. *Cognition* 94: 193–213.

Goodale, M. A., Milner, A. D., Jakobson, L. S., and Carey, D. P. (1991). A neurological dissociation between perceiving objects and grasping them. *Nature* 349: 154–156.

Gopnik, A. (1993). How we know our minds: The illusion of first-person knowledge of intentionality. *Behavioral and Brain Sciences* 16: 1–14.

Gopnik, A., and Astington, J. (1988). Children's understanding of representational change and its relation to the understanding of false belief and the appearance-reality distinction. *Child Development* 59: 26–37.

Gopnik, A., and Glymour, C. (2002). Causal maps and Bayes nets: A cognitive and computational account of theory-formation. In P. Carruthers, S. Stich, and M. Siegel, eds., *The Cognitive Basis of Science* (117–132). Cambridge: Cambridge University Press.

Gopnik, A., Glymour, C., Sobel, D. M., Schulz, L. E., Kushnir, T., and Danks, D. (2004). A theory of causal learning in children: Causal maps and Bayes nets. *Psychological Review* (111:3–32).

Gopnik, A., and Meltzoff, A. N. (1986). Words, plans, things, and locations: Interactions between semantic and cognitive development in the one-word stage. In S. A. Kuczaj and M. D. Barrett, eds., *The Development of Word Meaning: Progress in Cognitive Development Research* (199–223). New York: Springer-Verlag.

———. (1994). Minds, bodies, and persons: Young children's understanding of the self and others as reflected in imitation and theory of mind research. In S. Parker, R. Mitchell, and M. Boccia, eds., *Self-Awareness in Animals and Humans*. Cambridge: Cambridge University Press

———. (1997). *Words, Thoughts and Theories*. Cambridge, MA: MIT Press.

Gopnik, A., Meltzoff, A., and Kuhl, P. (1999). *The Scientist in the Crib*. New York: HarperCollins.

Gopnik, A., and Slaughter, V. (1991) Young children's understanding of changes in their mental states. *Child Development* 62: 98–110.

Gopnik, A., Sobel, D. M., Schulz, L. E., and Glymour, C. (2001). Causal learning mechanisms in very young children: Two, three, and four-year-olds infer causal relations from patterns of variation and covariation. *Developmental Psychology* 37: 620–629.

Gopnik, A., and Wellman, H. (1992). Why the child's theory of mind really *is* a theory. *Mind and Language* 7: 145–171.

———. (1994). The theory theory. In L. Hirschfeld and S. Gelman, eds., *Mapping the Mind: Domain Specificity in Cognition and Culture*. New York: Cambridge University Press.

Gordon, R. (1986). Folk psychology as simulation. *Mind and Language* 1: 158–171. Reprinted in Davies, M., and Stone, T., eds. (1995). *Folk Psychology* (60–73). Oxford: Blackwell.

———. (1992). The simulation theory: Objections and misconceptions. *Mind and Language* 7(1–2): 1–10.

———. (1995a). Sympathy, simulation, and the impartial spectator. *Ethics* 105: 727–742.

———. (1995b). Simulation without introspection or inference from me to you. In T. Stone and M. Davies, eds, *Mental Simulation* (53–67). Oxford: Blackwell.

————. (1996). "Radical" simulationism. In P. Carruthers and P. Smith, eds., *Theories of Theories of Mind* (11–21). Cambridge: Cambridge University Press.

————. (2005). Simulation and systematic errors in prediction. *Trends in Cognitive Sciences* 9:361–362.

Gould, J. L., and Marler, P. (1987). Learning by instinct. *Scientific American* 256: 74–85.

Gould, S. J., and Vrba, E. (1982). Exaptation: A missing term in the science of form. *Paleobiology* 8: 4–15.

Grandy, R. (1973). Reference, meaning, and belief. *Journal of Philosophy* 70: 439–452.

Greene, J. D., Sommerville, R. B., Nystrom, L. E., Darley, J. M., and Cohen, J. D. (2001). An fMRI investigation of emotional engagement in moral judgment. *Science* 293: 2105–2108.

Grèzes, J., and Decety, J. (2001). Functional anatomy of execution, mental simulation, observation, and verb generation of actions: A meta-analysis. *Human Brain Mapping* 12: 1–19.

Grush, R. (2004). The emulation theory of representation: Motor control, imagery, and perception. *Behavioral and Brain Sciences* 27: 377–396.

Gusnard, D. A., Akbudak, E., Shulman, G. L., and Raichle, M. E. (2001). Medial prefrontal cortex and self-referential mental activity: Relation to a default mode of brain function. *Proceedings of the National Academy of Sciences USA* 98: 4259–4264.

Hadfield, M. G. (1983). Dopamine: Mesocortical vs. nigrostriatal uptake in isolated fighting mice and controls. *Behavioral Brain Research* 7: 269–281.

Haidt, J. (2001). The emotional dog and its rational tail: A social intuitionist approach to moral judgment. *Psychological Review* 108: 814–834.

Halgren, E. (1992). Emotional neurophysiology of the amygdala within the context of human cognition. In J. P. Aggleton, ed., *The Amygdala: Neurobiological Aspects of Emotion, Memory, and Mental Dysfunction* (191–228). New York: Wiley-Liss.

Halle, M., and Stevens, K. N. (1964). Speech recognition: A model and a program for research. In J. A. Fodor and J. J. Katz, eds., *The Structure of Language: Readings in the Philosophy of Language*. Englewood Cliffs, NJ: Prentice-Hall.

Hamilton, D. L., and Sherman, S. J. (1996). Perceiving persons and groups. *Psychological Review* 103: 336–355.

Hare, B., Call, J., Agnetta, B., and Tomasello, M. (2000). Chimpanzees know what conspecifics do and do not see. *Animal Behavior* 59: 771–785.

————. (2001). Do chimpanzees know what conspecifics know? *Animal Behavior* 61: 139–151.

Hare, R. D. (1991). *The Hare Psychopathy Checklist—Revised*. Toronto, Ontario: Multi-Health Systems.

Hare, R. M. (1963). *Freedom and Reason*. Oxford: Clarendon.

————. (1981). *Moral Thinking*. Oxford: Clarendon.

Harman, G. (1973). *Thought*. Princeton, NJ: Princeton University Press.

————. (1978). Studying the chimpanzee's theory of mind. *Behavioral and Brain Sciences* 1: 576–577.

————. (1990). The intrinsic quality of experience. *Philosophical Perspectives* 4: 31–52.

Harris, P. (1991). The work of the imagination. In A. Whiten, ed., *Natural Theories of Mind* (283–304). Oxford: Blackwell.

Harris, P. L. (1992). From simulation to folk psychology: The case for development. *Mind and Language* 7: 120–144. Reprinted in Davies and Stone, eds. (1995). *Folk Psychology*. Oxford: Blackwell.

———. (2000). *The Work of the Imagination*. Malden, MA: Blackwell.

Harris, P. L., German, T., and Mills, P. (1996). Children's use of counterfactual thinking in causal reasoning. *Cognition* 61: 233–259.

Harris, P. L., and Leevers, H. J. (2000). Reasoning from false premises. In P. Mitchell and K. Riggs, eds., *Children's Reasoning and the Mind* (67–86). Hove, England: Psychology Press.

Harris, P. L., and Martin, L. (unpublished). From Little Red Riding Hood to Othello: Empathizing with a naïve protagonist.

Hatfield, E., Cacioppo, J. T., and Rapson, R. L. (1994). *Emotional Contagion*. Cambridge: Cambridge University Press.

Haugeland, J. (1985). *Artificial Intelligence, the Very Idea*. Cambridge, MA: MIT Press.

Hauser, M. D. (2000). *Wild Minds: What Animals Really Think*. New York: Henry Holt.

Heal, J. (1986). Replication and functionalism. In J. Butterfield, ed., *Language, Mind, and Logic*. Cambridge: Cambridge University Press.

———. (1994). Simulation vs. theory theory: What is at issue? In C. Peacocke, ed., *Objectivity, Simulation and the Unity of Consciousness* (129–144). Oxford: Oxford University Press.

———. (1996). Simulation and cognitive penetrability. *Mind and Language* 11: 44–67.

———. (1998). Co-cognition and off-line simulation: Two ways of understanding the simulation approach. *Mind and Language* 13: 477–98.

Hebb, D. O. (1949). *The Organization of Behavior*. New York: Wiley.

Heberlein, A. S., and Adolphs, R. (in press). Neurobiology of emotion recognition: Current evidence for shared substrates. In E. Harmon-Jones and P. Winkielman, eds., *Fundamentals of Social Neuroscience*. New York: Guilford.

Heberlein, A. S., Adolphs, R., Tranel, D., and Damasio, H. (2004). Cortical regions for judgments of emotions and personality traits from point-light walkers. *Journal of Cognitive Neuroscience* 16: 1143–1158.

Hegarty, M. (2004). Mechanical reasoning by mental simulation. *Trends in Cognitive Sciences* 8(6): 280–285.

Heider, F., and Simmel, M. (1944). An experimental study of apparent behavior. *American Journal of Psychology* 57: 243–259.

Hempel, C. G. (1958). The theoretician's dilemma: A study in the logic of theory construction. In H. Feigl, M. Scriven, and G. Maxwell, eds., *Minnesota Studies in Philosophy of Science*, Vol. 1 (37–98). Minneapolis: University of Minnesota Press.

Hess, U., and Blairy, S. (2001). Facial mimicry and emotional contagion to dynamic facial expressions and their influence on decoding accuracy. *International Journal of Psychophysiology* 40: 129–141.

Hodges, S. D., and Wegner, D. M. (1997). Automatic and controlled empathy. In W. Ickes, ed., *Empathic Accuracy* (311–339). New York: Guilford.

Hoffman, M. (2000). *Empathy and Moral Development*. New York: Cambridge University Press.

Holton, R. (1993). Intention detecting. *Philosophical Quarterly* 43: 298–318.

Holton, R., and Langton, R. (1999). Empathy and animal ethics. In D. Jamieson, ed., *Singer and His Critics* (209–232). Oxford: Blackwell.

Horgan, T., and Tienson, J. (2002). The intentionality of phenomenology and the phenomenology of intentionality. In D. Chalmers, ed., *Philosophy of Mind* (520–533). New York: Oxford University Press.

Hughes, C. (1998). Executive function in preschoolers: Links with theory of mind and verbal ability. *British Journal of Developmental Psychology* 16: 233–253.

Hughes, C., and Russell, J. (1993). Autistic children's difficulty with mental disengagement from an object: Its implication for theories of autism. *Developmental Psychology* 29: 498–510.

Hume, D. (1739/1958). *A Treatise of Human Nature*, 1st ed., L. A. Selby-Bigge, ed. New York: Oxford University Press.

Humphrey, N. (1984). *Consciousness Regained*. Oxford: Oxford University Press.

———. (1986). *The Inner Eye*. Oxford: Oxford University Press.

Hurlburt, R. (1990). *Sampling Normal and Schizophrenic Inner Experience*. New York: Plenum.

———. (1993). *Sampling Inner Experience in Disturbed Affect*. New York: Plenum.

———. (1997). Randomly sampling thinking in the natural environment. *Journal of Consulting and Clinical Psychology* 65(6): 941–949.

Hurlburt, R., Happé, F., and Frith, U. (1994). Sampling the form of inner experience in three adults with Asperger syndrome. *Psychological Medicine* 24: 385–395.

Hurlburt, R. T., and Heavey, C. L. (2001). Telling what we know: Describing inner experience. *Trends in Cognitive Sciences* 5: 400–403.

Hurley, S. (2005a). The shared circuits hypothesis: A unified functional architecture for control, imitation, and simulation. In S. Hurley and N. Chater, eds., *Perspectives on Imitation: From Neuroscience to Social Science*, Vol. 1 (177–193). Cambridge, MA: MIT Press.

———. (2005b). The shared circuits model. How control, mirroring, and simulation can enable imitation and mind reading. http://www.interdisciplines.org/mirror/papers/1.

———. (in press). The shared circuits model: How control, mirroring and simulation can enable imitation, deliberation and mindreading. *Behavioral and Brain Sciences*.

Hurley, S., and Chater, N., eds. (2005). *Perspectives on Imitation: From Neuroscience to Social Science* (2 vols.). Cambridge, MA: MIT Press.

Hurvich, L. M., and Jameson, D. (1957). An opponent-process theory of color vision. *Psychological Review* 64: 384–403.

Hutchison, W. D., Davis, K. D., Lozano, A. M., Tasker, R. R., and Dostrovsky, J. O. (1999). Pain-related neurons in the human cingulate cortex. *Nature Neuroscience* 2(5): 403–405.

Iacoboni, M. (2005). Understanding others: Imitation, language, and empathy. In S. Hurley and N. Chater, eds., *Perspectives on Imitation: From Neuroscience to Social Science*, Vol. 1 (76–100). Cambridge, MA: MIT Press.

Iacoboni, M., Molnar-Szakacs, I., Gallese, V., Buccino, G., Mazziotta, J. C., and Rizzolatti, G. (2005). Grasping the intentions of others with one's own mirror neuron system. *PLoS Biology* 3:529–535.

Imbens-Bailey, A. L., Prost, J. H., and Fabricius, W. V. (1997). Perception, desire and belief in me and you: Young children's reference to mental states in self and other. Unpublished manuscript, University of California, Los Angeles.

Jackendoff, R. (1996). The architecture of the linguistic-spatial interface. In P. Bloom, M. A. Peterson, L. Nadel, and M. F. Garrett, eds., *Language and Space* (1–30). Tucson: University of Arizona Press.

Jackson, F. (1982). Epiphenomenal qualia. *Philosophical Quarterly* 1982: 127–136.

———. (1986). What Mary didn't know. *Journal of Philosophy* 83(5): 291–295.

———. (1999). All that can be at issue in the theory-theory simulation debate. *Philosophical Papers* 28(2): 77–96.

Jackson, P. L., Meltzoff, A. N., and Decety, J. (2004). How do we perceive the pain of others? A window into the neural processes involved in empathy. *NeuroImage* 24:771–779.

Jacob, P., and Jeannerod, M. (2005). The motor theory of social cognition: A critique. *Trends in Cognitive Sciences* 9: 21–25.

Jankowiak, J., Kinsbourne, M., Shalev, R., and Bachman, D. (1992). Preserved visual imagery and categorization in a case of associative visual agnosia. *Journal of Cognitive Neuroscience* 4: 119–131.

Jeannerod, M. (2001). Neural simulation of action: A unifying mechanism for motor cognition. *NeuroImage* 14: S103–S109.

Jeannerod, M., and Pacherie, E. (2004). Agency, simulation and self-identification. *Mind and Language* 19: 113–146.

Johansson, G. (1973). Visual perception of biological motion and a model of its analysis. *Perception and Psychophysics* 14: 202–211.

Johansson, P., Hall, L., Sikstrom, S., and Olsson, A. (2005). Failure to detect mismatches between intention and outcome in a simple decision task. *Science* 310:116–119.

Johnson, S. C. (2003). Detecting agents. *The Neuroscience of Social Interaction* (219–240). Oxford: Oxford University Press.

Johnson, S. C., Baxter, L. C., Wilder, L. S., Pipe, J. G., Heiserman, J. E., and Prigatano, G. P. (2002). Neural correlates of self-reflection. *Brain* 125 (Pt 8): 1808–1814.

Johnson-Laird, P. N. (1983). *Mental Models: Toward a Cognitive Science of Language, Inference, and Consciousness*. Cambridge, MA: Harvard University Press.

Johnson-Laird, P. N., and Byrne, R. M. J. (1991). *Deduction*. Hillsdale, NJ: Erlbaum.

Kahneman, D., Slovic, P., and Tversky, A., eds. (1982). *Judgment under Uncertainty: Heuristics and Biases*. Cambridge: Cambridge University Press.

Kahneman, D., and Tversky, A. (1979). Prospect theory: An analysis of decision under risk. *Econometrica* 47: 263–291.

———. (1984). Choices, values and frames. *American Psychologist* 39: 341–350.

———, eds. (2000). *Choices, Values and Frames*. Cambridge: Cambridge University Press.

Kandel, S., Orliaguet, J. P., and Viviani, P. (2000). Perceptual anticipation in handwriting: The role of implicit motor competence. *Perception and Psychophysics* 62(4): 706–716.

Kant, I. (1781/1953). *Critique of Pure Reason*, 1st ed., trans. N. K. Smith. London: Macmillan.

————. (1785/1959). *Foundations of the Metaphysics of Morals*, trans. L. W. Beck. Indianapolis, IN: Bobbs-Merrill.

Kanwisher, N. (2000). Domain specificity in face perception. *Nature Neuroscience* 3: 759–763.

Kanwisher, N., McDermott, J., and Chun, M. M. (1997). The fusiform face area: A module in human extrastriate cortex specialized for face perception. *Journal of Neuroscience* 17: 4302–4311.

Kaplan, D. (1989). Demonstratives. In J. Almog, J. Perry, and H. Wettstein, eds., *Themes from Kaplan* (481–563). New York: Oxford University Press.

Kawada, C. L. K., Oettingen, G., Gollwitzer, P. M., and Bargh, J. A. (2004). The projection of implicit and explicit goals. *Journal of Personality and Social Psychology* 86: 545–559.

Keillor, J. M., Barrett, A. M., Crucian, G. P., Kortenkamp, S., and Heilman, K. M. (2002). Emotional experience and perception in the absence of facial feedback. *Journal of the International Neuropsychological Society* 8(1): 130–135.

Kellerman, J., Lewis, J., and Laird, J. D. (1989). Looking and loving: The effects of mutual gaze on feelings of romantic love. *Journal of Research in Personality* 23: 145–161.

Kelly, W. M., Macrae, C. N., Wyland, C. L., Caglar, S., Inati, S., and Heatherton, T. F. (2002). Finding the self? An event-related fMRI study. *Journal of Cognitive Neuroscience* 14: 785–794.

Keysar, B. (1994). The illusion of transparency of intention: Linguistic perspective taking in text. *Cognitive Psychology* 26: 165–208.

Keysar, B., and Bly, B. (1995). Intuitions of the transparency of idioms: Can one keep a secret by spilling the beans? *Journal of Memory and Language* 34: 89–109.

Keysar, B., Lin, S., and Barr, D. J. (2003). Limits on theory of mind use in adults. *Cognition* 89: 25–41.

Keysers, C., and Perrett, D. (2004). Demystifying social cognition: A Hebbian perspective. *Trends in Cognitive Sciences* 8: 501–507.

Keysers, C., Wicker, B., Gazzola, V., Anton, J.-L., Fogassi, L., and Gallese, V. (2004). A touching sight: SII/PV activation during the observation of touch. *Neuron* 42: 335–346.

Kieran, M. (2003). In search of a narrative. In M. Kieran and D. M. Lopes, eds., *Imagination, Philosophy, and the Arts* (69–87). London: Routledge.

Kim, J. (1993). The non-reductivist's troubles with mental causation. In J. Heil and A. Mele, eds., *Mental Causation* (189–210). Oxford: Oxford University Press.

————. (1998). *Mind in a Physical World*. Cambridge, MA: MIT Press.

Knoblich, G., and Flach, R. (2001). Predicting the effects of actions: Interactions of perception and action. *Psychological Science* 12(6): 467–472.

Knoblich, G., and Prinz, W. (2001). Recognition of self-generated actions from kinematic displays of drawing. *Journal of Experimental Psychology: Human Perception and Performance* 27: 456–465.

Koepp, M. J., Gunn, R. N., Lawrence, A. D., Cunningham, V. J., Dagher, A., Jones, T., Brooks, D. J., Bench, C. J., and Grasby, P. M. (1998). Evidence for striatal dopamine release during a videogame. *Nature* 393: 266–268.

Kögler, H. H., and Stueber, K. R., eds. (2000). *Empathy and Agency: The Problem of Understanding in the Human Sciences.* Boulder, CO: Westview.

Kohlberg, L. (1984). *The Psychology of Moral Development: The Nature and Validity of Moral Stages.* San Francisco: Harper and Row.

Kohler, E., Keysers, C., Umilta, M. A., Fogassi, L., Gallese, V., and Rizzolatti, G. (2002). Hearing sounds, understanding actions: Action representation in mirror neurons. *Science* 297: 846–848.

Kosslyn, S. M. (1978). Measuring the visual angle of the mind's eye *Cognitive Psychology* 7: 341–370.

———. (1980). *Image and Mind.* Cambridge, MA: Harvard University Press.

———. (1994). *Image and Brain: The Resolution of the Imagery Debate.* Cambridge, MA: MIT Press.

Kosslyn, S. M., Thompson, W. L., and Alpert, N. M. (1997). Neural systems shared by visual imagery and visual perception: A positron emission tomography study. *Neuro-Image* 6: 320–334.

Kosslyn, S. M., Pascual-Leone, A., Felician, O., and Camposano, S. (1999). The role of area 17 in visual imagery: Convergent evidence from PET from rTMS. *Science* 284: 167–170.

Krauss, R. M., and Glucksberg, S. (1969). The development of communication: Competence as a function of age. *Child Development* 40: 255–266.

La France, M. (1979). Nonverbal synchrony and rapport: Analysis by the cross-lag panel technique. *Social Psychology Quarterly* 42: 66–70.

———. (1982). Posture mirroring and rapport. In M. Davis, ed., *Interaction Rhythms: Periodicity in Communicative Behavior* (279–298). New York: Human Sciences.

La France, M., and Broadbent, M. (1976). Group rapport: Posture sharing as a nonverbal indicator. *Group and Organization Studies* 1: 328–333.

Lang, P., Levin, D., Miller, G., and Kozak, M. (1983). Fear behavior, fear imagery, and the psychophysiology of emotion: The problem of affective response integration. *Journal of Abnormal Psychology* 92: 276–306.

Langdon, R., and Coltheart, M. (2001). Visual perspective-taking and schizotypy: Evidence for a simulation-based account of mentalizing in normal adults. *Cognition* 82: 1–26.

Langdon, R., Michie, P. T., Ward, P. B., McGonaghy, N., Catts, S. V., and Coltheart, M. (1997). Defective self and/or other mentalizing in schizophrenia: A cognitive neuropsychological approach. *Cognitive Neuropsychiatry* 2: 167–193.

Latane, B., and Darley, J. M. (1968). Group inhibition of bystander intervention. *Journal of Personality and Social Psychology* 10: 215–221.

Laurence, S., and Margolis, E. (1999). Concepts and cognitive science. In E. Margolis and S. Laurence, eds., *Concepts: Core Readings* (3–81). Cambridge, MA: MIT Press.

Lawrence, A. D., and Calder, A. J. (2004). Homologizing human emotions. In D. Evans and P. Cruse, eds., *Emotions, Evolution and Rationality* (15–47). New York: Oxford University Press.

Lawrence, A. D., Calder, A. J., McGowan, S. M., and Grasby, P. M. (2002). Selective disruption of the recognition of facial expressions of anger. *NeuroReport* 13(6): 881–884.

Leaper, C. (1991). Influence and involvement in children's discourse: Age, gender, and partner effects. *Child Development* 62: 797–811.

Le Bon, G. (1896). *The Crowd: A Study of the Popular Mind.* London: Ernest Benn.

LePore, E., and Loewer, B. (1989). More on making mind matter. *Philosophical Topics* 17: 175–191.

Leslie, A. (1987). Pretence and representation: The origins of "theory of mind." *Psychological Review* 94: 412–426.

———. (1988). Some implications of pretense for mechanisms underlying the child's theory of mind. In J. Astington, P. Harris, and D. Olson, eds., *Developing Theories of Mind* (19–46). Cambridge: Cambridge University Press.

———. (1994). *Pretending* and *believing*: Issues in the theory of ToMM. *Cognition* 50: 211–238.

———. (2000). How to acquire a representational theory of mind. In D. Sperber, ed., *Metarepresentations: A Multidisciplinary Perspective* (197–223). New York: Oxford University Press.

Leslie, A., Friedman, O., and German, T. (2004). Core mechanisms in "theory of mind." *Trends in Cognitive Sciences* 8: 528–533.

Leslie, A., and German, T. (1995). Knowledge and ability in "theory of mind": One-eyed overview of a debate. In M. Davies and T. Stone, eds., *Mental Simulation* (123–150). Oxford: Blackwell.

Leslie, A., German, T., and Polizzi, P. (2005). Belief-desire reasoning as a process of selection. *Cognitive Psychology* 50: 45–85.

Leslie, A., and Polizzi, P. (1998). Inhibitory processing in the false belief task: Two conjectures. *Developmental Science* 1: 247–253.

Leslie, A., and Roth, D. (1993). What autism teaches us about metarepresentation. In S. Baron-Cohen, H. Tager-Flusberg, and D. Cohen, eds., *Understanding Other Minds: Perspectives from Autism* (83–111). Oxford: Oxford University Press.

Levelt, W. (1990). *Speaking: From Intention to Articulation.* Cambridge, MA: MIT Press.

Levine, D., Warach, J., and Farah, M. (1985). Two visual systems in mental imagery: Dissociation of "what" and "where" in imagery disorders due to bilateral posterior cerebral lesions. *Neurology* 35: 1010–1018.

Levine, J. (1993). On leaving out what it's like. In M. Davies and G. Humphries, eds., *Consciousness* (121–136). Oxford: Blackwell.

Lewis, C., Freeman, N., Hagestadt, C., and Douglas, H. (1994). Narrative access and production in preschoolers' false belief reasoning. *Cognitive Development* 9: 397–424.

Lewis, D. (1966). An argument for the identity theory. *Journal of Philosophy* 63: 17–25.

———. (1972). Psychophysical and theoretical identifications. *Australasian Journal of Philosophy* 50: 249–258. Reprinted in N. Block, ed., *Readings in Philosophy of Psychology*, Vol. 1 (1980). Cambridge, MA: Harvard University Press.

Lhermitte, F., Pillon, B., and Serdaru, M. (1986). Human autonomy and the frontal lobes. Part I: Imitation and utilization behavior: A neuropsychological study of 75 patients. *Annals of Neurology* 19(4): 326–334.

Lipps, T. (1903). Einfuhlung, innere nachahmung und organenempfindung. In *Archiv fur die Gesamte Psychologie*, Vol. 1, part 2. Leipzig: W. Engelmann.

Loar, B. (1990). Phenomenal states. In J. Tomberlin, ed., *Philosophical Perspectives* 4, *Action Theory and Philosophy of Mind* (81–108). Atascadero, CA: Ridgeview.

————. (2003). Phenomenal states (second version). In D. Chalmers, ed., *Philosophy of Mind* (295–311). New York: Oxford University Press.

Loewenstein, G., and Adler, D. (1995). A bias in the prediction of tastes. *Economic Journal: The Quarterly Journal of the Royal Economic Society* 105: 929–937.

Loewenstein, G., Prelec, D., and Shatto, C. (1998). Hot/cold intrapersonal empathy gaps and the prediction of curiosity. Working paper, Carnegie Mellon University.

Loewenstein, G., and Schkade, D. (1999). Wouldn't it be nice? Predicting future feelings. In D. Kahneman, E. Diener, and N. Schwartz, eds., *Well-Being: The Foundations of Hedonic Psychology* (85–105). New York: Russell Sage.

Lopes da Silva, F. H. (2003). Visual dreams in the congenitally blind? *Trends in Cognitive Sciences* 7(8): 328–330.

Lotze, M. and Montoya P. (1999). Activation of cortical and cerebellar motor areas during executed and imagined hand movements: An fMRI study. *Journal of Cognitive Neuroscience* 11: 491–501.

Loveland, K., and Landry, S. (1986). Joint attention and language in autism and developmental language delay. *Journal of Autism and Developmental Disorders* 16: 335–349.

Lundquist, L., and Dimberg, U. (1995). Facial expressions are contagious. *Journal of Psychophysiology* 9: 203–211.

Lycan, W. G. (1996). *Consciousness and Experience*. Cambridge, MA: MIT Press.

Lyons, W. (1986). *The Disappearance of Introspection*. Cambridge, MA: MIT Press.

Maccoby, E. E. (1998). *The Two Sexes: Growing Apart, Coming Together*. Cambridge, MA: Harvard University Press.

MacDonald, C. (1998). Externalism and authoritative self-knowledge. In C. Wright, B. C. Smith, and C. Macdonald, eds., *Knowing Our Own Minds* (123–154). Oxford: Oxford University Press.

Macrae, C. N., Moran, J. M., Heatherton, T. F., Banfield, J. F., and Kelley, W. M. (2004). Medial prefrontal activity predicts memory for self. *Cerebral Cortex* 14: 647–654.

Markram, H., and Lubke, J. (1997). Regulation of synaptic efficacy by coincidence of postsynaptic APs and EPSPs. *Science* 275: 213–215.

Marr, D. (1982). *Vision: A Computational Investigation into the Human Representation and Processing of Visual Information*. San Francisco: W. H. Freeman.

Maurer, D. (1985). Infants' perception of facedness. In T. Field and N. Fox, eds., *Social Perception in Infants*. Norwood, NJ: Ablex.

McCabe, K., Houser, D., Ryan, L., Smith, V., and Trouard, T. (2001). A functional imaging study of cooperation in two-person reciprocal exchange. *Proceedings of the National Academy of Sciences* 98: 11832–11835.

McDowell, J. (1991). Intentionality and interiority in Wittgenstein. In K. Puhl, ed, *Meaning Scepticism*. Berlin: de Gruyter.

————. (1998). Response to Crispin Wright. In C. Wright, B. C. Smith, and C. Macdonald, eds, *Knowing Our Own Minds*. Oxford: Oxford University Press.

McGee, V. (2005). Inscrutability and its discontents. *Nous* 39: 397–425.

McGinn, C. (1977). Charity, interpretation, and belief. *Journal of Philosophy* 74: 521–535.

McKinsey, M. (1991). Anti-individualism and privileged access. *Analysis* 51: 9–16.

McLaughlin, B. (1989). Type epiphenomenalism, type dualism, and the causal priority of the physical. *Philosophical Perspectives* 3: 109–136.

McLaughlin, B., and Tye, M. (1998). Externalism, Twin Earth, and self-knowledge. In C. Wright, B. C. Smith, and C. Macdonald, eds., *Knowing Our Own Minds* (285–320). Oxford: Oxford University Press.

Meltzoff, A. N. (1988). Infant imitation after a 1-week delay: Long-term memory for novel acts and multiple stimuli. *Developmental Psychology* 24: 470–476.

———. (1995). Understanding the intentions of others: Re-enactment of intended acts by 18-month-old children. *Developmental Psychology* 31: 838–850.

———. (1999). Imitation. In F. Keil and R. Wilson, eds., *The MIT Encyclopedia of the Cognitive Sciences* (389–390). Cambridge, MA: MIT Press.

———. (2005). Imitation and other minds: The "like-me" hypothesis. In S. Hurley and N. Chater, eds., *Perspectives on Imitation: From Neuroscience to Social Science*, Vol. 2 (55–77). Cambridge, MA: MIT Press.

Meltzoff, A. N., and Brooks, R. (2003). "Like-me" understanding in the development of gaze following. Paper presented at the Northwest Cognition and Memory Conference (NOWCAM). Seattle, WA, June 2003.

Meltzoff, A. N. and Decety, J. (2003). What imitation tells us about social cognition: a rapprochement between developmental psychology and cognitive neuroscience. *Philosophical Transactions of the Royal Society of London*, Series B, 358:491–500.

Meltzoff, A. N., and Moore, M. K. (1977). Imitation of facial and manual gestures by human neonates. *Science* 198: 75–78.

———. (1983). Newborn infants imitate adult facial gestures. *Child Development* 54: 702–709.

———. (1989). Imitation in newborn infants: Exploring the range of gestures imitated and the underlying mechanisms. *Developmental Psychology* 25: 954–962.

———. (1995). Infants' understanding of people and things: From body imitation to folk psychology. In J. Bermudez, A. J. Marcel, and N. Eilan, eds., *Body and the Self* (43–69). Cambridge: Cambridge University Press.

———. (1997). Explaining facial imitation: A theoretical model. *Early Development and Parenting* 6: 179–192.

Meltzoff, A. N., and Prinz, W., eds. (2002). *The Imitative Mind: Development, Evolution, and Brain Bases*. Cambridge: Cambridge University Press.

Mesulam, M. M. (1981). Dissociative states with abnormal temporal lobe EEG. Multiple personality and the illusion of possession. *Archives of Neurology* 38: 176–181.

Metzinger, T. (2003). *Being No One: The Self-Model Theory of Subjectivity*. Cambridge, MA: MIT Press.

Milgram, S. (1963). Behavioral study of obedience. *Journal of Abnormal and Social Psychology* 67: 371–378.

Millikan, R. (1989). Biosemantics. *Journal of Philosophy* 86: 281–297.

Milner, A. D., and Goodale, M. A. (1995). *The Visual Brain in Action*. Oxford: Oxford University Press.

Mitchell, J. P., Banaji, M. R., and Macrae, C. N. (2005). The link between social cognition and self-referential thought in the medial prefrontal cortex. *Journal of Cognitive Neuroscience* 17:1306–1315.

Mitchell, P., and Lacohee, H. (1991). Children's early understanding of false belief. *Cognition* 39: 107–127.

Monson, C. K., and Hurlburt, R. T. (1993). A comment to suspend the introspection controversy: Introspecting subjects did agree about "imageless thought." In R. T. Hurlburt, ed., *Sampling Inner Experience in Disturbed Affect*. New York: Plenum.

Montgomery, R. (1987). Psychologism, folk psychology, and one's own case. *Journal for the Theory of Social Behavior* 17: 195–218.

Moore, C., Jarrold, C., Russell, L., Lumb, A., Sapp, F., and MacCallum, F. (1995). Conflicting desire and the child's theory of mind. *Cognitive Development* 10: 467–482.

Morrison, I., Lloyd, D., de Pelligrino, G., and Roberts, N. (2004). Vicarious responses to pain in anterior cingulate cortex: Is empathy a multisensory issue? *Cognitive, Affective, Behavioral Neuroscience* 4:270–278.

Mundy, P., Sigman, M., Ungerer, J., and Sherman, T. (1986). Defining the social deficits in autism: The contribution of nonverbal communication measures. *Journal of Child Psychology and Psychiatry* 27: 657–669.

Nadel, J., and Butterworth, G. (1999). *Imitation in Infancy*. Cambridge: Cambridge University Press.

Newton, E. (1990). *Overconfidence in the Communication of Intent: Heard and Unheard Melodies*. Unpublished doctoral dissertation, Stanford University.

Nichols, K., and Champness, B. (1971). Eye gaze and the GSR. *Journal of Experimental Social Psychology* 7: 623–626.

Nichols, S. (2004a). Imagining and believing: The promise of a single code. *Journal of Aesthetics and Art Criticism* 62:129–140.

———. (2004b). *Sentimental Rules: On the Natural Foundations of Moral Judgment*. New York: Oxford University Press.

Nichols, S., and Stich, S. (1998). Rethinking co-cognition. *Mind and Language* 13(4): 499–512.

———. (2000). A cognitive theory of pretense. *Cognition* 74:115–147.

———. (2003). *Mindreading: An Integrated Account of Pretence, Self-Awareness, and Understanding of Other Minds*. Oxford: Oxford University Press.

Nichols, S., Stich, S. P., and Leslie, A. (1995). Choice effects and the ineffectiveness of simulation. *Mind and Language* 10(4): 437–445.

Nichols, S., Stich, S. P., Leslie, A., and Klein, D. (1996). Varieties of off-line simulation. In P. Carruthers and P. Smith, eds., *Theories of Theories of Mind* (39–74). Cambridge: Cambridge University Press.

Nickerson, R. S. (1999). How we know—and sometimes misjudge—what others know: Imputing one's own knowledge to others. *Psychological Bulletin* 125: 737–759.

———. (2001). The projective way of knowing. *Current Directions in Psychological Science* 10: 168–172.

Nietzsche, F. (1881/1977). Daybreak. In R. J. Hollingdale, trans., *A Nietzsche Reader*. Harmondsworth, England: Penguin.

Nisbett, R., and Wilson, T. (1977). Telling more than we can know. *Psychological Review* 84: 231–259.

Nozick, R. (1981). *Philosophical Explanations*. Cambridge, MA: Harvard University Press.

Nussbaum, M. (2001). *Upheavals of Thought: The Intelligence of Emotions*. New York: Cambridge University Press.

Oberman, L. M., Hubbard, E. M., McCleery, J. P., Altschuler, E. L., Ramachandran, V. S., and Pineda, J. A. (2005). EEG evidence for mirror neuron dysfunction in autism spectrum disorders. *Cognitive Brain Research* 24:190–198.

O'Craven, K. M., and Kanwisher, N. (2000). Mental imagery of faces and places activates corresponding stimulus-specific brain regions. *Journal of Cognitive Neuroscience* 12:1013–1023.

O'Neill, D. (1996). Two-year-old children's sensitivity to a parent's knowledge state when making requests. *Child Development* 67: 659–677.

Onishi, K. H., and Baillargeon, R. (2005). Do 15-month-old infants understand false beliefs? *Science* 308: 255–258.

O'Regan, J. K. (1992). Solving the "real" mysteries of visual perception: The world as an outside memory. *Canadian Journal of Psychology* 46: 461–488.

O'Regan, J. K., Rensink, R. A., and Clark, J. J. (1999). Change-blindness as a result of "mudsplashes." *Nature* 398: 34.

Orliaguet, J. P., Kandel, S., and Boe, L. J. (1997). Visual perception of motor anticipation in cursive hand writing: Influence of spatial and movement information on the prediction of forthcoming letters. *Perception* 26(7): 905–912.

Ozonoff, S., Pennington, B. F., and Rogers, S. J. (1991). Executive function deficits in high-functioning autistic individuals: Relationship to theory of mind. *Journal of Child Psychology and Psychiatry* 32: 1081–1095.

Papineau, D. (1987). *Reality and Representation*. Oxford: Blackwell.

Papousek, H., and Papousek, M. (1979). Early ontogeny of human social interaction: Its biological roots and social dimensions. In M. von Cranach, K. Foppa, W. Lepenies, and D. Ploog, eds., *Human Ethology: Claims and Limits of a New Discipline*. Cambridge: Cambridge University Press.

Parfit, D. (1984). *Reasons and Persons*. Oxford: Clarendon.

Parsons, L. M. (1987). Imagined spatial transformation of one's hand and feet. *Cognitive Psychology* 19: 178–241.

———. (1994). Temporal and kinematic properties of motor behavior reflected in mentally simulated action. *Journal of Experimental Psychology* 20: 709–730.

Parsons, L., Gabrieli, J., Phelps, E., and Gazzaniga, M. (1998). Cerebrally lateralized mental representations of hand shape and movement. *Journal of Neuroscience* 18: 6539–6548.

Peacocke, C. (1992). *A Study of Concepts*. Cambridge, MA: MIT Press.

———. (1996). Entitlement, self-knowledge and conceptual redeployment. *Proceedings of the Aristotelian Society* 96: 117–158.

———. (1998). Conscious attitudes, attention, and self-knowledge. In C. Wright, B. Smith, and C. Macdonald, eds., *Knowing Our Own Minds* (63–98). Oxford: Oxford University Press.

———. (1999). *Being Known*. Oxford: Oxford University Press.

Pearl, J. (2000). *Causality*. New York: Oxford University Press.

Pennington, B., Rogers, S. J., Bennetto, L., Griffith, E. M., Reed, D. T., and Shyu, V. (1997). Validity tests of the executive dysfunction hypothesis of autism. In J. Russell, ed., *Autism as an Executive Disorder* (143–178). Oxford: Oxford University Press.

Perky, C. W. (1910). An experimental study of imagination. *American Journal of Psychology* 21(3): 422–452.

Perner, J. (1991). *Understanding the Representational Mind*. Cambridge, MA: MIT Press.

———. (2000). About + belief + counterfactual. In P. Mitchell and K. Riggs, eds., *Children's Reasoning and the Mind* (367–401). Hove, England: Psychology Press.

Perner, J., and Howes, D. (1992). "He thinks he knows": and more developmental evidence against the simulation (role taking) theory. *Mind and Language* 7(1–2): 72–86.

Perner, J., and Lang, B. (2000). Theory of mind and executive function: Is there a developmental relationship? In S. Baron-Cohen, H. Tager-Flusberg, and D. Cohen, eds., *Understanding Other Minds: Perspectives from Developmental Cognitive Neuroscience*, 2nd ed (150–181). Oxford: Oxford University Press.

Perner, J., Leekam, S., and Wimmer, H. (1987). Three-year-olds' difficulty with false belief: The case for a conceptual deficit. *British Journal of Developmental Psychology* 5: 125–137.

Phillips, M. L., Young, A. W., Senior, C., Brammer, M., Andrew, C., Calder, A. J., Bullmore, E. T., Perrett, D. I., Rowland, D., Williams, S. C. R., Gray, J. A., and David, S. (1997). A specific neural substrate for perceiving facial expressions of disgust. *Nature* 389: 495–498.

Piaget, J. (1932/1948). *The Moral Judgment of the Child*. Glencoe, IL: Free Press.

Pitt, D. (2004). The phenomenology of cognition or what is it like to think that p? *Philosophy and Phenomenological Research* 69: 1–36.

Poe, E. A. (1845/1990). *Selected Works* (unabridged edition). New York: Gramercy.

Povinelli, D., and Eddy, T. J. (1996). What young chimpanzees know about seeing. *Monographs of the Society for Research in Child Development* 61: 1–152.

Premack, D., and Woodruff, G. (1978). Does the chimpanzee have a theory of mind? *Behavioral and Brain Sciences* 1: 515–526.

Preston, S., and de Waal, F. (2002). Empathy: Its ultimate and proximal bases. *Behavioral and Brain Sciences* 25: 1–20.

Prinz, J. J. (2004). The fractionation of introspection. *Journal of Consciousness Studies* 11(7–8): 40–57.

Prinz, W. (1990). A common coding approach to perception and action. In O. Neumann and W. Prinz, eds., *Relationships between Perception and Action: Current Approaches* (167–201). Berlin: Springer-Verlag.

———. (1997). Perception and action planning. *European Journal of Cognitive Psychology* 9: 129–154.

Pritchard, T. C., Macaluso, D. A., and Eslinger, P. J. (1999). Taste perception in patients with insular cortex lesions. *Behavioral Neuroscience* 113: 663–671.

Pronin, E., Puccio, C., and Ross, L. (2002). Understanding misunderstanding: Social psychological perspectives. In T. Gilovich, T. Griffin, and D. Kahneman, eds., *Heuristics and Biases: The Psychology of Intuitive Judgment* (636–665). Cambridge: Cambridge University Press.

Putnam, H. (1960). Minds and machines. In S. Hook, ed., *Dimensions of Mind*. New York: New York University Press.

———. (1975). The meaning of "meaning." In *Mind, Language and Reality: Philosophical Papers*, Vol. 2. (215–271). Cambridge: Cambridge University Press.

———. (1978). *Meaning and the Moral Sciences*. London: Routledge and Kegan Paul.

Pylyshyn, Z. W. (1981). The imagery debate: Analogue media versus tacit knowledge. *Psychological Review* 88: 16–45.

———. (1994). Some primitive mechanisms of spatial attention. *Cognition* 50(1–3): 363–384.

———. (1999). Is vision continuous with cognition? The case for cognitive impenetrability of visual perception. *Behavioral and Brain Sciences* 22(3): 341–423.

———. (2003a). Return of the mental image: Are there really pictures in the brain? *Trends in Cognitive Sciences* 7(3): 113–118.

———. (2003b). *Seeing and Visualizing: It's Not What You Think; An Essay on Vision and Visual Imagination.* Cambridge, MA: MIT Press.

Quine, W. V. O. (1960). *Word and Object.* Cambridge, MA: MIT Press.

———. (1990). *Pursuit of Truth.* Cambridge, MA: MIT Press.

Rall, J., and Harris, P. L. (2000). In Cinderella's slippers: Story comprehension from the protagonist's point of view. *Developmental Psychology* 36: 202–208.

Ramsey, F. P. (1931). *The Foundations of Mathematics.* R. B. Braithwaite, ed. London: Routledge and Kegan Paul.

Rawls, J. (1971). *A Theory of Justice.* Cambridge, MA: Harvard University Press.

Read, D., and van Leeuwen, B. (1998). Predicting hunger: The effects of appetite and delay on choice. *Organizational Behavior and Human Decision Processes* 78: 189–205.

Recanati, F. (2002). The Fodorian fallacy. *Analysis* 62: 285–289.

Reichenbach, H. (1956). *The Direction of Time.* Berkeley: University of California Press.

Repacholi, B., and Gopnik, A. (1997). Early understanding of desires: Evidence from 14 and 18 month olds. *Developmental Psychology* 33: 12–21.

Reynolds, C. W. (1987). Flocks, herds, and schools: A distributed behavioral model. *Computer Graphics* 21: 25–34.

———. (1993). An evolved, vision-based behavioral model of coordinated group motion. In J.-A. Meyer, H. L. Roitblat, and S. W. Wilson, eds., *From Animals to Animats* 2 (384–392). Cambridge, MA: MIT Press.

Riggs, K., Peterson, D., Robinson, E., and Mitchell, P. (1998). Are errors in false belief tasks symptomatic of a broader difficulty with counterfactuality? *Cognitive Development* 13: 73–90.

Rinck, M., and Bower, G. H. (1995). Anaphora resolution and the focus of attention in situation models. *Journal of Memory and Language* 34: 110–131.

Ripstein, A. (1987). Explanation and empathy. *Review of Metaphysics* 40: 465–482.

Rizzolatti, G. (2005). The mirror neuron system and imitation. In S. Hurley and N. Chater, eds., *Perspectives on Imitation: From Neuroscience to Social Science*, Vol. 1 (55–76). Cambridge, MA: MIT Press.

Rizzolatti, G., Fadiga, L., Gallese, V., and Fogasi, L. (1996). Premotor cortex and the recognition of motor actions. *Cognitive Brain Research* 3: 131–141.

Rizzolatti, G., Fogassi, L., and Gallese, V. (2001). Neurophysiological mechanisms underlying the understanding and imitation of action. *Nature Neuroscience Reviews* 2: 661–670.

Robbins, P. (2004). Knowing me, knowing you: Theory of mind and the machinery of introspection. *Journal of Consciousness Studies* 11(7–8): 129–143.

Robinson, E. J. (1994). What people say, what they think, and what really is the case: Children's understanding of utterances as sources of knowledge. In C. Lewis and P. Mitchell, eds., *Children's Early Understanding of Mind*. Hove: England: Lawrence Erlbaum.

Rogers, S. J., Hepburn, S. L., Stackhouse, T., and Wehner, E. (2003). Imitation performance in toddlers with autism and those with other developmental disorders. *Journal of Child Psychology and Psychiatry and Allied Disciplines* 44: 763–781.

Rogers, S. J., and Pennington, B. F. (1991). A theoretical approach to the deficits in infantile autism. *Developmental Psychopathology* 3: 137–162.

Rolls, E. T. (1994). Central taste anatomy and neurophysiology. In R. L. Doty, ed., *Handbook of Clinical Olfaction and Gustation*. New York: Dekker.

Rosen, C., Schwebel, D., and Singer, J. (1997). Preschoolers' attributions of mental states in pretense. *Child Development* 68: 1133–1142.

Rosenthal, D. M. (1993). Thinking that one thinks. In M. Davies and G. Humphreys, eds., *Consciousness* (197–223). Cambridge, MA: Blackwell.

Ross, L., Greene, D., and House, P. (1977). The false consensus effect: An egocentric bias in social perception and attribution processes. *Journal of Personality and Social Psychology* 13: 279–301.

Roth, M., Decety, J., Raybaudi, M., Massarelli, R., Delon-Martin, C., Segebarth, C., Morand, S., Gemignani, A., Decorps, M., and Jeannerod, M. (1996). Possible involvement of primary motor cortex in mentally simulated movement. A functional magnetic resonance imaging study. *NeuroReport* 7: 1280–1284.

Rozin, P., and Fallon, A. E. (1987). A perspective on disgust. *Psychological Review* 94: 23–41.

Rozin P., Haidt J., and McCauley, C. (2000). Disgust. In M. Lewis and J. Haviland, eds., *Handbook of Emotions*. New York: Guilford.

Rozin, P., and Nemeroff, C. (1991). The laws of sympathetic magic: A psychological analysis of similarity and contagion. In J. Stigler, G. Herdt, and R. A. Shweder, eds., *Cultural Psychology: Essays on Comparative Human Development*. Cambridge: Cambridge University Press.

Ruby, P., and Decety, J. (2001). Effect of subjective perspective taking during simulation of action: A PET investigation of agency. *Nature Neuroscience* 4(5): 546–550.

———. (2003). What you believe versus what you think they believe: A neuroimaging study of conceptual perspective-taking. *European Journal of Neuroscience* 17: 2475–2480.

———. (2004). How would *you* feel versus how do you think *she* would feel? A neuroimaging study of perspective taking with social emotions. *Journal of Cognitive Neuroscience* 16: 988–999.

Ruffman, T. (1996). Do children understand the mind by means of simulation or a theory? Evidence from their understanding of inference. *Mind and Language* 11: 388–414.

Ruffman, T., and Olson, D. R. (1989). Children's ascriptions of knowledge to others. *Developmental Psychology* 25: 601–606.

Russell, J., ed. (1997). *Autism as an Executive Disorder*. Oxford: Oxford University Press.

Russell, J., Mauthner, N., Sharpe, S., and Tidswell, T. (1991). The "windows task" as a measure of strategic deception in preschoolers and autistic subjects. *British Journal of Developmental Psychology* 9: 331–349.

Ryle, G. (1949). *The Concept of Mind*. London: Hutchinson.

Sacks, O. (1995). *An Anthropologist on Mars*. New York: Knopf.

Saltmarsh, R., Mitchell, P., and Robinson, E. (1995). Realism and children's early grasp of mental representation: Belief-based judgments in the state change task. *Cognition* 57: 297–325.

Samson, D., Apperly, I. A., Kathirgamanathan, U., and Humphreys, G. W. (2005). Seeing it my way: A case of a selective deficit in inhibiting self-perspective. *Brain* 128: 1102–1111.

Samuels, R. (2000). Massively modular minds: Evolutionary psychology and cognitive architecture. In P. Carruthers and A. Chamberlain, eds., *Evolution and the Human Mind* (13–46). Cambridge: Cambridge University Press.

Santos, L. R., Flombaum, J. I., and Webb, P. (in press). The evolution of human mindreading: How non-human primates can inform social cognitive neuroscience. In S. Platek, ed., *Evolutionary Cognitive Neuroscience*. Cambridge: MIT Press.

Saxe, R. (2005). Against simulation: The argument from error. *Trends in Cognitive Sciences* 9: 174–179.

Saxe, R., Carey, S., and Kanwisher, N. (2004). Understanding other minds: Linking developmental psychology and functional neuroimaging. *Annual Review of Psychology* 55: 87–124.

Saxe, R., and Kanwisher, N. (2003). People thinking about people: The role of the temporo-parietal junction in "theory of mind." *NeuroImage* 19: 1835–1842.

Saxe, R., and Wexler, A. (2005). Making sense of another mind: The role of the right temporo-parietal junction. *Neuropsychologia* 43: 1391–1399.

Schaffer, H. (1977). Early interactive development. In H. Schaffer, ed., *Studies in Mother-Infant Interaction*. New York: Academic Press.

Scheflen, A. E. (1964). The significance of posture in communication systems. *Psychiatry* 27: 316–331.

Schiffer, S. (unpublished). Comment on Jerry Fodor's "There are no recognitional concepts; not even red." New York University, Department of Philosophy.

Schmitz, T. W., Kawahara-Baccus, T. N., and Johnson, S. C. (2004). Metacognitive evaluation, self-relevance, and the right prefrontal cortex. *Neuroimage* 22: 941–947.

Scholl, B., and Leslie, A. M. (1999). Modularity, development and "theory of mind." *Mind and Language* 14: 131–153.

———. (2001). Minds, modules and meta-analysis. *Child Development* 72: 696–701.

Scholl, B., and Tremoulet, P. (2000). Perceptual causality and animacy. *Trends in Cognitive Sciences* 4: 299–309.

Schooler, J., Reichle, E. D., and Halpern, D. V. (2004). Zoning-out during reading: Evidence for dissociations between experience and meta-consciousness. In D. Levin, ed., *Thinking and Seeing: Visual Meta-Cognition in Adults and Children*. Cambridge, MA: MIT Press.

Schopenhauer, A. (1841/1965). *On the Basis of Morality*, A. F. J. Payne, trans. Indianapolis, IN: Bobbs-Merrill.

Schwarz, N., and Strack, F. (1991). Evaluating one's life: A judgment model of subjective well-being. In F. Strack, M Argyle, and N. Schwarz, eds., *Subjective Well-Being*. Oxford: Pergamon.

Schwebel, D. C., Rosen, C. S., and Singer, J. L. (1999). Preschoolers' pretend play and theory of mind: The role of jointly constructed pretence. *British Journal of Developmental Psychology* 17: 333–348.

Schwoebel, J., Boronat, C. B., and Coslett, H. B. (2002). The man who executed "imagined" movements: Evidence for dissociable components of the body schema. *Brain and Cognition* 50: 1–16.

Sebanz, N., Knoblich, G., and Prinz., W. (2003). Representing others' actions: Just like one's own? *Cognition* 88: B11–B21.

Segal, S. J., and Fusella, V. (1970). Influence of imaged pictures and sounds in detection of visual and auditory signals. *Journal of Experimental Psychology* 83: 458–474.

Sellars, W. (1955/1997). *Empiricism and the Philosophy of Mind*. Cambridge, MA: Harvard University Press.

Shah, A., and Frith, U. (1983). An islet of ability in autistic children: A research note. *Journal of Child Psychology and Psychiatry* 24: 613–620.

Shanton, K. (unpublished). A simulationist account of first-person past mindreading. Rutgers University, Department of Philosophy.

Shaw, L. L., Batson, C. D., and Todd, R. M. (1994). Empathy avoidance: Forestalling feeling for another in order to escape the motivational consequence. *Journal of Personality and Social Psychology* 67: 879–887.

Shepard, R., and Cooper, L. (1982). *Mental Images and Their Transformations*. Cambridge, MA: MIT Press.

Shepard, R., and Metzler, J. (1971). Mental rotation of three-dimensional objects. *Science* 171: 701–703.

Shoemaker, S. (1975). Functionalism and qualia. *Philosophical Studies* 27: 291–315.
———. (1996). *The First-Person Perspective and Other Essays*. New York: Cambridge University Press.

Siegman, A. W., Anderson, R. A., and Berger, T. (1990). The angry voice: Its effects on the experience of anger and cardiovascular reactivity. *Psychosomatic Medicine* 52: 631–643.

Siewert, C. P. (1998). *The Significance of Consciousness*. Princeton, NJ: Princeton University Press.

Sigman, M., Kasari, C., Kwon, J., and Yirmiya, N. (1992). Responses to the negative emotions of others by autistic, mentally retarded, and normal children. *Child Development* 63: 796–807.

Sigman, M., Mundy, P., Sherman, T., and Ungerer, J. (1986). Social interactions of autistic, mentally retarded, and normal children and their caregivers. *Journal of Child Psychology and Psychiatry* 27: 657–669.

Simner, M. L. (1971). Newborns' response to the cry of another infant. *Developmental Psychology* 5: 136–150.

Simons, D. J., and Rensink, R. A. (2005). Change blindness: Past, present, and future. *Trends in Cognitive Sciences* 9: 16–20.

Singer, P. (1981). *The Expanding Circle*. Oxford: Clarendon.
———. (1988). Reasoning towards utilitarianism. In D. Seanor and N. Fotion, eds., *Hare and Critics*. Oxford: Clarendon.

Singer, T., Seymour, B., O'Doherty, J., Kaube, H., Dolan, R., and Frith, C. (2004). Empathy for pain involves the affective but not sensory components of pain. *Science* 303: 1157–1162.

Sirigu, A., Duhamel, J., Pillon, B., Cohen, L., Dubois, B., and Agid, Y. (1996). The mental representation of hand movements after parietal cortex damage. *Science* 273: 1564–1568.

Sirigu, A., Duhamel, J., Pillon, B., Cohen, L., Dubois, B., Agid, Y., and Pierrot-Deseilligny, C. (1995). Congruent unilateral impairments for real and imagined hand movements. *NeuroReport* 6: 997–1001.

Small, D. M., Gregory, M., Mak, R., Gitelman, D., Mesulam, M. M., and Parrish, T. (2003). Dissociation of neural representation of intensity and affective valuation in human gestation. *Neuron* 39: 701–711.

Small, D. M., Zald, D. H., Jones-Gotman, M., Zatorre, R. J., Pardo, J. V., Frey, S., and Petrides, M. (1999). Brain imaging: Human cortical gustatory areas: A review of functional neuroimaging data. *NeuroReport* 10: 7–14.

Smith, A. (1759/1976). *A Theory of Moral Sentiments*. D. D. Raphael and A. L. Macfie, eds. Oxford: Clarendon.

Smith, B. C. (1998). On knowing one's own language. In C. Wright, B. Smith, and C. Macdonald, eds., *Knowing Our Own Minds* (391–428). Oxford: Oxford University Press.

Soja, N., Carey, S., and Spelke, E. (1991). Ontological categories guide inductions of word meaning: Object terms and substance terms. *Cognition* 38: 179–211.

Spelke, E. (1990). Origins of visual knowledge. In D. N. Osherson, S. M. Kosslyn, and J. M. Hollerbach, eds., *Visual Cognition and Action* (99–127). Cambridge, MA: MIT Press.

———. (1994). Initial knowledge: Six suggestions. *Cognition* 50: 431–445.

Spence, S. A., Brooks, D. J., Hirsch, S. R., Liddle, P. F., Meehan, J., and Grasby, P. M. (1997). A PET study of voluntary movement in schizophrenic patients experiencing passivity phenomena (delusion of alien control). *Brain* 120: 1997–2011.

Sperber, D. (1997). Intuitive and reflective beliefs. *Mind and Language* 12: 67–83.

———. (2005). The variety of human social cognition. http://www.interdisciplines .org/mirror/papers/3/1/3_1.

Spirtes, P., Glymour, C., and Scheines, R. (2001). *Causation, Prediction, and Search* (Springer Lecture Notes in Statistics, 2nd ed., rev.). Cambridge, MA: MIT Press.

Spivey, M., Tyler, M., Richardson, D., and Young, E. (2000). Eye movements during comprehension of spoken scene descriptions. In *Proceedings of the 22nd annual conference of the Cognitive Science Society* (487–492). Mahwah, NJ: Erlbaum.

Sprengelmeyer R., Young, A. W., Schroeder, U., Grossenbacher, P. G., Federlein, J., Buttner, T., and Przuntek, H. (1999). Knowing no fear. *Proceedings of the Royal Society, series B: Biology* 266: 2451–2456.

Sripada, C. S., and Goldman, A. I. (2005). Simulation and the evolution of mind-reading. In A. Zilhao, ed., *Evolution, Rationality and Cognition: A Cognitive Science for the Twenty-First Century* (148–161). London: Routledge.

Stanovich, K. (2004). *The Robot's Rebellion: Finding Meaning in the Age of Darwin*. Chicago: University of Chicago Press.

Stein, E. (1996). *Without Good Reason*. Oxford: Oxford University Press.

Stern, D. (1977). *The First Relationship: Infant and Mother*. Cambridge, MA: Harvard University Press.

Stich, S. (1981). Dennett on intentional systems. *Philosophical Topics* 12: 38–62.

Stich, S., and Nichols, S. (1992). Folk psychology: Simulation or tacit theory? *Mind and Language* 7: 35–71.

———. (1997). Cognitive penetrability, rationality and restricted simulation. *Mind and Language* 12(3–4): 297–326.

Strack, F., Martin, L., and Stepper, S. (1988). Inhibiting and facilitating conditions of the human smile: A nonobtrusive test of the facial feedback hypothesis. *Journal of Personality and Social Psychology* 54(5): 768–777.

Strack, F., Schwarz, N., and Gschneidinger, E. (1985). Happiness and reminiscing: The role of time perspective, mood, and mode of thinking. *Journal of Personality and Social Psychology* 49: 1460–1469.

Strawson, G. (1994). *Mental Reality*. Cambridge, MA: MIT Press.

Tager-Flusberg, H., and Sullivan, K. (2000). A componential view of theory of mind: evidence from Williams syndrome. *Cognition* 76:59–89.

Taylor, M., and Carlson, S. M. (1997). The relation between individual differences in fantasy and theory of mind. *Child Development* 68: 436–455.

Taylor, S. (1989). *Positive Illusions: Creative Self-Deception and the Healthy Mind*. New York: Basic Books.

Tolman, E. C. (1932). *Purposive Behavior in Animals and Men*. New York: Century.

Tomkins, S. (1963). *Affect, Imagery, Consciousness: The Negative Affects*, Vol. 2. New York: Springer.

Townsend, D. J., and Bever, T. G. (2001). *Sentence Comprehension: The Integration of Habits and Rules*. Cambridge, MA: MIT Press.

Treisman, A. (1996). The binding problem. *Current Opinion in Neurobiology* 6: 171–178.

Treisman, A., and Gelade, G. (1980). A feature integration theory of attention. *Cognitive Psychology* 12: 97–136.

Trout, D., and Rosenfeld, H. M. (1980). The effect of postural lean and body congruence on the judgment of psychotherapeutic rapport. *Journal of Nonverbal Communication* 4: 176–190.

Tversky, A., and Kahneman, D. (1974) Judgment under uncertainity: Heuristics and biases. *Science* 185: 1124–1131.

Tye, M. (1995). *Ten Problems of Consciousness: A Representational Theory of the Phenomenal Mind*. Cambridge, MA: MIT Press.

———. (1997). A representational theory of pains and their phenomenal character. In N. Block, O. Flanagan, and G. Guzeldere, eds., *The Nature of Consciousness* (329–340). Cambridge, MA: MIT Press.

———. (2002). Visual qualia and visual content revisited. In D. Chalmers, ed. *Philosophy of Mind* (447–456). New York: Oxford University Press.

Umilta, M. A., Kohler, E., Gallese, V., Fogassi, L., Fadiga, L., Keysers, C., and Rizzolatti, G. (2001). I know what you are doing: A neurophysiological study. *Neuron* 31(1): 155–165.

Van Boven, L., Dunning, D., and Loewenstein, G. (2000). Egocentric empathy gaps between owners and buyers: Misperceptions of the endowment effect. *Journal of Personality and Social Psychology* 79: 66–76.

Van Boven, L., and Loewenstein, G. (2003). Social projection of transient drive states. *Personality and Social Psychology Bulletin* 29(9): 1159–1168.

Vaughan, K. B., and Lanzetta, J. T. (1981). The effect of modification of expressive displays on vicarious emotional arousal. *Journal of Experimental Social Psychology* 17: 16–30.

Viviani, P. (2002). Motor competence in the perception of dynamic events: A tutorial. In W. Prinz and B. Hommel, eds., *Common Mechanisms in Perception and Action*, Vol. 19 (406–442). *Attention and Performance*. New York: Oxford University Press.

Vogeley, K., Bussfeld, P., Newen, A., Herrmann, S., Happe, F., Falkai, P., Maier, W., Shah, N. J., Fink, G. R., and Zilles, K. (2001). Mind reading: Neural mechanisms of theory of mind and self-perspective. *NeuroImage* 14: 170–181.

Vogeley, K., May, M., Ritzl, A., Falkai, P., Zilles, K., and Fink, G. R. (2004). Neural correlates of first-person perspective as one constituent of human self-consciousness. *Journal of Cognitive Neuroscience* 16: 817–827.

Vuilleumier, P., Richardson, M. P., Armony, J. L., Driver, J., and Dolan, R. J. (2004). Distant influences of amygdala lesion on visual cortical activation during emotional face processing. *Nature Neuroscience* 7: 1271–1278.

Vrana, S., Cuthburt, B., and Lang, P. (1989). Processing fearful and neutral sentences: Memory and heart rate change. *Cognition and Emotion* 3: 179–195.

Walton, K. (1990). *Mimesis as Make-Believe: On the Foundations of the Representational Arts*. Cambridge, MA: Harvard University Press.

———. (1997). Spelunking, simulation and slime: On being moved by fiction. In M. Hjort and S. Laver, eds., *Emotion and the Arts* (37–49). New York: Oxford University Press.

Webb, S. (1994). Witnessed behavior and Dennett's intentional stance. *Philosophical Topics* 22: 457–470.

Wegner, D. M. (1994). Ironic processes of mental control. *Psychological Review* 101: 34–52.

———. (2002). *The Illusion of Conscious Will*. Cambridge, MA: MIT Press.

Wegner, D. M., and Bargh, J. A. (1998). Control and automaticity in social life. In D. T. Gilbert and S. E. Fiske, eds., *The Handbook of Social Psychology*, 4th ed., Vol. 2 (446–496). New York: McGraw-Hill.

Wellman, H. (1990). *The Child's Theory of Mind*. Cambridge, MA: MIT Press.

Wellman, H. M., and Bartsch, K. (1988). Young children's reasoning about beliefs. *Cognition* 30: 239–277.

Wellman, H. M., Cross, D., and Watson, J. (2001). Meta-analysis of theory-of-mind development: The truth about false belief. *Child Development* 72: 655–684.

White, A. (1990). *The Language of Imagination*. Oxford: Blackwell.

Wicker, B., Keysers, C., Plailly, J., Royet, J.-P., Gallese, V., and Rizzolatti, G. (2003). Both of us disgusted in *my* insula: The common neural basis of seeing and feeling disgust. *Neuron* 40: 655–664.

Williams, J. H. G., Whiten, A., Suddendorf, T., and Perrett, D. I. (2001). Imitation, mirror neurons and autism. *Neuroscience and Biobehavioral Reviews* 25: 287–295.

Wilson, M. (2003). Imagined movements that leak out. *Trends in Cognitive Science* 7(2): 53–55.

Wilson, T. D. (2002). *Strangers to Ourselves: Discovering the Adaptive Unconscious.* Cambridge, MA: Harvard University Press.

Wimmer, H., Hogrefe, G., and Perner, J. (1988). Children's understanding of informational access as a source of knowledge. *Child Development* 59: 386–396.

Wimmer, H., Hogrefe, G., and Sodian, B. (1988). A second stage in children's conception of mental life: Understanding informational accesses as origins of knowledge and belief. In J. W. Astington, P. L. Harris, and D. R. Olson, eds., *Developing Theories of Mind* (173–194). Cambridge: Cambridge University Press.

Wimmer, H., and Perner, J. (1983). Beliefs about beliefs: Representation and constraining function of wrong beliefs in young children's understanding of deception. *Cognition* 13: 103–128.

Wittgenstein, L. (1953). *Philosophical Investigations*, trans. G. E. M. Anscombe. Oxford: Blackwell.

Wolf, D. P. (1982). Understanding others: A longitudinal case study of the concept of independent agency. In G. Forman, ed., *Action and Thought* (297–327). New York: Academic Press.

Wolpert, D. M. (1997). Computational approaches to motor control. *Trends in Cognitive Sciences* 1: 209–216.

Wolpert, D. M., Doya, K., and Kawato, M. (2004). A unifying computational framework for motor control and social interaction. In C. Frith and D. Wolpert, eds., *The Neuroscience of Social Interaction* (305–322). Oxford: Oxford University Press.

Wolpert, D. M., and Ghahramani, Z. (2000). Computational principles of movement neuroscience. *Nature Neuroscience* 3(suppl.): 1212–1217.

Wolpert, D. M., Gharamani, Z., and Jordan, M. (1995). An internal model for sensorimotor integration. *Science* 269: 1880–1882.

Wolpert, D. M., and Kawato, M. (1998). Multiple paired forward and inverse models for motor control. *Neural Networks* 11: 1317–1329.

Woodward, A. L. (1998). Infants selectively encode the goal object of an actor's reach. *Cognition* 69: 1–34.

———. (1999). Infants' ability to distinguish between purposeful and non-purposeful behaviors. *Infant Behavior and Development* 22: 145–160.

Woodward, A. L., Sommerville, J. A., and Guajardo, J. J. (2001). How infants make sense of intentional action. In B. Malle, L. Moses, and D. Baldwin, eds., *Intentions and Intentionality: Foundations of Social Cognition* (149–169). Cambridge, MA: MIT Press.

Wright, C. (1989). Wittgenstein's rule-following considerations and the central project of theoretical linguistics. In A. George, ed., *Reflections on Chomsky* (233–264). Oxford: Blackwell.

———. (1991). Wittgenstein's later philosophy of mind: Sensation, privacy and intention. In K. Puhl, ed., *Meaning Scepticism*. Berlin: de Gruyter.

———. (1998). Self-knowledge: The Wittgensteinian legacy. In C. Wright, B. C. Smith, and C. Macdonald, eds., *Knowing Our Own Minds* (13–45). Oxford: Oxford University Press.

Yablo, S. (1992). Mental causation. *Philosophical Review* 101: 245–280.

Yirmiya, N., Sigman, N., Kasari, C., and Mundy, P. (1992). Empathy and cognition in high-functioning children with autism. *Child Development* 63: 150–160.

Young, A. W., Humphreys, G. W., Riddoch, M. J., Hellawell, D. J, and deHaans, E. H. F. (1994). Recognition impairments and face imagery. *Neuropsychologia* 32: 693–702.

Youngblade, L. M., and Dunn, J. (1995). Individual differences in young children's pretend play with mother and sibling: Links to relationships and understanding of other people's feelings and beliefs. *Child Development* 66: 1472–1492.

Yue, G., and Cole, K. (1992). Strength increases from the motor program: Comparison of training with maximal voluntary and imagined muscle contractions. *Journal of Neurophysiology* 67: 1114–1123.

Zahn-Wexler, C., and Radke-Yarrow, M. (1982). The development of altruism: Alternative research strategies. In N. Eisenberg, ed., *The Development of Prosocial Behavior*. New York: Academic Press.

Zaitchik, D. (1991). Is only seeing really believing? Sources of the true belief in the false belief task. *Cognitive Development* 6: 91–103.

Zajonc, R. B., Adelmann, K. A., Murphy, S. T., and Niedenthal, P. M. (1987). Convergence in the physical appearance of spouses. *Motivation and Emotion* 11: 335–346.

Zysset, S., Huber, O., Ferstl, E., and von Cramon, D. Y. (2002). The anterior frontomedian cortex and evaluative judgment: An fMRI study. *Neuroimage* 15: 983–991.

Author Index

Aarts, H. 162
Adelmann, K.A. 277
Adelmann, P. 208
Adler, D. 173
Adolphs, R. 115, 117, 120–121,
  123, 127, 131
Agid, Y. 159
Agnetta, B. 145n19
Ahluwalia, J. 203
Akbudak, E. 163
Allen, D. 293
Alpert, N.M. 154
Altschuler, E.L. 206
Ames, D.R. 189n13
Anderson, A. 116
Anderson, R.A. 208
Andrew, C. 117
Aniskiewicz, A.S. 118
Anton, J.-L. 135, 137
Antoun, N. 117, 120, 122, 218
Apperly, I.A. 170–172, 190n16, 199
Armony, J.L. 121
Armstrong, D.M. 6, 25
Asch, S.E. 67n2
Asperger, H. 200–201
Astington, J. 12–13, 196, 235

Bachman, D. 154
Bacon, A. 293

Baillargeon, R. 77, 80, 86, 88,
  146n20, 292
Baird, G. 221n3
Baker, S. 141, 198
Baldwin, M.W. 208
Banaji, M.R. 51n8, 162–164, 189nn12, 14
Banfield, J.F. 163
Barbey, A.K. 145n16, 189n10
Bargh, J.A. 161, 162, 164, 207, 277–279
Barkow, J.H. 15
Baron-Cohen, S. 13–16, 19, 85, 95,
  109–110, 193, 200–207, 218,
  221nn2,3, 236
Barr, C.L. 207
Barr, D.J. 41, 166
Barrett, A.M. 131
Barsalou, L.W. 145n16, 189n10
Bartels, A. 119
Bartolomeo, P. 188n4
Bartsch, K. 76, 78–80, 93n6, 292
Basso, A. 153
Batkti, A. 203
Batson, C.D. 209, 290
Baxter, L.C. 163
Baynes, K. 231
Bechara, A. 115
Behrmann, M. 154
Bench, C.J. 219
Bennett, J. 11

Bennetto, L. 204
Benton, A.L. 120
Benuzzi, F. 122
Berger, T. 208
Bernieri, F.J. 276–277
Berntson, G.G. 126
Bertolo, H. 154
Beschin, N. 153
Bever, T.G. 184–185
Biederman, I. 260–262
Binkofski, F. 135
Birch, S.A.J. 41, 75, 165, 199
Bird, C.M. 141
Biro, S. 15, 53, 65–66, 68n
Bisiach, E. 153
Black, J.B. 288
Blackburn, S. 291
Blair, R.J.R. 116, 118, 122, 293, 303n5
Blairy, S. 130
Blakemore, S.-J. 144n9, 214
Blanchard, D.C. 219
Blanchard, R.J. 219
Block, N. 22n4
Bloom, P. 41, 72, 75, 165, 178, 199,
    303nn3,7
Bly, B. 41
Boe, L.J. 211
Boghossian, P. 62, 227–228
Boronat, C.B. 160
Botterill, G. 103, 105
Bower, G.H. 288
Brammer, M. 117
Brandt, S.A. 152
Broadbent, M. 276
Brockbank, M. 65
Brooks, D.J. 212, 219
Brooks, R. 194
Brouselle, E. 159
Brown, J. 228
Brugger, P. 155
Brunswick, N. 141, 198
Bryant, D.J. 288
Buccino, G. 122, 135, 138–140
Buchanan, T.W. 121
Buchel, C. 155
Budd, M. 188n1
Bullmore, E.T. 117
Burge, T. 177, 226–228, 255n5

Burrows, L. 161
Bush, L.K. 207
Bussfeld, P. 200
Butter, C. 188n3
Butterworth, G. 16, 196
Buttner, T. 116, 120–121
Byrne, R. 51n10, 218

Cacioppo, J.T. 126, 208, 277, 299
Caglar, S. 163
Calder, A.J. 116–118, 120–122,
    130–131, 218–219
Call, J. 145n19
Camerer, C. 41, 75, 165
Campbell, R. 130
Campbell, A. 301
Camposano, S. 154
Canessa, N. 122
Carrell, S.E. 208
Carey, S. 85, 88, 142, 178, 190n16,
    199–200
Carey, D.P. 264
Carlson S.M. 74, 196, 198–199
Carnap, R. 11
Carr, L. 130
Carroll, N. 286–287
Carruthers, P. 103, 105, 236
Casati, R. 178
Castelli, F. 141
Catts, S.V. 256n10
Chaiken, S. 207
Chalmers, D. 6, 250, 270–271,
    274–275nn11,12,14,17
Chaminade, T. 211–213
Champness, B. 16
Charman, T. 221n3, 293
Charney, E.J. 278
Chartrand, 162, 277–279
Chater, N. 195
Chatterjee, A. 154, 188n3
Chazot, G. 159
Chen, M. 161
Cherniak, C. 58
Chersi, F. 140
Chomsky, N. 85, 93n8, 102, 106
Chun, M.M. 154
Churchland, P.S. 217
Churchland, P.M. 6–7

Clark, F. 118, 122
Clark, J.J. 243
Clayton, N.S. 145n19
Clements, W.A. 77
Cohen, J.D. 291
Cohen, L. 159
Cole, J. 130
Cole, K. 158
Colledge, E. 116
Collingwood, R.G. 18
Coltheart, M. 171, 256n10
Condon, W.S. 276
Connellan, J. 203
Coplan, A. 286–287
Cooper, G. 127
Cooper, L. 39, 157
Corcoran, R. 237, 256n10
Corkum, V. 193
Coslett, H.B. 160
Cosmides, L. 15
Cox, A. 221n3
Craig, A.D. 252, 257n23
Craik, K. 51n10
Craver-Lemley, C. 152
Crelier, G. 155
Cross, D. 75–76, 91–92
Crucian, G.P. 131
Csibra, G. 15, 53, 65, 68n5
Cunningham, V.J. 219
Currie, G. 52n21, 112n, 188n1, 189n9, 220, 283, 286–288, 303n2
Cuthburt, B. 283

Dagher, A. 219
Damasio, A.R. 115–117, 120–121, 127, 154
Damasio, H. 115, 120, 127, 131, 154
Danks, D. 83–89
Darley, J.M. 161, 291
Darwin, C. 114
Dasheiff, R.M. 156
Dasser, V. 15
David, S. 117
Davidson, D. 8–9, 22n5, 53–54, 58–63
Davies, M. 32–33
Davis, M.H. 278
Davis, K.D. 136
de Pellegrino, G. 136

de Villiers, J. 87–88
de Villiers, P.A. 87–88
de Waal, F. 145n16, 207
Decety, J. 91, 136, 138, 144n9, 159, 160, 211–213, 221n9
Decorps, M. 160
deHaans, E.H.F. 154
Delon-Martin, C. 160
Dennett, D. 8–9, 11, 23, 31–32, 53–58, 60–64, 66, 220
Descartes, R. 5
Diamond, A. 198
Dijksterhuis, A. 161–162
Dilthey, W. 18
Dimberg, U. 129–130, 207
Dolan, R. 121, 136–137, 141, 198
Dominey, P. 159
Dostrovsky, J.O. 136
Douglas, H. 73
Doya, K. 215, 216–217, 221–222n9
Dretske, F. 109, 241–242, 250, 268
Drew, A. 221n3
Driver, J. 121
Dubeau, M.-C. 130
Dubois, B. 159
Duhamel, J. 159
Dunn, J. 197
Dunning, D. 166–167, 175

Eddy, T.J. 145n19
Egeth, H.E. 207
Eisenberg, N. 291
Ekman, P. 116, 125–126
Elmehed, K. 130
Emery, N.J. 145n19
Epley, N. 169
Eslinger, P.J. 218
Evans, G. 32, 240

Fabricius, W. 74, 92
Fadiga, L. 128, 130, 134–135
Falkai, P. 163, 171–172, 200
Fallon, A.E. 218
Farah, M. 153–154, 156
Feagin, S. 286, 288
Federlein, J. 116, 120–121
Fein, D. 293
Felician, O. 154

Ferrari, P.F. 140
Ferstl, E. 163
Festinger, L. 67n2
Fink, G.R. 135, 163, 171–172, 200
Flach, R. 145n16, 221n19
Flanagan, O. 250
Flavell, E.R. 12
Flavell, J.H. 12
Fletcher, P. 141, 198
Flombaum, J.I. 145n19
Fodor, J.A. 43, 95–98, 101–106,
    112nn2,3, 190n19, 225, 250, 268–269,
    272, 274nn2,5
Fogassi, L. 128, 130, 134–135,
    137, 140
Forguson, L. 12
Frackowiak, R.S. 155
Frackowiak, R. 141, 198
Franklin, N. 288
Freeman, N. 73
Frege, G. 259, 269
Freud, S. 164, 245
Freund, H.-J. 135
Frey, S. 117
Fricker, E. 226, 255n3
Friedman, O. 97
Friesen, W.V. 116, 126
Friston, K. 155
Frith, C. 136–137, 141, 198, 214
Frith, U. 13–14, 85, 141, 198, 200,
    204–205, 221n3, 237
Frye, D. 74, 198–199
Funk, M. 155
Fuller, G. 25
Fusella, V. 152

Gabrieli, J. 158
Gale, E. 87
Gallagher, H.L. 141, 198
Gallese, V. 117, 122, 124, 128, 132,
    134–137, 138–140, 189n10, 210–211,
    214–216, 218. 221nn6,9
Gallistel, C.R. 84–85, 145n19
Garcia, J. 218
Garcia, S.M. 161
Gazzaniga, M. 158, 231–232
Gazzola, V. 135, 137
Gelade, G. 255

Gelman, R. 93n
Gemignani, A. 160
Gendler, T. 284
Gergely, G. 15, 53, 65–66, 68n5
German, T. 72–73, 92, 93n3, 96–100,
    104–105
Gernsbacher, M.A. 288
Gesierich, B. 140
Ghahramani, Z. 213–214, 216
Gibbard, A. 291
Gilbert, D.T. 169–170
Gill, M.J. 169–170
Gilovich, T. 56, 169
Gitelman, D. 117
Glucksberg, S. 165
Glymour, C. 83–89
Goel, V. 141
Goldenberg, G. 153
Goldie, P. 303n4
Goldman, A. 19, 31, 42, 55–56, 81, 136,
    144n1, 145n15, 196, 211, 219, 220,
    230, 243, 248, 250, 255n2, 275n15,
    290, 295
Goldsmith, H.H. 288
Gollwitzer, P.M. 164
Goodale, M.A. 264
Gopnik, A. 12–13, 25, 70, 80, 83–91,
    195, 235–236, 256n9, 274n3
Gordon, R. 18–19, 82, 144n10, 185–188,
    240, 256n12, 259, 290
Gosselin, F. 121
Gould, J.L. 93n8, 219
Gould, S.J. 219
Grafman, J. 141
Grandy, R. 59
Grasby, P.M. 118, 131, 212, 219
Gray, J.A. 117
Green, F.L. 12
Greene, D. 167
Greene, J.D. 291
Gregory, M. 117
Grèzes, J. 212, 221n9
Griffin, D. 56
Griffith, E.M. 204
Grossenbacher, P.G. 116, 120–121
Grush, R. 217
Gschneidinger, E. 301
Guajardo, J.J. 22n7, 193

Gunn, R.N. 219
Gusnard, D.A. 163

Hadfield, M.G. 219
Hagestadt, C. 73
Haidt, J. 117, 291
Halgren, E. 144n3
Hall, L. 233
Halle, M. 184
Hallett, M. 141
Halpern, D.V. 243
Hamann, S. 116
Hamilton, D.L. 67n2
Hammer, J. 201
Hamsher, K. 120
Happé, F. 141, 198, 200, 237
Hare, B. 145n19
Hare, R.D. 293, 118
Hare, R.M. 290, 294–296
Harman, G. 11, 56, 250
Harris, P. 19, 25–26, 81, 93n3, 181,
    196, 284, 287–288
Hatfield, E. 126, 208, 277, 299
Haugeland, J. 35
Hauser, M.D. 303n3
Heal, J. 19–20, 36, 189n10, 190n17
Heatherton, T.F. 163
Heavey, C.L. 242–243, 245
Hebb, D.O. 142
Heberlein, A.S. 123, 131
Hegarty, M. 51n10
Heider, F. 15, 31
Heilman, K.M. 131
Heiserman, J.E. 163
Hellawell, D.J. 154
Hempel, C.G. 11
Hepburn, S.L. 205
Hepp-Raymond, M.-C. 155
Herrmann, S. 200
Hess, U. 130
Hirsch, S.R. 212
Hix, H.R. 74
Hodges, S.D. 207–209
Hoffman, M. 290, 303n7
Hogrefe, G. 81, 236
Holmes, J.G. 208
Holton, R. 256– 257n14, 295–297
Horgan, T. 250

House, P. 167
Houser, D. 279
Hubbard, E.M. 206
Huber, O. 163
Hughes, C. 74, 198–199, 204
Hume, D. 17, 22n, 144n, 150, 290
Humphrey, N. 19, 217–218,
    222n10
Humphreys, G.W. 154, 170–172,
    190n16, 199
Hurlburt, R. 229, 237, 242–243, 245
Hurley, S. 195, 216, 221n8
Hurvich, L.M. 274n4
Husain, M. 141
Hutcheson. 294
Hutchison, W.D. 136

Iacoboni, M. 130, 138–140, 206
Imbens-Bailey, A. 74, 92
Inati, S. 163
Isard, S. 185

Jackendoff, R. 262–263, 266
Jackson, F. 30–31, 270, 274n6
Jackson, P.L. 136, 138
Jacob, P. 211
Jakobson, L.S. 264
Jameson, D. 274n4
Jankowiak, J. 154
Jarrold, C. 74–75
Jeannerod, M. 42, 52n16, 159–160,
    211, 221n7
Jenkins, J.M. 196
Johansson, G. 144n13
Johansson, P. 233–234
Johnson, S.C. 85, 163, 193
Johnson-Laird, P.N. 51n10
Jones, L. 118, 122
Jones, T. 219
Jones-Gotman, M. 117
Jordan, M. 213, 216

Kahneman, D. 56, 182–183, 191n, 301
Kandel, S. 211
Kanner, L. 200
Kant, I. 18, 290, 294
Kanwisher, N. 88, 119, 141–142, 154,
    190n16, 199–200

Kaplan, D. 270
Kasari, C. 293
Kathirgamanathan, U. 170–172, 190n16, 199
Kaube, H. 136–137
Kawada, C.L.K. 164
Kawahara-Baccus, T.N. 163
Kawato, M. 213, 215–217, 221–222n9
Keane, J. 117, 120, 122, 130, 218
Keillor, J.M. 131
Kellerman, J. 208
Kelly, W.M. 163
Kelly, S. 116
Keysar, B. 41, 166, 169
Keysers, C. 117, 122, 124, 128, 132, 135, 137, 142–143, 210–211, 218
Kieran, M. 288–289
Kim, J. 247, 268
Kinsbourne, M. 154
Klein, D.J. 126
Klein, D. 150
Knoblich, G. 145n16, 221n9, 301
Koepp, M.J. 219
Kögler, H.H. 22n10
Kohlberg, L. 290
Kohler, E. 135
Kollias, S.S. 155
Koos, O. 65
Kortenkamp, S. 131
Kosslyn, S.M. 153–156, 188n3, 189n6
Kozak, M. 283
Krauss, R.M. 165
Kuhl, P. 13
Kushnir, T. 83–89
Kwon, J. 293

La France, M. 276, 278
Lacohee, H. 73
Lagravinese, G. 122
Laird, J.D. 208
Landry, S. 193
Lang, B. 75
Lang, P. 283
Langdon, R. 171, 256n10
Langton, R. 295–297
Lanzetta, J.T. 207
Latane, B. 161
Laurence, S. 258

Lawrence, A. 116, 118, 120–121, 131, 218–219
Le Bon, G. 299
Leaper, C. 203
LeDoux, J.E. 232
Lee, G.P. 116
Leekam, S. 12, 235
Leevers, H.J. 93n3
Lenzi, G.L. 130
Leonard, A. 116
Leonard, R.A. 116
Lepore, E. 190n19, 250
Leslie, A. 13–16, 22n8, 46, 50n3, 73, 75–76, 85, 92, 95–102, 104–109, 112n5, 150, 173, 175, 200, 274n3
Levelt, W. 230
Levenson, R.W. 126
Levin, D. 283
Levine, D. 153
Levine, J. 250
Lewis, C. 73
Lewis, D. 6–8
Lewis, J. 208
Lhermitte, F. 134
Liddle, P.F. 212
Lin, S. 41, 166
Lipps, T. 18
Lloyd, D. 136
Loar, B. 265–267, 269–270, 273, 274n6
Loewenstein, G. 41, 75, 165–168, 173, 175, 191n24
Loewer, B. 250
Lopes da Silva, F.H. 155
Lopez, D.E. 208
Lotze, M. 160
Loveland, K. 193
Lozano, A.M. 136
Lubke, J. 143
Lui, F. 122
Lumb, A. 74–75
Lundquist, L. 130
Luzzatti, C. 153
Lycan, W. G. 25, 109, 250, 260
Lyons, W. 228

Macaluso, D.A. 218
Maccoby, E.E. 203
MacCallum, F. 74–75

MacDonald, C. 255n
Macrae, C.N. 51n8, 162–164,
    189nn12,14
Maier, W. 200
Mak, R. 117
Malik, O. 141
Manes, F. 117, 120, 122, 218
Margolis, E. 258
Markram, H. 143
Marler, P. 93n8
Marques, R. 154
Marr, D. 260
Martin, L. 126, 288
Massarelli, R. 160
Maurer, D. 16
Mauthner, N. 74
May, M. 163, 171–172
Mazziotta, J.C. 130, 138–149
McCabe, K. 279
McCauley, C. 117
McCleery, J.P. 206
McDermott, J. 154
McDowell, J. 226
McGee, V. 190– 191n22
McGinn, C. 60
McGonaghy, N. 256n10
McGowan, S.M. 118, 131
McHugo, G.J. 207
McKinsey, M. 228
McLaughlin, B. 228, 250, 268
Meary, D. 211
Medvec, Y.H. 169
Meehan, J. 212
Meltzoff, A.N. 13, 50n2, 89–91,
    112n6, 129–130, 136, 138,
    172, 193–195, 235
Mestre, T. 154
Mesulam, M.M. 117, 212
Metzinger, T. 221n7
Metzler, J. 157
Michie, P.T. 256n10
Mijovic-Prelec, D. 188n3
Milgram, S. 174
Miller, G. 185, 283
Millikan, R. 274n9
Mills, P. 93n3
Milner, A.D. 264
Mitchell, D.G.V. 116

Mitchell, J.P. 51n8, 162–164,
    189nn12,14
Mitchell, P. 73–74, 93n3
Molnar-Szakacs, I. 138–140
Monson, C.K. 229
Montgomery, R. 22n11
Montoya, P. 160
Moore, C. 74–75, 193
Moore, M.K. 90, 129–130, 194
Moran, J.M. 163
Morand, S. 160
Morewedge, C.K. 169
Morris, R. 293
Morrison, I. 136
Moscovitch, M. 154
Moses, L.J. 74, 198–199
Moskowitz, G.B. 161
Muellbacher, W. 153
Mundy, P. 193, 293
Müri, R.M. 155
Murphy, S.T. 277
Murray, L.K. 116

Nadasdy, Z. 15, 53, 65–66, 68n
Nadel, J. 195
Nemeroff, C. 284
Newen, A. 200
Newman, C. 116
Newton, E. 166
Nichols, K. 16
Nichols, S. 25, 35, 43, 46, 51n15, 81, 92,
    93n6, 105, 150, 167, 173, 175, 181,
    190n17, 236–239, 245, 254, 256n7,
    281–283, 291–294, 303nn1,2,5
Nickerson, R.S. 41
Niedenthal, P.M. 145n16, 189n10, 277
Nietzsche, F. 17–18
Nisbett, R. 231, 233
Nowak, A. 153
Nozick, R. 22n11
Nussbaum, M. 290
Nystrom, L.E. 291

Oberman, L.M. 206
O'Craven, K.M. 154
O'Doherty, J. 136–137
Oettingen, G. 164
Ogston, W.D. 276

Olson, D.R. 81
Olsson, A. 233
O'Neill, D. 86
Onishi, K.H. 77, 80, 86, 88, 146n20, 292
O'Regan, J.K. 243
Orliaguet, J.P. 211
Ozonoff, S. 198, 204

Pacherie, E. 42, 52n16, 221n7
Paiva, T. 154
Palfai, T. 74, 198–199
Papineau, D. 274n9
Papousek, H. 16
Papousek, M. 16
Pardo, J.V. 117
Parfit, D. 298, 303n
Parrish, T. 117
Parsons, L. 158
Pascual-Leon, A. 154
Patteri, I. 122
Pavesi, G. 130, 134
Peacocke, C. 190n18, 250, 254, 255n5
Pearl, J. 83
Pennington, B. 198, 204–205
Perky, C.W. 152
Perner, J. 12–13, 19, 22n6, 71–72, 75,
    77–78, 81, 235
Perrett, D.I. 116–117, 205, 210
Perrett, D. 142–143
Peschardt, K.S. 116
Pessoa, L. 154
Peterson, D. 93n3
Petrides, M. 117
Phelps, E.A. 116, 121
Phelps, E. 158
Phillips, M.L. 117
Piaget, J. 290
Pierrot-Deseilligny, C. 159
Pillon, B. 135, 159
Pineda, J.A. 206
Pipe, J.G. 163
Pitt, D. 250
Plailley, J. 117, 122, 124, 128, 132,
    137, 218
Poe, E.A. 17–18
Polizzi, P. 75, 99–100
Porro, C.A. 122
Povinelli, D. 145n19

Preblanc, C. 159
Prelec, D. 167
Premack, D. 5, 10–11, 15
Preston, S. 145n16, 207
Price, C. 155
Prigatano, G.P. 163
Prinz, J. 246, 256n11
Prinz, W. 145n, 195, 216, 221n,
    277, 301
Pritchard, T.C. 218
Pronin, E. 166
Prost, J.H. 92
Przuntek, H. 116, 120–121
Puccio, C. 166
Putnam, H. 22n11, 25, 177, 228
Pyers, J. 87
Pylyshyn, Z. 155–156, 188nn4,5

Quine, W.V. 18, 22n5, 94n11, 179–180,
    190–191n22, 191n23

Radke-Yarrow, M. 292
Raichle, M. 163
Rall, J. 288
Ramachadran, V.S. 206
Ramsey, F.P. 7
Rapson, R.L. 208, 277, 299
Ravenscroft, I. 52n21, 188n1,
    189n9, 283
Rawls, J. 294
Raybaudi, M. 160
Read, D. 167
Recanati, F. 275n18
Reed, D.T. 204
Reeves, A. 152
Regard, M. 155
Reichenbach, H. 83
Reichle, E.D. 243
Rensink, R.A. 234, 243
Repacholi, B. 80
Reynolds, C.W. 279
Richardson, D. 152
Richardson, M.P. 121
Richell, R.A. 116
Riddoch, M.J. 154
Riffle, A. 188n3
Riggs, K. 93n3
Rinck, M. 288

Ripstein, A. 22n11
Ritzl, A. 163, 171–172
Rizzolatti, G. 117, 122, 124, 128,
    130, 132, 134–135, 137–140, 206,
    210–211, 218
Robbins, P. 94n9, 237
Roberts, N. 136
Robertson, R.R.W. 288
Robinson, E. 73–74, 93n3
Rockland, C. 115
Rogers, S.J. 198, 204–205
Rolls, E.T. 117
Rosen, C. 196, 236
Rosenfeld, H.M. 278
Rosenthal, D.M. 250, 256n13
Ross, L. 166–167
Roth, D. 96–97
Roth, M. 160
Rowland, D. 117
Royet, J.-P. 117, 122, 124, 128, 132,
    137, 218
Rozin, P. 117, 218, 284
Rozzi, S. 140
Ruby, P. 212–213
Ruffman, T. 81–83
Ruppert, J.A. 145n16, 189n10
Russell, J. 74, 198, 204
Russell, L. 74–75
Ryan, L. 279
Ryle, G. 4–6

Sacks, O. 221n3
Sadato, N. 141
Sala, S.D. 153
Saltmarsh, R. 73–74
Samson, D. 170–172, 190n16, 199
Samuels, R. 106–107
Santos, L.R. 145n19
Santos, R; 154
Sapp, F. 74–75
Savitsky, K. 169
Saxe, R. 81–82, 88, 94n12, 141–142,
    174, 190n16, 199–200
Schaffer, H. 16
Scheflen, A.E. 276
Scheines, R. 83
Schiffer, S. 275n18
Schkade, D. 168

Schmitz, T.W. 163
Scholl, B. 75–76, 102, 108, 110, 274n3
Schooler, J. 243
Schopenhauer, A. 290
Schroeder, U. 116, 120–121
Schulman. 163
Schulz, L.E. 83–89
Schwarz, N. 301
Schwebel, D.C. 196, 236
Schwebel, D. 236
Schwoebel, J. 160
Schyns, P. 121
Scott, S.K. 116
Sebanz, N. 301
Segal, S.J. 152
Segebarth, C. 160
Seitz, R.J. 135
Sellars, C. 118, 122
Sellars, W. 7, 25
Senior, C. 117
Serdaru, M. 135
Seymour, B. 136–137
Shah, A. 204
Shah, N.J. 200
Shalev, R. 154
Shanton, K. 190n15
Sharpe, S. 74
Shatto, C. 167
Shaw, L.L. 209
Shepard, R. 39, 157
Sherman, S.J. 67n2
Sherman, T. 193
Shiffrar, M. 155
Shine, J.H. 116
Shoemaker, S. 25, 227–228, 242, 244,
    256–257n14
Shulman, G.L. 163
Shyu, V. 204
Siegman, A.W. 208
Siewert, C.P. 250
Sigman, M. 193
Sigman, N. 293
Sikstrom, S. 233
Simmel, M. 15, 31
Simons, D.J. 234
Singer, J. 236
Singer, J.L. 196
Singer, P. 295–297

Singer, T. 136–137
Sirigu, A. 159
Slaughter, V. 235–236
Slovic, P. 56
Small, D.M. 117
Smith, A. 17–18, 276, 294, 299
Smith, B.C. 62
Smith, M. 118, 122
Smith, V. 279
Sobel, D.M. 83–89
Sodian, B. 81, 236
Soja, N. 178
Sommerville, J.A. 22n7, 193
Sommerville, R.B. 291
Soso, M.J. 156
Southwood, M. 154, 188n3
Spelke, E. 178
Spence, S.A. 212
Sperber, D. 176–177, 210
Spirtes, P. 83
Spivey, M. 152
Spreen, O. 120
Sprengelmeyer, R. 116, 120–121
Stevens, K.N. 184
Sripada, C.S. 144n1, 145n15, 219
Stackhouse, T. 205
Stanovich, K. 207
Stark, L.W. 152
Stein, E. 58
Stepper, S. 126
Sterelny, K. 112n
Stern, D. 16
Stich, S. 25, 35, 43, 46, 51n15, 55, 60,
    81, 92, 93n6, 105, 150, 167, 173, 175,
    181, 190n17, 236–239, 245, 254,
    256n7, 281, 283
Stone, T. 33
Strack, F. 126, 301
Strawson, G. 250
Strayer, J. 291
Strickland, I. 118, 122
Stueber, K.R. 22n10
Suddendorf, T. 205, 210
Sullivan, K. 94n9
Swettenham, J. 221n3

Tager-Flusberg, H. 94n9
Tasker, R.R. 136

Taylor, C. 198
Taylor, M. 196
Taylor, S. 302
Thompson, W.L. 154
Thunberg, M. 129–130
Tidswell, T. 74
Tienson, J. 250
Todd, R.M. 209
Tolman, E.C. 83
Tomasello, M. 145n19
Tomkins, S. 218
Tooby, J. 15
Townsend, D.J. 184–185
Tranel, D. 115–117, 120–121, 127,
    131, 154
Treisman, A. 255
Tremoulet, P. 110
Trope, Y. 207
Trouard, T. 279
Trout, D. 278
Turner, T.J. 288
Tversky, A. 56, 182–183, 191n25, 301
Tversky, B. 288
Tye, M. 109, 228, 250, 252, 254, 257n21
Tyler, M. 152

Ulbaek, K. 15
Umilta, M.A. 135
Ungerer, J. 193

van Boven, L. 166–169, 175
van Knippenberg, A. 162
van Leeuwen, B. 167
Varney, N.R. 120
Vaughan, K.B. 207
Viviani, P. 145n16, 211
Vogeley, K. 163, 171–172, 200
von Cramon, D.Y. 163
Vrana, S. 283
Vrba, E. 219
Vuilleumier, P. 121

Walton, K. 284–285, 287
Warach, J. 153
Ward, P.B. 256n10
Waterhouse, L. 293
Watson, J. 75–76, 91–92
Weaver, K. 161

Webb, P. 145n19
Webb, S. 63
Weber, M. 41, 75, 165
Wegner, D.M. 207–209, 256n8
Wehner, E. 205
Wellman, H. 13, 76, 78–80, 93n6,
  274n3, 292
Wellman, H.M. 75–76, 91–92
Wexler, A. 141
Wheelwright, S. 203
White, A. 188n1
Whiten, A. 205, 210, 218
Wicker, B. 117, 122, 124, 128, 132, 135,
  137, 218
Wilder, L.S. 163
Williams, A.O. 118, 122
Williams, E. 93n
Williams, J.H.G. 205, 210
Williams, S.C.R. 117
Wilson, M. 160, 189n8
Wilson, T.D. 169–170, 231–233,
  235, 256n8
Wimmer, H. 12, 19, 22n6, 81, 235–236
Winocur, G. 154
Wittgenstein, L. 4, 22n5, 225–226

Wolf, D.P. 196
Wolpert, D.M. 213–217, 221–222n9
Woodruff, G. 5, 10–11
Woodward, A.L. 22n7, 77, 193
Wright, C. 226, 256–257n14
Wyland, C.L. 163

Yablo, S. 250
Yantis, S. 207
Yirmiya, N. 293
Young, A.W. 116–117, 120–122, 130,
  152, 154, 218
Young, E. 152
Youngblade, L.M. 197
Yue, G. 158

Zahn-Waxler, C. 292
Zaitchik, D. 73–74
Zajonc, R. 208, 277
Zald, D.H. 117
Zatorre, R.J. 117
Zeki, S. 119
Zelazo, P. 74, 198–199
Zilles, K. 135, 163, 171–172, 200
Zysset, S. 163

Subject Index

Altruistic motivation 290–296, 298, 302
Amygdala 115–117, 120–124, 221n4
Anchoring and adjustment 169–170
Animal mindreading 3, 5, 10–11, 140,
  145n19
Appearance-reality distinction 12, 71,
  198, 237
Asperger's syndrome. *See* autism
Attention 16, 193–195, 205, 242–246
Attributional accuracy 128–129,
    149–150, 157, 173–175
  and E-imagination 148–150, 157–158,
    160, 173–175
  and empathy 296
  of FaBER 128–129
  and input inadequacy 38, 48,
    173–175
  of introspection 223–224, 247
  and quarantine failure 40–42, 148,
    170–173, 187
Autism 13–15, 21, 85, 192, 200–206,
    236–237, 297
  domain-specific impairment in 14, 85,
    87, 102, 193
  and empathizing 201–206, 221n3,
    292–294
  executive dysfunction theory of
    198, 204
  extreme-male-brain theory of 200–204

  and false-belief tasks 13–15, 19,
    106–107, 198
  and mirror-neuron dysfunction
    205–206
  and self-other asymmetry 236–237
  and systemizing 201–203, 205
  and ToMM 15–16, 102
  weak central coherence theory of
    204–205

Bayes nets 83–87, 89
Belief box 47, 238–240, 254, 281–282
Binding problem 253, 255

CST. *See* child-scientist theory
Chameleon effect 277–279
Charity theory. *See* rationality theory
Child-scientist theory (CST) 17, 69–94
  and acquisition of mentalizing skills
    69, 83–89, 91, 97
  and analogy to science 13, 69–71,
    85–88, 90, 111
  and Bayes nets 83–87, 89
  and conceptual deficit 12–13, 71–80,
    99. *See also* conceptual deficit
  and domain-general learning
    mechanisms 70, 83–89, 91, 93
  of first-person mindreading 69–71,
    90–93, 235

353

Child-scientist theory (CST) (*continued*)
and folk psychological laws 69,
81–83, 89
and inference neglect 80–83
and introspection 69–70, 90–93, 111,
234–236
and language 87–89
of mental concepts 69–71, 93,
111–112
and misrepresentation 13, 71–73, 76
and representational model of mind
12–13, 70–72, 76, 78–80, 172
See also theory theory
Cogito judgments 226–227
Cognitive contagion 207–209
Common-coding theory 145n16
Concept epistemicism 272–275
Concept pragmatism. *See* concept
epistemicism
Concepts 177, 258–259. *See also* mental
concepts
Conceptual deficit 12–13, 71–80, 99–100
and appearance-reality tasks 12
avoidance-desire evidence against
92, 99
and connectionist conception of desire
78–80
and false belief tasks 12–13, 70–73,
75–77, 88
early success evidence against
76–78, 80
inhibitory control evidence against
74–76, 197–199
linguistic evidence against 88–89
memory evidence against 72–73,
92, 236
neurological evidence against 171–172
reality bias evidence against 93n3
and unfulfilled desire 78–80, 86, 89
Conceptual structure module (CS)
262–264, 266
Concern mechanism 293–294, 303n5
Confabulation 62, 231–234,
255–256n6, 263
Control theory 192, 213–217,
221–222n9
Cooperation, of simulation and theory.
See ST-TT hybrids

CS. *See* conceptual structure module
Curse of knowledge 41, 75, 165–166,
171, 199. *See also* egocentric bias

Decision-making mechanism 20, 27, 29,
34, 43–44, 131, 183
Default attribution 51n15, 105, 167, 169
Desire box 281
Development 8–9, 19, 113, 192
of altruistic motivation 290–293, 302
and domain-general learning
mechanisms 83–89, 91, 93
and egocentric bias 40–42, 75, 80
and Hebbian learning 142–144
of intention tracking 195
of joint visual attention 16, 193–195
and language 87–89
and mental concept acquisition 69–70,
96–97, 101
of mirror systems 142–144
of role play 15, 195–197
and self-other symmetry 234–238
and whole-object bias 178–179
Domain-general learning mechanisms
70, 83–89, 91, 93, 106, 115. *See also*
Bayes nets
Domain specificity 14, 101–104,
110–111, 112n2
Dopamine 118, 120–121, 131, 219
Dualism 5, 257n22, 267
Dual process theories 207–210

E-imagination. *See* enactment
imagination
EDD. *See* eye-direction detector
Egocentric bias 50, 148, 160, 164–165,
176, 187, 199
and input inadequacy 166, 173–175
and morality 296–297
in predicting feelings 42, 167–169
in predicting knowledge 165–166
in predicting valuations 80, 166–167
and self-perspective inhibition
172–173
See also curse of knowledge,
endowment effect, projection,
quarantine
Egocentric empathy gaps 167–168, 175

Egocentric shift 186–188
Emotion 3, 20, 47, 109, 111, 213,
    258, 278
    and autism 202, 206
    E-imagination of 47–48, 167–168, 284
    and egocentric bias 172
    and empathy 209–210, 278–279,
        290–292, 297
    and fiction 196, 282–289
    and introspection 224–225, 245
    See also emotional contagion,
        face-based emotion recognition
Emotional contagion 125–128, 207–208,
    218–220, 299–300
    and altruistic motivation 291–294
    and empathy 207–209
    evolution of 218–220
    and mirroring 132–133, 218, 286
    reciprocal hedonic 299–300, 302
    See also emotion
Empathy 4, 11, 21–22, 136, 201–204,
    206–209, 286, 290–292, 295–298
    and autism 201–206
    automatic 207–209
    cognitive 208, 278–279
    controlled 207, 209
    dual-process theory of 207–210
    emotional 207–210, 278–279
    as epistemic tool 295–298
    and fiction 284–290
    and morality 209, 290–298
    neural correlates of 213
    and social bonds 276–280
    and well-being 299–302
    See also E-imagination, mirroring,
        perspective taking, simulation
Empathy theory. See simulation theory
Enactment imagination (E-imagination)
    47–48, 147–162
    and attributional accuracy 148–150,
        157–158, 160, 173–175
    conceptual 160–162
    control of 151, 158, 161, 210,
        220, 221n5
    definition of 47–48, 147, 151
    and fiction 281–290
    and genuine states 147–151, 156–158
    and input inadequacy 173–175

knowledge-guided 149–150, 175
    and moral psychology 290–291,
        294, 297–298
    motor 151, 157–160
    and pretend states 147–151, 156–158,
        173–175
    and resemblance 48–49, 148–151,
        155–157, 160
    visual 149–157, 175
    See also empathy, high-level
        mindreading, imagination,
        perspective taking, pretense,
        suppositional imagination
Endowment effect 42, 166–167, 173–175
Evolution 15, 21, 61, 113, 117, 179–180,
    183, 192, 217–220, 239
Executive function 74–75, 171, 197–199,
    204. See also inhibitory control
Eye-direction detector (EDD) 15–16, 110

FaBER. See face-based emotion
    recognition
Face-based emotion recognition
    (FaBER) 110, 113–132, 245
    and amygdala 115–117, 120–124
    of anger 113, 116, 118–119, 121,
        218–219
    and anterior insula 117–118, 120, 124,
        215, 218
    of disgust 113, 116–118, 121–122,
        128, 137, 215, 218–219
    and facial mimicry 129–130, 138
    of fear 113, 115–119, 121–122, 294
    generate-and-test model of 124–125,
        129, 132, 138, 184
    and mirroring 20, 50, 113, 130–133,
        137, 140
    modularity of 110–111
    and psychopathy 116, 294
    reverse simulation models of 125–127,
        129–131, 138, 207–208
    unmediated resonance (mirroring)
        model of 127–129, 131–132, 207
    and visual processing deficiency
        121–123
    See also low-level mindreading,
        mirroring, paired deficits
Factual reasoning mechanism 27–28, 34

False belief tasks 11–14, 19, 70–78,
    87–89, 92, 106–107, 171–172,
    197–200, 234–236, 292
  and autism 13–14, 19, 106–107, 198
  early success on 76–78, 80, 86, 88–89,
    93, 292
  and inhibitory control 74–76,
    171–172, 197–200, 292
  and language 87–89
  and memory 72–73, 92, 236
  and performance deficit 72–76,
    171–172, 197–200
  and representational model of mind
    12–13, 70–72, 76, 78–80
  and role play 196–197
  and self-other symmetry 92, 234–236
  as test of belief concept 11–13
  and theory of mind mechanism
    (ToMM) 13–14, 106–107
  See also conceptual deficit,
    development
Fiction 281–290
First-person mindreading 21–22, 23–26,
    223–257, 263–264, 273
  by ascent routine 240–241
  and confabulation 231–234,
    255–256n6, 263
  of mental state content 241, 246–247,
    253–255
  of mental state intensity 246–247,
    251, 255
  of mental state type 224–226, 239–240
  and monitoring mechanism 238–239
  reliability of 223–224, 229–230, 232,
    247, 273
  RT account of 23–24, 61–63, 67, 69
  by special method 224–228
  TT account of 25, 69–71, 90–92,
    234–236
  See also introspection, self-other
    asymmetry
Folk psychological laws 7–8, 24–26, 30,
    44, 69–70, 96–97
  and choice prediction 180, 182–183
  and decision prediction 19, 29, 44,
    180–182
  and functionalism 7, 25, 50n3
  and inference neglect 80–83

  and introspection 25–26, 89–92
  acquisition of 26, 69–70, 83–87,
    96–97
  and mental concepts 26, 50n3, 97, 172,
    178–180
  and threat of collapse 30–34, 43–44,
    46, 50n3, 163–164
  and theoretical inference 25–28, 69,
    89, 95–98
  See also folk psychology
Folk psychology 6–7, 10, 15, 19,
    31, 53
  and eliminativism 6
  and evolution 15, 61
  and functionalism 6–7, 19
  and mental concepts 9, 63–65, 95–98,
    109, 181
  and myth of rationality 4, 54–58
  and ToMM 109, 111
  See also folk psychological laws
Format distinctiveness problem
    269–270, 272
Forward models 214–217, 221–222n9
Functionalism 6–8, 19, 25–26, 50n3
  and introspection 25–26, 239,
    247–249
  and mental concepts 6–8, 47, 50n3, 64,
    69, 264–265, 269
  and pretense 46–47, 281–283
  as origin of TT 7–8, 10
Functional properties 247–249. See also
    introspection

Gaze following. See attention
Generate-and-test 45, 124–125, 129, 132,
    184–185
Genuine states 29–30, 41, 48–49,
    147–148, 151
  and E-imagination 48–49, 147–148,
    151, 156–158, 160
  and fiction 283–287
  and quarantine failure 40–42, 165–172
  resemblance of pretend states to
    48–49, 149–151, 156–158, 211–212
  and shared representations 211–213
Geometrical ions (geons) 260–261
Geonic code 260–264
Golden rule 294

Hebbian learning 142–144
High-level mindreading 21, 113,
    131–132, 147–191
  and altruistic motivation 292–294
  characterization of 132, 147, 149–150
  consciousness of 147, 151, 161
  control of 132, 147, 207
  vs. low-level mindreading 113,
    140–142, 220
  and moral rationalism 294–295
  neural loci of 140–142
  and social coordination 279
  See also E-imagination, simulation
    theory, third-person mindreading
Hybrids. See ST-TT hybrids

I-code. See introspective code
ID. See intentionality detector
Imagery. See imagination
Imagination 19, 48–49, 149–162
  conceptual uses of 160–162
  enactment 47–49, 149–151
  and fiction 281, 283–286, 289
  and morality 294–296
  motor 157–160
  resemblance to genuine states 38, 49,
    149–151, 158, 160
  suppositional 47–48, 281–283
  visual 38, 151–157, 261, 289
  and well-being 300–302
  See also enactment imagination,
    pretense, suppositional imagination
Imitation. See mimicry
Implementation, of simulation by theory.
    See ST-TT hybrids
Independence, of simulation and theory.
    See ST-TT hybrids
Inexpressibility problem 269, 272
Inference neglect 80–83
Information encapsulation 101–106,
    110–111, 112n3
Inhibitory control 74–75, 99–100, 135,
    170–172, 198–200
  and autism 198, 204
  and belief-desire reasoning 99–100
  and egocentric bias 148, 170–173
  and false-belief tasks 74–76, 99–100,
    172, 197–200, 292

  and imagination 160
  See also executive function,
    quarantine
Input inadequacy 38, 41, 48, 82, 166,
    173–175
Insula, anterior 117–118, 120, 124, 136,
    215, 218
Intention tracking 193–195
Intentional stance theory 8, 23–24,
    53–68
  in infancy 65–67
  and mental-state concepts 63–65
  and myth of rationality 54
  and self-other symmetry 61–62
  See also rationality theory
Intentionality detector (ID) 15, 110
Interoception 252–254, 257n23
Interpretivism 8, 58–60
Introspection 187, 229–231, 242–257
  and attention 242–246
  and binding problem 253, 255
  cognitive scientific objections to
    229–238
  and concept epistemicism 272–274
  and consciousness 242–243, 245–246,
    249–251
  descriptive experience sampling
    242–243
  displaced-perception theory of
    241–242
  independence condition objection to
    227–228, 242, 244–245
  methodological doubts about 229–231
  monitoring mechanism account of
    238–241, 245, 254
  phenomenology of 228, 261, 264, 266
  philosophical objections to 225–229
  properties that serve as inputs to
    246–253
  and recognition 246–247, 253–255,
    273–274
  and redeployment 238–241, 247,
    253–255
  reliability of 9, 38, 229–230,
    241–242, 273
  and self-blindness 227–228, 244
  as a transduction process 246–247
  and translation 253–255

Introspection (*continued*)
  See also first-person mindreading,
    introspective code, mental concept
    contents, mental concept vehicles
Introspective code (I-code) 261, 263–267
  analogous to visual code 260–261, 264
  and concept epistemicism 272–274
  and format distinctiveness problem
    269–270, 272
  and inexpressibility problem 269, 272
  and natural language 264–265,
    267, 269
  parameters of 261, 263
  and recognitional concepts 265–267,
    269, 273
  and representational modularity
    262–265
  See also introspection, mental concept
    vehicles

Left temporoparietal junction (LTPJ) 141
Like-me premise. *See* resemblance-to-
  self premise
Logical behaviorism 5–7
Low-level mindreading 21, 113–146
  and altruistic motivation 292–294
  automaticity of 49, 113, 132, 147,
    207–208, 220
  characterization of 113, 133–134
  generate-and-test model of 124–125,
    129–130, 132, 138
  mirroring model of 127–129,
    131–140
  modularity of 43, 109–111
  neural loci of 140–142
  and paired deficits 115–119, 125,
    127–128
  primitiveness of 113, 140–142
  and psychopathy 116, 118–119,
    122, 294
  and reciprocal hedonic contagion
    299–300
  reverse simulation model of 125–131,
    138, 207–208
  reverse simulation model of, with as-if
    loop 127–129, 131
  and somatosensory cortices 127,
    131, 135

  See also face-based emotion
    recognition, mirroring, simulation
    theory, third-person mindreading
LTPJ. *See* left temporoparietal junction

M-representations. *See* modularity
  theory, metarepresentations
Medial prefrontal cortex (MPFC)
  141–142, 162–164, 279
Mental concept content 21–22, 267–272
  causal-covariation approach to
    267–270
  definition of 259
  format distinctiveness problem for
    269–270, 272
  inexpressibility problem for
    269, 272
  information-theoretic approach to
    268–269
  and ontological preferences 178–180
  and pure phenomenal concept
    270–271
  two-dimensional approach to 267,
    270–272
  See also mental concepts
Mental concept vehicles 259, 260–264
  and analogy to vision 260–262, 264
  definition of 259
  and multiple formats of representation
    262–264
  and self-directed recognitional
    concepts 265–267, 269, 273
  type-demonstrative theory of 265–267,
    269–270
  See also introspective code,
    introspection, mental concepts
Mental concepts 9, 21, 258–275
  development of 12–13, 70–72, 75–77,
    86, 89, 97
  and functionalism 6–8, 25–26, 46–47,
    50n3, 64, 69
  non-introspectability of 9
  and philosophy of mind 4–8
  rationality theory account of 63–65
  theory theory account of 26
  See also concepts, conceptual deficit,
    mental concept contents, mental
    concept vehicles

Metaethics 290–295
Mimicry 17–18, 20, 134–135
    and autism 205–206
    behavioral 276–279
    and intention tracking 193, 195
    and joint visual attention 193–195
    and mirror neurons 205–206
    and role play 195–197
    See also mirroring
Mindblindness 200, 202
Mirror neurons 127, 130, 132–136,
    205–206
    autism and dysfunction of
        205–206, 293
    discovery of 134–136
    and evolution of mindreading
        219–220
    for hand action 134
    and Hebbian learning 142–144
    and imitation 205–206
    for mouth and foot action 135
    and mu suppression 206
    origins of 142–144
    and simulation theory *vi*, 132–136
    See also mirroring
Mirroring 4, 50, 113, 117–118, 147,
    132–140
    automaticity of 130, 132, 158,
        207–210, 220
    as basis for mindreading 128,
        131–134, 136–140, 143
    and control theory 214–215
    definition of 133, 137
    of disgust 117–118, 132,
        137, 143
    and empathy 136–138, 143, 206–209,
        292, 297
    and intention ascription 137–140
    motor 130, 134–135, 138–140,
        143–144, 211
    of pain 136–138, 206, 215
    resonance model of emotion
        recognition 127–129, 131–132, 207
    and the unity of social cognition
        210–211, 278
    as species of simulation 132–136
    of touch 135–137, 143
    and well-being 299–300

See also empathy, face-based emotion
    recognition, low-level mindreading,
    mimicry, mirror neurons, simulation
Misrepresentation 13, 71–73, 76, 268
Modality-neutral representation 260–261
Modes of presentation 269–270
Modularity theory (MT) 13–16, 95–112
    and acquisition of mentalizing skills
        15, 96–97
    and autism 13–16, 102, 106–107, 193
    and Chomskian modules 102, 106–107
    commitment to TT of 95–98, 100
compatibility with ST of 99–101,
        110–111
    and EDD 15–16, 110
    and false-belief tasks 13–14, 96,
        99–100, 106–107
    and Fodorian modules 101–102,
        106–107
    and ID 15, 110
    and inhibitory control 99–100
    and metarepresentations 16, 97, 102,
        104–105, 107–109, 114
    minimal modularity 107–109
    origins of 13–16
    and pretense 14–16, 97–99, 105, 107
    and processing encapsulation 105–106
    and SAM 16, 110, 193
    and SP 98–100, 108
    and theoretical inference 95–98,
        105, 111
    and third-person mindreading 16,
        96–97, 101–102, 107–109, 111
    See also modularity, theory of mind
        mechanism (ToMM), theory theory
Modularity 101–111
    Chomskian 106–107
    criteria for 101
    and domain specificity 14, 84,
        101–104, 106, 112n2
    of face-based emotion recognition 43,
        109–111
    Fodorian 101–107, 111
    and informational encapsulation
        101–106, 110–111, 112n3
    representational 262–265
    of theory of mind mechanism (ToMM)
        95, 98, 101–109

Monitoring mechanism (MM) 238–241,
245, 254
Moral theory and moral psychology 3,
22, 290–302
and altruistic motivation 291–294,
298, 302
and autism 292–293
and empathy 209, 276, 290–292,
295–298
and golden rule 294
and moral rationalism 290, 294
and moral sentimentalism 290–291,
294–295
and perspective-taking (simulation)
292–294
and psychopathy 293–294
social determinants of hedonic
experience 298–302
MPFC. *See* medial prefrontal cortex
MT. *See* modularity theory

Neural properties 247, 251–253, 268.
See also introspection

Off-line simulation theory. *See*
simulation theory
Ontogeny. *See* development
Other minds, problem of 5, 194

Pain. *See* sensations
Paired deficits in emotion experience
and recognition 110–111,
115–132
accidental colocalization explanation
of 114–115, 119
for anger 110, 113, 116, 118–119, 121
for disgust 110, 113, 116–118,
121–122, 128, 137
for fear 110, 113–119, 121–122, 294
generate-and-test explanation of
124–125, 129, 132, 138
for guilt 116, 118–119, 122
information deficit explanation of
119–121
resonance (mirroring) explanation of
127–129, 131–132, 207
reverse simulation explanation of
124–125, 129, 132, 138, 207–208

visual processing deficit explanation of
121–124
See also face based emotion
recognition
PC. *See* posterior cingulate
Performance deficit. *See* false-belief
tasks
Perspective taking 168–172, 209–210,
212–213, 287–294
and egocentric bias 168–172
evolution of 220
and fiction 287–290
and the golden rule 294
and ironic process theory 209
and moral psychology 290–294
and self-other asymmetry 236, 238
See also empathy, enactment
imagination, simulation
Phenomenal properties 247, 249–250.
See also introspection
Phylogeny. *See* evolution
Physicalism 5–6, 267
Possible world box (PWB) 46–47,
181–182, 281–282
Posterior cingulate (PC) 141
Predictive attribution
of choice 180–183
of decision 19–20, 27–30, 40, 43–44,
186, 223
of desire 80, 89, 103
of emotion 169–170
of inference 148, 180–182
by rationalizing 8, 53, 57, 63–64, 66
of sensation 214–215
by simulating 43, 100, 170, 173–175,
184, 210
by theorizing 26, 83, 72, 96, 100, 174
Pretend box. *See* possible world box
Pretense 46–49, 147–151, 186–188
characterization of 46–49
and decision-prediction 19–20, 27–30,
43–45, 131, 187
and egocentric shift 186–188
and false-belief tasks 197–199
and fiction 281–285, 287
and input inadequacy 38, 41, 48, 82,
173–175
process vs. product 47–48

as propositional attitude 46–47
resemblance of pretend states to
    genuine states 48–49, 147–151,
    152–160
and role play 14–16, 195–197, 200
and tagging 28, 160, 186–187,
    211–213
See also enactment imagination
Private language argument 225–226
Privileged access 224. *See also*
    introspection
Projection 40–42, 164–173, 175–180
of conceptual content 175–180
and egocentric bias 164–173
of feelings 167–168
and failure of inhibitory control
    170–173
and intention tracking 195
of knowledge 165–166
and self-directed recognitional
    concepts 266–267
simulation-plus- 40–42
of valuations 166–167
See also simulation
Propositional attitudes 6–7, 9, 20, 53,
    102, 249–250
and domain-specificity of mentalizing
    102, 109
and folk psychology 20
and intentional stance theory 53, 64
ontological status of 6–7, 9, 53
phenomenology of 249–250
Quine on 180
and single-code hypothesis 282–283
and ToMM 16, 102, 109
Proprioceptive mapping 91, 129, 194
Psychopathology 21, 85, 236–237,
    290–294
See also autism, psychopathy,
    schizophrenia
Psychopathy 118–119, 290–294, 296
and concern mechanism 293–294
and fear 116, 294
and guilt 118–119, 122
and moral motivation 290,
    293–294
and perspective taking 290,
    293–294

See also psychopathology
Pure phenomenal concept 270–271
PWB. *See* possible world box

Quarantine 29–30, 41, 148, 164, 296–297
curse-of-knowledge and failure of
    165–166
endowment effect and failure of
    166–167
neuropsychology of 148, 170–173,
    197–198
successful 29–30
See also egocentric bias, inhibitory
    control
Quasi-perceptual model, of introspection.
    See introspection

Rationality, myth of 4, 54–58
Rationality theory (RT) 4, 23–24, 53–68
collapse into simulation theory 57, 183
of first-person mindreading 23–24,
    61–63
and folk psychology 9, 31, 53–54
incompleteness of 23–24, 61
and introspection 23–24, 61–63
and irrationality 55–58
and logical rules 55–56
of mental concepts 63–65
strong vs. weak versions of 54–60
and teleological stance 66
and truth-maximization 58–60
See also intentional stance theory,
    interpretivism
Reciprocal hedonic contagion
    299–300, 302
Recognition, face-based. *See* face-based
    emotion recognition
Recognitional concepts 265–267,
    269, 273
Redeployment 238–241, 247, 253–255
ascent-routine version of 240–241
introspection version of 240, 247
monitoring mechanism version of
    238–241, 245, 254
Replication. *See* simulation
Representational model of mind 12–13,
    70–71, 76, 78–80, 172, 241. *See* also
    misrepresentation

Representational properties 247,
    250–251. *See also* introspection
Resemblance-to-self premise 30–31, 51n,
    90–91, 163–164, 172, 187, 194
Resonance. *See* mirroring
Retrodictive mindreading 44–45, 148,
    183–185
Right temporoparietal junction (RTPJ)
    141–142
Role play 14–16, 193, 196–197, 200
RT. *See* rationality theory
RTPJ. *See* right temporoparietal junction

S-imagination. *See* suppositional
    imagination
SAM. *See* shared attention mechanism
Schizophrenia 212, 237. *See also*
    psychopathology
Seeing = knowing rule 81
Selection processor (SP) 98–100, 108
Self-attribution. *See* first-person
    mindreading
Self-knowledge, problem of 5
Self-other asymmetry, evidence for
    236–237
    from autism 236–237
    from false-belief tasks 92, 236
    from knowledge attribution 236
    from pretense 236
    from schizophrenia 237
    See also introspection, self-other
        symmetry
Self-other problem 212–213
Self-other symmetry, evidence for
    234–236
    from autism 236
    from false-belief tasks 234–235
    See also self-other asymmetry
Self-monitoring. *See* introspection
Self-reflection 148, 162–164, 187
Sensations 15, 20, 47, 196, 258, 261
    and control theory 214–215
    and functionalism 6, 25, 248
    and interoception 252–254
    mirroring of 133, 135–138, 143, 215
    representational account of
        238–239, 268
    and social cognition 292, 298

Shared attention mechanism (SAM) 16,
    110, 193
Shared manifold hypothesis 128, 215
Shared representations 159,
    211–213, 277
Simulation 23, 50
    attempted vs. successful 29, 36–39, 41,
        150, 177
    automatic 37, 40, 49, 210, 225
    and behavioral mimicry 276–279,
        299, 302
    controlled 147, 210, 220
    generic 36–38, 132, 156
    and enactment imagination 49,
        149–151, 289, 294, 302
    as an epistemic tool 25, 291,
        295–298, 302
    knowledge-guided 149–151, 175
    mental 36–38
    low-level vs. high-level 49, 113, 147,
        149–151
    mental, for mindreading 36, 39–40,
        42, 46, 50
    plus-projection 41, 45, 164, 169, 237
    process-driven 32, 34, 132
    replication vs. computation
        interpretation of 4, 36, 46, 216–217
    See also empathy, mirroring,
        projection, simulation theory of
        mindreading
Simulation theory of mindreading (ST) 4,
    11, 17–21, 26–42
    competing version of 148,
        185–188, 259
    comprehensiveness of 20–21, 23–24,
        223, 274
    negative approach to 34
    origins of 5, 17–19, 23, 276
    partial compatibility with modularity
        approach 99–101, 110–111
    positive approach to 34–35, 46
    reframed debate with theory theory
        45–46
    threat of collapse from resemblance-
        to-self premise 30–31, 163–164
    threat of collapse from tacit theory
        32–33, 46
    varieties of simulationist theses 42–43

See also high-level mindreading, low-level mindreading, simulation, ST-TT hybrids

Simulation-neglecting theory theory. *See* theory theory

ST-TT hybrids 4, 21, 89, 113, 122, 150, 263

  simulation implemented by theory 42–43, 207, 209–210, 292–293

  simulation and theory cooperate 44–46

  simulation and theory operate independently 45–46

  See also ST, TT

Social cognition 3, 21–22

  autism as impairment in 205, 297

  and celebrity 279–280

  and chameleon effect 277–279

  and erotic stimulation 279–280, 300

  and mimicry 21, 276–279, 302

  and mirroring 132–140, 205–206, 210–211, 278

  and reciprocal hedonic contagion 298–300, 302

  and social bonds 276–279, 302

  and social coordination 279, 297

  and well-being 298–302

  See also empathy, fiction, moral theory and moral psychology

Somatosensory cortices 127, 131, 136

Spatial representation module (SR) 262–263, 266

Special method theory, of first-person mindreading. *See* introspection

SR. *See* spatial representation module

ST. *See* simulation theory

Suppositional imagination (S-imagination) 47–48, 175, 281–283, 290. *See also* E-imagination

Tacit theory 95–96

  of grammar 181

  of ontology 178–179

  opacity of concept of 32–33, 46

  and ST-TT implementation 43–44

  and ST-TT threat of collapse 30, 32–34, 46

Tactile empathy. *See* mirroring, of touch

Tagging 28, 160, 186–187, 211–213

Theory of mind mechanism (ToMM) 15, 98, 102, 104–105, 107–111

  adaptiveness of 15

  and autism 13–14

  and false-belief tasks 99–100

  and M-representations 16, 104, 107–109

  modularity of 95, 98, 101, 104–105, 107–111

  and pretense 15–16

  and propositional attitudes 16, 102, 109, 218

  See also modularity theory

Theory theory (TT) 4, 10, 13, 17, 23, 50, 67, 69, 289

  child-scientist variant of 69–89

  completeness of 24–26

  of first-person mindreading 25–26, 69–70, 89–92, 173, 237

  and folk-psychological laws 4, 8, 31

  and functionalism 8, 25–26, 69

  and mental concepts 13, 69–70

  modularity variant of 95–109

  origins of 8, 10

  paradigm version of 26, 91, 97–98, 173

  reframed debate between ST and 45–46

  of third-person mindreading 19, 24–26, 40, 69, 148, 173, 224, 237

  and unobservability of mental states 111, 259

  See also child-scientist theory, modularity theory, ST-TT hybrids

Third-person mindreading 4, 7–9, 19, 26–30

  via high-level simulating 28–30, 40–42, 164–168, 175–183

  via hybrid methods 43–46, 169–170

  via low-level simulating 124–132, 136–140

  via rationalizing 8–9, 54–61, 65–67

  via theoretical inference 27–28, 80–81, 83–84, 90–92, 97–98

Third-person mindreading (*continued*)
    See also child-scientist theory,
       high-level mindreading, low-level
       mindreading, modularity theory,
       perspective taking, rationality
       theory, simulation
ToMM. *See* theory of mind mechanism
Touch. *See* sensations
Truth-maximization, principle of 58–60

TT. *See* theory theory

Universalizability 294–295
Unmediated resonance. *See* mirroring

Visualization. *See* enactment
    imagination

Well-being 291, 298–302